TO BRING THE GOOD NEWS
TO ALL NATIONS

A volume in the series

The United States in the World

edited by David C. Engerman, Amy S. Greenberg, and Paul A. Kramer

A list of titles in this series is available at cornellpress.cornell.edu.

TO BRING THE GOOD NEWS TO ALL NATIONS

Evangelical Influence on Human Rights and U.S. Foreign Relations

Lauren Frances Turek

Cornell University Press
Ithaca and London

Cornell University Press gratefully acknowledges receipt of a grant from Academic Affairs of Trinity University, which aided in bringing this book to publication.

First published 2020 by Cornell University Press

Library of Congress Cataloging-in-Publication Data

Names: Turek, Lauren Frances, 1983– author.
Title: To bring the good news to all nations : evangelical influence on
   human rights and U.S. foreign relations / Lauren Frances Turek.
Description: Ithaca [New York] : Cornell University Press, 2020. | Series:
   The United States in the world | Includes bibliographical references
   and index.
Identifiers: LCCN 2019035834 (print) | LCCN 2019035835 (ebook) |
   ISBN 9781501748912 (hardcover) | ISBN 9781501748936 (pdf) |
   ISBN 9781501748929 (ebook)
Subjects: LCSH: Christianity and international relations—United States. |
   Evangelicalism—Political aspects—United States. | Evangelicalism—
   United States—Influence. | Christianity and politics—United States. |
   Human rights—Religious aspects—Christianity. | United States—
   Foreign relations.
Classification: LCC BR115.I7 T87 2020 (print) | LCC BR115.I7 (ebook) |
   DDC 261.8/70973—dc23
LC record available at https://lccn.loc.gov/2019035834
LC ebook record available at https://lccn.loc.gov/2019035835

Contents

Acknowledgments

We often think of researching and writing a book as a solitary task, but I have found the opposite to be true. Throughout this endeavor, I have been blessed with more help and support than I could possibly deserve from many wonderful advisers, colleagues, archivists, family members, and friends.

I could not have researched and written this book without the generous financial support that I received from Trinity University, the Institute for Political History, The John C. Danforth Center on Religion and Politics at Washington University in St. Louis, The Institute for Advanced Studies in Culture at the University of Virginia, the Society for Historians of American Foreign Relations, the American Historical Association, the Lynde and Harry Bradley Foundation at the University of Virginia, the University of Virginia Society of Fellows, the Billy Graham Center Archives / The Torrey M. Johnson, Sr. scholarship fund, The Institute of the Humanities and Global Cultures at the University of Virginia, the Corcoran Department of History at the University of Virginia, and the Robert J. Huskey Travel fund at the University of Virginia.

I am grateful to Melvyn Leffler, who has been a tireless champion of this project from the very beginning. Mel is an unparalleled scholar, thinker, and adviser, and I consider myself lucky to have had the honor of working with him. During my time as a graduate student, he provided me with the right mix of encouragement and advice, as well as the intellectual freedom I needed to develop as a scholar. His generous and rigorous feedback encouraged me to write clearly and think incisively. The insights that he provided have improved my work—and this book—immeasurably. I cannot imagine a better mentor or role model.

I also owe a debt of gratitude to other scholars who aided me in my studies at the University of Virginia, including Brian Balogh, Marc Selverstone, Matt Hedstrom, Phyllis Leffler, Jennifer Burns, Sophia Rosenfeld, J.C.A. Stagg, Mark Thomas, Stephen Schuker, Charles Mathewes, Ethan Schrum, and Christopher Nichols. Valarie Cooper introduced me to the fascinating world of Pentecostalism and played a significant role in shaping this project. I also benefited greatly from discussions with Brian Owensby about Latin American history and with John Edwin Mason about South African history. I received much good advice on the manuscript, as well as much needed merriment, from my UVA colleagues, including Stephen Macekura, James Wilson, Brent Cebul, Harold Mock, Evan McCormick, Mary Barton, Kelly Winck, Alexandra Evans, Joseph Scott, Philip Herrington, Cecilia Márquez, Tamika Richeson, Alec Hickmott, Mary Hicks, Willa Brown, and Chris Cornelius. Brian Rosenwald, Rhonda Barlow, Kate Geoghegan, and Emily Senefeld deserve special thanks—I will cherish their support and the friendships we forged in graduate school forever.

I had the good fortune to spend the 2014–15 academic year at the John C. Danforth Center on Religion and Politics at Washington University in St. Louis. The faculty and staff there provided me with a congenial intellectual home, and I thank Darren Dochuk, Laurie Maffly-Kipp, Leigh Schmidt, Marie Griffith, Mark Valeri, Lerone Martin, Rachel Lindsay, Ronit Stahl, Maryam Kashani, Stephanie Wolfe, Sheri Peña, and Debra Kennard for their invaluable help and feedback on my work.

My colleagues at Trinity University also deserve special thanks. Carey Latimore has cheered me on and supported me from the moment I arrived in the department. Jason Johnson, Aaron Navarro, Gina Tam, Nicole Marafioti, David Lesch, Anene Ejikeme, Ken Loiselle, Erin Kramer, Linda Salvucci, Todd Barnett, Emilio de Antuñano, Michael Hughes, Claudia Stokes, and Angela Tarango have provided generous feedback on my work and a truly gratifying work environment. I am also appreciative of the research assistance I received from my students Katie Welch and Meg Chase, who gathered interesting reading material for me.

Countless archivists assisted me in my research. All deserve commendation, but I owe special thanks to Bob Shuster and Katherine Graber at the

Billy Graham Center Archives, Keith Call at the Wheaton College Special Collections Buswell Library, Thelma Porres, Blanca Velásquez, Anaís García Salazar, and all of the other staff members at the Centro de Investigaciones Regionales de Mesoamérica, as well as the staff at the National Archive of South Africa for their tremendous help and patience. They went above and beyond to aid me in my research. I am also thankful to the Billy Graham Evangelistic Association for granting me permission to reference their materials in this book.

Many colleagues and scholars read chapters, commented on conference papers, or provided advice or feedback in other ways. I thank Melani McAlister, Sarah Snyder, Andrew Preston, Cara Burnidge, Mark Edwards, Emily Conroy-Krutz, John Wilsey, Dan Hummel, Amanda Demmer, Rasmus Søndergaard, Hideaki Kami, Michael Cangemi, Susie Colbourn, Simon Miles, Mitch Lerner, Andy Johns, Jeff Engel, Kyle Longley, Liz Borgwardt, Vanessa Walker, Bob Brigham, Mark Philip Bradley, Virginia Garrard-Burnett, and Randall Balmer, among many others.

A version of chapter 5 appeared in the September 2015 issue of *Diplomatic History*, under the title "To Support a 'Brother in Christ': Evangelical Groups and U.S.-Guatemalan Relations during the Ríos Montt Regime." The author thanks the editors of *Diplomatic History* for their permission to republish this material.

My deepest thanks to Michael McGandy, Karen Laun, Irina Burns, and the other members of Cornell University Press who nurtured this project. Their tireless work, candid suggestions, and careful editing made the final manuscript much better, and they have been a joy to work with every step of the way. I also very much appreciate Sandy Aitken, who did the painstaking work of preparing the index.

Finally, I thank the dear friends and family who supported me through this process. Rachel Rehl, Chris and Doreen Siciliano, Brian and Kelly Hargraves, Michael and Lindsay Burke, Lucy Kwon, Karena Wong, Lauren Hunter, Nicole Gitau, Greg Schiller, and Natalie Belew have all cheered me on and offered words of encouragement as I worked on this book. My family deserves special recognition. My parents, Thomas and Jayne, and my sister, Sara, offered their unwavering support; their love and faith in me sustained me throughout this project. I would not have been able to complete this book without them behind me. Finally, my husband Jeffrey has been my rock, reading drafts of every chapter, offering incisive suggestions, and providing constant reassurance. His love and support have meant everything to me. This book is dedicated to him, to my parents, and to my sister.

Abbreviations

ABM	Anti-Ballistic Missile
AE	African Enterprise
AFM	Apostolic Faith Mission
ANC	African National Congress
AUCECB	All-Union Council of Evangelical Christians and Baptists
BGEA	Billy Graham Evangelistic Association
CAAA	Comprehensive Anti-Apartheid Act
CCECB	Council of Churches of Evangelical Christians-Baptists
CIS	Commonwealth of Independent States
CREED	Christian Rescue Effort for the Emancipation of Dissidents
CRI	Christian Response International
CSCE	Conference on Security and Cooperation in Europe
CSI	Christian Solidarity International
ECWA	Evangelical Church of West Africa
ELWA	Eternal Love Winning Africa
EWNS	East/West News Service
FEBC	Far East Broadcasting Company
HCJB	Heralding Christ Jesus' Blessings network
ICOWE	International Congress on World Evangelization

IGE	Iglesia Guatemalteca en el Exilio
IRCEBCSU	International Representation for the Council of Evangelical Baptist Churches of the Soviet Union
ISEES	Institute of Soviet and East European Studies
LCWE	Lausanne Committee for World Evangelization
MARC	Missions Advanced Research and Communication Center
MFN	Most Favored Nation
MLN	Movimiento de Liberación Nacional
NAE	National Association of Evangelicals
NCC	National Council of Churches
NRB	National Religious Broadcasters
NSC	National Security Council
NSDD	National Security Decision Directive
RSA	Republic of South Africa
SACC	South African Council of Churches
SACLA	South African Christian Leadership Assembly
SALT	Strategic Arms Limitation Treaty
SBC	Southern Baptist Convention
SGA	Slavic Gospel Association
SWAPO	South West Africa People's Organization
TWR	Trans World Radio
UDHR	Universal Declaration of Human Rights
WCC	World Council of Churches
WEF	World Evangelical Fellowship
WEFCC	World Evangelical Fellowship Communications Commission

TO BRING THE GOOD NEWS
TO ALL NATIONS

Introduction

Defining and Defending Rights

It is the God-appointed duty of every government to secure conditions of peace, justice, and liberty in which the church may obey God, serve the Lord Christ, and preach the Gospel without interference. We, therefore, pray for the leaders of the nations and call upon them to guarantee freedom of thought and conscience, and freedom to practice and propagate religion in accordance with the will of God and as set forth in The Universal Declaration of Human Rights.

—*The Lausanne Covenant*, International Congress
on World Evangelism, 1974

A world adrift and full of suffering. The forces of tyranny gaining steady ground, ready to crush the fragile promise of human freedom and democracy. When Carl F. H. Henry sat down in late 1956 to pen his inaugural editorial essays for a new evangelical magazine, *Christianity Today*, he could not help but consider the place of his faith and the responsibilities he and his fellow believers had in confronting what he saw as "a decaying and darkening world."[1] An infant when the Great War erupted in Europe in 1914, a teenager when the world plunged into a cataclysmic economic depression, and a student of theology throughout World War II, Henry had come of age in an era of bloodshed, privation, and global atrocity. As an adult, he watched with increasing anxiety as totalitarian states amassed power and suppressed dissent, imperiling peace as well as the postwar order. Indeed, within days of the release of that first issue of *Christianity Today*, the Soviet Union sent tanks and soldiers into Hungary to quell a popular revolution against a repressive, Soviet-backed government. In his principal essay "Fragility of Freedom in the West," Henry expressed a profound pessimism about the state of global human rights, which he counterbalanced with the hope that evangelical Christianity might hold the key to shoring up freedoms in the world.

Anticommunism informed Henry's perceptions of liberty and the threats it faced. In his view, human rights were synonymous with democratic governance, free enterprise, and religious liberty, and in the context of the Cold War, the United States and its allies were losing the battle of ideas. For Henry, individual rights and the individual responsibility to protect those rights lay at the heart of the contest between Western freedom and totalitarian statism. Yet he argued that "the West's concept of liberty is indefinite and fuzzy," which made it hard to capture the allegiance of the masses, especially given the clear and direct appeals that communist nations offered to a world in transition after a totalizing war and ongoing decolonization.[2] He chided the West for its failure to counter communist propaganda with a positive, fixed "philosophy of human freedom," noting that the Western nations lacked agreement on the meaning of human dignity and thus struggled to mount an adequate defense of their cherished civil liberties.[3] The West had to demonstrate that human rights were rooted in clear-cut and eternal truths, he said. Henry reasoned that "the only compelling basis for speaking of inherent rights is the theological fact that man is a creature bearing the image of God," and therefore the "fate of freedom" in the world hinged on humanity's embrace of God's word and commandments: the Christian faith.[4] Accordingly, since human rights came from God, salvation through Jesus Christ offered the means to achieve global freedom.

From its debut issue under Henry's editorship then, *Christianity Today* linked Christianity and evangelism with the spread of liberty worldwide. Henry and the other founders of the magazine, which included the renowned evangelist Billy Graham, hoped to bring evangelicals together, giving them a stronger voice in their contemporary culture as well as direction as they lived their faith and pursued their spiritual mission to share the gospel.[5] Despite the establishment of the National Association of Evangelicals (NAE) in 1942, evangelical Christians in the United States remained divided along denominational lines in the 1940s and 1950s, a reality that undermined their ability to influence public life and spread their faith to nonbelievers. Eschewing rigid denominationalism for an emphasis on biblical "truths," evangelism, and an evangelical perspective on political affairs, *Christianity Today* complemented the (ultimately successful) efforts of the NAE to bring cohesion and greater public influence to U.S. evangelicals.[6] Furthermore, from the outset, the magazine included an international focus, consummate with Graham's belief "that people all over the world are hungry to hear the Word of God" and that evangelicals had a biblical mandate to fulfill this need.[7] This focus often came in the form of reports about suffering and human rights abuses, especially religious persecution, abroad. The perspectives that Henry, Graham, and other influential evangelicals brought to bear on their fellow believers and U.S. political culture at large shaped national thinking about human rights, especially among politically and theologically conservative Christians. Yet it took several decades before the ideas about human rights that Henry articulated in his first *Christianity Today* essay found their expression in effective evangelical foreign policy activism.

Evangelical human rights thought evolved in tandem with larger, society-level changes in how most Americans understood and defined human rights. Throughout much of the 1940s, 1950s, and early 1960s, rights-related social activism centered on ending racial segregation and promoting civil rights in the United States, as historian Barbara Keys demonstrates.[8] This was certainly true for the NAE; its first "Human Rights" resolution, issued in 1956, addressed domestic civil rights exclusively.[9] Only in the mid-1970s did the U.S. public begin to focus on human rights in an international context.[10] For U.S. evangelicals, this shift in thinking about human rights and human rights activism emerged alongside two significant developments in evangelicalism in the last quarter of the twentieth century: a massive revival in evangelical foreign missionary work and the bourgeoning domestic political power of the Christian right.

The causes that evangelical activists took up in the 1970s reflected a blend of political and spiritual beliefs that together defined a new conservative "Christian" foreign policy and human rights agenda. U.S. evangelicals approached the waning decades of the millennium with grave concern for the "unredeemed" souls of the world. With their belief in the Bible as the inspired word of God, evangelicals took the Great Commission, or the scriptural mandate to "go into all the world and proclaim the good news to the whole creation" in order to "make disciples of all nations," seriously.[11] They believed earnestly that by following this biblical command to share the gospel throughout the world, they offered all of mankind the opportunity to achieve eternal salvation through faith in Jesus Christ. Evangelicals thus viewed freedom of conscience—their freedom to evangelize and the freedom of the unreached to hear the gospel—as the most vital of all human rights. For evangelicals, no earthly privation compared to the loss of the potential for ultimate salvation.

The evangelistic task loomed large and grew more urgent in the aftermath of the cultural revolutions of the 1960s and 1970s. As Protestant missionaries from mainline denominations began to retreat from their mission fields in the 1960s amid concerns about cultural imperialism, U.S. evangelicals lamented the fact that, in their estimate, more than two billion people in the world had not yet heard the Christian gospel of salvation.[12] At the same time, innovations in communications technology and the dawning of a new era of economic globalization brought forth waves of urbanization, mass migration, and Western corporate expansion across the Global South. The social dislocation that these changes wrought created a tremendous opening for evangelism.[13] Evangelical missions proliferated as Pentecostals, Southern Baptists, and other U.S. evangelical groups flocked to Latin America, Africa, Asia, and Eastern Europe in an effort to spread the gospel and fulfill the "Great Commission."

By evangelizing and planting churches, these missionaries and the denominations that they belonged to forged close relationships with their brethren abroad. They also witnessed religious persecution, state violence, and acts of genocide against inhabitants in their new mission fields firsthand. In regions such as the Soviet bloc, where Western evangelicals could not proselytize openly, radio evangelism and clandestine contacts created a robust yet dispersed network for exchanging information about Christian life behind the Iron Curtain. These interactions, in tandem with deep-seated anticommunism, shaped the opinions that U.S. evangelicals held about foreign affairs and international human rights. Contacts in the Soviet Union and Eastern Europe provided detailed reports of totalitarian repression and other threats to religious liberty. Western evangelical organizations used such reports to raise awareness about Christian suffering abroad and to spur grassroots political action to counter it. Likewise, when evangelicals identified anticommunist or pro-evangelical leaders in other parts of the world, they relied on reports from local Christians to build support for U.S. policies that would benefit those regimes.

With the rise of the religious right in the 1970s, evangelicals enjoyed increased visibility and influence that provided them with a commanding platform for promoting their internationalist objectives. This powerful coalition of politically conservative Protestants (including conservative evangelical and fundamentalist Christians) and right-leaning Catholics coalesced around hot-button domestic social issues in the United States, including abortion and prayer in schools.[14] Although the desire to preserve so-called traditional family values defined the movement, conservative evangelicals evinced an enduring interest in foreign affairs rooted in their commitment to global evangelism and the sense of connection they felt with brethren overseas. During the Jimmy Carter and Ronald Reagan administrations, evangelical interest groups such as the NAE drew on their growing political clout to address concerns about the rights of religious believers throughout the world and their own rights to engage in foreign missionary work. Through presidential and congressional lobbying, as well as national and international public awareness campaigns, they influenced official decision making on a number of foreign policy initiatives. They lent support to authoritarian regimes that welcomed evangelism and offered a bulwark against atheistic communism. With their advocacy for hardline policies to counter totalitarian expansion, evangelical interests especially complemented the ideology and foreign policy objectives of the Reagan administration. Although evangelical and administration goals did not overlap on all issues, the core values that they shared created interdependence. Evangelical leaders reinforced presidential policies in the Soviet bloc, Central America, and Southern Africa just as President Reagan bolstered and legitimized evangelical interests in proselytizing throughout these regions.

Ultimately, evangelical lobbying efforts in the 1970s and 1980s influenced congressional and presidential decision making on a number of foreign policy initiatives, including legislation related to foreign military aid, international trade relations, and human rights, especially religious freedom. Through their advocacy work, evangelical interest groups developed a human rights vision that reflected their spiritual beliefs as well as their evangelistic mission. In contrast to liberal human rights activists, who emphasized economic and social justice, evangelicals espoused a commitment to protecting freedom of conscience as the most fundamental human right.[15] Writing again about human rights in 1992 for an issue of *Christianity Today* dedicated to the theme of "Freedoms under Fire," Henry reiterated his belief that religious liberty was the "first freedom," a requirement for functioning democracies as well as for the success of evangelism.[16] Another contributor to the special issue noted that religious liberty and other individual human rights provided essential "immunities from coercive state power."[17] Evangelicals embedded this perspective on religious liberty and, by extension, on human rights abuses in the Soviet bloc and the Global South, in their political lobbying.

This strain of conservative Christian human rights thought interacted in important ways with the revival of human rights activism that began in the 1970s and shaped U.S. foreign relations through the end of the Cold War and beyond.[18]

Indeed, by 1996, evangelical efforts to promote religious liberty abroad as part of a larger strategy for achieving global evangelism had developed into a full-blown, high-profile campaign. That year, the NAE released a lengthy resolution on religious liberty and universal human rights. The "Statement of Conscience Concerning Worldwide Religious Persecution" demanded government action to counter the violent repression that evangelicals throughout the world suffered under antidemocratic, communist, and militant Islamist regimes. According to the NAE, a combination of anti-Western and anti-Christian sentiment motivated oppressive foreign governments to terrorize evangelical Protestants and Catholics. Such violations of individuals' freedom of conscience threatened human rights in general within these countries.[19] The NAE argued that "persons of evil intent rightly understand that the survival of churches undermines their aims, because these churches affirm the human dignity of all persons created in God's image and acknowledge their ultimate accountability to a transcendent God."[20] Legislators proved receptive to the connections that the NAE and other evangelical interest groups drew between the rights of believers to practice their religion and the protection of other forms of human rights. Evangelical lobbyists promoted and helped draft the International Religious Freedom Act, which both houses of Congress passed by an overwhelming majority in 1998.[21]

The central role that evangelicals played in the passage of the International Religious Freedom Act attracted sustained attention from scholars of U.S. religion, politics, and foreign policy.[22] Some commentators found evangelical activism on human rights surprising, viewing politically conservative Christians as strange bedfellows with the progressive religious groups and advocacy organizations more commonly associated with human rights, such as Amnesty International. Yet evangelicals had long engaged with human rights questions, particularly those centered on issues of religious freedom, which they regarded as the "first" or most fundamental right. Nearly four decades after penning an editorial on human rights for the inaugural issue of *Christianity Today*, Henry reminded readers that "the human right of religious liberty" was essential for sharing the gospel and achieving the Great Commission.[23] Peoples living under regimes that mandated adherence to one faith or restricted religious practice entirely were unlikely to convert to Christianity.[24] This basic belief motivated evangelicals to lobby persistently for human rights as they interpreted them beginning in the late 1970s. Pursuing global evangelism under the banner of human rights enabled U.S. evangelical Christian groups to exercise influence on U.S. foreign relations, including decisions on trade, aid, and military assistance, diplomatic exchanges, and bilateral negotiations with allies and adversaries alike. In this way, internationalist evangelical groups transformed society, culture, and politics at home as well as abroad through their overseas missionary work and foreign policy activism.

This book delves into this story, examining how U.S. evangelical groups operated abroad, forged transnational cultural ties and, at times, shaped official U.S. foreign policy in the decades surrounding the end of the Cold War. In contrast to scholarship on the ascendancy of the religious right as a domestic political force, this book focuses on how foreign missionary work contributed to the creation of an influential evangelical lobby with distinct interests in the trajectory of U.S. foreign relations.[25] It reveals that the vast expansion of evangelical Christianity throughout the world during the 1970s and 1980s nurtured ties between U.S. evangelicals and their coreligionists abroad, creating a diffuse yet energetic global network of faith-based non-state organizations and actors. American missions in the Global South and efforts to support persecuted Christians in the Soviet bloc informed evangelical views of Christian life abroad and the prospects for evangelism, both of which shaped evangelical perspectives on how the United States should interact with other nations.

By the late 1970s, U.S. evangelicals had the political power necessary to advocate effectively for policies that they believed would nurture global Christendom. Their activism drew on and expanded their connections with Christians in other countries, and involved massive media-driven campaigns intended to shape broad public opinion as well as presidential, congressional, and state department thinking about human rights and international religious liberty. As their concerns about these issues intensified in the late 1970s and 1980s, evangelical leaders and activists coordinated ever more closely with their Christian brethren abroad and began communicating more extensively with policymakers. They exhorted the White House to protect the freedom of conscience worldwide and, in some cases, to intervene on behalf of foreign religious prisoners. They persuaded Congress to grant aid to favored yet repressive regimes in countries such as Guatemala while imposing economic and diplomatic sanctions on nations that persecuted Christians, such as the Soviet Union. In the process, they used their interpretations of scripture to develop a limited and particularistic perspective on human rights abuses in the Soviet bloc and the Global South, which they used to marshal support for their foreign policy positions.

Before proceeding further, a definitional note on evangelicalism is in order. "Evangelical" and "evangelicalism" are broad terms, encompassing a range of Christian denominations, beliefs, and practices that vary considerably across ethnic and geographic boundaries.[26] From tiny storefront assemblies in urban strip malls filled with gospel music, ecstatic dancing, and worshippers who speak in tongues to enormous megachurches in the Midwest featuring Christian rock performances and charismatic preachers who use PowerPoint to enhance their sermons, the lived experience of evangelical religion varies tremendously. Scholars have likened the modern evangelical movement to a "mosaic," a "patchwork quilt," or a "kaleidoscope," analogies that speak to the diverse array of churches, parachurch groups, and subcultures that make up global evangelicalism.[27] The influential religious historian George Marsden characterized evangelicalism as a style of U.S. Christianity as well as a religious movement, and he described evangelicals as sharing "common heritages, common tendencies, an identity, and an organic character" despite their great diversity.[28]

At the most basic level, the term "evangelical" derives from the Greek word *evangelion*, which is typically translated as "gospel" or "good news." All evangelicals share a commitment to evangelize, or to spread the "good news" throughout the world. Still, scholars continue to debate the defining characteristics of evangelicalism beyond this fundamental commitment to evangelism. For the purposes of this book, I rely on the concise yet comprehensive definition that sociologist Mark Shibley offers in his article "Contemporary Evangelicals: Born-Again and World Affirming," which ably summarizes the definitions that scholars of the evangelical movement such as Marsden, David Bebbington, and Mark Noll have employed in their seminal works. According to Shibley, "the term 'evangelical' refers to a broad group of believers who (1) have had a born-again (conversion) experience resulting in a personal relationship with Jesus Christ; (2) accept the full authority of the Bible in matters of faith and the conduct of everyday life; and (3) are committed to spreading the gospel by bearing public witness to their faith."[29] This definition captures the core beliefs that guided evangelical missionary activity and explains the individualistic and trans-denominational nature of the movement. It also illuminates why evangelical religious expression is so diverse; adherence to biblical authority does not necessarily imply the existence of a systematic evangelical theology. These core characteristics, along with the syncretic nature of evangelicalism, inspired followers to export their faith to all reaches of the globe during the late twentieth century.[30]

Evangelicalism, which dates back to the revivals of the First Great Awakening in colonial America and eighteenth-century Europe, profoundly shaped culture and politics in the United States.[31] As the evangelical movement spread rapidly throughout the American colonies in the eighteenth century, it contributed to the emergence of republican ideals and "the new rights-based American ideology" of the revolutionary era, according to Thomas S. Kidd.[32] In the decades that followed the revolution, evangelicals spearheaded the foundation of voluntary societies, Bible schools, missionary organizations, and political advocacy movements such as abolitionism, imparting a deep imprint on the civic culture and associational life of nineteenth- and early twentieth-century United States.[33]

This legacy of political engagement notwithstanding, one must approach comparisons between evangelicals from the late twentieth century and those who lived in earlier periods with circumspection given that a number of theological and political debates have cleaved the movement throughout its history.[34] While current U.S. evangelicals share a genealogical connection with their forebears of the eighteenth and nineteenth centuries, the modern movement traces its origins to the 1940s. Historian Larry Eskridge suggests that contemporary U.S. evangelicalism "came into being as a reaction against the perceived anti-intellectual, separatist, belligerent nature of the fundamentalist movement in the 1920s and 1930s."[35] Although evangelicals sought to remain engaged with the world as they worked toward fulfilling the Great Commission, fundamentalists tended to eschew secular society.[36] The establishment of parachurch organizations such as the NAE in 1942 and the rise to national prominence of leaders such as Billy Graham by 1949 reinforced the outward-looking, ecumenical character of this new strand of evangelicalism.[37] In this book, I focus on the organizations, leaders, and denominations that fall under this broad category of "modern U.S. evangelicalism" because these groups functioned as a relatively cohesive body with a distinct set of interests and an openness to civic engagement crucial to effective political mobilization.[38]

As such, I begin with an analysis of the religious and political beliefs that inspired the drive for overseas evangelism, as well as the scriptural interpretations that informed evangelical notions about the role that the United States should play in the world. Following the work of Philip Jenkins, Mark Shaw, Robert Wuthnow, and Dana Robert, I survey the social, economic, and political changes of the 1970s that led evangelicals to a renewed sense of missionary urgency and a newly internationalist outlook, comparing the effects of decolonization on the missionary agendas of mainline and evangelical Protestant churches.[39] As Paul Pierson has noted, by the end of the twentieth century some 150,000 Americans engaged in overseas evangelistic work each year on either a short-term or a long-term basis.[40] With mainline organizations turning to humanitarian rather than missionary activity in the 1970s, evangelicals made up a significant portion of this growing population.[41] When overseas, these missionaries wrote letters to their congregations at home describing their interactions with the people they met. Upon their return to the United States, they shared further details about their evangelistic experiences with their churches, prayer groups, and friends.[42] Andrew Preston has argued that in this way, evangelicals acted as internationalist agents who "[brought] the world to Americans" as they spread their religion—and U.S. culture—to the world.[43] I draw on this concept of "evangelical internationalism" that Preston and Melani McAlister have introduced to describe how overseas evangelistic work, combined with the growing domestic political power of the religious right, led to the emergence of an evangelical foreign policy consciousness.[44]

Anxieties about religious repression in totalitarian regimes and the threat it posed to the global missionary agenda led to the establishment of a powerful evangelical foreign policy lobby in the United States.[45] Evangelicals, with their millennial orientation, privileged religious freedom, and the freedom to evangelize as the most fundamental human rights.[46] Concerns about religious persecution and other abuses against the faithful led these groups to advocate for a "Christian" U.S. foreign policy—one that upheld core religious values and protected the country's missionaries and those they evangelized. These views also led many evangelicals to perceive authoritarian and other expressly antitotalitarian regimes as friendly to their objectives. This perception enabled evangelicals to interpret state violence in authoritarian countries as an acceptable or even desirable effort to combat the spread of communism. Even as movements for social justice multiplied, diversified, and internationalized in the 1970s, human rights—as concept and praxis—remained contested and open to interpretation. This fluidity, in concert with the power of Christian advocacy to shape the contours of congressional debate and public opinion on human rights issues, allowed evangelical foreign policy interest groups to adopt human rights language to promote an effective conservative Christian foreign policy agenda.

To gauge the extent of evangelical influence on U.S. foreign policy and the outcome of these policies on society and politics abroad, this book studies three cases where evangelical engagement abroad proved consequential. Although evangelical missions proliferated throughout the entire world and attracted sustained interest from U.S. believers in the affairs of nations in all corners of the globe, I have chosen to focus on regions of particular significance to U.S. foreign policy during the late Cold War: the Soviet Union, Central America, and Southern Africa. To this end, I examine evangelical policy engagement with the USSR during the late 1970s through the 1990s, with Guatemala following the 1976 earthquake and during the ascendance of evangelical dictator Ríos Montt in 1982, and with late apartheid-era South Africa. In each case, I identify the major evangelical leaders and organizations involved in each country, discuss the policy issues that they tackled, and uncover their interactions with fellow believers, foreign officials, and U.S. policymakers as they worked to make all nations of the world into safe havens for evangelism.

While recognizing that evangelicalism alone did not steer U.S. foreign relations in the late twentieth century, this book takes seriously the power of domestic social, religious, and political forces to shape and constrain policymaking. Diplomatic historians who have embraced the field's cultural turn have demonstrated that factors such as race, class, and gender have at times exerted noteworthy influence on U.S. policy. More recently, Andrew Preston, Andrew Rotter, and other scholars have begun to incorporate religion as a category for analysis in the history of twentieth-century foreign relations.[47] Reflecting on the profound intertwinement of culture, politics, and religion in the United States, these historians suggest that deeply held religious beliefs molded the worldview of U.S. leaders as well as the public, shaping how Americans perceived threats abroad and setting the parameters for acceptable foreign policy responses.[48]

Examining the emergence of evangelical foreign policy lobbying adds new layers to this story. It underscores key historical moments when religious and ethical values infused U.S. foreign policy, adding an important cultural dimension to the study of diplomatic history. It also reminds us that the rise of the religious right in the United States operated within a global context. Evangelicals viewed themselves as members of a transnational community of believers, and this identity provided the foundation for their human rights activism. When Christian interest groups blended their religious beliefs and conservative political ideology, they added their new but powerful voice to the national discourse about U.S. foreign relations. As evangelical lobbyists adopted and adapted human rights language in their advocacy campaigns and congressional testimonies, they helped to shape how policymakers interpreted state violence and repression abroad. Ultimately, evangelical interest groups influenced official decision making on a range of vital issues starting in the late 1970s, including foreign military aid, trade relations, and diplomatic negotiations, and the outcomes of these decisions effected society and politics in other countries. Evangelical foreign policy activism and global networking mattered.

The first three chapters of the book link the global expansion of evangelical Christianity with the concomitant rise in evangelical political influence in the United States. These chapters examine the interplay of religious and political beliefs that underpinned the push for overseas evangelism, the technological mechanisms that fostered evangelical internationalism, and the scriptural interpretations that informed evangelical notions about human rights and the role that the United States should play in the world. The book then offers three regional examples that reveal how evangelical leaders, missionaries, and interest groups drew on their political power and the international evangelical network they had helped build to shape international relations and national policies in the United States, the Soviet Union, Guatemala, and South Africa. The timelines of many of the chapters overlap, a structure that reflects the layered and multimodal nature of evangelical internationalist development and of the foreign policy challenges that evangelical activists confronted.

Chapter 1 traces the development of a global network of mission-minded evangelicals in the 1970s. It identifies the International Congress on World Evangelization that Billy Graham organized in 1974 as a landmark event that touched off a new era in evangelical missionary work and cross-cultural cooperation. This chapter delves deeply into the debates and new relationships that emerged from the congress, and explains how the economic, political, and social changes of the 1970s led to a renewed sense of missionary urgency among evangelicals throughout the world. It demonstrates that active involvement in this new global Christian network cultivated an internationalist outlook among U.S. evangelicals. The subsequent chapter overlaps with this story, explaining the practical mechanisms by which evangelical organizations expanded their reach. Many scholars of Christianity have attributed the global expansion of evangelicalism to "new technology" without adequately demonstrating how technological innovations made evangelical Christianity appealing to its new adherents throughout the world. This chapter illuminates the strategic approach of U.S. evangelical organizations in using electronic communications to spread the gospel.

It shows how individuals and local communities abroad interacted with Christian media and details how evangelicals throughout the world came to view themselves as members of a transnational community of believers by the early 1980s.

Chapter 3 adds another overlapping layer, exploring how nascent evangelical internationalism developed into a focused vision for U.S. foreign relations that provided the foundation for political advocacy on a wide range of global issues by the late 1970s and early 1980s. It argues that a powerful evangelical foreign policy lobby emerged in response to growing anxieties about developments in international relations, especially the perceived uptick in Soviet human rights abuses that accompanied détente with the Soviet Union and the 1975 Helsinki Accords. Evangelicals drew on their connections with coreligionists abroad and combined their spiritual beliefs with human rights language to build support among policymakers for the cause of international religious liberty, shaping how members of congress discussed human rights issues in the process.

Having explained how evangelical lobbying and evangelical internationalism developed, this book then transitions into three chapters that show the lobby at work. Here, I seek to answer a set of interrelated questions: How effective were Christian efforts to attain foreign aid for favored regimes and to impose economic and diplomatic sanctions on those nations that persecuted Christians and stifled evangelism? Why did U.S. evangelicals so often lend support to repressive authoritarian regimes in the name of human rights, and how did their stance on human rights evolve over time? Finally, what influence did evangelical involvement and U.S. policy have on society and politics abroad, particularly on human rights issues?

Next, Chapter 4 examines evangelical interest group lobbying on behalf of persecuted Soviet Pentecostals and Baptists during the Reagan administration. This chapter shows that evangelicals combined human rights activism at home with focused network building in the Soviet bloc to support their suffering brethren and lay the foundation for expanded evangelistic opportunities in the communist world. As the Soviet Union began to collapse during the George H. W. Bush administration, evangelical organizations and missionary groups moved in immediately to ensure that the postcommunist states would guarantee religious liberty for their citizens and allow foreigners to evangelize.

Chapter 5 turns to Guatemala, where evangelical dictator General José Efraín Ríos Montt seized power in a coup in 1982. Ríos Montt's religious beliefs, coupled with his staunch anticommunism, led politically influential evangelical leaders and nongovernmental organizations in the United States to support and promote his regime. In addition to direct fundraising, evangelical organizations lobbied Congress to restore military aid to Guatemala, which Carter had suspended due to ongoing human rights violations. Despite mounting evidence that Ríos Montt's military campaign against the "communist insurgency" in his country involved the mass killing of indigenous Mayans, many evangelical groups argued that the dictator's Christian faith would compel him to improve the human rights situation in Guatemala. The chapter thus demonstrates how evangelical engagement with Ríos Montt reshaped society and politics in Guatemala, as well as policymaking in the United States.

Finally, Chapter 6 explores the evangelical contribution to the debate over U.S. relations with the apartheid government of South Africa and the global anti-apartheid movement. While some members of the Southern Baptist Convention joined progressive religious groups to protest U.S. involvement with the regime, many evangelicals urged the Reagan administration to refrain from imposing sanctions on South Africa or pursuing disinvestment strategies. These groups claimed that these policies would have dire effects on the fragile human rights situation in South Africa, and expressed concern about the potential for a communist takeover. Evangelical antisanctions rhetoric employed a paradoxical blend of human rights language, religious beliefs, and anticommunism that had an important influence on conservative discourse and provided moral backing to the Reagan administration and Republican leaders who opposed the Comprehensive Anti-Apartheid Act of 1986.

The conclusion returns to the influential role that evangelical lobbyists played in shaping human rights legislation during the Clinton and George W. Bush administrations, placing their work on the International Religious Freedom Act within a larger historical context. The first part of the book traced the early history of effective evangelical lobbying efforts on matters related to human rights and U.S. foreign policy. The second part illuminated key moments when evangelical activism actually influenced the specific policy directions that government leaders pursued or the manner in which they discussed and understood global issues. The conclusion reflects on the legacy of earlier evangelical foreign policy engagement in building the political capital and international networks necessary for effective advocacy at the turn of the twenty-first century.

By interrogating the complicated interweaving of evangelical religious convictions, overseas missions, human rights, anticommunism, and foreign affairs, this book advances our understanding of the diverse factors that drove international relations in the late twentieth century. It also offers insight into how nonstate actors exert influence in global politics. Situating the understudied phenomenon of Christian foreign policy engagement during the late twentieth century within the framework of the human rights movement exposes how evangelical interest group activism helped to shift the meaning and content of U.S. human rights policy so that it aligned with conservative political objectives. When U.S. evangelicals collaborated with their brethren in Eastern Europe and the Global South to navigate the rapidly shifting social and economic conditions of the late twentieth century, they revealed that shared religious identity has tremendous power to forge connections—and political influence—across national borders.

Chapter 1

A Global Shift in
Missionary Christianity

In a 1974 article published in *Christianity Today*, Billy Graham issued a
call to evangelicals throughout the world to join together and renew their
commitment to global evangelism. Humanity teetered on a precipice,
he suggested, and only Christian salvation could prevent it from toppling
into the abyss. Casting his gaze over the events and transformations of the
two preceding decades, Graham saw a world increasingly open to evangelism,
yet also beset by structural crises, natural and manmade disasters, and spiritual malaise. Citing rampant inflation, wars, poverty, floods, and famine, not
to mention the cultural revolutions that shook Western societies in the 1960s
as well as the 1973 oil shocks and the Watergate scandal, he warned his readers that "our world may be standing at the very brink of Armageddon."[1] For
Graham and like-minded evangelicals who viewed such social ills through the
lens of apocalyptic biblical prophecies, these changes and challenges made the
evangelistic mission of the church seem especially urgent. As he exclaimed in
the article, "God is giving his people an opportunity for world-wide witness—
perhaps a last chance!"[2] Graham also acknowledged that a serious rift within
Christianity itself threatened to undermine this core spiritual duty.

Through the 1960s, evangelical leaders had grown increasingly concerned about what they perceived as a trend toward secularization and

liberalization (theological as well as political) within the major Protestant denominations, the Catholic Church, and interchurch organizations such as the World Council of Churches (WCC). This trend grew out of a constellation of political, social, economic, and religious forces that led Western church leaders to question the efficacy and morality of traditional modes of evangelism. The movements for self-determination and decolonization in the Global South that followed World War II, with their attendant critiques of Western colonialism and imperialism, also contributed to a "crisis of missions" by the mid-1960s.[3] As indigenous church leaders called for greater autonomy and liberal theologians rejected the "imperialist" nature of Western missionary work, a sharp divide emerged between those who sought to broaden the mission of the church to promote social justice and self-determination and those committed to the primacy of sharing the gospel. Liberal and mainline Protestants tended to embrace this more socially aware redefinition of the church's mission. Western evangelicals did not deny the importance of social action, but they did perceive the reorientation from evangelism to social justice as "a radically changed view of the mission of the Church" that threatened their efforts to advance Christianity throughout the world.[4]

This debate crystallized at the Fourth Assembly of the WCC, which convened in Uppsala, Sweden in 1968. The theme of the assembly, "Behold, I make all things new," and the major program sections, titled "renewal in mission," "world economic and social development," and "towards justice and peace in international affairs," left no doubt as to the perspective and objectives of the WCC leadership. Evangelicals voiced strident opposition to the working drafts and final statement on the mission that the World Council produced. In the article "Will Uppsala Betray the Two Billion?," Fuller Theological Seminary professor Donald McGavran argued that forsaking the traditional evangelistic mission of the church would condemn "inconceivable multitudes [to] live and die in a famine of the Word of God, more terrible by far than the sporadic physical famines which occur in unfortunate lands."[5] Despite their efforts to influence the drafting process, evangelical leaders did not believe that the World Council's "Final Pronouncement on Mission" placed adequate emphasis on the imperative of global evangelism.[6] They decried the WCC for its determination "to subordinate evangelism to service."[7] As John Stott, one of England's leading evangelical thinkers, noted:

> The assembly was preoccupied with the hunger, poverty, and injustices of the contemporary world. I myself was deeply moved and challenged by it.

And I do not want to see it diminished. What worried me is that I found no comparable compassion or concern for the spiritual hunger of the unevangelized millions.[8]

The outcome of the Uppsala Assembly and the trajectory of the debate over the crisis of missions left evangelicals feeling besieged and anxious to reassert the primacy of what they viewed as their biblical mission to spread the gospel. The actions they took in response forged a new internationalist outlook and activist sensibility among evangelicals.

The break between mainline and evangelical Protestants on questions of theology and the nature of world missions came amid significant demographic changes within the major churches. Lutheran, Episcopalian, and other mainline denominations in the United States experienced a steady decline in membership over the course of the twentieth century.[9] These churches, which had engaged in extensive missionary work during the nineteenth century, grew increasingly critical of foreign missions by the 1960s and participated actively in the WCC meeting at Uppsala. According to historian Dana Robert, as these denominations "attempt[ed] to shift from paternalistic to partnership models of mission, they began cutting back on Western missionary personnel."[10] This reduction in missionaries helped to dissociate indigenous Protestant churches from the Christian colonizers of the past, which allowed local evangelization to flourish.[11] Meanwhile, the more theologically conservative evangelical churches such as the Southern Baptists and Pentecostals grew exponentially—both in the United States and abroad.[12] Pentecostalism in particular spread rapidly through Latin America, Asia, and Africa, the result of missionary fervor from Pentecostals in the West and burgeoning indigenous evangelism coupled with explosive population growth.[13] The population boom in these regions, which significantly outstripped the growth rate in the West, made the Global South a particularly appealing mission field for U.S. evangelicals, who moved in quickly as mainline missionaries moved out.[14]

Against this backdrop of perceived missionary crisis and opportunity, evangelical leaders began an effort in the early 1970s to establish a global and interdenominational network of evangelicals to work together toward the goal of bringing the Christian gospel to all unreached peoples. Although the aim of achieving world evangelization through ecumenical collaboration did not originate in this period—the 1910 Edinburgh Missionary Conference had initiated the movement for Protestant cooperation in evangelism decades earlier—the 1970s represented a turning point in the history of evangelical missions, a moment when cooperative internationalization became paramount. Though some evangelical leaders had held conferences in the 1950s and 1960s in an attempt to develop a unified response to the crisis of missions, before the 1970s most of these efforts remained uncoordinated and small in scale. Indeed, in his memoirs, Billy Graham recalled that "part of the problem was that there was no real worldwide network—formal or informal—of evangelicals or evangelists" at that time.[15]

In 1966, the Billy Graham Evangelistic Association (BGEA) and *Christianity Today* began the process of rectifying this problem by organizing a World Congress on Evangelism in Berlin. This event, though U.S.-led, brought evangelical leaders from around the world together for the first time, and signaled, but did not fulfill, the latent potential of an internationalist evangelical network.[16] The fragile unity that the Berlin congress and subsequent regional conferences inspired helped precipitate the evangelical break with mainline Protestants at the 1968 WCC assembly in Uppsala and led to calls for more serious efforts to foster world evangelical cooperation. At the 1971 meeting of the National Association of Evangelicals (NAE), Graham reiterated the need for a global "evangelical superstructure" to fulfill the Great Commission.[17] By then, the world situation and the perceived crisis of missions lent even greater urgency to the task. Evangelicals responded with several overlapping initiatives, some church or denomination specific, some interdenominational, and, in keeping with the tremendous expansion of independent evangelical churches in this period, some nondenominational. Beginning with the 1974 International Congress on World Evangelization (ICOWE), the ongoing Lausanne Movement that it generated, and the resurgence in missions and outreach activity from churches, mission boards, and nondenominational evangelical organizations, a loosely connected, but significant internationalist evangelical network took hold.[18]

This global and transnational network flowered in the 1970s. A series of international conferences brought evangelicals from all continents together to debate the theological basis for foreign missions and to develop new strategies for cross-cultural outreach. As evangelical leaders and church members from the United States deepened their engagement with their brethren abroad through cooperative missionary and humanitarian aid ventures, prayer, and the social, political, and theological disputes that unfolded at these conferences, they cultivated enduring connections with Christians from all over the world. These connections affirmed their belief in the bib-lical mandate to proclaim the gospel to all nations and their aspiration to achieve this Great Commission within their lifetimes. The renewed sense of missionary urgency and millennial expectation, the rapid expansion of evangelical denominations in the Global South, and the creation of a global evangelical network fostered a robust, focused internationalist outlook among U.S. evangelicals.[19] This nascent evangelical internationalism sowed the seeds for the emergence of a powerful body of U.S. evangelical Christian activists focused on global issues and foreign affairs by the late 1970s and 1980s. Furthermore, the debates about mission and social justice that occurred within the context of this process helped to shape evangelical conceptions of human rights, religious freedom, and the world order.

Confronting the Crisis of Missions

On August 25, 1972, after several days of deliberations with religious lead-ers hailing from every continent, Billy Graham announced plans to hold an ICOWE in 1974 to expand on the work initiated at the 1966 Berlin Con-gress.[20] Graham anticipated that this event, one of five major conferences on Christian evangelism slated for that year, would "bring evangelicals of all denominations to a new obedience that would result in worldwide evange-lization," and asserted, "it is my prayer that this meeting will . . . lead to the evangelization of every person on earth before the end of this century."[21] The flurry of excitement and publicity surrounding the ICOWE and other inter-national evangelical gatherings, such as Campus Crusade for Christ's Explo '74 in Seoul, South Korea—which attracted well over a million attendees—led the *Los Angeles Times* to declare that "world evangelization is in vogue this year."[22] Still, commentators singled out the ICOWE Planning Commit-tee's effort to foster evangelical unity by including representatives from a broad array of countries and organizations as unprecedented.[23] Reporters emphasized that the upwelling interest in evangelization stemmed from global Christian demographic changes as well as from the traditional biblical mandate to spread the gospel.[24] The efflorescence of interdenominational conferences on cross-cultural evangelism also reflected roiling fears that the foreign mission model faced an existential crisis.

Overseas evangelistic work had long provided U.S. Protestants a window to the wider world, forging connections between missionaries, converts abroad, and brethren at home. Throughout the nineteenth and twentieth centuries, missionaries had served as conduits of cultural exchange between evangelists and evangelized, as well as between mission-sending and receiving nations. Evangelists from the United States sent news about their overseas experiences home, educating other Americans about the people and cultures of foreign nations, not to mention the domestic and international issues that affected them.[25] Information exchange notwithstanding, much of the transmission of culture flowed in one direction. As Andrew Preston and other scholars note, missionary efforts to introduce Christianity abroad also tended to propagate U.S. cultural, political, and economic values.[26] Critiques of this tendency as cultural imperialism triggered the debates over mission that caused Graham and others such anguish about the future of evangelism.

Seeking to reconcile the realities of a rapidly changing postcolonial world with their biblical imperative to spread Christianity, evangelicals in the 1970s worked to change the dynamics of the intercultural relationships they built through missionary work. At international conferences, they consulted with indigenous Christians to develop appropriate means for sharing what they perceived as a universal message of salvation across national and cultural boundaries. These collaborative efforts to reach unreached peoples and share in international fellowship did not eliminate the charges or reality of cultural imperialism. They did, however, deepen relationships between evangelical leaders in the United States and abroad, enhancing the web of connections that made up the nascent world evangelical network.

The sense of embattlement, angst, and opportunity that surrounded the crisis of missions and inspired the organization of international conferences on evangelism reflected the powerful pull that the core theological and eschatological tenets of evangelical Protestantism exerted on its adherents. With their unwavering belief in the authority of the Bible, evangelicals interpreted key scriptures as evidence that believers must engage in missionary work or evangelism to spread the gospel. Chief among these was Matthew 28:16–20, in which a resurrected Jesus commissioned his followers to "go therefore and make disciples of all nations, baptizing them in the name of the Father and of the Son and of the Holy Spirit, and teaching them to obey everything that I have commanded you."[27] Scriptural authority also shaped the millenarianism of the evangelical faith. Accepting biblical prophecies, followers trusted that "Jesus Christ will return personally and visibly, in power and glory, to consummate his salvation and his judgment," after which he would reign the Kingdom of God on Earth for a millennium of peace.[28] Mark 13:10 and 13:26, which assert, respectively, that "the good news must first be proclaimed to all nations," and "then they will see 'the

Son of Man coming in clouds' with great power and glory," led some evangelicals to conclude that they must achieve the Great Commission before that second coming could occur.[29] The centrality of these scriptures to evangelicalism helps explain the vehemence with which evangelicals from the West as well as the Global South responded to the 1968 WCC program on mission. It also explains why they viewed the rapid expansion of Christianity in Africa, Asia, and Latin America with such great millennial expectation.

By the 1970s, many observers recognized that the locus of Christianity had begun to move southward. David Barrett, an influential Anglican missiologist, published a statistical study in 1970 that projected explosive growth in the Christian populations of Africa, Asia, and Latin America—which evangelicals often referred to as the "two-thirds world."[30] One table, titled "Southwards Shift in Christian World, 1900–2000," estimated that the Christian populations of Northern America, Europe, and Russia would grow from approximately 637 million in 1965 to 796 million by 2000, whereas the combined population of Christians in Asia, Africa, Latin America, and Oceania would grow from 370 million to 1.1 billion over the same time period.[31] Barrett argued that this demographic growth "might well tip the balance and transform Christianity permanently into a primarily non-Western religion."[32]

For Christians enmeshed in the debate over the crisis of missions, this projected transformation seemed at once tremendously hopeful from a millennial standpoint as well as indicative of the need for new cross-cultural approaches to evangelism.[33] At the 1971 meeting of the National Association of Evangelicals, Billy Graham, *Christianity Today* editor Harold Lindsell, and NAE president Hudson Armerding described these shifts in global Christianity as "a necessary prelude to completing the Church that Christ established at Pentecost," emphasizing the relationship between the propagation of the gospel and the proximity of Christ's return to earth.[34] By embracing these demographic changes, the ICOWE played a crucial role in fostering evangelical unity in the 1970s.

Planning an International Congress

From the planning stage forward, the ICOWE aimed to connect evangelical leaders from the United States and Europe with evangelical leaders from Africa, Asia, and Latin America in order to advance global evangelism. Graham conceived of the congress as the first of many gatherings that would unite evangelicals "just like at Pentecost, where you hear one voice. Where all these divergent groups could meet."[35] The thirty-one-person planning committee, which included Graham as honorary chairman, Anglican bishop A. Jack Dain of Australia as executive chairman, and U.S. missionary to Japan Donald Hoke as director, began meeting regularly in 1970 to develop the format of the congress and to select evangelical leaders from a variety of countries to conduct studies, submit papers, and attend the gathering.[36] Though Western evangelicals held leadership positions, several members of the planning committee, including Peruvian theologian and head of the Inter-Varsity Christian Fellowship Samuel Escobar, hailed from the Global South. Their inclusion on the committee, and the direction of discussions at the early meetings, revealed the self-conscious effort the committee made to include non-Western voices at the ICOWE and avoid the appearance of U.S. or European dominance. In this manner, they hoped to articulate their objective for the congress: to "Let the Earth hear His Voice," and to develop the means to reach all people throughout the world by the end of the century.[37]

A number of the conference planners suggested that holding the congress in a non-Western nation might facilitate this objective. In a meeting held in Washington, D.C., in February 1970, planning committee member Victor Nelson asserted: "I don't think it should be a foregone conclusion that the next congress must be on European soil. In fact, I'm not sure but what this might be a mistake. Should it not be somewhere where we could bring together Latin America, Africa, the Middle East, India, the Far East into an area down there? This is the developing area. This is the area where now evangelism is moving and there is a thrust there."[38] Nelson's statement was met with considerable agreement among the meeting participants, as it alluded both to the significant growth of evangelical Christianity in what they termed the "developing" world and to the tremendous number of people who had yet to hear the gospel.

Much to the disappointment of the planning committee, the BGEA staff could not find a location outside of Europe capable of accommodating an international conference of the scope that they had in mind. Nevertheless, the sentiments that Nelson and others expressed revealed that evangelical leaders had internalized the seismic changes that demographic projections implied for the future of Christianity. In their conversations, they tacitly acknowledged that close association with U.S. or Western missionary efforts often had an injurious effect on indigenous evangelism.[39] As such, they viewed the projection of an inclusionary and egalitarian vision as essential not just for fostering evangelism, but for connecting with leaders in these "developing areas" as well.

Attentive to the importance of cultivating a positive public image for the ICOWE, the planning committee emphasized the central role that two-thirds world evangelical voices would have at the congress.[40] After the organizers settled on the Palais de Beaulieu conference center in Lausanne, Switzerland as the best available location, they directed advisory groups to begin selecting evangelical leaders from as many countries as possible to attend and contribute to the proceedings.[41] More than half of the Christian leaders, invited by the planning committee to the Lausanne Congress, hailed from an African, Asian, or Latin American country. Graham ensured that even those from the poorest regions could attend by devoting a significant portion of the $3.2 million he raised for the ICOWE to scholarships for travel expenses.[42] In addition to connecting with indigenous evangelical church leaders, the committee invited representatives from some "300 non-North American, non-European, non-Caucasian foreign-missionary sending agencies . . . to share their insights and to wrestle with problems that are common to any cross-cultural communication of the Good News."[43] Mission historians have commented extensively on the revolutionary character that this level of representation from the developing world imparted to the congress and the Lausanne Movement that it inspired.[44] More significant, by placing their imprimatur on emerging models of indigenous evangelism, Congress organizers brought these otherwise independent enterprises under the aegis of the ICOWE and into the consciousness of evangelicals throughout the world.

The inclusivity of the plans for the congress received wide coverage in Christian periodicals and news outlets, many of which highlighted the relationship between the internationalism of the congress and its stated goal of advancing evangelism. Commentators and committee members alike noted that the active participation of representatives from outside of North America and Europe signaled a momentous and opportune break from the past. One article suggested that in gathering diverse evangelicals together to discuss cross-cultural evangelism, the ICOWE had the potential to build "a clear biblical foundation for world evangelization, declared not by east or west, north or south, but by representatives of evangelical Christians worldwide," as well as "a new sense of cooperation in strategic planning" to fulfill the Great Commission.[45] Eager to extend a sense of ownership over the outcome of the congress beyond the direct participants, organizers promoted the formation of prayer groups throughout the world "to intercede for God's direction and power in the congress preparation, program, and results."[46] U.S. evangelical organizations, including the National Religious Broadcasters and Campus Crusade for Christ, publicized the congress as well, producing promotional materials for radio and television broadcast on foreign, domestic, and missionary networks, reaching believers throughout the world.[47] The final invitation list for the congress included 2,473 delegates representing 150 countries, 1,300 observers, guests, and consultants, a number of journalists, and an army of student volunteers.[48]

In advance of the ICOWE, eighteen plenary speakers submitted papers on the goals, theology, and methodology of world evangelization to the entire body of participants for their review and response. Hundreds of respondents weighed in on these papers, some of which generated thousands of comments.[49] Taking the principal messages expressed in these papers and comments into account, a small contingent of committee members drafted a brief document that affirmed the centrality and necessity of evangelism in the Christian faith. Several months before the congress convened, they shared this document with a group of advisers to solicit feedback and proposed revisions. The document and the comments it generated formed the foundation of the Lausanne Covenant, a set of fourteen principles intended

Figure 1. Anglican bishop A. Jack Dain of Australia and evangelist Dr. Billy Graham signing the Lausanne Covenant on the last day of the International Congress on World Evangelization. Courtesy of the Billy Graham Center Archives, Wheaton College, Wheaton, IL.

to guide the renewed crusade for world evangelization.[50] In addition, the participants began compiling strategic profiles of every nation and culture to quantify the scope of the evangelical task.[51]

Debating Foreign Evangelism

Billy Graham opened the ICOWE with a speech that celebrated the inclusivity of the gathering and the promise it held to bring greater coherence to the world evangelical movement. He credited the growth of Christianity in the two-thirds world, including the rapid expansion of Charismatic and Pentecostal sects, with bringing a new and welcome dimension to global evangelism. He also asserted that in uniting these "younger churches in Africa, Asia, and Latin America who have taken up the torch and are sending missionaries to other nations" with the "older churches that have witnessed and evangelized for centuries," the congress would expedite the fulfillment of the Great Commission.[52] The speech identified Social Gospel, with its "preoccupation with social and political problems" rather than with the souls of individuals, as a threat to this goal and a contributor to the relative decline of Protestantism in the West.[53] After reaffirming evangelism as the primary Christian responsibility—and the tie that bound "younger" and "older" churches together—Graham told the audience, "I hope that a new 'koinonia' or fellowship among evangelicals of all persuasions will be developed throughout the world" as a result of the congress.[54] He articulated a vision for evangelical cooperation based on the idea that, whatever doctrinal and cultural differences existed, all Christians belonged to one church and had one task: "to proclaim the message of salvation in Jesus Christ."[55] Accordingly, evangelicals must prioritize this mission over other important and necessary Christian duties, including fighting injustice.[56]

The strategy papers and reports that the working groups at the congress developed revealed a broad consensus among the participants on the goal of world evangelization as well as Graham's prescription for evangelical cooperation as a means to this end. In one such paper, David Cho, an evangelical Presbyterian missionary originally from North Korea who dedicated his life to promoting non-Western missions, advocated a reciprocal approach to missionary work, with Western and non-Western nations alike sending missionaries out to evangelize the world.[57] Other Congress participants, including Ernest Oliver, secretary of the Evangelical Missionary Alliance of Britain, and S. O. Odunaike of the Nigeria Evangelical Fellowship, echoed the call for cooperation and reciprocality among missions, going so far as to suggest creating an international evangelical missionary body.[58]

Yet the plenary papers, which formed the intellectual foundation of the congress, revealed conflicting opinions about how to approach global evangelism. All of the speakers addressed the Christian duty to evangelize and agreed that "world evangelization requires the whole church to take the whole Gospel to the whole world," yet their papers revealed significant cleavages between Western and non-Western conceptions of this core mission.[59] The discussants diverged over two major issues: the role of nonindigenous missionaries in Third World evangelism and the place of social justice in the mission of the church. The avowed anti-imperialism of speakers such as C. René Padilla, who advocated a moratorium on Western missions and called evangelicals to make a radical commitment to fighting oppression, jolted many participants. Some U.S. and European speakers rushed to defend their ongoing involvement in foreign missionary work. Others labored strenuously throughout the congress to bring the two sides together, hoping to find points of unity that would enable evangelicals to go forth collectively and "let the Earth hear His voice."

Padilla, the associate general secretary for Latin America of the International Fellowship of Evangelical Students, presented a controversial essay titled "Evangelism and the World," which pointedly condemned U.S. cultural imperialism as counterproductive to the advance of world evangelism. He recounted the role that Roman Catholicism played in facilitating the Spanish conquest of Latin America and argued that by the nineteenth century, "Christian missionary outreach was so closely connected with European colonialism that in Africa and Asia Christianity would become identified as the white man's religion."[60] Drawing parallels between nineteenth-century European imperial powers and the twentieth-century United States, Padilla accused U.S. evangelicals of propagating "another form of 'culture Christianity,'" which he defined as "the identification of Christianity with a culture or a cultural expression."[61] He noted that this association of the Christian faith with the culture of a hegemonic power made it difficult for local religious leaders to communicate the universality of Christianity to the unevangelized, decreasing the likelihood of their conversion.

In the case of the United States, argued Padilla, the Cold War imperative to maintain economic and military supremacy over the USSR necessitated the export of certain elements of U.S. ideology and culture to the periphery. Yet preponderant U.S. influence in the Global South meant that Latin American evangelists often faced "innumerable prejudices that reflect the identification of Americanism with the Gospel in the minds of [their] listeners."[62] Padilla contended that, intentionally or not, white American evangelicals often transmitted their own national values along with the gospel in their missionary work, conveying the notion that Christianity and the "American Way of Life" were inextricably linked.[63] Insisting that the church "be not *of* the world but to be *in* the world," Padilla declared that Christians had to sever this association between Americanism and the gospel.[64]

Although he shared with Graham a deep conviction in the need to spread the Good News throughout the developing world, Padilla feared that U.S.-style evangelism missed the mark. Among other concerns, he believed the Western obsession with using the latest technological innovations to blanket the earth with the gospel demonstrated a fundamental ignorance of the pressing spiritual and material needs of humankind.[65] Repudiating the influence and methods of U.S. missionaries, Padilla stressed that "we urgently need to recover an evangelism that . . . is oriented toward breaking man's slavery in the world."[66] His vision for world evangelization entailed a radical reorientation of Christian missionary work towards an organic, local style of evangelism with a greater focus on the biblical principles of social justice.[67] Replacing Western missionaries with local religious leaders would allow an authentic and truly universal Christianity to flourish in all cultural contexts.

Padilla's paper elicited a tremendous outpouring of opinion from the participants at the ICOWE. Some commenters felt his notion of "culture Christianity" created unnecessary discord that diverted attention from the core objectives of the congress, while others believed his critique "[had] not gone far enough" to address the creeping imperialism of Western evangelicals.[68] In an oral history interview, Padilla recalled, "I found that unwittingly I had been voicing something that an awful lot of Third World people wanted to say themselves. I was surprised at the number of Asians and Africans and Latin Americans who felt represented by what I said."[69] The sense of solidarity that developed as a result of Padilla's paper contributed to growing calls for a moratorium on Western-led foreign missions and cemented connections between two-thirds world evangelicals. Yet it also prompted a backlash. Though Padilla insisted that he "[had] no intention of judging the motives of the propounders of American culture Christianity," he acknowledged that many Americans "felt attacked" by his comments.[70] Ultimately, consensus around the need for cooperative efforts to achieve the Great Commission did not translate into an agreed on framework for achieving this goal.

Many presenters framed their papers in response to Padilla's allegations of cultural imperialism, defending the role and methods of Western evangelism. McGavran acknowledged that European colonialism had abetted earlier evangelism but argued that the breakup of empires had erased the link between imperialism and Christianity. He divided the world into two spheres: the largely evangelized "Eurican" nations (those in Europe, the United States, and the developed world) and the "Latfricasian" countries (those in Latin America, Africa, and Asia) where most of the "unreached peoples" resided.[71] The church, McGavran insisted, had to find new methods for spreading the gospel to the unreached regions. He took issue with the concept of "culture Christianity," maintaining that "a pernicious notion that world evangelism is a concealed form of Eurican imperialism and will destroy the beautiful cultures of Asia, Africa and Latin America has recently been retarding world evangelism. The idea is false and must be cleared out of the way. It is not in harmony with the revealed will of God. World evangelism has nothing to do with Eurican imperialism, past or present. This Congress does not believe that Eurican culture is God's chosen culture."[72]

McGavran insisted that modern evangelism could and did account for the changed geopolitical order of the postcolonial era. He stressed that Western

Figure 2. Ecuadorian theologian Dr. C. René Padilla addressing the International Congress on World Evangelization in 1974. Courtesy of the Billy Graham Center Archives, Wheaton College, Wheaton, IL.

evangelicals celebrated indigenous cultures and realized that local church growth in Africa, Asia, and Latin America offered the most effective way to evangelize the two billion unreached people in their midst.[73] As such, he argued that "God is calling for . . . churches from *every* land to send their best sons to carry the Gospel across cultural frontiers," asserting that "the day is too urgent to quibble over words."[74] In essence, McGavran rejected Padilla's characterization of U.S. evangelism because the immensity of the Christian task required all believers everywhere to cross national and cultural boundaries to spread the Good News. He, therefore, urged cooperation between Eurican and Latfricasian missionary societies, calling for increased indigenous evangelism with continued missionary and monetary support from Western churches.[75] Without churches and "reborn men" proliferating the world in a coordinated effort, McGavran believed no hope existed for fostering the Kingdom of God—or for the social justice that leaders like Padilla sought.[76]

McGavran built on the framework for world evangelism that Ralph Winter, also a professor at the socially and theologically conservative Fuller Theological Seminary, presented in his paper "The Highest Priority: Cross-Cultural Evangelism." Winter argued that the major obstacle to achieving world evangelization lay in the "truth that most non-Christians in the world today are not culturally near neighbors of any Christians, and that it will take a special kind of 'cross-cultural' evangelism to reach them."[77] He acknowledged that Christians should support local evangelism wherever possible, but maintained that the lack of "cultural near neighbors" in many parts of the Global South rendered indigenous or even regional evangelism "literally impossible."[78] Winter effectively sidestepped the question of cultural imperialism, appealing instead to practicality and efficacy in tackling the project of reaching the unreached two billion.

Some participants questioned Winter's pessimistic assessment of the reach of Christian "near neighbors" though. Jacob Loewen, a Canadian anthropologist and Mennonite missionary working in Zambia as a translation consultant for a Bible society, argued that near-neighbor proselytism was the most feasible and biblical strategy for achieving genuine conversions in the Global South.[79] He worried that too often, Western missionaries conflated their "cultural models for conversion, church, and Christian living" with Christianity itself, a situation that made true cross-cultural communication impossible and pushed the evangelized "to become imitation Europeans rather than spiritually reborn nationals."[80] Unless the evangelized embraced the universal gospel in their own local context, they would neither experience a full conversion nor fan out to evangelize others, Loewen asserted.[81]

Winter retorted that the tremendous number of unreached peoples in the world necessitated cross-cultural evangelism, though he reassured critics that he saw near-neighbor evangelism as preferable and foreign missions as a last resort.[82] This concession allowed for some measure of agreement as it acknowledged the desirability of indigenous evangelism without conceding to the need for a moratorium on foreign missions.[83]

Although this effort to find common ground sidestepped many of the underlying grievances that evangelists such as Padilla raised, John Stott, Hudson Armerding, and Samuel Escobar drew on Winter's formulation as they revised the Lausanne Covenant. This declaration of shared evangelical beliefs and evangelistic goals gave rise to the influential Lausanne Movement and shaped the trajectory of global evangelicalism for decades to come. In addition to praising God and affirming the primacy and universality of scripture, the final version of the document emphasized the critical need to reach the multitudes who had not yet heard the gospel.[84] Article 9, "The Urgency of the Evangelistic Task," acknowledged that the continued presence of foreign missionaries in evangelized regions hindered the ability of local churches to spread the gospel. As such, the covenant recommended greater autonomy for non-Western churches. Yet it also accepted Winter's basic assertion that the sheer number of unreached people necessitated a continued reliance on cross-cultural missionary efforts in some regions.[85] Stott noted that this compromise ensured a more efficient use of resources and expanded the evangelistic reach because it encouraged non-Western churches to engage in their own local missionary work, freeing up Western missionaries to evangelize elsewhere.[86]

The covenant also accepted the need for social justice. Escobar reminded Congress participants that the legacy of cultural imperialism in Western missionary work, coupled with Western evangelical indifference to authoritarian rule, social inequality, and human rights abuses in the Global South contributed to the perception that evangelization constituted "an 'imperialist plot.'"[87] The covenant took these concerns into account, stating "although reconciliation with man is not reconciliation with God, nor is social action evangelism, nor is political liberation salvation, nevertheless we affirm that evangelism and socio-political involvement are both part of our Christian duty."[88] These affirmations notwithstanding, outside observers noted that the covenant promoted social action only as a means of supporting evangelism.[89]

The revisions that the ICOWE organizers made to the Lausanne Covenant reflected the powerful critiques of the foreign missionary model that

Padilla, Escobar, and other Christians from the Global South offered. In the years following the congress, Western evangelicals began to encourage greater autonomy and indigenous evangelism in Africa, Asia, and Latin America, a dramatic break from earlier decades. Indigenous evangelism supported the overarching goal of achieving the Great Commission and contributed to closer partnerships between Western and non-Western evangelical leaders. These relationships formed the core of a burgeoning evangelical network that shaped Christian practice and politics throughout the world.

Launching the Lausanne Movement

Billy Graham, along with the vast majority of the other Congress participants, signed the Lausanne Covenant before leaving the ICOWE. Many more signatures trickled in after the congress ended.[90] Although Graham expressed misgivings over the anti-Western content of some of the congress papers, he still oversaw the drafting and revisions of the covenant and expressed pride in the document, which he termed "a classic statement on evangelism."[91] Despite his long-standing refusal to sign "manifestos or documents or petitions of any sort," he made an exception for the Lausanne Covenant, perhaps because he felt it necessary for the congress to release a unified statement on the aims and urgency of evangelism.[92] In addition to embracing the covenant, a majority of the congress participants also supported plans to establish a formal evangelistic organization to fulfill the promise of the ICOWE.[93] The Lausanne Movement, which grew out of these proposals, guided world evangelical relations throughout the rest of the twentieth and into the twenty-first centuries.

To launch this new global enterprise, the ICOWE Planning Committee appointed a continuation group, later known as the Lausanne Committee for World Evangelization (LCWE), comprised of forty-eight representatives from Asia, Africa, Latin America, the Middle East, North America, Europe, and Oceania. In 1975, this group met in Mexico City to formalize the organization and create a plan for supporting the many evangelical initiatives the congress had inspired.[94] Working under the leadership of chairman A. Jack Dain and executive secretary Gottfried Osei-Mensah—with Billy Graham serving as honorary chairman to confer "authenticity and credibility" to the proceedings—the committee created the administrative structure and agenda for the movement.[95]

Over the objections of some members, the LCWE decided it would focus exclusively on the task of evangelism, a decision that minimized the parts of the Lausanne Covenant that emphasized social justice.[96] It created working groups that would collaborate with parachurch organizations such as World Vision's Missions Advanced Research and Communication Center (MARC) and the World Evangelical Fellowship (WEF) to develop tactics for more effective cross-cultural evangelism and to organize evangelistic conferences.[97] Osei-Mensah believed that this cooperative approach would allow the Lausanne Movement, MARC, and WEF to provide more comprehensive global outreach than any single organization could provide on its own.[98] Likewise, LCWE-organized meetings such as the 1980 Consultation on World Evangelization in Pattaya, Thailand, created opportunities for evangelical leaders and parachurch organizations to work together on new evangelistic ventures.[99] Gathering believers from across the globe in these ways centered the Lausanne Movement in the new evangelical network and nurtured a renewal in missionary fervor in the late 1970s and 1980s.

As debates about foreign missions and social justice unfolded among leading evangelical thinkers, a wave of indigenous and cross-cultural evangelism surged through Africa, Asia, and Latin America. Within a month of the ICOWE, the *Christian Messenger* in Ghana reported that "plans for the evangelization of all Ghana and neighbouring countries have been mapped up by Ghana's 16 participants to the International Congress on World Evangelization," who returned home eager to share the tactics they learned at the congress with local church leaders.[100] Numerous delegations from other African, Asian, and Latin American nations followed suit. In 1977, Osei-Mensah hailed conferences organized by two-thirds world Christians, such as the 1976 Pan-African Christian Leadership Assembly and the All-India Congress on Mission, as evidence that "the vision of world evangelism is now descending to grass-roots levels, especially in Third World churches."[101] Evangelicals in Africa, Asia, and Latin America seized on the covenant's mandate to exercise local leadership and evangelize, working independently in their home countries as well as abroad to promote the mission of the church. At the same time, they remained connected to evangelicals in the United States and other parts of the Western world through the LCWE and the larger evangelical network.

Thus, the ICOWE helped to usher in a new era of evangelism and evangelical connectivity. Although a number of evangelical groups convened major conferences in the mid-1970s, the ICOWE proved unusual and momentous. Its cosmopolitan participants—brought together for the first time—engaged with the vital social, political, and religious issues of the decade to produce perhaps the most influential evangelical statement of the modern era. The debates over mission and social justice that shaped the Lausanne Covenant laid bare the extraordinary changes of the postwar years, as anticolonial nationalism led to the proliferation of powerful, independent churches in Africa, Asia, and Latin America. As evangelicals from throughout the world grappled with what they wanted these changes to mean for the future of evangelism, they collectively gave birth to an enduring mass evangelical association.

Denominational Internationalism

The ecumenicism of the ICOWE merited comment in the press and elsewhere in part because evangelicals and evangelical denominations had historically functioned so independently from one another. Evangelicalism, a pluralistic movement within Protestantism, encompassed groups as disparate as the Southern Baptists, the Presbyterian Church in America, and the Church of God, a Pentecostal denomination.[102] The inclusion of Pentecostals, neo-Pentecostals, and Charismatics at the congress proved particularly noteworthy at the time, as those groups had not participated extensively in earlier ecumenical Protestant gatherings yet comprised the most rapidly growing evangelical denominations in the world.[103] Bringing together all of these major streams of evangelicalism was significant, and it created a new cooperative consciousness among evangelicals.

That said, evangelical internationalism and network building also developed in new ways within these diverse denominations during the 1970s. U.S. evangelical churches entered the decade with aggressive overseas missionary agendas either in place or in development. Recognizing that in the United States individual believers felt most connected to Christians who shared their denomination, mission boards worked actively to win souls to their own individual denominations, even as they agreed that spreading the gospel remained the universal goal of all evangelical churches. As Southern Baptists and Pentecostals forged closer relationships with their denominational brethren abroad, they confronted the same social and political issues related to foreign missionary work that the ICOWE sought to address through the Lausanne Covenant. Questions about the need for indigenous evangelism, local autonomy, and social justice reverberated throughout denominational discussions and strategic planning efforts for overseas missionary work.

Foreign mission boards and church leaders took pains to affirm the centrality of evangelism to the mission of the church and to ensure that missionaries remained on message as they entered their mission fields, but they also began to build more robust relationships with local church leaders. Strengthening cross-cultural relationships within denominations acted as a necessary corollary to the interdenominational cooperation of the ICOWE because it instilled both a sense of belonging and a responsibility to the global church among individual believers, which fostered the emergence of an internationalist outlook.

In regions where they had a long-established church presence, Pentecostals and Baptists in the United States began promoting indigenous evangelism and greater autonomy for national churches as a means to free up resources for U.S. missionaries to do more work in unevangelized areas. For example, Church of God Foreign Missions Board member W. E. Johnson cheered the growth of his denomination abroad and urged continued expansion into unevangelized areas of the world. Hoping to make the Church of God "truly worldwide in its outreach" so it could fulfill its evangelistic mission and function as a universal church, he called for more indigenous evangelism and praised foreign brethren for their zeal and efficacy in spreading the gospel.[104] Similarly, the Southern Baptist Foreign Mission Board held meetings throughout 1975 and 1976 to hammer out new strategies for promoting indigenization and the growth of autonomous national churches, inviting contributions from U.S. and overseas church leaders.[105] Through this strategic planning process, the Southern Baptists launched a new program called the "Bold Mission Thrust," which involved evangelizing in "neglected" areas of the world, building new churches, and then stepping aside to allow "indigenous" Christians to take on the leadership positions missionaries had once held.[106] Missionaries would also rotate into different jobs to ensure that they did not become entrenched in any one role or location.[107] In this manner, the churches would develop in their own national context—not as "colonial extensions of an American denominational entity"—but remain linked to Baptists in the United States and throughout the world.[108]

This turn toward supporting local church leadership rather than seeking to retain external control reflected the influence of the ideas that animated the ICOWE and the Lausanne Covenant. Yet discussions within each denomination about indigenization reveal that this goal evolved gradually over the decade, an unfolding process of negotiation, reflection, and policy review. Writing in early 1970, one Church of God foreign mission analyst opined, "As we move toward the indigenous church on the mission field, we must decide to what degree these churches should be self-governing. We must take care not to cling to a continuing parental approach and attitude toward our foreign churches. Rather, we must become partners with them in the gospel, allowing them to reach maturity in Christ."[109] These recommendations gained greater traction in the years following the ICOWE, thanks in part to the powerful influence of the covenant and the Lausanne Movement. Throughout the decade, missionary superintendents and the regional division heads of the Church of God Foreign Mission Board devised and implemented plans for transitioning "nationals" into leadership roles through expanded biblical educational opportunities and active mentorship.[110]

As Southern Baptists and Pentecostals expanded their overseas missionary outreach efforts and forged closer, more collaborative relationships with brethren and church leaders abroad during the 1970s, they grew more aware of and attuned to the social ills that plagued the Global South. To be sure, these denominations still viewed evangelism as their primary responsibility and believed that salvation through Christ offered suffering people the best hope for a better life.[111] Nevertheless, through the Bold Mission Thrust program, the Southern Baptists pledged to implement new initiatives to ease the human suffering they observed in their mission fields.[112] Referencing the "two great commandments," the foreign mission board made clear that it understood social ministry to follow closely behind evangelism in the hierarchy of Christian responsibility.[113] As such, they asserted that benevolent ministries formed an important, if subsidiary, part of their evangelistic strategy. Ministering to human need, according to the foreign mission board report, served "a two-fold purpose: (1) to demonstrate the love and concern of God through Christ for the whole person, and (2) to provide an opportunity to proclaim the redeeming, liberating, and sustaining power of the gospel."[114] Attending to the physical needs of the poor, sick, and disaster-stricken of the world thus gave Southern Baptists and their local partners another avenue for evangelism.[115] This fusion of humanitarian concern and evangelistic fervor formed the core of global evangelical engagement in this period. When the foreign mission board pledged to keep Southern Baptists in the United States apprised of global needs and its efforts to meet those needs, it wove webs of connectivity between U.S. Baptists and those living abroad, fostering an expansive and international Baptist identity.[116]

The major U.S. evangelical churches also developed new methods for evangelization through mass media, which linked them to brethren (and potential brethren) throughout the world. Evangelical denominations and broadcasting companies had produced radio shows for international audiences since the 1930s, but the renewed sense of missionary urgency, coupled with improving radio, television, and communications technology, led to an explosion of interest in "the electric church" in the 1970s, as the next chapter discusses in more detail.[117] Pentecostals expanded their global electronic reach exponentially in this decade, using radio broadcasts in dozens of foreign languages as a means to provide Bible training to listeners, who could then evangelize their family members, friends, and neighbors.[118] Similarly, the Southern Baptists declared that "the recent technological revolution, transistor radios, jumbo jets, satellites, and computers should be made the servants of Christian missions."[119] The Bold Mission Thrust program included plans to adopt new technologies in evangelism, such as the use of shortwave radio to beam the gospel into communist and Muslim countries that barred missionaries.[120]

The sense of urgency that overcame evangelicals as they surveyed the massive task of spreading the gospel to the 2.7 billion unevangelized motivated evangelical denominations to make significant changes in their approaches to foreign missions in the 1970s. Their efforts to develop new evangelization methods reflected the intellectual and emotional ferment of church leaders and laity alike as they confronted a rapidly changing world and sought to secure their churches' place in it. As one prominent evangelical leader admonished, "to meet the demands of an exploding world population we need dynamic new methods . . . The communication of the Good News of salvation through Jesus Christ cannot be delayed. We must do it now. . . . It is ten minutes to midnight on the clock of the world."[121] Discussions about improving missionary outreach filtered down from leaders to laity through the denominational press, the resolutions they signed at national convention meetings, and radio and television broadcasting. In reciprocal fashion, these concerns also reached up to the leadership from the grassroots as individual ministers, missionaries, and laypeople weighed in through letters, radio station call-ins, and local initiatives.

For Southern Baptists and Pentecostals in particular, these endeavors paid great dividends. Their churches expanded rapidly, attracting millions of new members in the United States and throughout the world in the 1970s and 1980s.[122] As these denominations grew, they disseminated a wealth of information about overseas evangelism to their followers through a variety of media, keeping them apprised of and deeply engaged with the evangelistic mission of their churches. Over time, adherents developed a profound interest in and sense of connection with fellow believers living in other countries. The initiatives that these denominations launched in the 1970s to expand foreign missionary work, encourage indigenous evangelism, and employ new communications technology to share the gospel reinforced the diffuse intradenominational bonds that linked their churches in the United States with those they established abroad.

Nondenominational Network Building

The 1970s also witnessed the flourishing and expansion of nondenominational evangelical churches, movements, and organizations. Future mega churches, such as Joel Osteen's Lakewood Church, large-scale nondenominational associations such as Calvary Chapel and the Vineyard Christian Fellowship, and the Jesus Movement began to elicit great attention in mainstream U.S. culture.[123] As nondenominational evangelical entities, these churches and movements blended multiple strands of Protestant belief—often with a mix of Pentecostal and Charismatic worship forms—and took seriously their responsibility to evangelize throughout the world to achieve the Great Commission. They also possessed a global outlook and sought to cultivate relationships with evangelicals abroad.

One of the most politically influential nondenominational U.S. evangelical organizations of the twentieth century, the Fellowship Foundation, gained new leadership in the 1970s and began to work more discreetly and powerfully in Washington, D.C., to expand its reach throughout the world. Unlike the other nondenominational ministries mentioned above, which sought to cultivate broad audiences, the Fellowship Foundation focused exclusively on bringing national elites into its fold. Working on the assumption that creating a worldwide evangelical fellowship of political and religious leaders would bring about greater evangelization and Christian commitment in all nations, the Fellowship Foundation developed and maintained extensive connections with global elites through its ministries. Although it operated behind the scenes, the Fellowship Foundation tied non-evangelical political leaders to the burgeoning global evangelical network by bringing them together with evangelical legislators, businessmen, and church leaders who were part of that network (such as Billy Graham) at national and legislative prayer breakfasts.[124] These political connections lent increased power and influence to the evangelical movement as it gained visibility and reach in the late 1970s and 1980s.

Doug Coe assumed leadership of the Fellowship Foundation in 1969, after the death of founder Abraham Vereide, who had established the foundation in 1935 to serve as a vehicle for spreading the gospel through regular prayer meetings with business and government leaders.[125] By the time Coe took control, the Fellowship Foundation had hosted seventeen Presidential Prayer Breakfasts in the United States, organized numerous Christian conferences overseas, and exported the prayer breakfast concept to seventy other countries.[126] Vereide had tended to emphasize the national, rather than international, aspects of the group's work though.[127] Under Coe's leadership, the Fellowship Foundation placed a greater emphasis on internationalism and made a considerable commitment to establishing autonomous yet coordinated ministries and prayer groups overseas.[128] He led the revision of the organization's by-laws, which instructed members to "work together to bring about a spiritual awakening throughout the world through prayer, discussion and analysis," to hold prayer and discussion groups to help men throughout the world develop their leadership skills, and to "commit themselves daily through the power of Christ to being and building bridges of communication and understanding between disparate peoples."[129] At its core then, and in keeping with the efforts of other evangelical groups in this period, the Fellowship Foundation sought to create a network with Christians throughout the world in order to share the gospel.

The Fellowship Foundation built and nurtured its overseas network in two key ways. First, Fellowship members, including and especially those hailing from the U.S. Congress, established personal connections with political leaders abroad either through letters or in-person meetings and encouraged those leaders to form cells or prayer groups with other influential citizens in their country. The foundation developed this strategy through meetings of its Congressional Core, a group of legislators, which included Harold Hughes (D-IA), John Dellenback (R-OR), and Mark Hatfield (R-OR), who took on an active role in expanding the fellowship worldwide by meeting and praying with heads of state, influential businessmen, and religious figures abroad.[130] In one typical letter, Senator Hughes provided prominent South African businessman H. F. Oppenheimer an introduction to the Fellowship Foundation and the prayer groups. Hughes described the structure of the weekly Senate and House prayer meetings and stated that "from these and other leadership groups, a fellowship of men and women with its center in Jesus Christ has been developing in many nations around the world."[131] He encouraged Oppenheimer to visit with and consider joining the new cell developing at that time in South Africa, as well as to meet with Congressman Dellenback during his visit to the country with Doug Coe.[132]

Oppenheimer did so, joining Fellowship cell leader Rev. I. Ross Main of the Evangelical Fellowship of Anglican Churchmen of South Africa, and Dellenback at a meeting in November 1973.[133] In a subsequent letter to the foundation, Rev. Main celebrated this visit from Dellenback for helping the South African group expand its membership, noting: "The men in our core have realised that to get through to the leaders of the Government on a personal relationship basis in any really meaningful way can only be done with the help of God and we have been especially careful to follow His leading step by step . . . John and Dick's visit has certainly played a very important part both in accelerating and in making this penetration into Government circles at the highest level."[134]

Inspired, Main and the other core members expanded the reach of the Fellowship Foundation further into Southern Africa by helping to set up prayer breakfasts in Botswana and in the KwaZulu nation in 1973.[135] Eager to remain in contact with the Washington Core, Main asked his correspondent to keep him apprised of the Fellowship Foundation's "contacts and plans concerning Africa especially, within the great commission to make disciples of all nations," and requested their prayers as he worked to consolidate the new relationships he had developed in his country.[136] The Fellowship Foundation's files are full of letters of this nature from evangelicals and political leaders from all over the world who had met Coe or another Fellowship member. These letter writers described founding cell or national prayer breakfast programs in their own country and corresponded regularly with the Washington Core.[137]

The Fellowship Foundation also grew its international network by inviting leaders from overseas to attend the National Prayer Breakfast in the United States. Attending the prayer breakfast gave these individuals the opportunity to meet with the president of the United States, members of Congress, businessmen, and key U.S. religious leaders, as well as with other international members of the Fellowship. In 1974, for example, Howard Hughes invited Yakov Malik, the Soviet Union's deputy minister of foreign affairs and ambassador to the United Nations, along with other UN ambassadors, to attend the National Prayer Breakfast as well as a smaller, more private associated luncheon. Hughes stated in his invitation that "our desire is to find a way to meet on a more informal basis to build the ties of friendship which are so needed. It is our feeling that our common spiritual bond can be the basis of this friendship."[138] In a follow-up letter to Malik and the other attendees, Doug Coe expressed his desire to stay in touch and, if possible, to arrange a visit to their home countries.[139] The Fellowship Foundation also arranged for foreign leaders visiting the United States to attend a weekly Senate or House prayer breakfast. In a memorandum to President Richard Nixon, Doug Coe indicated that Emperor Haile Selassie I of Ethiopia had twice attended these breakfasts in the United States. According to Coe, Emperor Selassie had subsequently started his own prayer breakfast in Ethiopia and appointed a committee "to discuss how these links of friendship through the Spirit of Christ can be developed among the leaders of all Africa."[140]

In 1977, the Fellowship Foundation engaged in a strategic planning effort to improve communications and strengthen the web of connections between various core groups operating throughout the world. The foundation articulated a set of goals for reaching out to these cores, which it described as "family" or "key" groups, under its new global communications policy. In addition to enhancing each core members' faith and love for God, the program aimed to cultivate "the feeling of being part of the worldwide family of Christ."[141] The policy encouraged the core groups to share information about their local projects in order to foster collaboration, prayer, and other support from the larger foundation network. It also recommended that the Washington Core encourage members of other core groups to write to "brothers" living in other parts of the world.[142] In this manner, the Fellowship Foundation hoped to instill in its dispersed membership the "feeling that they're part of an intimate family of brothers and sisters in Christ."[143]

Although the Fellowship Foundation operated a somewhat unusual ministry in that it established nondenominational prayer groups rather than full-fledged congregations, its theological underpinnings and overarching goals aligned closely with the larger evangelical movement. As such, it contributed in significant ways to global evangelical networking building in the 1970s. Despite working clandestinely, the Fellowship Foundation fostered deep connections not only between evangelicals in the United States and abroad but also between evangelicals and nonevangelicals in positions of power in government and business. Furthermore, many evangelicals who belonged to or led other parachurch and denominational organizations attended the National Prayer Breakfasts and events at the Fellowship Foundation house and corresponded with Doug Coe, Richard C. Halverson, and other members of the group. Although the Fellowship Foundation remained a shadowy institution unknown to most rank-and-file evangelicals, it nevertheless integrated itself into the vanguard of international evangelicalism. The relationships the Fellowship built with congressional and world leaders also played an important role in shaping evangelical policy activism in the later decades of the twentieth century.

A Global Evangelical Network

Evangelical Christians approached the 1970s with a complicated mix of mil-lennial hope and profound anxiety. From their perspective, the world seemed to be descending into depravity and chaos, signaling the approach of the end times. Billy Graham summed up the evangelical mind-set when he observed: "Most of us hold the view of Scripture that teaches that as we approach the end of history things will get worse. Our Lord predicted in Matthew 24 that false prophets, earthquakes, famines, wars, betrayals, moral permissive-ness, persecution, and apostasy would precede his return."[144] Graham and his fellow evangelicals viewed the tribulations of the decade as a sign that humanity was hurtling toward this apocalyptic end. Indeed, many evangeli-cals welcomed the fulfillment of these biblical prophecies.

At the same time, Matthew 24 also promised believers that "the one who endures to the end will be saved. And this good news of the kingdom will be proclaimed throughout the world, as a testimony to all the nations; and then the end will come."[145] Many evangelicals interpreted this scripture as evidence that the end of the world would not come until everyone in the world had heard the gospel.[146] For this reason, they felt compelled to redou-ble their efforts to take the gospel of salvation to all nations. Yet the global political changes and revolutions in communications technology that shaped the 1970s at once complicated and transformed their traditional approaches to evangelism.

In response to these staggering changes and spiritual callings, a global evangelical network emerged over the course of the decade through inter-national conferences such as the ICOWE, as well as through intradenomina-tional strategic missions planning and nondenominational ministries. This network, more broad than dense, did not erase all disagreements between Western and two-thirds world evangelicals, or between evangelical denom-inations. It did, however, create an unprecedented sense of shared evangeli-cal identity that transcended national and cultural boundaries. It also led to a tremendous upwelling of missionary fervor, which contributed to the dramatic expansion of evangelicalism throughout the world. The strat-egies that Western evangelical leaders used to spread their faith created new relationships with church members abroad. These relationships wove the emergent global community tighter together. In linking evangelicals from the United States—the leadership as well as rank-and-file believers—to their brethren in other countries, this global network inspired a newly internationalist outlook among U.S. believers. With their gaze turned outward to the world, evangelical internationalists focused their energies on reaching the unreached and supporting fellow Christians as they worked to achieve the Great Commission. In time, this internationalist orientation bred political activism as well.

Chapter 2

The Communications Revolution and Evangelical Internationalism

The urgent task of evangelizing the world required collaborative action and bold experimentation. Evangelical leaders, including many of the participants at the International Congress on World Evangelization (ICOWE), believed that in order to "Let the Earth Hear His Voice" they had to build a robust global Christian community that extended even into countries hostile to missionaries. They embraced Ralph Winter's contention that near-neighbor and indigenous evangelism offered a key avenue for reaching the unreached, particularly in more remote parts of the world. Jacob Loewen, Donald McGavran, C. René Padilla, and other influential evangelical thinkers had argued persuasively that Christians could not propagate the gospel effectively unless non-Christians could hear it in their own languages and grasp its transformative potential on the basis of their own cultural terms. Yet the impassioned debates that erupted at the congress over how to cultivate local churches in countries where few if any Christians lived revealed the challenges many Western evangelicals saw in pursuing fully indigenous evangelism. Committed evangelists thus explored a range of strategies to aid them in their task of trans-cultural communication. Increasingly, they looked to communications technology, along with mass media techniques, audience research, and creative adaptations of various modes of transportation, to establish contact with the unreached and strengthen their existing connections with Christians abroad.

With these goals in mind, the organizers of the ICOWE arranged for one of the conference's strategic study groups to explore how Christians should use new and old technology to narrow the distances that separated them and gain entrance to countries otherwise closed to the gospel. The six sessions that the communications strategy group held during the congress proved unexpectedly popular. More than three hundred participants attended, eager to hear the prepared papers and to brainstorm. Around two-thirds of these attendees already used some form of media and technology in their witness, yet few felt they had adequate training in the techniques and technical aspects of the field.[1] The sessions reflected this commingling of ambition and anxiety, praising fellow evangelicals for their tendency to be early adopters of new media while emphasizing the dangers of failing to keep up with accelerating technological change.[2] Phillip Butler, an *ABC News* correspondent and the founder of the short-term missionary recruitment organization Intercristo, argued in his presentation that "the Scripture gives a mandate for the use of the media—woe be to us if the church does not use these resources placed in our hands by God."[3] Other presenters echoed this fretful sentiment, imploring the evangelical community to "exploit urgently the vast communication networks available today . . . with vision and an aggressive spirit" so as to tap into the divine power and potential these networks held for spreading their Christian faith worldwide.[4]

The communication committee's discussions ranged widely, addressing practical means for creating effective cross-cultural radio and television programming as well as raising broad questions about the theological basis for adopting new technologies for evangelistic outreach. Together, the strategy group members developed a set of recommendations to share with the congress and with external evangelical organizations involved in media production and global communications, including the World Evangelical Fellowship (WEF) and the National Religious Broadcasters (NRB). In line with the broader discussions unfolding at the congress, the committee recommended the establishment of "cooperative communications entities" in every country and the close involvement of local churches in integrating media into their evangelistic outreach.[5] The ever-expanding assortment of available media and media organizations necessitated greater coordination through regular national and international conferences as well as the creation of an international resource center for sharing information and materials. Greater coordination would also help facilitate one of the most crucial goals: convincing the church as a whole to "grasp *new* media," including "satellites, computer networks, [and] data transmission," and to figure out how to deploy these emerging technologies for global evangelism.[6] Equally important, according to the committee, was the belief that evangelicals must develop a theology of mass media communications to provide a biblical foundation for training Christians to witness via media.

The evangelical embrace of technology was not new, but the communications committee recommendations epitomized an emerging trend in how evangelical communications leaders thought about technology, mass media, and the mission of the church in the 1970s. These leaders, which included individuals in executive positions at evangelical organizations such as Phillip Butler of Intercristo and Ben Armstrong of the NRB as well as Christian academics, publishers, and media evangelists, sensed that they lived in a decade of rapid technological innovation that held both promise and peril. They recognized the uneven distribution of technology across their mission fields— the fact that few countries in the Global South had wide access to television, for example—and the need for evangelists to use multiple modes of communication simultaneously. Yet nurturing old media tools, while developing programming and infrastructure to take advantage of the new generated strategic and financial pressures, especially given the atomized nature of the evangelical media landscape and the vital imperative for world evangelism. The media strategy discussions at the ICOWE highlighted ongoing evangelical efforts to grapple with these challenges, bringing together and drawing more focused attention to the range of proposals that Christian communications professionals had produced on this topic by the early 1970s, but not yet implemented effectively. The emphasis the committee recommendations placed on local participation, coordination, and leadership spoke to the Lausanne Movement's vision for a fully internationalized and interconnected world evangelical community.

The ICOWE media strategy recommendations signaled a turning point for the establishment of this global evangelical network, unleashing the momentum necessary to coordinate disperse evangelical groups. Christian mass media and communications networks bound evangelicals together across national borders, as U.S. and non-U.S.-based individuals alike served as producers and consumers of print media, television, and radio programs. The need to develop community distribution networks and compelling programming in local languages created indispensable roles for local church leaders. It also built reciprocal links between believers in the United States and in Latin America, Asia, Africa, and the Soviet bloc. These relationships did not erase the tensions that emerged at the congress between those committed to evangelism above all else and those seeking indigeneity, social justice, and a moratorium on missions. Yet they did bring greater attention to the particular challenges that evangelicals living in the Global South and the communist world faced in seeking to practice and propagate their faith. Increasingly robust communications networks proved crucial for spreading the news about religious repression and evangelistic opportunities, which mobilized foreign policy activism in the United States on behalf of brethren abroad in the decades that followed.

This chapter explains the practical mechanisms by which evangelical organizations expanded their international reach. Many scholars of Christianity have attributed the global explosion of evangelicalism in the 1970s to "new technology" without adequately demonstrating how evangelicals used technological innovations to make Christianity appealing to potential adherents throughout the world.[7] U.S. evangelical organizations used electronic communications and cheaper, faster modes of travel strategically to spread the gospel and to create new networks for sharing information. They set up study groups and commissions to coordinate their efforts and train media providers. They also came to view technological innovations such as satellites and television through a prophetic lens. This lent further urgency to their use of new technology. The interactions that developed between U.S. and foreign evangelicals as they consumed and created Christian media helps to explain, in part, how evangelicals throughout the world came to view themselves as members of a transnational community of believers by the early 1980s.

Organizing and Internationalizing Mass Media Christianity

Whenever a new form of communications technology appeared, evangelical media and missionary organizations embraced them. In January 1921, just two months after airing the first ever commercial radio program, station KDKA in Pittsburgh, Pennsylvania began broadcasting Sunday services from the Calvary Episcopal Church on a weekly basis.[8] Domestic religious radio programs proliferated as U.S. radio set ownership mushroomed over the next decade. Christians also moved swiftly to use radio broadcast technology for international missionary work. The Heralding Christ Jesus' Blessings (HCJB) network, which the U.S. evangelist Clarence W. Jones founded in Quito, Ecuador in 1929, began broadcasting evangelistic programs on the

"Voice of the Andes" on Christmas Day in 1931. In the years that followed, missionary radio stations multiplied. Emergent networks such as Far East Broadcasting Company (FEBC) and Trans World Radio (TWR) established posts in far-flung parts of the globe after World War II, often using army surplus equipment to set up short wave stations that could reach listeners in Eastern Europe, the Soviet Union, and China.[9] It was a period of tremendous experimentation, with nearly nonexistent coordination. Still, Ben Armstrong looked back on the success of early missionary radio fondly, noting that "the technological advances of postwar broadcasting enabled the home-grown electric church to accomplish a worldwide mission that surpassed the missionary efforts of the previous century."[10]

Armstrong's bold assertion rested in part on the astounding growth that these missionary radio stations experienced. HCJB made its first broadcast over a 250-watt transmitter that Jones had set up in a converted sheep shed, with a wire strung between two 85-foot tall telephone poles as an antenna.[11] The hymns and Christmas Day sermon that the small HCJB staff shared over the airwaves in Spanish and English reached all six of the radio sets that existed in Quito in 1931. By 1967, HCJB had multiple transmitters in Ecuador, including a 500,000-watt transmitter in Pifo—the most powerful transmitter in Latin America—and employed a large enough staff that it could develop and broadcast programming in more than a dozen languages.[12] Its signal reached all of Latin America as well as Europe, the Soviet Union, and Japan. HCJB also ran a television station, airing four hours of Christian programming each night for the residents of Quito, hundreds of whom called the station during these programs, according to HCJB reports.[13]

Likewise, the FEBC began broadcasting from a modest 1,000-watt transmitter in the Philippines in 1948, initially reaching only those listeners who lived in Manila. Within a year, its signal extended into mainland China, a goal that had acquired considerable urgency after the Chinese Communist Party triumphed in the revolution and expelled Christian missionaries from that country. The FEBC built new stations and increasingly powerful transmitters across Asia and the West Coast of the United States. In 1967, the network covered Latin America, Asia, and the Soviet Union, broadcasting in dozens of different languages and regional dialects. The FEBC reported that it received thousands of letters from listeners across the globe each month.[14] TWR, Eternal Love Winning Africa (ELWA), and others experienced similarly meteoric growth rates.

This growth depended on continued financial support from individuals, churches, and missionary organizations in the United States. In addition to touting the wide potential audiences their stations could reach and the number of individuals they brought to Christ each month, FEBC, HCJB, and other networks appealed to donors by framing their programming as central to the mission of global evangelism, especially behind the Iron and Bamboo Curtains. One FEBC fundraising brochure highlighted the network's reach into China, the Soviet Union, North Vietnam, and Cuba, setting the names of these communist nations in a different color typeface from the many other nations that it listed within its coverage zone. The brochure promised potential donors that "the message of hope in Christ is being heard in lands where unrest and conflict have taken hold," and noted that the broadcasts introduced the unreached to the gospel, won listeners to Christ, and provided spiritual solace to followers throughout the world.[15] The networks also assured their evangelical donor base that local Protestant churches in the regions they broadcast to reacted warmly to their presence and programming.[16] Support rolled in from individual Christians, congregations, and parachurch groups across the United States, allowing for the expansion of missionary radio operations large and small. These donations also knit U.S. evangelicals together with their brethren living and working abroad by creating a literal sense of investment in the success of the stations as well as in the people who tuned in to listen to them.

Donations poured in to support ongoing experimentation with other forms of technology as well, including television, film, and audio recordings. Missionary supply companies touted novel devices such as the "Portable Preacher," a battery and hand-crank-operated tape and record player that included a public-address system and built-in speakers, as a way for evangelists to increase their productivity and efficiency in the field. Indeed, the creator of the Portable Preacher, Missionary Electronics, Inc., asserted that these units would hasten total world evangelization at a fraction of the estimated cost and manpower that the 1960 Congress on World Missions had calculated for the task.[17] According to the company, evangelists could preach on street corners using the PA function or play a record from Gospel Recordings in one of 2,300 languages, enabling the Christian message to penetrate language barriers as well as "any 'curtains,' whether of iron or bamboo, demoniac or 'religious.'"[18] Missionaries could thus gain purchase in countries they perceived as hostile to evangelicals, including those with powerful Catholic, Muslim, or indigenous faith leadership as well as communist governments.

These apparent benefits led other groups to develop similar devices. Eager to reach communities in remote areas that lacked radios, the FEBC distributed what it called "Portable Missionaries"—radio sets pretuned to receive FEBC broadcasts.[19] To aid them in face-to-face evangelism, missionaries in the field also requested less high-tech communications tools such as typewriters, film projectors, mimeograph machines, and copiers, as well as cars, helicopters, and small planes to ease travel.[20] The range of technological and transportation equipment that evangelists sought out created extraordinary opportunities for fundraising and increased demand for products tailored to their needs. This spurred the growth of technology-focused parachurch groups and new mission-adjacent industries, just as it had facilitated the rapid expansion of missionary radio stations.

Despite the pride, excitement, and investment that these experiments generated, Christian media experts grew increasingly concerned by the late 1960s that the ad hoc nature of evangelical technology deployment posed a threat to the mission of the church. Without a coordinated, comprehensive strategy for multimedia evangelism, they feared that Christian radio and television stations might lose their audiences to secular or competing religious programming or that missionaries might fail to take full advantage of all of the tools at their disposal. Missionary media organizations working independently of one another also risked duplicating efforts and thus wasting resources.[21]

Concerned about this and dismayed that so many of his fellow Christians seemed "completely unaware of and unprepared" for the communications revolution, Scottish missionary and journalist George Patterson underscored the need for an international communications clearinghouse.[22] In 1968, he published an article in *Christianity Today* that detailed advances in satellite and network technology that would make it possible to connect with "anyone, anywhere at any time, by voice, sight, or document" within the decade.[23] The crisis of missions firmly in mind, Patterson argued that this technology combined with fundraising acumen, mass media expertise, and appropriate cultural training would make it "possible to present the Christian Gospel in any form . . . to any country, tribe, or class," in the world.[24] It also held great promise for indigenous evangelism and "the universal cross-fertilization of believers" wherein Christian leaders from India or other parts of Asia might spread their message to regional neighbors as well as to Americans.[25] Yet the window of opportunity appeared distressingly narrow. As satellites grew more powerful, the receiving stations on the ground would become less expensive; cheaper radio and television sets would follow and proliferate. Patterson noted that at that point even "under-developed" countries would be able to construct national communications networks, which might make missionary broadcasting more difficult. More threateningly, the strongest, most advanced nations might seek to exert control over satellite systems or the programming that flowed through them. Patterson asserted that the church had to get in at the outset or risk losing access to the networks and the governing bodies that would regulate them.[26]

The same month his article appeared in *Christianity Today*, Patterson joined twelve other Christian media leaders at a meeting in Chicago to lay the groundwork for greater evangelical cooperation in the communications field. Representatives from Campus Crusade for Christ, the Evangelical Foreign Missions Association, Wheaton College, Evangelical Literature Overseas, International Christian Broadcasters and other media and missionary organizations gathered in a conference room at O'Hare airport with the aim of creating "an overall 'umbrella' fellowship" that would bring focus and efficiency to mass media evangelism.[27] Together, they founded the Evangelical Communications Commission, a loose consortium they hoped would encourage member organizations to collaborate on research, share information, host conferences, and help missionaries develop strategies for more effective global evangelism.[28]

The organization struggled to get off the ground. According to a report from the Evangelical Press Association, "the group could not nail down the specific role the commission would play or the extent of its authority in serving its member agencies," even though the participants agreed on the need for a coordinating body.[29] Still, they met regularly through the early 1970s. In 1971, the group reorganized and renamed itself the Christian Communications Council, adding key members such as the NRB and the Missions Advanced Research and Communications Center, hosting seminars, and launching a newsletter. Member organizations continued to undertake their own initiatives but kept the Christian Communications Council involved or at least apprised of their projects. Wheaton College, which had launched a graduate program in communications in 1968 to provide training in cross-cultural media evangelism, received funding from the council to support a graduate student intern at the ELWA radio station in Liberia, for example.[30] Nevertheless, with its limited staffing and financing, the council found it difficult to achieve its stated mission of bringing "consensus and cooperation" to evangelical and missionary media agencies throughout the world.[31]

The WEF and the ICOWE helped to turn the tide for the project of global evangelical communications coordination that the Christian Communications Council and its member agencies sought. In 1973, the head of both the WEF and the NAE Clyde Taylor approached several leaders involved with the council with the idea of forming a new communications body under the auspices of the WEF.[32] This commission, global in scope, would include representatives from evangelical communications organizations in each participating country. For the United States, this meant the NRB and the media arm of the National Association of Evangelicals.[33] Planning for the commission proceeded apace with preparation for the ICOWE communications strategy group and included input from Butler and other strategy group participants.

At its July 1974 meeting, the General Assembly of the WEF announced the founding of its Communications Commission. The WEF appointed Dr. Ben Armstrong of the NRB as chairman, with Rev. Fred Magbanua of the FEBC in the Philippines and Rev. Horst Marquardt of Evangeliums-Rundfunk, the German branch of TWR as members of the commission steering committee.[34] This steering committee met with Christian media leaders from each continent, taking steps to establish the WEF Communications Commission (WEFCC) as a central coordinating body for global mass media. In addition to working closely with the Christian communicators already operating in Asia, Africa, and Latin America, the WEFCC aimed to gather and share technical strategies with affiliated evangelistic agencies. It also made a plea for regular reports and local news from members abroad, reminding recipients of its newsletter that "as you share information and ideas, you will be advancing the world-wide task of communicating the Gospel."[35]

Both the membership and the goals of the WEFCC overlapped with the ICOWE communications strategy group and the recommendations it advanced, and thus the two bodies worked together closely after the congress. The strategy group elected an eight-member task force under Butler's chairmanship to implement its recommendations. This task force included representatives from the WEFCC and three member organizations of the Christian Communications Council—Evangelical Literature Overseas, Wheaton College, and the International Christian Broadcasters. Timothy Yu of Hong Kong Baptist College, Menkir Esayas of Radio Voice of the Gospel in Ethiopia, and Peter Church of Go-Tell Communications in South Africa—who were all also members of the WEFCC—rounded out the group. The recurrence of these individuals and agencies across multiple communications bodies thickened the network of evangelical media leaders, connecting national groups in the United States such as the NRB with their counterparts throughout the world. Indeed, the task force requested that in selecting their reps, the WEFCC and other U.S.-based communications organizations "appoint a third-world representative wherever possible" to ensure a truly international approach to their efforts to nurture mass media evangelism.[36] Butler, in particular, stressed the need for developing "a local-church centeredness to our use of the media" through the development of communications groups in each country, as well as the creation of regional training centers and conferences.[37]

The international scope and interconnected membership of the ICOWE task force and the WEFCC, coupled with the momentum for world evangelism that the Lausanne Movement inspired, brought renewed attention and cohesion to missionary radio, television, and media. These organizations supported regional initiatives, such as the creation of an All Asia Communications Fellowship, as well as international Christian communications conferences, and provided subsidies so that media practitioners from the Global South could attend.[38] They also ensured that their conferences included demonstrations of new technologies and sessions on how to apply for "TV and radio time, newspaper space, licenses and permits."[39] The pointed efforts to attract rank-and-file media workers, rather than famous televangelists, and offer practical "how-to" sessions on navigating legal and regulatory processes underscored the WEFCC's desire to expand global accessibility to evangelical media. Without access to state-regulated media channels in Africa, Latin American, and Asia, the gospel message would spread only as far as an individual mission field. Christian broadcasts over powerful transmitters blanketed entire countries though and extended into states that banned missionaries and their media entirely.

Through newsletters, publications, and conference announcements, which they circulated to their massive international mailing lists, the WEFCC and the task force helped forge new transnational relationships among evangelical leaders. Christian communicators living in Africa, Asia, and Latin America expressed their desire to collaborate with the organization, to attend its conferences, and to share news about their local media projects.[40] Many, including the founders of the All Asia Communications Fellowship, looked to the WEFCC and its affiliated organizations in the United States for funding to expand their local and regional evangelistic efforts.[41] Closer coordination allowed individual Christian communicators to become nodes in a larger global evangelical network that connected media, parachurch, and denominational leaders with ordinary believers across national boundaries. These connections brought coherence to their global communications efforts and a new attentiveness among U.S. evangelicals to the work that African, Asian, and Latin American Christians were doing to advance the mission of the church. With the values of partnership and reciprocity that the global Lausanne Movement inspired in mind, evangelical leaders in the United States embraced media technologies as essential tools to support cross-cultural evangelism and their Christian brethren living abroad.

A Theology of Mass Media

Having set the wheels of global collaboration in motion, Christian communicators turned their attention to developing more effective evangelistic programming and media strategies. In part, this required the articulation of a new theology of mass media, which would ensure that broadcast organizations and individual producers took a systematic approach to sharing the gospel through media. Mass media theologies wedded the ultimate goal of the ICOWE—achieving the Great Commission—with the recognition that in the postcolonial era, missionaries had to try to avoid cultural chauvinism and find new ways to package their message. By aligning communications practices with evangelical tenets and the spiritual underpinnings of the Lausanne Movement, media proponents ensured that communications technology became a central component of cross-cultural missionary outreach.[42] In time, some evangelical media leaders, including Ben Armstrong, even began ascribing prophetic qualities to new communications technology. This development made mass media evangelism seem all the more essential to the mission of the church.

The Bible contained ample guidance on how to use television, radio, and emerging computer networks to share the gospel globally, according to Phillip Butler. His paper for the ICOWE, "Evangelism and the Media: A Theological Basis for Action," used extensive scriptural exegesis to make a case for constant innovation in missionary communications technology and messaging. Butler began with Genesis, arguing that by granting man "dominion over the natural fruit of this world's element," God had also charged humanity with the responsibility to use those fruits—including those that man assembled into new forms, such as media—to bring "redemption" to the world.[43] Responsible dominion required efficiency though, per the "command for wise stewardship found in Matthew 25:14–30."[44] Butler viewed novel technologies as a means for increasing efficiency. He read Ephesians 5:16–17 and Colossians 4:5 (both of which entreated believers to make "the most of the time") as having a direct connection to mass media since radio and television could introduce the gospel to "large numbers at low cost" and at remarkable speed.[45] Beyond conceiving of communications technology as a form of wise resource stewardship, Butler interpreted biblical stories of God using "many types of communications through the centuries"—from Jesus as described in John 1 to "plagues, pillars (of salt, fire, cloud), animals (remember the ass that spoke?), rainbows, and manna"—as evidence that man too should use all available means to share the Christian faith.[46]

In Butler's estimation, the Bible gave clear instructions on how to reach a range of different audiences, and thus provided a foundation for effective cross-cultural and indigenous media evangelism. Setting goals, and conducting audience research to decide how to best meet those goals, were the necessary first steps in any successful media campaign. Butler referenced the admonition for planning in Luke 14:28–30 to remind readers that unless evangelists started off with a defined outcome in mind in terms of how they hoped their audience would receive and understand their message, they would fail in their mission of evangelizing the world.[47] Referencing 1 Corinthians, Acts 17, and Acts 26, he suggested that the apostle Paul knew, given the vast diversity of the world's cultures, that "the form for the message may have to be modified to meet different audiences, even within a single geographic location."[48] Butler viewed these scriptures as "a plea" that fellow believers should heed "to break down the audience into its natural segments—by language, education, ethnic or religious patterns—whatever is necessary for effective communication."[49] Many of the other participants on the ICOWE task force and the WEFCC agreed and called for greater investment in audience research.[50]

If, as Butler argued, the Bible called on Christians to match the medium they used to share their message with the cultural context of each given audience, he also cautioned his readers that mass media programming had to meet potential followers where they were in their individual spiritual journeys. Although those eagerly seeking out the Christian faith might prove receptive to a worship service broadcast over the radio, individuals who were indifferent or hostile to Christianity likely would not be. Even those who listened to or watched missionary programming attentively might not become committed to the faith. Butler viewed mass media evangelism as a multistep process that must include "sowing, watering, and reaping," as described in First Corinthians.[51] He worried that media evangelists focused too much on creating programming for individuals that were already open to the gospel, a tendency that allowed them to "reap" a small number of converts quickly, but not cultivate the seed of the faith deeply in the larger community.

As such, he contended that evangelists should develop holistic mass media programs *"specifically* targeted" to the tasks of sowing, watering, and reaping.[52]

Butler believed that if missionaries could develop a strong bond with evangelicals in Africa, Asia, Latin America, and the Soviet bloc through media, while also providing them with tools and other support to build and expand their own local churches (to sow and water), the Christian faith would flourish. He and his fellow ICOWE presenter David Chao reasoned that radio and television programming were the first step "to make contact with the listener—allowing literature, personal follow-up, or other media to carry the process of evangelism to its conclusion."[53] Radio, television, and print programming tailored to nurture the gospel at multiple stages and in collaboration with local Christians formed the centerpiece of the mass media theology that Butler and his contemporaries articulated at Lausanne.

By the late 1970s, the growth and influence of the Lausanne Movement had helped to embed these core ideas in evangelical thinking about global media and strategies for witness. In 1979, James F. Engel, a professor in the Wheaton College graduate program in communications, published *Contemporary Christian Communications: Its Theory and Practice.* The book expanded on a paper he had given at the ICOWE that discussed potential media strategies for evangelizing culturally diverse audiences.[54] Both the original paper and *Contemporary Christian Communications* blended mass media theology with concepts drawn from professional, secular communications practices. Engel, like Butler, interpreted the role of media in evangelism through the lens of First Corinthians, referencing the apostle Paul to assert that "the mass media are useful in planting or seed sowing, whereas personal influence is the primary means of watering and reaping."[55] He combed through studies on the efficacy of mass media in overseas and domestic evangelism and concluded that media typically played a key "contributory" (rather than a "decisive") role in conversion.[56] The studies Engel cited suggested to him that religious broadcasting supported evangelism by "creating a climate of acceptance of the standards of Christian life and conduct," with face-to-face witness providing the final, determinative factor in gaining new adherents to the faith.[57]

Yet Engel acknowledged that in areas that lacked an active local church, media proved crucial. He observed that "shortwave radio, in particular, appears to have played a more decisive role in the communist countries," though he conceded it was difficult to get conclusive evidence about audience reception from behind the Iron Curtain.[58] The studies that Engel discussed dovetailed with the debates over the future of missions at the ICOWE, leading him to conclude that missionaries had to integrate mass media with face-to-face evangelism conducted through local churches. These findings reflected the ideas generated in the papers and discussions from his fellow media strategy group members at the Lausanne Congress.[59]

In this way, Engel saw great promise for shortwave radio as an evangelistic tool, and he offered his readers and students a set of instructions for using the medium effectively for cross-cultural evangelism. First, he noted that offering a balance of content, including news and entertainment as well as religious programming, provided the most effective means for building an audience. Attracting secular listeners through "general airfare" while still providing for the needs of Christian listeners was essential.[60] Yet for the religious programming to appeal to believers and receptive nonbelievers, it had to make sense in the local context. Engel argued that simply translating the Bible word-for-word into another language stripped the text of its meaning, which made it difficult for listeners to see Christian teachings as relevant to their lives.[61] He urged Christian media producers to focus instead on what he called "dynamic equivalence" to convey the core messages of the Bible.[62] Here he blended new media theology with practical instruction. Rather than direct word-for-word translations, Engel believed that finding the "linkages between Christian ways and cultural patterns" that existed in each country or mission field would allow Christian communicators to make the faith legible and familiar for all audiences.[63]

Engel's suggestions mirrored those of other influential evangelists. Ted Engstrom, an executive with the missionary and humanitarian organization World Vision International, emphasized the same need for cross-cultural evangelism. In his 1978 book on missionary work, he advocated partnering with local Christians to discern which aspects of a given culture evangelists might draw on to convey the gospel message in the most resonant, effective way.[64] World Vision, and its research arm the Missions Advanced Research and Communication Center (MARC), played a vital role in gathering data on unevangelized peoples for the Lausanne Movement and had long advocated using technology to discover these points of resonance and thus foster cross-cultural evangelism.[65] The conversations that unfolded at the ICOWE both reflected and shaped Engstrom's thinking about the need to merge cross-cultural communications with new media.

Furthermore, he and Engel expanded on these core concepts in their respective work, developing new strategies for the Lausanne Movement and disseminating them for wider practice. Engstrom brought these ideas into his influential writings on missions and his work with World Vision. Engel, in his role as a communications professor at Wheaton College, shaped future Christian communicators through his teaching. He also served energetically on the WEFCC. The confluence of thinking on the theological underpinnings of media and mission among U.S. evangelical leaders lent great credibility to the project of Christian communications. With the Lausanne Movement and the WEFCC acting as unifying, galvanizing forces, the theology of mass media that Butler, Engel, Engstrom, and the strategy group members generated guided evangelical outreach abroad throughout the late 1970s and 1980s.

Linking evangelism and communications technology through scripture also contributed to the prophetic language that Christian media influencers, particularly Ben Armstrong, began to use when discussing new communications tools such as satellites and computer networks. Armstrong had an extensive background in Christian media and enjoyed wide authority as an evangelical opinion leader. After serving as the director of radio for TWR from 1958 until 1966, and earning a PhD in mass communications from New York University along the way, Armstrong took over as director of the NRB.[66] He handled global television and radio coverage for the ICOWE in 1974; that same year, the WEFCC elected him as its chairman. In 1979 he published *The Electric Church*, which traced the history of radio and television evangelism, casting religious broadcasting as the titular "electric church" that made worship at once global and local. He believed that this aspect of Christian broadcasting reestablished "conditions remarkably similar to the early church," a restorationist goal many evangelicals sought to realize.[67] Armstrong closed the book with a chapter on the future of religious broadcasting, focusing on satellites that would allow "television, radio, computers, and other information-processing devices to become an all-encompassing communications resource" within just a few years.[68] After describing the first religious broadcast ever transmitted over satellite, which he participated in with the NRB and TWR in 1971, he launched into an expansive prophecy about the role of satellites in the fulfillment of the Great Commission.

Armstrong believed that satellite broadcasting might be a pivotal piece of the end times, as depicted in the Book of Revelation. He viewed satellite broadcasting initiatives such as "Project Look Up," which sought to beam "seminary teaching and lay leader institutes" to receivers installed in underserved communities in Latin America, as the beginning of a promising new global evangelistic strategy.[69] Project Look Up fit in neatly within WEFCC objectives too, providing Bible education to local Christians who could then evangelize in their own communities, without requiring much if any direct involvement on the ground from Western missionaries. Armstrong saw larger eschatological implications. He argued that the existence of satellite technology made it possible for evangelicals to blanket the earth with the gospel, bringing the good news to all nations and then the end times, as described in Matthew 24:14.[70]

Trusting that he was living in this apocalyptic period, Armstrong conflated the angel described in Revelation 14:6, who preached the gospel from heaven to all peoples on earth, with communications satellites. These satellites, he argued, would help ensure that all of the peoples on earth "experience the fulfillment of the next verse of Revelation" by proclaiming the glory of God.[71] He developed this idea further, stating:

> Is it possible that the angel specified in Revelation 14:6, 7 is a heavenly body weighing forty-seven hundred pounds, measuring eighteen feet in length and eight feet in width, flying in geosynchronous orbit twenty-two thousand miles above the earth? . . . Only in recent years has it been possible technologically for a heavenly body to 'fly in the midst of heaven' with a message for those who dwell on earth. With several communications satellites in operation today, it does not seem altogether unreasonable to assume that the communications satellite may become the fulfillment of the prophecy of John who saw the vision of the "other angel" almost two thousand years ago.[72]

Having suggested that God may have sent satellite technology as this prophesied angel, Armstrong hoped that evangelicals would invest in their own satellites, which they could use exclusively for global preaching without government oversight or competition from other faiths or secular sources.[73]

When the WEFCC met in London in March 1980, Armstrong convened a "New Technology Study Group" to discuss communications satellites and the creation of a new evangelical satellite broadcast network. During the meeting, the group debated the feasibility of such a network at length, and Armstrong introduced his idea for fulfilling Revelation 14:6–7 by funding three satellites named Angel I, II, and III to beam the gospel to all reaches of the globe.[74] Ultimately, the proposal for purchasing satellites did not get too far, but the discussions on satellite networks and communications more generally did lay the groundwork for WEFCC coordination on broadcasting throughout the 1980s.

Indeed, the London WEFCC meeting proved crucial in setting up technology training for evangelicals throughout the world as well as in raising awareness about and financial support for Christian radio stations and other media operations in Muslim, Catholic, and communist nations. Representatives from Brazil, India, Spain, and Nigeria balanced their excitement about the expansion of Christian communications in their countries with the challenges that a lack of trained personnel and competition (or regulation) from government, secular, and other religious media posed.[75] Reverend Panya Baba of Nigeria noted that both Christians and Muslims in his country clamored for religious radio and television; with training, he believed he and his team could develop Christian programming more efficiently, and thus gain greater market share for evangelistic channels.[76] In a similar vein, a representative of the European Evangelical Communicators Association praised Christian radio programming for contributing to revivals in the Soviet Union and parts of the Eastern bloc but noted the difficulty that Christian broadcasters in Europe experienced in terms of amassing financing for their endeavors.[77] The meeting participants gave the impression that evangelicals throughout the world were eager to put media to use to "let the earth hear His voice," just as soon as they received technical training, funding, and the autonomy to create programs that reflected their local cultural contexts.

In response to such requests, the WEFCC created a new training committee, which included Phillip Butler and James Engel, to study contemporary media training and implement new programs.[78] One committee member, Gladys Jasper, highlighted the Asia Christian Communications Fellowship, which provided technical instruction in theological schools, as well as tape recording ministries that served illiterate populations, as exemplars for media leaders in other countries to emulate.[79] Concerned that providing an "exclusively Western model" of communications training would hinder evangelism and receptivity to this training, members of the WEFCC also pushed for culturally specific models, including the use of "folk media," such as dance dramas in India.[80] Reverend Baba and others recommended that local Christians take charge of programming wherever possible, rather than Western evangelists or media organizations.[81] These recommendations made manifest the influence of the ICOWE, both in terms of the emphasis they placed on embracing all means available to spread the gospel and in reflecting, at least to some extent, the voices and expertise of Latin American, African, and Asian evangelicals.

Establishing a theological basis for mass media evangelism, along with extensive work on audience research, programmatic strategies, and technical training, created common ground for Christian communicators operating throughout the world. As these media workers organized and attended conferences, drafted and shared training manuals, and developed new techniques for expanding their audiences, they became points of contact and information exchange in a larger global network of evangelicals. The WEFCC did not direct the activities of Christian broadcasters, but it did provide a clearinghouse of information that organizations large and small could consult. Its core members generated important ideas at their meetings that percolated into books, articles, and the classroom, establishing best practices as well as future goals for evangelical technology use. The sense that evangelicals must embrace emerging technology to achieve the Great Commission spread from the upper echelons of organizations such as the WEFCC and the NRB to the operators of even the smallest, most remote missionary radio stations. As this process unfolded, Western evangelical communications leaders acknowledged the ideals of "cultural sensitivity" and local control that many members of the Lausanne Movement advocated. Yet they embraced them imperfectly at best, as European and U.S. evangelicals continued to hold most positions of authority in organizations such as the WEF and in missionary broadcasting more generally. Still, the advances in radio, television, tape, and other technology-based ministries had a profound effect, expanding the reach of evangelical missions to peoples in a range of regions, including previously unreached areas and countries that Western evangelicals viewed as hostile.

Media Evangelism in "Hostile" Lands

The attention that the WEFCC and the Lausanne Movement brought to Christian communications lent credibility and a strong sense of shared purpose to the many evangelistic media enterprises that had emerged by the 1970s. According to historian Timothy Stoneman, the programmatic and logistical strategies that evangelical media producers adopted in this period had helped to "legitimize evangelicalism" among people living in predominantly Catholic and Islamic nations as well as those under communist rule.[82] This legitimization facilitated the growth of churches and helped amplify receptivity to the gospel message.[83] Yet it also brought increased scrutiny from political and religious leaders who opposed the spread of evangelical Christianity in their countries. Western evangelicals took note of worsening political circumstances for their brethren in these so-called hostile nations, concerned that restrictive regulations and outright religious persecution would hinder the achievement of the Great Commission. At the same time, Christian mass media acted as a form of two-way communication, connecting believers in the United States with those who lived abroad, as well as forging links among evangelicals living in Asian, Latin American, African, and Soviet bloc states. As Christian communicators learned more about the struggles their coreligionists faced in other countries, they adapted their media programming, communications techniques, and use of technology accordingly. The challenges that these evangelists sought to overcome by broadcasting the gospel made the scale and threat of religious repression abroad all the more manifest to believers in the United States. In time this knowledge mobilized evangelical activism and advocacy for global religious freedom.

Christian expatriates from Soviet bloc countries formed an important base of evangelistic broadcasting and media distribution to the USSR and Eastern Europe. Organizations such as Word to Russia, the Voice of Salvation, Inc., Eastern European Missions, and the Slavic Gospel Association (SGA), which Russian immigrant Peter Deyneka Sr. founded in 1934, embraced radio evangelism early on as a means to minister to their brethren in the communist world. Deyneka, who traveled to Quito in 1941 to record sixteen sermons in Russian for global broadcast from the HCJB station, claimed he was the first minister to preach the gospel over shortwave radio to Soviet audiences.[84] Listener response to these sermons encouraged him to recruit other Russian-speaking Christian expats and immigrants to produce radio shows that would air at regular intervals.[85] In the decades that followed, SGA significantly expanded its operations, offering programming in multiple Slavic languages and recording material for broadcast over HCJB, Trans World Radio, Far East Broadcasting, and eight other missionary radio stations.[86] By the mid-1970s, the SGA was a major player in the field of Christian mass media, as well as a steadfast advocate for believers behind the Iron Curtain who were suffering from state persecution.

The SGA, along with Word to Russia and similar groups, shared reports from Baptists, Pentecostals, and other unregistered or "underground" Christian sects in the Soviet Union that painted a picture of religious life that was at once exuberant and forcefully constrained. One Associated Press article reported that despite bans on printing Bibles and religious literature, Soviet evangelicals "publish thousands of religious books from secret printing plants and distribute them all over the country. They [also] circulate newsletters clandestinely to their members and collect money" to fund their work.[87] In addition to risking arrest to practice and propagate their faith as they saw fit, some of these underground evangelicals printed books about human rights abuses in the Soviet Union, which they distributed alongside their religious texts.[88] Such enterprises attracted unwanted attention from state security agents. The KGB frequently raided and harassed underground Christian publishers, shutting down presses, confiscating Bibles, and arresting those involved, not to mention targeting evangelical ministers who refused to register their churches with the state or who ran "illegal Sunday schools."[89]

Russian and Eastern European expats in the United States drew attention to these raids to remind U.S. evangelicals of the persecution their coreligionists faced in the communist world. One Word to Russia newsletter queried readers, "Would secret printing presses be necessary if freedom of worship existed behind the Iron Curtain? Would secret printing presses be necessary if Bibles and other Christian materials could be purchased in their own cities?"[90] Beyond raising awareness about infringements on religious liberty, these organizations encouraged readers to provide spiritual support to persecuted Christians abroad by funding missionary radio, television, and mass communications.

In this way, U.S. evangelicals came to believe that radio evangelism, tape cassette ministries, and other means of sharing the word via unofficial channels might help circumvent the restrictions communist governments imposed on religious believers, services, and education. Radio ministers such as Earl Poysti attracted significant followings among Soviet Christians and carried on an extensive correspondence with fans.[91] Newsletters printed testimonials from Baptist, Pentecostal, and Seventh-Day Adventist listeners living and ministering in the Soviet bloc who attested to the benefits of Russian-language programming while also revealing the depth of spiritual need. One Russian listener wrote to Word to Russia to ask for a copy of the New Testament and to praise the organization for its programs: "Your broadcasts are coming in very clear. Our brethren are recording them on magnetic tape and sending them to other places."[92] After receiving reports that listeners were sharing radio broadcasts, U.S. organizations raised money to send tape recorders to Christians in Bulgaria and other Soviet bloc countries, so they might record and send radio sermons to believers "in isolated areas where no churches exist."[93] This allowed local Christians to support and reach out to individuals that U.S. missionaries would never be able to contact directly on their own. Evangelical media producers still expressed anxiety about their ability to make religious broadcasts appealing to nonbelievers, yet their radio programs helped them build important relationships with existing Soviet Christians. These relationships gave listeners a sense of belonging to a larger, global community of the faithful, and the programs steeled their resolve to evangelize their countrymen.

Figure 3. Peter Deyneka Jr. of the Slavic Gospel Association working with radio recording equipment in January 1965. Tapes of the SGA's evangelistic radio programs line the shelves behind him. Courtesy of Special Collections, Buswell Library.

This was true for Christians in Communist China and Southeast Asia as well. In 1971, the FEBC launched what it called the "Open Door" project to construct two 250,000-watt transmitters to blanket China, Vietnam, Cambodia, Laos, and North Korea with the gospel. Although the network had been broadcasting into the region for more than twenty-five years, almost around the clock, it sought to extend and expand its operations as much as possible. After the completion of these transmitters in 1975, FEBC fundraising letters announced "MISSION ACCOMPLISHED! . . . ? In one way, yes . . . but from another perspective the battle is NOW engaged!" as they could now attempt to evangelize the "921 million people in Asia behind atheistic curtains."[94] The FEBC assured potential funders that their support was generating conversions and providing a haven for Christians suffering persecution in China.[95] The director of the FEBC in Hong Kong reported to evangelical news agencies that "nearly half of the mail response from Mainland China [that he received] [was] generated by the three hours of Mandarin programming broadcast" from just one of the two new transmitters.[96]

Supporters of missionary radio networks believed that radio programs provided concrete tools to help these listeners become lay leaders and local evangelists. The Slavic Gospel Association received letters from believers in Russia and Eastern Europe who claimed that, due to isolation and restrictions on church building and evangelism, "the radio programs are their only church."[97] Lacking access to printed religious texts in their language, these listeners asked for more programs with dictation-speed readings of the Bible, so they might "write down portions of the Holy Writ into notebooks and have part of the Bible for their very own."[98] They could then exchange these hand-copied scriptures with friends, family members, and fellow believers. Peter Deyneka Jr., who took over from his father as the head of the SGA in 1975, asserted that ministers of underground Soviet churches welcomed the broadcasts, viewing them as a vital counterpart to their ministry and essential for reaching potential followers in remote areas.[99] They also considered broadcasts aimed explicitly at nonbelievers crucial, as they helped pave the way for more effective local evangelism.[100] Noting that Soviet law banned Bible schools for children and seminaries for ministers, the SGA reported that listeners relied on its "Bible Institute of the Air," which offered Bible training for lay leaders and ministers alike, and that Soviet Christians expressed a strong desire for children's educational programming.[101] Such letters proved invaluable for evangelical broadcasters eager to gauge local reactions to their programming, especially given the methodological challenges they encountered when conducting audience research in the Soviet Union and other closed societies.

While letters from listeners provided guidance on producing programs that would nurture the spiritual lives of existing believers and facilitate their evangelistic efforts, broadcasters also studied state reactions for evidence of their reach and influence on nonbelievers. The Institute of Soviet and East European Studies (ISEES), part of the Slavic Gospel Association, collected and translated articles from Russian newspapers that revealed Soviet frustrations with Western Christian media providers. The ISEES seemed particularly keen on gathering articles that complained about the SGA as a subversive foreign group, likely because such articles ensured domestic supporters that the organization was effective.[102] As Peter Deyneka noted, "if Christian radio were having no effect upon Russian citizens then the Russian government would not be attacking religious broadcasts from the West in their atheistic magazines and newspapers as they do."[103] Missionary radio stations carefully avoided political commentary on the air, fearful that communist

Figure 4. Peter Deyneka Jr. of the Slavic Gospel Association standing in front of a map of Eastern Europe and Russia plotted with pushpins representing listener responses to SGA evangelistic radio programs. Deyneka holds a stack of letters from Soviet bloc listeners. Courtesy of Special Collections, Buswell Library.

governments would have even more reason to try to jam their broadcasts. Nevertheless, Christian media organizations viewed Russian complaints about the "anti-Soviet" nature of the hours of religious programming beamed into their country each day as evidence of success in their mission.[104]

According to the news articles that the ISEES gathered, Soviet leaders regarded shortwave religious broadcasts as a threat to their national security. One reporter culled quotes from *Trud*, a Russian trade union newspaper, which revealed that government officials described radio evangelism as "purposeful propaganda of militant anti-communists trying to undermine Socialism from within," and complained that "the voices of religious radio advocates cease neither by day nor night."[105] They also decried evangelical efforts to smuggle in Bibles. An article in *Komsomolskaya Pravda* described in bitter detail the methods by which evangelicals distributed religious literature from the ship *Logos* to Russian sailors docked in a nearby port in Singapore: "Naturally, our foes see our seaman as a special target. He is not just an isolated object to be bombarded by 'agitators' on the land and on the high seas. Our seaman's families and friends are scattered over the length and breadth of our country. Therefore a package of 'Christ's teachings' in a seaman's chest can be distributed far and wide."[106] This was exactly the effect that the evangelical broadcasters and missionary organizations that collected and shared such reports hoped for, and official concern about it suggested they were reaching at least some nonbelievers in addition to their already-committed audience of Soviet Christians.

Missionary broadcasters also aroused suspicions from government officials in parts of the Middle East, despite their stated efforts to craft programming and materials with "a sensitivity to people of Islamic background."[107] In 1979, a former Learjet executive named George K. Otis Sr. founded Voice of Hope, a Christian radio station based in Southern Lebanon, just a few miles from the border with Metula, Israel. In an interview for the WEFCC newsletter right before launching the venture, Otis reported that the signal from his station could reach "into Turkey, Egypt, Iraq, and Iran as well as covering Israel, Lebanon, Syria and Jordan."[108] Voice of Hope played a mix of country music and newscasts, but Otis assured readers that "each 15-minute segment will include one Gospel number and what we call 'God's commercial,' a 60-second reading of the Word. This will offer Old Testament passages . . . starting with Psalms, Proverbs, then Isaiah."[109] Much like radio evangelists beaming the word into the Soviet Union, Otis claimed that he wanted to avoid antagonizing non-Christians, so as to increase his chances of winning new adherents and providing spiritual succor to existing believers.[110]

Voice of Hope did help its parent organization, the California-based High Adventure Ministries, forge deeper connections with Lebanese Christians, but it also exacerbated tensions in a country in the midst of a civil war. By early 1981, the news it broadcast over the airwaves was "decidedly slanted in favor of" Major Saad Haddad, the "born-again" leader of an Israeli-backed Lebanese Christian militia that was locked in violent conflict with its Palestinian neighbors.[111] The militia leader had welcomed Otis and Voice of Hope with open arms in 1979, claiming that the Christian station would "bring light in our darkest hour and help to save my people."[112] As the civil war intensified, Haddad sometimes came on the radio station himself to issue warnings to members of the Palestine Liberation Organization (and any Lebanese civilians in their midst) about impending artillery fire and shelling.[113] This led many in the region to conclude that Voice of Hope was actually a "U.S. government connivance" intended to lend support to Israel at the expense of the Palestinians and the Lebanese.[114] The State Department despaired in its inability to curb the relationship between the U.S. evangelical radio program and the Christian militia leader. Otis informed State Department officials that he saw his mission in Lebanon as one that promoted "human rights and good work" because he was spreading the gospel in a region he viewed as "hostile" to his faith.[115] Despite assaults on the station at various points during the civil war, Voice of Hope continued to broadcast from its post on the border.[116] It also maintained strong support from evangelicals in the United States, including televangelist Pat Robertson, and operated as a base for missionary communications throughout the Middle East.[117]

In parts of the world that U.S. evangelicals considered "open" or at least more readily accessible to evangelism, Christian communicators steadily expanded their mass media offerings and the networks of local personnel needed to produce the programs during the late 1970s. The Evangelical Church of West Africa (ECWA), an indigenous organization that grew out of the Sudan Interior Mission, set up a training program to ensure that Nigerian Christians could produce programming to air on the nineteen satellite-linked state television stations in Nigeria by 1980. These programs, which ranged from television dramas to newscasts to educational shows for children, all featured a "Christian, church-building emphasis."[118] In addition, the ECWA oversaw a range of other outreach efforts, including Bible correspondence courses, bookstores, tape ministries, and Radio ELWA. Derek Frost, a U.S. missionary with the Sudan Interior Mission who directed the television training course, hoped that by putting West Africans in charge of producing their own media programs, they might succeed in "reaching the 20 million pagans and 35 million Moslems in Nigeria . . . while benefiting the 25 million Christians."[119] Besides their belief in the greater efficacy of local evangelism, media leaders working on the African continent also sensed that local control of radio and television programs would help them establish friendlier relationships with the government officials who regulated the stations. A meeting between African church leaders and members of TWR in Swaziland emphasized this point in particular, concluding that locals rather than expats should run each country's stations as well as the regional offices that coordinated TWR efforts across the continent.[120] Similar impulses informed the development of Christian communications in Latin America and Southeast Asia.[121]

By the early 1980s then, evangelicals who supported the use of novel communications technology had developed a thick, cross-woven global network of indigenous, expatriate, and Western believers who operated media enterprises and remained in regular contact with one another. Radio, television, satellites, and tape cassette ministries were just the beginning though. Newsletters from organizations as diverse in their approaches to evangelism as the Mission Aviation Fellowship and Intercessors for the Suffering Church boasted about their adoption of emerging computer technology in the late 1970s through the 1980s. The former began programming its own micro-computers to process data and schedule flights for its helicopter-based ministry in Africa, Asia, and Latin America.[122] Intercessors for the Suffering Church meanwhile used its then state-of-the-art Apple II computer to circulate newsletters and calendars for prayer on behalf of persecuted Christians, as well as to engage in "electronic evangelism" through the online bulletin board systems on CompuServe.[123] Evangelicals tended to see a divine purpose in the new media and technology that flooded the consumer markets in the 1970s and 1980s. This perception encouraged them to master and sometimes repurpose technology to fulfill their mission of sharing the gospel with all peoples of the world. Whether they embraced this technology as a tool to foster missionary work in remote areas or as a means of connecting with persecuted brethren from afar via computer, radio, or television, evangelicals used modern communications to create unprecedentedly cross-cultural and transnational communities.

The Limits of Technology

Evangelicals had emerged from the 1974 International Congress on World Evangelization with a capacious vision for achieving the Great Commission.

Global cooperation, local and "culturally sensitive" spiritual outreach, and technological innovation were key pillars of the strategy that they developed in Lausanne and implemented at continuation meetings and international congresses over the ensuing decades. The Lausanne Movement provided direction, encouragement, and loose coordination to the diverse organizations and individuals that identified themselves as evangelical and committed themselves to the project of world evangelism. The sense of connection and common purpose that Lausanne generated meant that even small organizations that did not participate directly in the congress or its affiliated offshoots still understood themselves as part of a networked evangelical whole. They were discrete, independent entities, yet members of a global church. Modern communications technology provided the conduits necessary to link them together despite the distances that separated them, whether those distances were geographical, cultural, or political.

Technology took on new forms and applications in the 1970s, but evangelicals had long embraced new media tools in their missionary work. Still, the ICOWE was a technology incubator of sorts, acting as a catalyst for more rigorous study into which types of media, communication methods, and programs were best for reaching unreached or restricted populations. On a philosophical level, the major debates that defined the congress and revealed the growing consensus in favor of indigenous evangelism and local church control also had a signal effect on conversations among Christian communicators as they considered how to deploy technology and develop cross-cultural programs. Even though Western missionaries or expatriates living in the United States or Europe controlled many religious radio and television stations, they had an acute understanding that they could not simply translate Christian programming designed for Western audiences into foreign languages and expect it to resonate in other cultural contexts. They also recognized the desirability of local control in both open and closed societies and sought out the means to support those developments. These were often halting and imperfect efforts. Nevertheless, the outcome of these efforts and the push for more coordinated, expanded communications technology in missionary work was significant. Through communications and mass media, evangelicals in the United States and abroad developed a sense of internationalism and a shared global identity; they also greatly increased their knowledge about the lives of believers in other nations, including repressive or otherwise "hostile" ones.

This knowledge encouraged greater evangelical attention to international affairs and the domestic political climates of foreign countries, inasmuch as they effected missionary work or the freedom to practice Christianity. It also intersected with concurrent political and foreign policy developments in the United States that attracted increasing concern among evangelicals in the 1970s. Ultimately, while communications and mass media offered a vital means for evangelizing and connecting with the unreached and the persecuted, technology provided only a partial solution to the challenges that evangelical leaders encountered in their mission to bring the gospel to all nations. As such, even as they developed radio and television stations, programming, and novel evangelistic devices in the years following the ICOWE, evangelicals pursued other measures to ensure that they could propagate their faith worldwide.

The limits of technology, coupled with the mix of threats and opportunities that emerged in international politics in the late 1970s, led U.S. evangelicals to engage more directly with foreign policy and with policymakers. The advent of evangelical lobbying in this period proved particularly significant as a means for advancing broader missionary objectives, and powerful Christian mass media and communications tools rendered these lobbying efforts all the more effective and influential. As evangelicals gained clout as a domestic political movement over the course of the 1970s and 1980s, their internationalist outlook and connections informed their perspective on a wide range of global issues, from human rights (specifically religious freedom) to arms control and state-to-state relations.

Chapter 3

Religious Freedom and the New Evangelical Foreign Policy Lobby

Two weeks before the election that brought Southern Baptist Jimmy Carter into the White House, *Newsweek* declared 1976 the "Year of the Evangelicals," and emblazoned the cover of the magazine with a photograph of evangelicals at worship.[1] The cover story asserted that Carter's presidential nomination had "focused national attention on the most significant—and overlooked—religious phenomenon of the '70s: the emergence of evangelical Christianity into a position of respect and power."[2] During the presidential campaign, both Gerald Ford and Carter referenced their evangelical faiths in interviews and made explicit appeals to evangelical groups. President Ford even addressed the Southern Baptist Convention, the National Association of Evangelicals (NAE), and the National Religious Broadcasters in an effort to convince voters of his evangelical bona fides.[3] Recognition from political leaders and strategists as well as from the media that evangelicals constituted an increasingly powerful presence in U.S. politics reflected the success that conservative Christian groups had experienced in mobilizing support and garnering attention for a range of national policy issues by the mid-1970s.

Scholars have focused considerable attention on the rise of the religious right as a domestic political force, seeking to explain the evolution of grassroots Christian activism and the powerful influence it exerted on U.S.

culture and politics during the late twentieth century. The prevailing narrative traces the origins of evangelical and fundamentalist Christian political mobilization to the broad conservative backlash that erupted in response to the rights revolutions of the 1960s and early 1970s.[4] Perceiving the social and cultural changes of the era as a sweeping assault on their "traditional" religious values, evangelicals and other conservative Christians rallied to protest legislation and Supreme Court rulings that they found threatening or morally objectionable, including *Engel v. Vitale, Griswold v. Connecticut, Green v. Connally,* and *Roe v. Wade.*[5] Scholars such as Daniel K. Williams note that although evangelicals had involved themselves in the political process on issues of importance to them in the past, their political engagement did not often translate to meaningful influence prior to the 1970s.[6] A culmination of factors, including the increasing proportion of the U.S. population that identified as "born-again" or evangelical and the proliferation of grassroots conservative activism, contributed to a key shift by the mid-1970s.[7] Only then, with the rise of conservatism and the religious right more generally, did evangelical Christians become an influential and visible political entity with solid ties to the Republican Party.[8]

Although domestic issues played a central role in mobilizing the Christian right—and as such, dominate the literature—international and foreign policy concerns also held significance for evangelicals and inspired them to greater involvement in politics. Few historians have explored this dimension of evangelical political engagement fully, however. Most of the accounts of the rise of the religious right that discuss foreign policy issues focus narrowly on anticommunism.[9] Those works that move beyond anticommunism to delve more deeply into the global concerns of evangelicals tend to emphasize the post–Cold War decades of the 1990s and 2000s.[10] Yet, as the previous chapters discussed, evangelicals in the early 1970s articulated a strongly internationalist outlook and built a robust global network of fellow believers based on their firm commitment to fulfill the biblical mandate to evangelize all nations. Evangelicals drew on the political power that they amassed through their lobbying efforts on domestic political issues during the 1970s to advocate for foreign policy positions that would further their global evangelistic agenda. This nascent evangelical foreign policy lobby came into its own during the Reagan administration, when the influence of the Christian right as a whole reached an apex. It thus laid the foundation for the powerful evangelical lobbying efforts that shaped U.S. policy on global religious freedom, human trafficking, and AIDS during the Clinton and George W. Bush administrations.

This chapter provides this crucial missing narrative, supplementing the literature on the rise of the religious right and providing the backstory necessary to place recent works that focus on contemporary evangelical foreign policy lobbying in their proper historical context. It illuminates how anxieties about the ways in which key global developments, such as the emergence of the international human rights regime, postcolonial nationalist movements, and efforts to achieve superpower détente, affected world evangelism and led to the genesis of an evangelical foreign policy lobby during the Ford and Carter administrations. Deeply held religious beliefs shaped evangelical interpretations of foreign policy issues, and evangelicals translated their concerns about world affairs into political action through issue-specific advocacy groups that coordinated with national lobbying and parachurch organizations. A fundamental commitment to advancing evangelism motivated evangelicals to promote religious freedom abroad by supporting policies that punished nations for persecuting believers. Initially, evangelical human rights activists focused on abuses in the Soviet bloc. Yet evangelicals remained attentive to religious persecution and foreign policy issues in other regions as well, and the geographic scope of their activism began expanding in the late 1970s, then blossomed in the 1980s once Reagan came into office. As they extended their political outreach, evangelicals articulated the biblical roots of Christian anticommunism and drew on their sense of religious mission to develop a unique, if conservative, vision of human rights.

Détente and Religious Freedom

When evangelicals from across the globe gathered at the International Congress on World Evangelization (ICOWE) in 1974 to launch their movement for global evangelism, they pushed for the inclusion of a resolution in the Lausanne Covenant that both called on all nations to guarantee religious freedom and committed believers to work on behalf of their persecuted brethren.[11] This resolution, adopted as article 13 of the covenant, along with the accompanying study papers and reports on evangelism in communist, Muslim, and other hostile states, indicated the acute threat that evangelicals believed religious persecution posed to achieving the Great Commission. The biblical mandate for world evangelism united evangelicals with a shared vision and duty to promote adherence to the principle of religious freedom—specifically the "freedom to practice and propagate religion in accordance with the will of God."[12] Thus, at Lausanne, evangelicals affirmed the fundamental right to religious freedom, first set forth in the 1948 UN Universal Declaration of Human Rights (UDHR), as a necessary standard in international law for advancing evangelism throughout the world.[13] That they defined "religious freedom" not just as the right to *hold* a belief in a particular faith, but the right to *practice* that faith as they saw fit is significant.[14] Free religious practice, including the right to evangelize, took on an outsize role in how evangelicals in the 1970s understood religious freedom. The freedom to believe was not sufficient; evangelicalism required evangelism. Evangelicals viewed regimes that targeted the "practice and propagation" of faith as the most repressive in part because they posed the most vital threat to the goal of achieving world evangelization. Given this sense, U.S. evangelicals embraced the Lausanne Movement's call for the promotion of international religious freedom and began to agitate for its inclusion in the making of U.S. foreign policy.

Accounts of religious persecution, especially in communist nations, had distressed evangelicals in the United States since the 1940s, occasionally even making their way into media reports and congressional testimony.[15] In the early years of the Cold War, U.S. evangelicals worked to combat persecution and to raise awareness about the "suffering church" abroad through congressional lobbying and the foundation of private advocacy organizations such as Religion in Communist-Dominated Areas and Jesus to the Communist World. These efforts expanded tremendously in scope and influence during the mid-1970s and 1980s.[16] The urgency of the evangelistic task, coupled with the perception that communist officials in Eastern Europe and the Soviet Union were escalating their repression of Christians, underlay the rapid growth and visibility of evangelical advocacy groups.[17] So, too, did the sweeping changes to U.S. relations with the Soviet Union that President Richard Nixon and his National Security Adviser Henry Kissinger implemented through their policy of détente, which raised considerable congressional and public concern about religious persecution in the USSR.

Détente, a multifaceted effort to relax tensions between the United States and the Soviet Union, involved a series of bilateral agreements and negotiations including the Anti-Ballistic Missile Treaty, the first Strategic Arms Limitation Treaty (SALT I), and various accords on trade and scientific exchange. Nixon and Kissinger pursued détente to counter a number of fundamental threats to U.S. power that had emerged by 1969: the intractable war in Vietnam that sapped U.S. strength and dealt a blow to domestic consensus about the nation's role abroad; the advent of strategic parity between the United States and the USSR that jeopardized national security; and the ascendance of smaller powers clamoring for a greater role in international affairs, which heralded an increasingly multipolar world order and complicated the traditional bipolar conflict between the superpowers.[18] Yet the accords and agreements that détente diplomacy produced did not and could not alter the ideological and political differences that divided the superpowers. Nor did they halt superpower competition in the periphery or decrease ongoing political and religious repression in the Soviet bloc. These limitations contributed to a groundswell of public and congressional disillusionment with détente, out of which emerged a powerful and influential movement to impose values-based restrictions on U.S. foreign relations.[19] This movement, spearheaded by Congress and Jewish lobbying groups, proved extremely effective at restraining U.S. foreign policymaking.[20] It also served as an inspiration and exemplar to evangelical Christian groups as they embarked on their own efforts to combat the persecution of Christian dissidents in the Soviet Union and Eastern Europe.

In 1972, as the United States and USSR negotiated a trade agreement that would grant the Soviet Union most favored nation (MFN) trading status and Export-Import Bank credits in return for the repayment of its lend-lease debts, the Kremlin introduced an exorbitant "diploma tax" intended to discourage its educated Jewish citizens from emigrating. This act of persecution provided Senator Henry Jackson (D-WA) an opening to impose limitations on Nixon's détente strategy, which he believed weakened the United States vis-à-vis the Soviet Union. Jackson especially wanted to extract concessions from the USSR on human rights issues.[21] In late 1972, he and Representative Charles Vanik (D-OH) introduced an amendment to the trade act that made the extension of MFN status and trade credits to any nonmarket country incumbent on the freedom of that country's citizens to emigrate. Influential Jewish groups, concerned about the persecution that their coreligionists faced in the Soviet Union, mobilized to support the Jackson-Vanik amendment and efforts to fight for the civil and human rights of Soviet Jewry.[22] They conducted extensive letter-writing campaigns, held demonstrations, testified before Congress, and made crucial connections with other interest groups and sympathetic congressional leaders.[23] Congress passed the Jackson-Vanik amendment, which became section 402 of the Trade Act of 1974, with overwhelming support.[24] The amendment scuttled the trade agreement with the Soviet Union and imposed restrictions on trade with communist nations deemed guilty of human rights abuses. Although most historians credit Jackson for the passage of the amendment, the public and congressional backing that the Jewish lobby cultivated proved critical as well.[25] Indeed, the public viewed Jewish lobbying and outreach efforts as the most powerful force behind Jackson-Vanik's passage.

Evangelical Christians concerned about the persecution of their brethren abroad took particular notice of the methods and achievements of Jewish lobbying efforts. As the Jackson-Vanik amendment worked its way through Congress in 1973, some evangelicals began to remark on the efficacy of Jewish and congressional advocacy on behalf of the Soviet Jewry and expressed concern that evangelicals had not mobilized in a similar fashion on behalf of Soviet Christians. As one *Christianity Today* editorial lamented: "American diplomats have been able to put the plight of Jews on their agenda for discussion with Soviet leaders—and, indeed, Soviet Jews have been granted some concessions—largely because American Jews have made the matter a major issue. Christians have *not*. Until we do, we deprive our government of the leverage it needs to demand redress."[26]

Although Christians had made efforts throughout the postwar years to call attention to the plight of the "suffering church," they had mostly done so through appeals to fellow believers in published accounts, conference presentations, and sermons rather than through overt political advocacy.[27] This outreach often remained within or focused on specific denominations.[28] It also typically took the form of prayer requests rather than concerted political action.[29] Evangelicals living under repressive regimes requested prayers from Western Christians in part because they believed that prayer itself had the power to improve their situation and in part because they realized that global prayer networks raised awareness in the West about their plight.[30] Many Western Christians asserted that prayer, along with "aggressive evangelism" in hostile states, offered the best hope for combating government abuses against their brethren.[31] Evangelicals in the United States did not broaden their reach or begin to organize politically in a cohesive and effective manner on the issue of religious persecution until after 1974.

This lack of political cohesion, and thus efficacy, reflected the fact that even into the early 1970s evangelicals did not yet embody or see themselves as a coherent political coalition. Though many evangelicals espoused conservative views, liberal evangelicals and the evangelical radical left represented a small but not insignificant Christian population through the late 1960s.[32] Consequently, between the 1940s and 1960s, evangelicals had not voted in a reliable or monolithic bloc.[33] Nor had they exerted much influence on the platform or legislative agenda of either political party.[34] As cultural issues came to the fore at the close of the 1960s, however, conservative Christians began to cultivate stronger connections with each other and with the

Republican Party.[35] When they went to the polls in 1968, most conservative evangelicals supported Richard Nixon, whom they viewed as a champion of morality, "traditional values," and "law and order."[36] Though Nixon courted the votes of specific evangelical denominations during the election and during his time in office, their value as a political constituency did not translate into influence on the policies that he implemented.[37] As the political coalition of conservative Christians grew larger and more closely allied with the Republican Party through the decade, it exerted greater influence on policymaking.[38] This growing power, in concert with the example of the movement for the Soviet Jewry, the burgeoning international human rights movement, and mounting public disillusionment with détente, helped to bring evangelicals together as a nascent interest group around the issue of Christian persecution, especially in the Soviet bloc. The addition of more formal political action beginning in the mid-1970s represented a crucial shift in the nature and objective efficacy of evangelical foreign policy engagement.

The debate over Jackson-Vanik between Congress and the policymaking establishment forced the U.S. public to grapple with the mismatch between the pursuit of détente and the government's ability to promote American ideals abroad. It also drew greater national and international attention to the significance of religious freedom as a foundational foreign policy value and to reports of egregious violations of religious freedom in the Soviet Union.[39]

These core issues played out on the global level through the Conference on Security and Cooperation in Europe (CSCE) negotiations that took place between 1973 and 1975, concluding with the signing of the Helsinki Final Act on August 1, 1975. Part of the multilateral CSCE effort to achieve détente, the Helsinki Accords included significant provisions for the protection of human rights. Borrowing language and ideas from the 1948 UN Declaration of Human Rights, Principle VII of Basket I pledged the thirty-five signatories to respect the freedom of religion and the freedom of individuals "to profess and practice, alone or in community with others, religion."[40] Basket III, reflecting the tremendous concerns in the United States and other Western countries about restrictions on emigration in the Soviet bloc, called on all participants "to facilitate freer movement and contacts" within and between their respective nations.[41] Although Secretary of State Henry Kissinger dismissed such provisions as a meaningless "grandstand play to the left," the Helsinki Accords played a crucial role in reinforcing the notion that religious persecution violated internationally accepted human rights norms.[42] Resistance to these principles in the USSR on the grounds that they encroached on Soviet sovereignty and internal affairs, as well as the U.S. perception that the Final Act had codified Soviet control over Eastern Europe, heightened widespread disillusionment with détente in the United States.[43]

Evangelicals participated avidly in the public discourse about foreign policy that emerged out of the intensifying disenchantment with détente. They voiced grave concerns about the plight of the Soviet Jewry while also sharing an increasing volume of information about the persecution of Christian dissidents, particularly unregistered Baptists and Pentecostals, in the USSR and Eastern Europe.[44] As one evangelical commenter noted, "Jews have raised the matter of religious freedom to the level of a major world issue, and Christians should do all they can to keep it there."[45] Evangelical efforts to do so gathered steam after the passage of the Jackson-Vanik amendment and the signing of the Helsinki Accords.

Evangelical groups took advantage of the increased attention paid to religious freedom. Initially, their advocacy focused on abuses in the Soviet bloc, although they remained concerned about religious persecution in China, Vietnam, and elsewhere in the world.[46] In part, this emphasis reflected the greater availability of information that evangelicals had about conditions for Christians in the Soviet bloc, not to mention congressional interest in and hearings on human rights violations in the region in the years after the passage of the Jackson-Vanik amendment and the signing of the Helsinki Accords. Evangelical activists compiled reports about persecuted Christians and publicized them in both the secular and religious media, drawing on newly salient human rights language to elicit wider support.[47] They formed NGOs and parachurch organizations, expanded existing ones, and built connections with suffering coreligionists abroad. Many of these organizations, such as Voice of Salvation and the Society for the Study of Religion Under Communism, originated in the United States. Others, including the influential Keston Institute that Reverend Michael Bordeaux founded in England in 1969 as an academic center for the study of religion in communist countries, operated abroad but shared information extensively with U.S. believers. Evangelical magazines and news services made liberal use of the information that these organizations disseminated in their newsletters and press releases. The work of the Keston Institute received particularly frequent attention in *Christianity Today*, the *Baptist Press*, secular newspapers, and in Congress.[48] As U.S. evangelicals began testifying more frequently in hearings before Congress about Soviet abuses, they drew on the vast research that these Christian advocacy organizations conducted on church life in the USSR and Eastern Europe.[49]

Jews and Christians faced similar forms of persecution in the USSR, yet evangelicals focused more on the rights of believers in the Soviet Union and Eastern Europe to practice their religion and evangelize openly than on their right to emigrate. This reflected the nature of the restrictions on religious expression in the Soviet bloc as well as the global evangelistic goals of Western Christians. The Kremlin allowed Christians in registered churches to worship (with some restrictions and only in government-provided spaces), but not to evangelize.[50] Given the centrality of spreading the Good News to the Christian faith, these constraints rankled evangelicals in the West as well as in the Soviet Union. Although many Soviet evangelicals belonged to the registered All-Union Council of Evangelical Christians and Baptists, a number of Baptists, Pentecostals, and others chose to worship clandestinely in unregistered underground churches. There, they could practice their faith and evangelize, but they faced a greater risk of suffering from state harassment, violence, imprisonment, and exile.[51] In spite of such persecution, reports suggested that most evangelicals living in the Soviet Union and Eastern Europe wanted to stay in their home countries, work to gain greater freedom there to worship and evangelize, and continue to win new believers.[52] Roger Hayden, an associate of the Centre for the Study of Religion in Communist Countries whom U.S. evangelical sources cited widely, told the Baptist and Pentecostal church groups he visited in the United States in 1975 that, "the word from Christians inside Russia is that they want outsiders to petition the Russian government for greater religious freedom and freedom from persecution."[53] Statements from evangelicals in Romania and other communist states suggested that they shared this desire with their Russian brethren.[54]

With such information in mind, evangelicals in the United States began to come together in a more unified manner to push Congress and the president to address issues related to religious freedom, particularly in the Soviet bloc. After receiving reports about ongoing persecution in Romania, individual evangelicals as well as Jesus to the Communist World, Inc., and other similar organizations, penned letters to their state legislators, members of Congress, President Ford, and the Romanian ambassador calling on policymakers to take action.[55] Several dozen members of Congress urged the president to discuss human rights abuses against Christians with Romanian president Nicolae Ceaușescu during scheduled trade talks in 1975.[56] For its part, the Ford administration offered reassurances that it "[was] deeply concerned for those unable to exercise fundamental human rights, including the freedom of religion," but suggested that "an expanding and improving

U.S.-Romanian relationship will provide the best framework to convey U.S. views on this."[57] Such assertions fell far short of the level of engagement that concerned evangelicals sought, but they lacked the necessary political clout with the Ford administration to force the issue.

Evangelicals found greater purchase for their concerns about religious persecution with members of Congress, in part because of the extant congressional advocacy on human rights issues, the Jackson-Vanik amendment, and the movement to protect the Soviet Jewry. The rise of international human rights activism more broadly by 1975 brought greater visibility to political and religious dissidents in the Soviet Union, elevating congressional attention through high-profile cases such as those of Aleksandr Solzhenitsyn and Andrei Sakharov. This attention, and the bipartisan appeal of congressional activism on Soviet human rights abuses, primed lawmakers—especially Christian lawmakers—for appeals from evangelical NGOs, denominational leaders, and rank-and-file believers.

The case of Soviet Baptist pastor Georgi Vins, for example, mobilized Baptists and other evangelical groups in the United States and aroused intense ire in Congress. In March 1974, the Soviet government arrested, jailed, and exiled Vins, the general secretary of the unregistered Council of Churches of Evangelical Christians-Baptists (CCECB), for "illegal religious action."[58] The Southern Baptist Convention, Baptist World Alliance, and a number of nondenominational Christian activist groups from throughout the United States and the rest of the world promptly condemned the action. Representatives of these organizations met with Soviet officials from the Board of International Affairs of the USSR to plead for clemency for Vins and for hundreds of other jailed religious prisoners.[59] When the Soviet Union refused to release the pastor, the Lausanne Continuation Committee of the ICOWE called on the international community of evangelicals to intercede on behalf of Vins and other persecuted Christians.[60] Christian Prisoners' Release International, an organization with offices in California, Calgary, and London founded shortly after Vins's arrest, held a series of demonstrations and petition drives throughout the world to protest Soviet persecution and demand Vins's release.[61] In the United States, a diverse coalition of Baptist leaders presented petitions at the Soviet embassy in Washington, testified before Congress, and sent inquiries to the State Department.[62]

The uproar and activism ensured that Vins's arrest received considerable congressional attention, including a hearing before the House Committee on International Relations at which the chairman of the CCECB and former Soviet religious prisoners testified.[63] In their testimony, they detailed the nature of religious repression in the Soviet Union, which included job discrimination, beatings, imprisonment, and the forced removal of children from religious homes. They argued that the United States and the international community should compel the Soviet Union to comply with the international human rights norms it agreed to in the Helsinki Accords.[64] John Buchanan, a Republican congressman from Alabama and a practicing Baptist, testified extensively at the hearing, referencing reports he had received from evangelical organizations about Vins and other persecuted Christians.[65] He urged his colleagues to put pressure on the Soviet Union to allow its Christian citizens to freely practice their religion, including the freedom to evangelize.[66]

The hearings proved effective. In October 1976, the House and Senate passed Concurrent Resolutions, sponsored by John Buchanan and Henry Jackson respectively, which called on the Soviet Union to release Georgi Vins from jail. Crucially, the resolutions also called on the USSR to allow Vins "and all other Christians and other religious believers within its borders to worship God freely according to their own consciences."[67]

H. Con. Res. 726 did not immediately bring forth the release of Vins or usher in a new era of religious freedom in the Soviet Union. Nor did it push the Ford administration or the leading officials at the State Department to embrace punitive sanctions and public denunciations over quiet diplomacy on these matters.[68] Indeed, after dismissing the efficacy of congressional resolutions and the Jackson-Vanik amendment to change international behavior, Coordinator for Human Rights and Humanitarian Affairs James M. Wilson Jr. recounted that "it was the nearly unanimous view of our Ambassadors overseas . . . that public flagellation of offenders in official U.S. Government reports would badly strain our relations with most of the countries concerned and reduce our future ability to persuade them to mend their ways."[69] Yet Congress and the growing body of human rights activists in the United States disagreed with such assessments, viewing the efficacy of quiet diplomacy skeptically while championing the trade restrictions of the Jackson-Vanik amendment.[70] This bipartisan congressional commitment to human rights grew stronger through the end of the decade, undermining détente and imposing critical constraints on executive power over foreign policy.[71]

At the same time, the rise of the religious right as a visible domestic force by 1976 had brought at least some new conservative evangelical legislators into Congress, where, in addition to pushing a conservative domestic agenda, they provided a critical reception for evangelical foreign policy interests. During the congressional and presidential campaigns in 1976, Campus Crusade for Christ International director Bill Bright wrote and distributed two million copies of a booklet on Christian political engagement that encouraged evangelicals to pray, register, become informed, help elect godly people, and vote.[72] Newspapers reporting on the 1976 election provided evidence of "a wave of Christian political activity to endorse and support particular candidates who were avowedly Christian."[73] Although they did not manage to get all of the candidates they endorsed elected, groups such as Third Century, Campus Crusade for Christ International, and state-level groups such as California Christians Active Politically, reported success in electing at least some "Christ-centered" candidates to the House and Senate.[74]

Evangelicals enjoyed even greater success in the 1978 electoral cycle when they helped bring Senator Roger Jepsen (R-IA) and Gordon J. Humphrey (R-NH) into office. Both senators served on the board of the evangelical organization Christian Voice, an influential political advocacy group that disseminated "moral report cards" grading elected officials on their adherence to Christian values.[75] Jepsen and Humphrey used their influence in Congress to act as stalwart defenders of religious liberty abroad and to promote other evangelical foreign policy interests during their time in office, Humphrey as a member of the Senate Committee on Foreign Relations and Jepsen as one of the founding members of the Christian Rescue Effort for the Emancipation of Dissidents (CREED).

Having identified sympathetic members of Congress, evangelical leaders and interest groups kept up the flow of information about Christians suffering persecution abroad. They also continued their activism on behalf of Vins and other imprisoned evangelicals, steadily building a base of support among rank-and-file believers, key Christian congressmen, and the broader electorate for the cause of religious freedom behind the Iron Curtain. That blend of grassroots and congressional action proved crucial to mobilizing supporters and influencing policy during the Carter and Reagan administrations.

The Carter Years

Although the election of a Southern Baptist and self-proclaimed "born-again" Christian to the presidency in 1976 seemed to presage a greater evangelical influence in government, Carter's management of domestic and foreign policy issues proved disappointing to conservative Christians. One prominent theologian mused in 1979 that "Carter has failed to demonstrate any significant Christian influence on the federal administration, in spite of his noble-minded human rights campaign," a shortcoming he feared called into question the ability of evangelicals to exert sufficient influence on the country's future.[76] Carter's well-known commitment to human rights and his Baptist identity had raised the hopes of Pentecostals, Baptists, and other Christian denominations in the United States and in the Soviet bloc that his administration would make significant strides toward ameliorating religious persecution.[77] Yet, despite his close association with the human rights movement and his efforts to compel repressive autocratic leaders to abide by international norms, evangelicals found Carter's handling of human rights compliance in the communist world frustrating. By the end of his presidency, these frustrations, in tandem with ongoing congressional human rights activism, contributed to the development of a biblically based evangelical human rights vision and the establishment of several key Washington-based evangelical foreign policy lobbying organizations.

Functionally, little changed between the Ford and Carter administrations with regard to presidential and State Department thinking about the issue of religious persecution in the Soviet bloc. The emphasis on quiet diplomacy held sway. In his early communications about human rights and the Helsinki Accords with General Secretary Leonid Brezhnev, Carter assured the Soviet leader that: "It is not our intention to interfere in the internal affairs of other nations. We do not wish to create problems with the Soviet Union but it will be necessary for our government to express publicly on occasion the sincere and deep feelings of myself and our people. Our commitment to the furtherance of human rights will not be pursued stridently or in a manner inconsistent with the achievement of reasonable results. We would also, of course, welcome private, confidential exchanges on these delicate areas."[78] In subsequent meetings, Carter stressed that he had exercised great discretion when discussing human rights, seeking to avoid embarrassing Brezhnev and noting that he "recognized the difficulty for the Soviet Union posed by the human rights question."[79] Likewise, when U.S. evangelical groups approached the State Department and the White House about supporting the small number of Soviet Baptists and Pentecostals who had begun to express an interest in emigrating, U.S. officials "urged private efforts" and confidential discussions with Soviet ambassador Anatoly Dobrynin rather than overt protests or sanctions.[80] This discrete approach contrasted significantly with the Carter administration's forceful handling of authoritarian regimes guilty of human rights violations, such as Chile and Argentina.[81]

Carter attributed the Soviet Union's release of persecuted Baptist pastor Georgi Vins to quiet diplomacy and behind-the-scenes negotiations. In April 1979, the Soviet Union agreed to free five of its political prisoners, including Vins, and allow them to emigrate to the United States in exchange for the return of two captured Soviet spies.[82] On April 26, 1979, Soviet officials transported Vins from his prison in Tyumen to Moscow. Several days later, they stripped him of his Soviet citizenship and expelled him and several members of his family from the country, sending them to the United States.[83] In a meeting with Brezhnev two months later, Carter lavished the Soviet leader with praise, noting that "the people of our nation had been warmly gratified by the actions the Soviet Union had taken on its own initiative and without any pressure from us. . . . Fourteen million Baptists had been very happy to welcome Mr. Vins in our country."[84] Carter indicated that releasing other high-profile religious and political prisoners would further improve relations between the two superpowers.[85] For evangelical activists in the United States, however, the release of Vins and the prospective improvement of superpower relations did not counterbalance the continued persecution in the Soviet Union. The high-level negotiations required to free Vins demonstrated how far they had to go to nurture religious freedom in nations hostile to Christians, and highlighted the frustrating gradualness inherent in quiet diplomacy.

Figure 5. President Jimmy Carter meeting with dissident Soviet Baptist pastor Georgi Vins at the First Baptist Church in Washington, D.C., in April 1979, shortly after Carter negotiated Vins's release from a Soviet prison camp. Photograph #NLC 10489, frame 19a, courtesy of the Jimmy Carter Library.

When Carter attributed the exchange to Soviet initiative, he downplayed the significance of evangelical political action and international publicity on behalf of Vins and other Christian prisoners. Underground Evangelism, Christian Prisoners' Release International, Jesus to the Communist World, Christian Solidarity International, and a number of other evangelical organizations had kept up a steady drumbeat of petitions, press releases, and prayer vigils since the pastor's arrest in 1974.[86] In interviews with Christian media in the United States, Vins asserted that "whenever there was support action in the West, I was treated better by prison administrators. . . . Western support to some degree influences the authorities, making them feel under obligation."[87] Additionally, without sustained pressure from interest group lobbying, the U.S. State Department would not likely have pursued Vins's release as part of the prisoner-spy exchange.

Although Baptists and other evangelicals in the United States welcomed Vins with open arms, they had not sought his forced emigration from the Soviet Union. Rather, Baptist and evangelical activists had hoped to exert enough pressure on the USSR to get Vins released back into Soviet society and to allow him and all members of evangelical churches, registered and unregistered, to evangelize and practice their religion freely in their home country. The outcome had not sat well with the pastor initially, either. Vins noted that after his release he had first felt "very sorrowful, for I did not want to leave my work and my brothers in Russia."[88] He viewed evangelism in Russia as his calling and life's work, stating that despite the persecution he faced in his country, he would prefer to live there than in the United States if he could share the gospel without restraint.[89] Given the reality of his exile, however, the pastor pledged "from here I shall help my brethren in Russia to preach Christ."[90]

Once settled in the United States, Vins tapped into the nascent network of evangelical activism to continue to advocate for his imprisoned brethren and for religious freedom in the Soviet Union, asserting that he believed that "the Lord has sent me here to establish relationships with Christians in the United States on behalf of the Reform Baptists in Russia."[91] He reaffirmed his commitment to evangelism in the USSR and throughout the world, and determined to pursue this goal through political advocacy.[92] Shortly after he arrived in the United States, Vins met with Carter's national security adviser Zbigniew Brzezinski and testified before Congress as well as before the Commission on Security and Cooperation in Europe about his experiences as a persecuted believer and religious prisoner.[93] His testimony, in concert with that of other evangelical witnesses, moved Congress deeply.[94] In 1980, Vins founded an evangelical NGO, International Representation for the Council of Evangelical Baptist Churches of the Soviet Union (IRCEBCSU), with a group of other concerned evangelical leaders in the United States. He and the IRCEBCSU sent frequent, sometimes daily updates about Soviet Baptists facing persecution or imprisonment to President Carter's Special Assistant for Religious Liaison Bob Maddox. Many of these communiques bore instructions to pass the information on to the Commission on Security and Cooperation in Europe as part of the Helsinki monitoring process.[95] Because of Vins's visibility and leadership, the IRCEBCSU exerted an important influence on congressional and evangelical opinion on issues related to religious life and persecution in the Soviet Union throughout the 1980s.[96]

In addition to their primary objective of promoting evangelism and religious freedom in the Soviet Union, Christians in the United States also rallied during the Carter presidency to support Baptists, Pentecostals, and members of other persecuted evangelical denominations who wished to emigrate from the Soviet bloc. As persecution in the Soviet Union against unregistered sects escalated in the late 1970s, a greater number of Russian, Ukrainian, Latvian, and other Soviet evangelicals sought to emigrate to nations where they could practice their religion and evangelize freely.[97] In reports to the Carter administration and in official cables, the State Department, National Security Council (NSC), and Central Intelligence Agency (CIA) detailed the challenges that individual Soviet Pentecostals and Baptists faced in their efforts to secure the right to emigrate.[98] The State Department also made a note of congressional, public, and international inquiries that poured into its offices about stymied would-be emigrants.[99]

The case of the Siberian Seven, two families of Russian Pentecostals who sought refuge from persecution by hiding in the basement of the U.S. embassy in Moscow from 1978 until 1983, became a flashpoint for evangelical and congressional advocates for religious freedom. Refused the right to emigrate, and suffering from decades of ill-treatment from Soviet officials for practicing their faith, the Vashchenko and Chmykhalov families became international emblems of human rights abuses in communist regimes. One congressional resolution described the families as "a living sign of the Soviet war on the God given human rights of tens of thousands of Evangelical Christians."[100] Their presence in the embassy and the perceived inattention of the Carter administration to their plight spurred significant organizing by evangelicals and generated broad support and interest from the general public. Amnesty International and mainline Christian organizations joined with evangelical groups such as Religion in Communist-Dominated Areas in calling on the U.S. government to sanction or cut off trade to the Soviet Union in order to demonstrate U.S. support for human rights, including rights of religious practice and emigration.[101] Congressional leaders referenced the plight of the Siberian Seven frequently in discussions of SALT II, the Commission on Security and Cooperation in Europe, human rights, and trade relations with the USSR. In 1980, fifty senators sent a letter to Brezhnev urging him to release the Vashchenko and Chmykhalov families and to comply with the guarantees of religion freedom agreed to in the UDHR and the Helsinki Final Act.[102] The broad resonance that the case of the Siberian Seven had with the U.S. public enabled evangelicals and their supporters in Congress to fundraise, expand their organizations, and lobby more effectively on behalf of the Vashchenkos, Chmykhalovs, and other persecuted Christians living under repressive regimes.

Despite the ferment in Congress and among the public, the Carter administration seemed reticent to highlight the matter of evangelical

Figure 6. The Siberian Seven took refuge in the U.S. embassy in Moscow from 1978 until 1983. Front row from left to right are Timofei Chmykhalov, Lidiya Vashchenko, Liliya Vashchenko, and Lyuba Vashchenko. Back row are Mariya Chmykhalov, Augustina Vashchenko, and Pyotr Vashchenko. Courtesy of Special Collections, Buswell Library.

emigration and referred all appeals to the State Department.[103] Patt Derian, the assistant secretary of state for Human Rights and Humanitarian Affairs under Carter, coordinated with private organizations to aid in the emigration effort but chose to eschew publicity. She hoped that discretion would "result in substantial numbers of the Pentecostals being able to leave."[104] It did not. Appeals from congressmen, constituents, and NGOs met with noncommittal replies from Brzezinski and other State Department officials. They deflected pressure, stating that "human rights and religious freedom are a primary concern of this Administration, and you can be assured that these issues will continue to be a focus of U.S.-Soviet relations."[105] Yet, with the collapse of détente in 1979, human rights ceased to be the major focus of the Carter administration.[106] When the Soviet Union invaded Afghanistan, even backchannel efforts to spur emigration from the USSR for religious dissidents dropped off as the president, State Department, and NSC grappled with policy issues and national security threats they deemed more critical.

Evangelical Human Rights and CREED

As hopeful as evangelicals had felt at the outset of Carter's presidency, by 1979 most recognized that lobbying Congress and publicizing human rights abuses through their own organizations were more effective than appeals to the president. In addition to the proliferation of evangelical NGOs around the country and the world committed to promoting religious freedom, several new Washington-based organizations emerged out of the congressional concern for Georgi Vins and the Siberian Seven. Around the same time, the new director of the NAE, Robert P. Dugan, expanded the NAE's Office of Public Affairs. He started publishing a monthly newsletter, *NAE Washington Insight*, and hired policy analysts and lobbyists to increase evangelical influence in Washington.[107] These developments made manifest the new level of comfort with lobbying and political activism that had arisen among evangelical leaders by 1980 and heightened the deep connections that they had built with sympathetic members of Congress.[108]

In March 1980, Senator Roger Jepsen (R-IA) and Representative Jack Kemp (R-NY) incorporated the CREED to coordinate the dozens of religious organizations working at that time to pray and advocate for Christian dissidents living under communist or otherwise hostile regimes. The congressmen attributed their decision to found the organization to their earlier work on behalf of the Soviet Jewry and their desire to see a similar level of political commitment to aid persecuted Christians.[109] Jepsen, a Pentecostal and a member of the Assemblies of God, and Kemp, a Presbyterian, appointed Dr. Ernest Gordon as the president of the new organization, and held an inaugural meeting at the Fellowship Foundation's headquarters in Washington, D.C., in October.[110] The seventy-five attendees represented a diverse body of Christian denominations and organizations, including Christian Solidarity International, the NAE, and the Religious News Service. At the initial meeting, these individuals codified the core values that would define the new organization, values shared across denominational lines. These values reflected an ethos of freedom and human rights particular to evangelicals and other conservative Christians. Thus, the founding documents of CREED illuminate the intellectual and theological basis of the evangelical understanding of human rights that evolved over the course of the 1970s.

The coordinators of the inaugural meeting noted that, although the organization originated from concern about Christians in the Soviet bloc, CREED sought to promote religious freedom in all nations and did not aim to become an anticommunist group. Board of Trustees member Lt. Col. Paul Roush avowed that, above all else, CREED intended to marshal the support of Congress, NGOs, and individual laypeople in order "to influence repressive societies to abide by international agreements and their own national laws regarding religious freedom."[111] This stated goal encompassed a range of communist and noncommunist nations while referencing not only the UDHR and the Helsinki Accords, but the Soviet constitution as well. While CREED affirmed its intention to promote the freedom of emigration, its members hoped that by encouraging nations to abide by international human rights norms, they would ensure that Christian dissidents would no longer feel compelled to emigrate. Roush emphasized that he hoped that Soviet Christians would be able to practice their faith freely so that they could "transform" their society rather than leave their homeland, a view that many evangelicals shared.[112] Finally, CREED pledged "to affirm the uniqueness of Biblical understanding of human freedom as a divine gift that is differentiated from a gift of the state."[113] CREED's founders believed this biblical focus distinguished their organization from secular human rights organizations and would inspire its members to persevere in their activism despite the powerful challenges they faced.[114]

These fundamental principles reflected the evangelical understanding of freedom and human rights that had developed by 1980 through the work of advocates for religious liberty and for global evangelism. The association of Christian faith with spiritual freedom had a long history in evangelical thought, but the connection between these concepts and the idea of human rights came only with the rise of human rights discourse more broadly in the 1970s. As the global conversation about human rights unfolded between national governments, the UN and other international bodies, and a growing number of activist NGOs, evangelical groups began to articulate their own human rights vision, a vision based in scripture and informed by the escalation of evangelical concern about religious persecution.

Many core, interlocking beliefs about the relationship between God, man, and government informed this shared evangelical perspective on the meaning of human rights. First, the belief in the divinely granted dignity of human beings, drawn from Genesis 1:26–27 wherein "God created humankind in his image," led Christians to conclude that God had granted them their essential rights.[115] This concept of the *imago dei* connected closely with the Christian faith in eternal salvation through Jesus Christ, derived from John 3:16: "for God so loved the world that he gave his only Son, so that everyone who believes in him may not perish but may have eternal life."[116] Salvation in Christ also promised believers an expansive freedom from sin and death; as noted in 2 Corinthians 3:17, "where the Spirit of the Lord is, there is freedom."[117] In his analysis of the Southern Baptist Convention's 1978 "Declaration on Human Rights," theologian Ronald D. Sisk referenced *The Baptist Faith & Message* of 1963 to elucidate this connection, noting that the Southern Baptist statement of faith asserts, "the sacredness of human personality is evident in that God created man in His own image, and in that Christ died for man; therefore every man possesses dignity and is worthy of respect and Christian love."[118] The Baptist World Alliance took this connection one step further in the conclusion of its 1980 "Declaration on Human Rights," wherein it linked these biblically based beliefs about the meaning of human rights with a call to political action: "Because we are being set free by the power of God through faith in Jesus Christ as Lord, we pledge to use our freedom responsibly to help free others. Individually as well as through our churches and institutions we promise to pray and work for the defense of human rights, to strive to avoid violating the rights of others, and to serve him from whom all human rights come, the only One who is Righteous, Just, and Merciful, the Father of our Lord Jesus Christ."[119]

The conviction that God, rather than the state, served as the ultimate authority and granter of rights—as well as the path to salvation—led many evangelicals to believe that religious freedom—the freedom to follow God's will, to worship, and to spread the gospel—constituted the most primary of human rights, from which all other rights derived.[120]

Thus, CREED's foundational principles reflected the broad move of evangelical thought about human rights that had coalesced across denominational lines by 1980 as a result of concerted advocacy on behalf of Christian dissidents. CREED's strategic planning efforts also revealed another significant development that had emerged by 1980: the connections across national borders that religious leaders, NGOs, and missionary organizations had forged through the evangelistic campaigns of the decade. Activities as diverse as radio evangelism, Bible smuggling, and even letter-writing and coordinated prayer vigils brought believers throughout the world, and especially those behind the Iron Curtain, into contact with Christians in the West. CREED acknowledged the power of these networks. It sought to integrate itself with evangelical NGOs and missionary groups that had strong contacts with believers in the Soviet bloc, including Christian Solidarity International and Keston College, among others.[121]

CREED's leaders drew on these connections and the evangelical human rights vision as they began to advocate in Congress for the passage of legislation on behalf of persecuted Christians. Senate Concurrent Resolutions 60 and 61, which Senator Jepsen first introduced in December 1979, formally expressed the sense of the Congress that the president, State Department, and other policymakers must "affirm the support of the United States for full implementation of all the provisions of . . . the Helsinki Accords," and to "make it known" to the Soviet Union that the United States "strongly disapproves of the religious harassment of Christians."[122] During hearings before the Committee on Foreign Relations, Jepsen and the international witnesses he invited to testify emphasized the immensity of the restrictions and abuses Soviet Christians faced. These witnesses stressed the Kremlin's prohibitions against "teaching their children about God."[123] They also focused on the laws that barred children from attending church until they turned eighteen.[124] The evangelicals who gave testimony stated explicitly that these injunctions against religious education, and by extension, evangelism, contravened the essential human rights that they believed God had granted to all people.[125] Soviet Christians who wrote appeals to the Senate noted the double-bind they faced: "if we submit to the government, we sin against our God, since by its laws on religion the government forces us to break Christ's fundamental commandments. If we remain faithful to our God, the government treats us like criminals."[126]

An Effective Lobby Emerges

When S. Con. Res. 60 passed in November 1980, commenters remarked that it was a momentous milestone. One article in the conservative tabloid

Human Events described the Senate action as "a long-awaited resolution of enormous importance to the Christian community—one that officially sanctions and thereby strengthens a key element of its campaign for religious human rights."[127] The passage of the resolution demonstrated the power of evangelical organizing, the resonance of their message in Congress, and the crystallization of an evangelical human rights vision. It also served as a strong rebuke of President Carter, whom Jepsen had lambasted in hearings for failing to take sufficient action on behalf of Christian dissidents. Jepsen argued U.S. officials knew full well the extent of Soviet violations of the Helsinki Accords and other international agreements, yet they responded to the pleas of Soviet Christians and their advocates "with near silence and passive acquiescence."[128]

For this reason, among others, Jepsen and his fellow evangelicals threw their support behind Ronald Reagan in the 1980 presidential election. One journalist commented that

> the advent of the new Administration is being eagerly awaited to help add new momentum to the drive. President-elect Reagan has let it be known that he is "very interested and very supportive" of the campaign to assist persecuted Christians. This, unfortunately, was not the case under President Carter. In fact, despite all its rhetoric about promoting human rights, the Carter Administration largely turned a blind eye and a deaf ear to the plight of persecuted believers. Letters to the White House often went unanswered. At times they were simply carted to the State Department and dumped on an office floor.[129]

U.S. evangelicals looked to Reagan, with his promise of a more aggressive stance toward the Soviet Union, to lend visible U.S. support not just to the Christian dissident movement in the USSR, but to the resurgence of Christianity behind the Iron Curtain that that movement revealed.[130] Evangelicals entered the 1980s prepared to advocate effectively for their brethren abroad in order to ensure their ability to practice and propagate their faith throughout the world.

By the time Ronald Reagan entered the White House in January 1981, evangelical Christians in the United States had come together to form a large number of organizations focused on protecting the freedom of religion and evangelism. They lobbied on key foreign policy issues and expanded their contacts with brethren overseas through their missionary work and advocacy for persecuted Christians, including the Siberian Seven, which the next chapter will explore. This activity, coupled with the broad public concern about the repression of religious minorities and political dissidents in the Soviet Union, encouraged the development of an evangelical perspective on human rights and highlighted a language for discussing human rights abuses rooted in scripture. During the 1980s and 1990s, evangelicals drew on this perspective to guide their involvement and lobbying efforts on a range of global and foreign policy issues, not just in the Soviet bloc but in Central America, Southern Africa, and other major geopolitical hotspots throughout the world.

Chapter 4

Fighting Religious Persecution behind the Iron Curtain

In November 1985, U.S. president Ronald Reagan and Soviet general secretary Mikhail Gorbachev met for the first time at a summit in Geneva, Switzerland, where they discussed arms control and efforts to improve superpower relations. At dinner on November 20, Secretary of State George Shultz asked the Soviet leader and his wife, Raisa, about the religious revival sweeping Russia and Eastern Europe.[1] Gorbachev tried to downplay the magnitude of Christian renewal and religious dissidence in the Soviet Union, claiming that "true believers are dying out with the older generation."[2] Yet he admitted that many Soviet citizens still found traditional religious practices appealing. Despite his country's state-sponsored atheism, the general secretary estimated that one-third of the population got married in the Russian Orthodox Church and had their children baptized in that faith.[3] Raisa acknowledged the large and growing number of Baptist, Pentecostal, and other evangelical denominations active in Russia.[4]

These evangelical churches appealed to young and old alike, and their vitality belied the Gorbachevs' insistence that religious belief in the Soviet Union was headed toward extinction. In fact, when the NSC briefed President Reagan before the Geneva summit, it highlighted the "extraordinary burgeoning of religion" in the USSR as "by far the most dramatic development in Soviet dissent in recent years."[5] The NSC suggested that many Eastern bloc citizens yearned for "spiritual refuge from . . . the drabness and moral emptiness of contemporary Soviet life," and argued that this impulse explained the extraordinary expansion of underground Protestant, Catholic, and Muslim sects in the region.[6] Soviet media, such as the *Communist Youth League Daily*, cited evangelistic radio programs and other Christian mass media as major contributors to Christian renewal.[7] State crackdowns on religious expression, which intensified after 1979 in response to this religious revival, led many Soviet Christians to grow bolder in their protests against repression, demands to practice their faith freely, and contacts with brethren in the West.[8]

Evangelicals in the United States publicized the concurrent rise of repression and revival in Russia and Eastern Europe as part of their ongoing efforts to support persecuted Christians in the Soviet bloc and advance global evangelism.[9] As noted in the previous chapter, these campaigns on behalf of Baptists and Pentecostals in the communist world gained considerable political traction during the late 1970s. While the two Pentecostal families who fled to the basement of the U.S. embassy in Moscow to seek refuge from Soviet persecution in 1978 garnered perhaps the most public attention, evangelical activists lobbied on behalf of hundreds of other, lesser known believers as well.[10] By the time that Reagan assumed the presidency in 1981, evangelicals had a defined foreign policy agenda that underscored religious freedom and a robust network of contacts in Eastern Europe and the USSR that documented Soviet abuses.

This chapter examines how U.S. evangelicals put their human rights vision into action during the Reagan administration through their engagement with Baptists and Pentecostals living in the Soviet Union. In the early 1980s, evangelical activists focused their attention on Congress and the State Department, pushing U.S. officials to highlight human rights concerns when discussing trade and diplomatic relations. They also used a variety of means to expand their communications with registered and unregistered Christian sects in Eastern Europe and the Soviet Union—from clandestine meetings and radio evangelism to state-sanctioned visits from religious leaders such as Billy Graham. As the internal political conditions of the Soviet Union began to shift in reaction to Gorbachev's policies of perestroika and glasnost, U.S. evangelicals drew on their network of regional contacts to navigate the changing social context and uncover new opportunities for evangelism. They also adapted their lobbying strategy in response to the rapidly evolving conditions abroad. After the Soviet

Union collapsed in 1991, evangelicals accelerated their efforts to expand their spiritual influence in the region.

Examining U.S.-Soviet relations during the Reagan administration through the lens of evangelical nonstate actors offers a more nuanced interpretation of the role of religion at the end of the Cold War. Beyond the simplistic yet powerful Reagan-era rhetoric about the "evil empire," U.S. evangelicals saw themselves as members of a global Christian community with a shared mandate for evangelism. Their internationalist outlook, rooted deeply in scripture as well as in U.S. Cold War ideology, spurred their political mobilization as a foreign policy lobby with a specific focus on religious human rights in the Soviet bloc.

A Human Rights Vision

In 1979, Evangelism Center International, a large nondenominational Christian umbrella agency that coordinated groups such as Underground Evangelism, founded the East/West News Service (EWNS) to report on the increasing frequency of Soviet crackdowns on religion.[11] The EWNS filled its newsletters with vivid "eye-witness reports" of beatings, forced psychiatric treatments, and other human rights abuses in order to "make known the problems confronting Believers in the East."[12] Soviet Christians described raids on worship services where police attacked them "with bestial fury," detailing how "they were kicked, thrown against walls, trampled on, dragged by the feet with their heads banging against the concrete," as the officers arrested them.[13] Baptists and Pentecostals, particularly those from unregistered churches, stated that government officials routinely detained and harassed believers, confiscated their property, and demolished churches.[14] These accounts, which framed such abuses as attacks on the entire global community of believers, galvanized evangelicals in the United States, encouraging them to expand their ongoing efforts to pressure and shame offending countries into improving their human rights records.[15] Although grassroots evangelical activist organizations lacked central coordination, their strategies for political action coalesced into a fairly cohesive, if multifaceted, campaign for religious liberty throughout the world in the early 1980s.

In Congress, evangelicals sought to reorient U.S. human rights policy so that it focused more attention on promoting religious freedom for persecuted Christians abroad. Groups such as the Christian Rescue Effort for the

Emancipation of Dissidents (CREED) organized briefings for pastors and lay leaders in advance of key congressional hearings on trade and human rights so that they could rally their flocks and contact their representatives to take action on behalf of persecuted Soviet Christians.[16] Evangelical lobbyists used reports of religious persecution in the Soviet bloc from the EWNS and other organizations to make emotionally charged pleas before Congress. They intended their testimony to push legislators to impose sanctions on nations guilty of persecuting Christians, as well as to expose the Soviet leadership to international ridicule. Similarly, these activists hoped that by including accounts of attacks on the Christian revivals taking place in the Eastern bloc in reports for the Conference on Security and Cooperation in Europe (CSCE) follow-up meetings, they would "shame the Soviets into relaxing their grip on religious believers."[17]

Evangelical activists also worked from within the Soviet bloc to compel change. Some used controversial tactics, such as Bible smuggling, to highlight limits on religious expression while also spreading the gospel. This proved attractive for fundraising within the United States but tended to escalate tensions with communist authorities. Other groups worked to facilitate cooperation with registered Baptist and Pentecostal churches, coordinating visits to the USSR from Billy Graham and other well-known religious leaders as well as visits by leaders of the All-Union Council of Evangelical Christians-Baptists to the United States. Evangelical political advocacy kept religious human rights abuses in the public eye, preventing Congress, the administration, and Soviet leaders from avoiding these issues.

Reagan established himself as an ally in the evangelical fight to promote religious liberty abroad early on in his presidential campaign against Carter. When he accepted the Republican nomination in July 1980, he pledged to promote "world peace and freedom" through his foreign policy if elected and, in a departure from his prepared text, called explicit attention to religious persecution in the Soviet Union.[18] Reagan won evangelicals over with his appeals to biblical principles and "traditional" moral values, and they voted for him by a significant margin in the 1980 election.[19] His stated commitment to religious freedom gave evangelicals hope that the Reagan administration would take strong action to address Soviet human rights abuses.

Reagan's concern for Christians suffering behind the Iron Curtain—and his views on human rights and opposition to communism more generally—originated in part from his deeply held, if slightly unorthodox, religious beliefs.[20] As a devout Christian, Reagan believed that God had created mankind in his image and thereby bestowed equality and dignity on all human beings. In speeches and public statements, Reagan often merged this biblical notion of human dignity with "eternal" U.S. values, including the freedom of conscience.[21] He reviled Soviet communism for its atheism as well as its statist repression. Throughout his career as a public speaker and politician, Reagan counterposed the United States as the "shining city upon a hill" against the bleak, totalitarian Soviet Union.[22] He saw the United States as the world's beacon of freedom and expressed confidence in the broad appeal of U.S. democratic values.[23]

During the 1980 presidential campaign, Reagan drew on these core religious and ideological beliefs to mount an attack on President Carter's approach to international relations and human rights. He railed against détente and the Strategic Arms Limitation Treaty, advocating for a more muscular foreign policy that would bolster U.S. strength and negotiating power vis-à-vis its major adversary. On human rights, Reagan alleged that Carter had applied foreign policy pressure inconsistently, targeting authoritarian regimes for their violations yet ignoring abuses in the Soviet Union. In his campaign speeches, he called for a reappraisal of how human rights issues fit into U.S. policymaking—though not for their wholesale removal from the decision-making process.[24]

During his first term as president, Reagan and his advisers advanced a human rights vision that distinguished between and emphasized human rights violations in totalitarian as opposed to authoritarian regimes, and sought change through quiet diplomacy rather than congressional pressure.[25] In an interview with Walter Cronkite on *CBS News* in March 1981, Reagan explained his position: "I think human rights is very much a part of our American idealism. . . . My criticism of them, in the last few years, was that we were selective with regard to human rights. We took countries that were pro-Western, that were maybe authoritarian in government, but not totalitarian . . . and we punished them at the same time that we were claiming détente with countries where there are no human rights. The Soviet Union is the greatest violator today of human rights in all the world."[26] In downplaying the abuses of authoritarian regimes, this distinction troubled many liberal human rights activists. For evangelical groups such as CREED, however, Reagan's statements aligned with their policy objectives and seemed to indicate that he planned to champion religious liberty abroad while in office.[27]

Eager to protect their brethren behind the Iron Curtain, evangelicals rallied during the first months of Reagan's presidency to defend his administration's stated plan to prioritize human rights abuses in totalitarian rather than authoritarian regimes. In February 1981, Reagan nominated Ernest Lefever to serve as assistant secretary of state for Human Rights and Humanitarian Affairs. This decision triggered serious opposition from liberal members of Congress and the public. Lefever, the founder of a think tank "dedicated to applying the Judeo-Christian moral tradition to critical issues of public policy" called the Ethics and Public Policy Center, advocated a conservative reorientation of human rights policy that corresponded closely with Reagan administration foreign policy goals.[28] Critics expressed concerns about Lefever's commitment to upholding human rights principles, noting congressional testimony that he gave in a 1979 hearing wherein he recommended repealing certain human rights statutes.[29] Although Lefever tried to backtrack on these earlier statements in his 1981 nomination hearing, ultimately he shared with Reagan appointees Alexander Haig and Jeane Kirkpatrick the belief that U.S. human rights policy should deal with totalitarian abusers forcefully yet utilize quiet diplomacy with friendly authoritarian regimes. That he downplayed authoritarian violations as only "minor abridgement[s] of certain rights" did not win him any favors with most members of Congress.[30]

Yet evangelical activists defended Lefever against his critics, sending in numerous letters ahead of his nomination hearing as well as testifying on his behalf.[31] Supportive letters from the founding editor of *Christianity Today* and the directors of evangelical NGOs such as World Concern and World Relief claimed that Lefever's perspective on human rights had a strong biblical foundation.[32] Robert P. Dugan Jr. the director of the National Association of Evangelicals, submitted a request to testify during the hearing in order to "address the philosophical basis of Dr. Lefever's position on human rights," a position that he and the NAE believed "to be in concurrence with the thinking of most evangelical Christians."[33]

The testimonials that evangelicals submitted did not allay congressional opposition to Lefever, but they did articulate a coherent and well-developed evangelical human rights vision. At the nomination hearing, Dugan asserted that evangelicals derived their belief in the innate, universal nature of human dignity from the Book of Genesis and identified "God as the source and sanction of human rights."[34] Rejecting the emphasis that liberal human rights activists placed on economic justice as a "rationalization for socio-political revolution in Third World countries," Dugan complained that concerns about "relatively minor abridgments of rights" should not supersede action for the millions of individuals suffering under totalitarianism.[35] He also argued that conservative Christians promoted human rights more effectively than other groups because they sought to fulfill the biblical mission of the church. For Dugan, salvation offered the promise of eternal life and ultimate (spiritual) freedom to the oppressed.[36] Furthermore, he claimed that evangelical beliefs offered more realistic guidance for how national leaders should handle human rights violations than did liberal theological perspectives. To wit, Dugan opined, "evangelical recognition of man's sinful nature and its consequences compels acceptance of the view that the world political arena is a tough arena where coercive power counts more than good intentions."[37] For this reason, he and other evangelical leaders advocated a strong national security policy and called on U.S. leaders to hold the Soviet Union to the UN Declaration of Human Rights, the Helsinki Accords, and other international agreements.[38] Dugan also affirmed the desirability of a U.S. foreign policy that differentiated between human rights abuses in authoritarian and totalitarian regimes, in part because he believed that authoritarian regimes allowed for greater freedom of religious practice.[39]

Ultimately, the Senate Foreign Relations Committee rejected Lefever's nomination. In response, the State Department and the Reagan administration launched a campaign to counter congressional claims that their foreign policy objectives lacked a commitment to human rights concerns.[40] In their discussion of how to best accomplish this goal, they asserted that "'human rights'—a somewhat narrow name for our values—gives us *the best opportunity to convey what is ultimately at issue in our contest with the Soviet bloc.*"[41] A State Department memorandum affirmed the basic premises of the administration's human rights policy, including its focus on Soviet abuses of individual liberties and the grave threat that it believed totalitarian expansion posed to world freedom. However, it noted that the United States must also respond when friendly nations violated human rights, as otherwise "no one will take seriously our words about Communist violations."[42] The administration leaked selected parts of this memorandum to the *New York Times* in an effort to convey to the public that it had made a meaningful shift in its stance on human rights, even though the shift was mostly rhetorical.[43] This maneuver succeeded.

Reagan's subsequent appointee for the position, Elliot Abrams, promoted a human rights policy that corresponded well with the evangelical objectives Dugan outlined in his testimony on behalf of Lefever, yet framed the issues in language more palatable to Congress and the public.[44] Abrams, then serving as assistant secretary of state for International Organization Affairs, had a good working relationship with a number of the legislators who were most outspoken on human rights issues.[45] These connections, along with the perception that he would promote human rights issues actively at the State Department and had a clear plan for how to do so, helped him sail through his confirmation hearings in November 1981.[46] Yet his preferred approach to human rights, as illustrated in his congressional testimony and in leaked State Department documents, emphasized civil and political rights over social and economic rights.[47] He called for quiet diplomacy with authoritarian allies, while urging a mix of diplomacy and public pressure with totalitarian adversaries.[48] Breaking from administration orthodoxy, Abrams indicated that he would resist efforts to repeal the Jackson-Vanik amendment, a statement that many legislators—and Christian human rights activists—cheered.[49]

The Siberian Seven

As the Reagan administration worked to reorient U.S. relations with the Soviet Union and pursue "peace through strength," evangelical activists ramped up their lobbying efforts on behalf of members of the suffering Soviet church—especially the Siberian Seven.[50] The Vashchenko and Chmykhalov families had taken refuge in the basement of the U.S. embassy in Moscow in 1978, after Soviet authorities repeatedly denied their requests to emigrate.[51] Once there, they refused to leave, fearing state reprisal. As group leader Pyotr Vashchenko noted, "we have been through their prisons, their labor camps, their psychiatric wards. . . . Do you think that after we have been living in the American Embassy . . . they will let us go home and do nothing to us?"[52] Timofei Chmykhalov reported that the authorities in his hometown "continue agitating against us," threatening to imprison family members still living there and seeking to turn the townspeople against them.[53] Although the U.S. embassy staff hoped they would leave, they nonetheless provided food and medical care to the seven family members, allowing them to stay in a small room with two beds and to have access to a radio.[54]

Since 1978, evangelical groups from the United States had petitioned the Soviet government to allow the two Pentecostal families to emigrate and urged U.S. policymakers to take action on their behalf. They had also remained in regular contact with the Siberian Seven, sharing updates about the case and statements from the families with the U.S. public.[55] The plight of the Vashchenko and Chmykhalov families received sympathetic coverage in the U.S. media and attracted bipartisan support in Congress as well as close attention from President Reagan, who had long advocated for their right to emigrate.[56] During Reagan's first term in office, the ongoing saga of the "Embassy Pentecostals" offered evangelicals a high-profile case to use as a platform for their arguments that U.S. foreign policy should promote religious freedom abroad.[57]

Representatives from CREED, Religion in Communist-Dominated Areas, and other evangelical organizations testified at the numerous congressional hearings held between 1981 and 1983 to discuss how to pressure the Soviet Union to allow the Vashchenko and Chmykhalov families to emigrate. In addition to attesting to the families' piety and suffering, these witnesses drew key conceptual links between religious freedom, human rights, and U.S. values.[58] At a November 1981 hearing before the Subcommittee on Immigration and Refugee Policy to support a bill that would grant visas and permanent residency in the United States to the Siberian Seven, CREED cofounder and Senator Roger Jepsen declared: "To not take a stand resolutely behind the families that have come to be known as the 'Siberian Seven' would be to encourage forces of religious repression throughout the world to move against people of faith without fear of serious or sustained American protest. At issue is not only the freedom of seven individuals, Mr. Chairman. As leaders of the free world, will America stand up and speak out against a violation of the most basic human right—the freedom of thought and of worship."[59]

These sentiments struck a chord with Congress. The bill passed the Senate in July 1982, and the linkage between freedom to practice religion and freedom in general as a universal value cropped up frequently in other related hearings.[60] When the deputy director of Religion in Communist-Dominated Areas, Olga Hruby, testified before Congress in a hearing on religious persecution throughout the world, she argued that the U.S. government should cut off aid to the Soviet Union in order to demonstrate U.S. support for human rights and "adherence to the ideals which inspired and created this great democracy."[61] Likewise, the executive director of Christian Solidarity International (CSI) concluded his testimony before the House Foreign Affairs Committee by citing the need to bring "world public opinion to bear against violations" of religious freedom, and by quoting Abraham Lincoln: "Those who deny freedom to others deserve it not for themselves, and, under a just God, cannot long retain it."[62]

The firsthand accounts that Christian human rights groups gathered from their brethren in the USSR and shared in their testimony in Congress convinced many legislators of the need for continued action on behalf of the Siberian Seven and other persecuted Christians. When Representative Barney Frank (D-MA) and Senator Carl Levin (D-MI) introduced legislation in the House and Senate to extend United States constitutional protections to the two families, Levin stated that he was inspired by the testimony he had heard about Christian suffering, as well as by his interactions with the

Siberian Seven, who he visited at the embassy in 1979.[63] During the hearings on religious persecution, Representative Don Bonker (D-WA) praised the Christian activists who spoke for awakening his conscience and for making the Congress "more fully committed to getting something done."[64]

Figure 7. Anita and Peter Deyneka of the Slavic Gospel Association, Soviet dissidents Igor Gerashchenko and Irina Ratushinskaia, an unidentified U.S. official, Kent Hill of the Institute on Religion and Democracy, and Democratic congressman Tom Lantos stand on the steps of the U.S. Capitol. Courtesy of Special Collections, Buswell Library.

In addition to their congressional lobbying efforts, evangelical activists worked to keep the case in the public eye. In 1982, the National Religious Broadcasters (NRB), whose members hailed from a diverse array of evangelical missionary, media, and humanitarian organizations, signed a resolution that called on the U.S. government to take stronger action on behalf of the Pentecostal families and sent a petition to President Reagan.[65] The NRB, along with religious media organizations throughout the world, also pushed secular press outlets to highlight the case.[66] The extensive press coverage called greater attention to Soviet persecution of Christians, garnering additional support for evangelical efforts to help all victims of religious repression.

So too did Billy Graham's controversial visit to the Soviet Union in 1982. Ilya Orlov, a leader in the registered All-Union Council of Evangelical Christians and Baptists (AUCECB) of the Soviet Union, invited Graham and several representatives from the Baptist World Alliance to participate in a peace conference organized by Patriarch Pimen of the Russian Orthodox Church.[67] Given Soviet government involvement in the affairs of registered churches, the Department of State, not to mention many Christians in the United States, opposed the visit thinking that Graham's participation would hasten the "achievement of Soviet foreign policy and propaganda aims."[68] Graham recognized that the Soviet government might use his presence for propaganda purposes, but felt the opportunity to establish direct contacts would benefit the cause of religious freedom and evangelism behind the Iron Curtain in the long run.[69] Many U.S. evangelicals, committed to spreading the gospel throughout the communist world, agreed.[70] After President Reagan encouraged Graham to make the trip, the Department of State briefed the preacher on the administration's stance on nuclear arms reduction to help him prepare for his conference address.[71] The White House also helped Graham arrange a personal, pastoral visit with the Siberian Seven as part of his agreement to attend the peace conference.[72]

Graham stated that he viewed his visit to Moscow primarily as an opportunity to preach the gospel to public audiences as well as to government leaders in the Soviet Union. His address on "The Christian Faith and Peace in a Nuclear Age" focused on achieving world peace through obedience to God. Affirming his belief that "peace is possible, if we will humble ourselves and learn again God's way of peace," Graham called on world leaders to make meaningful progress toward nuclear arms reductions and urged the conference members to "call the peoples of the world to prayer."[73] He also insisted on preaching during church services at a Russian Orthodox as well as a Baptist church.[74] According to Alexei Bychkov, general secretary of the AUCECB, Graham built important connections with Orthodox leaders, setting the stage for productive future visits from the preacher to the Soviet Union. His presence nurtured unprecedented cooperation between the AUCECB and the Orthodox Church, in part by helping to dignify and legitimize evangelicalism in the eyes of Orthodox leaders.[75] The local media aired extensive coverage of Graham's public appearances, expanding the reach of his message widely throughout the Soviet Union.[76]

Most significant, Graham met privately with officials from the Foreign Affairs Committee of the Soviet Parliament and the Central Committee of the Communist Party to discuss the fate of the Siberian Seven and the prospects for religious freedom in the Soviet Union more generally.[77] According to Alexander S. Haraszti, who coordinated Graham's visits throughout Eastern Europe and the Soviet Union in the 1970s and 1980s, Graham's tact and grace engendered good will from the Soviet authorities, influenced their policies, and helped him secure future invitations to evangelize in the Soviet Union.[78]

Yet Graham's intervention did not bring the release of the Siberian Seven, and the Vashchenko and Chmykhalov families made it clear from the outset that they did not see his visit as particularly desirous. Although Graham spent an evening at the U.S. embassy praying with them, offering them counsel, and reading passages from the Bible, they expressed dismay that he had accepted the invitation to come to the USSR, as they believed the Soviet government would exploit it for propaganda.[79] Several Western news reporters took a similar view of his trip, critiquing Graham for not rebuking Soviet authorities for their abridgements of religious rights.[80] Nevertheless, as he and his defenders noted at the time, Graham made a strategic decision not to embarrass his Soviet hosts by engaging in angry polemics, thereby paving the way for ongoing evangelical foreign policy engagement.[81]

The controversy over Graham's visit highlighted the tensions within the evangelical community over how the United States should best address Soviet human rights violations. A large contingent of activists believed that change would only come with sustained public pressure on the Soviet Union from the international community as well as from the United States government. These individuals saw little utility in pursuing the private diplomacy that Graham employed during his visit, or that the State Department advocated. In addition to their efforts to levy international opprobrium through congressional action, these groups attempted to smuggle Bibles into the Soviet Union and then widely publicized their interactions with the authorities if caught.[82] Other evangelicals promoted a less bombastic approach to dealing with Soviet authorities, such as working through official channels to distribute Bibles.[83] Ultimately, the combination of public pressure and private diplomacy had an impact. In late 1982, for example, the Central Committee of the Communist Party of the Soviet Union consented to a recommendation from the Council for Religious Affairs to print and distribute one hundred thousand Bibles to give at least the outside appearance of compliance with their own state policies on religious practice.[84]

Reagan and his top advisers pursued a similar mix of restrained public statements and serious private negotiations with Soviet leadership to push the USSR to allow the families to emigrate. In 1981, Secretary of State Alexander Haig discussed the Vashchenko case with Soviet foreign minister Andrei Gromyko repeatedly in private meetings, stressing that Reagan and many members of Congress viewed progress on the case as a foreign policy imperative.[85] When Reagan met with Soviet ambassador Anatoly Dobrynin for the first time in 1983, he focused on the Siberian Pentecostals as part of a larger discussion about how human rights abuses in the Soviet Union made it difficult from a domestic political standpoint to improve the U.S.-Soviet relationship.[86] Domestic political mobilization in the United States against Soviet abuses of religious freedom made it hard for the administration to disaggregate human rights concerns from national security issues such as arms control in bilateral negotiations.[87]

Yet Soviet leaders viewed these concerns as unwarranted intrusions into their internal affairs. In an effort to elicit concessions from the Soviet Union, Reagan addressed human rights issues quietly. He assured Dobrynin that his administration would greet positive outcomes "with appreciation but not with any sense of victory" and expressed his disinclination to use the trade sanctions of the Jackson-Vanik amendment to compel Soviet human rights compliance.[88] At the same time, the president sent a public letter to the Siberian Seven, expressing his concern for their wellbeing and urging them "to continue your courageous course, a struggle that is an inspiration to all who value religious freedom and individual human rights."[89] The combination of quiet diplomacy with the Soviet Union and public statements of support to temper public frustrations panned out; in April 1983, the Siberian Seven left the embassy.[90] By July, members of both families had emigrated to Israel.[91] In his diary, Reagan heralded the quiet deal the administration negotiated with the Soviet Union for their freedom.[92]

The success that the administration had in nudging the Soviet Union to allow the Siberian Seven to emigrate influenced its handling of similar cases throughout the mid-1980s. Reagan refrained from commenting publicly on the U.S. role and deflected suggestions that he meet with the Vashchenko and Chmykhalov families.[93] He recognized that attempting to capitalize on the Soviet decision to allow the Pentecostals to emigrate would violate the tacit agreement that had brought their release, and would undermine administration efforts to achieve similar results in the future.[94] Yet in private meetings and summits with Soviet leaders, Shultz and Reagan continued to emphasize human rights issues, particularly those related to religious freedom.[95] Furthermore, his description of the Soviet Union as an "evil empire" in his March 1983 speech to the National Association of Evangelicals made clear that Reagan still held the USSR in contempt for infringing on basic human freedoms.[96] For their part, evangelical activists kept up a steady drumbeat of letters and petitions to the president and the State Department urging them to continue to press Soviet bloc leaders to improve their treatment of Christians in their countries.[97]

Targeting Religious Rights Violators

Despite the emigration of the Siberian Seven in 1983, religious leaders and lobbyists found considerable evidence to suggest that human rights abuses were on the uptick in the Soviet Union and Eastern bloc countries. Senate human rights hearings and the State Department *Country Reports on Human Rights Practices* catalogued ongoing repression and widespread religious persecution. In testimony before the Senate Committee on Foreign Relations, Jerry K. Rose, the Pentecostal president of Christian Communications of Chicagoland, argued that throughout the communist world, "believers are subjected to a variety of persecutions, including the imposition of large fines, the dispersal of prayer meetings, weddings and funerals, the deprivation of parental rights, psychiatric confinement, punitive conscription, and criminal prosecution."[98] Though thankful for the Siberian Seven's release, he urged Congress not to mistake this positive development as a sign that the Soviet Union had made a substantive shift in its policy toward religious believers. Rather, he suggested that the assembled senators and representatives view it as an inducement to continue to apply legislative and public pressure to promote human rights compliance in the Soviet bloc.[99]

The leading congressional supporters of human rights corroborated the case that various Christian groups presented. Senator Charles H. Percy (R-IL), for example, opened a Senate Foreign Relations Committee hearing on human rights in the USSR and Eastern Europe by noting that "the human rights situation in the Soviet Union is by all accounts worse today than at any time in the past decade," owing to ongoing emigration restrictions, harassment, and repression.[100] He called on Congress to continue to introduce resolutions condemning religious persecution in the Soviet bloc and implored the president and his advisers to push the Soviets to improve their human rights record and ensure that their citizens could worship freely. After the hearing, Percy formed the Advisory Council on Religious Rights in Eastern Europe and the Soviet Union in order to better address the escalating abuse of Christians, Jews, and other religious minorities. This council, which included a diverse group of religious leaders including Jerry K. Rose as well as former secretaries of state Alexander Haig, Cyrus Vance, William Rogers, and Dean Rusk, sent letters to Soviet leaders, submitted reports to Congress, and raised the issue of religious persecution at meetings of the North Atlantic Assembly.[101]

Other congressional leaders made direct contacts with persecuted Christians in the Soviet Union, and used these relationships to press for diplomatic sanctions against countries that violated international agreements to protect human rights and religious freedom. In September 1983, Senator Kemp sent Secretary of State Shultz a lengthy missive about the religious persecution he witnessed during a visit to the USSR in July 1983 with his wife, Senator and Mrs. Bill Armstrong, and twenty members of the House of Representatives.[102] Kemp reported meeting with Christians who had grown up in orphanages while their parents endured long prison sentences for preaching the gospel, and described the indignant speeches about these violations that he and his colleagues gave before the admittedly indifferent Supreme Soviet.[103] With these poignant personal experiences in mind, he urged Shultz to take the Soviet Union's "shocking record of Helsinki violations" into consideration while preparing for his meetings with Soviet Foreign Minister Gromyko during the conference on East-West cooperation in Madrid.[104] In similar letters throughout the early 1980s, Kemp implored Shultz, as well as the foreign ambassadors he met with, to intervene on behalf of suffering Christians in the Soviet bloc.[105]

Introducing these concerns into diplomatic exchanges did facilitate the emigration of a limited number of families, though it did not immediately bring greater freedoms to Christians living behind the Iron Curtain. For this reason, evangelical advocates also pursued legislative means to compel Soviet compliance with human rights norms. Although the State Department and the Reagan administration made clear their disinclination to use trade sanctions for this purpose, many evangelical activists and members of Congress viewed restrictions on U.S. trade as an effective inducement for offending countries to improve their treatment of religious minorities.[106] Throughout the 1980s, evangelical human right groups and their congressional allies offered testimony and eyewitness evidence of increasing religious persecution in the Soviet Union and Eastern Europe to build a case for denying most favored nation (MFN) trading status to the worst offenders per the terms of the Jackson-Vanik amendment.

After the Soviet Union, the Socialist Republic of Romania ranked topmost on the list of transgressors that these activists targeted. Despite having the second highest rate of church attendance in Eastern Europe as well as one of the fastest growing evangelical populations, Romania had one of the most dismal records on religious freedom in the region, according to human rights organizations such as Helsinki Watch and the Christian Legal Defense and Education Fund.[107] Reports from contacts within Romania to evangelicals in the United States and Great Britain indicated that Romanian Baptist and Pentecostal denominations had begun to experience a revival between 1973 and 1974.[108] Increased church attendance, particularly among young Romanians, created tensions between believers and government leaders. In response to the religious revival, as well as to the outspoken activism of evangelical leaders such as Baptist Josef Ton and Pentecostal Vasile Rascol, state officials intensified their persecution and surveillance of believers.[109] To counter these abuses, evangelicals in the United States mounted effective campaigns during the mid- to late-1970s to pressure the Romanian government to release Ton, Rascol, and other imprisoned leaders.[110] In the 1980s, evangelical activists and members of the Christian media in the United States expanded these efforts, embarking on a more holistic campaign to protect Romanian believers and the ongoing religious revival. Convincing Congress and the president to link the extension of MFN trading status to human rights compliance and religious freedom in Romania formed the centerpiece of their crusade.

In congressional hearings on trade with Romania, evangelical lobbyists and sympathetic state and national legislators shared disturbing reports of Romanian religious persecution and other human rights abuses. Jeffrey Collins, director of Christian Response International (CRI) and EWNS, testified in numerous hearings about Romanian officials razing churches, torturing religious activists, and imprisoning Christians for distributing Bibles.[111] He and Calvinist minister Alexander Havadtoy condemned the Romanian government for recycling for use as toilet paper some twenty thousand

Bibles that the Baptist World Alliance had sent to Romanians desperate for religious materials.[112] Other Christian leaders testified about the "mysterious deaths" of ministers, discrimination in employment and education, and emigration bans that Romanian Christians faced.[113] They also referenced the Romanian government's refusal to grant the growing Baptist and Pentecostal congregations permission to expand their church facilities.[114]

Much as in the case of the Siberian Seven, evangelicals identified religious liberty as a core value that the United States government needed to defend abroad in order to advance global human rights. In so doing, they put forth a human rights policy that would promote evangelism and revival within the communist world, rather than just emigration to more open societies. Collins stressed that while freedom to emigrate remained an important measure of human rights compliance, U.S. policymakers should focus on creating "a political climate, an economic climate, a religious climate in these nations that we might create a reverse migration, where people would be able to leave the United States and return to their homelands and enjoy the human freedoms that they so deserve."[115] Collins and other activists emphasized the desire of Romanian Baptist and Pentecostal pastors to stay in their own countries and evangelize, stating that these individuals only sought emigration when the abuses they suffered became overwhelming.[116] They and their congressional allies stressed that the Reagan administration should interpret the Jackson-Vanik amendment broadly by considering the rights of believers in the Soviet bloc to practice their religion as well as to emigrate when deciding on MFN status.[117] The rhetorical link that activists drew between religious liberty and broader notions of freedom and human rights proved powerful. Employing vivid, emotional evidence of Christian suffering, evangelical activists attracted sustained bipartisan support in Congress.

CRI also arranged guided visits to Romania so that sympathetic legislators and White House officials could witness the revival and repression of Christian life there firsthand and then use their experiences to build the case for congressional and presidential action. In April 1985, Collins and representatives from Campus Crusade for Christ and the Christian Legal Society led an eight-day trip to Romania for U.S. and British government officials. Trip participants included Representative Mark Siljander (R-MI), White House associate director of public affairs Carolyn Sundseth, and two state representatives from Kentucky—Baptist Tom Riner and Pentecostal Gene Huff, both of whom had traveled to Romania on a CRI trip in 1982 as well.[118]

In a letter to President Reagan, Siljander described the experience of visiting the ruins of a Baptist church in Bistrita, Romania that the authorities had razed with a bulldozer in November 1984. Commenting on the emotional scene, he noted, "we stood with other CRI delegates on the ruins of that church and were joined by 300 members of the church. We joined hands, singing and praising God for three hours in freezing temperatures. . . . We all wept together—we were one in Christ."[119] Afterward, the delegation spoke with Baptist and Pentecostal congregants to assess church-state relations in Romania. They then met with local officials, seeking to intervene on behalf of the Bistrita church and other endangered congregations.[120] Siljander pledged to monitor the situation and praised CRI's advocacy for persecuted Christians, whom, he stated, "depend[ed] on CRI staff to represent them before the governments and courts of the world."[121] He called on his fellow Christians to support CRI based on "the biblical mandate to support those . . . who are suffering because of their faith (Hebrews 13:3)."[122] Siljander also suggested that the state demolition of the church building in Bistrita—and the outpouring religious faith he witnessed—typified the dissident Christian experience in Romania. CRI and its backers vowed to testify in Congress to recommend against renewing Romania's MFN status if the government did not end religious persecution.[123]

True to their word, Collins and his fellow activists repeatedly testified during the hearings on Romanian trade and human rights violations that took place between 1982 and 1988, with considerable support from Siljander, Kemp, and other like-minded Christian legislators. Their efforts to use the Jackson-Vanik amendment to punish Romania for its religious persecution met with resistance from the State Department and the Reagan administration, which continued to renew Romania's MFN status year after year. In statements to Congress justifying these decisions, Reagan argued that trade agreements fostered "important productive exchanges on human rights and emigration matters," affording the administration leverage to press the Ceauşescu government for change.[124] Reagan and his advisers also claimed that they feared that rescinding MFN would lead the Romanian government to retaliate against its already vulnerable and suffering Christian population.[125] Some evangelical leaders, including National Association of Evangelicals executive director Robert P. Dugan, acknowledged the Reagan administration's fears and desire to maintain leverage. Despite his sensitivity to the president's concerns though, he still wanted the administration to suspend Romania's MFN, even if only temporarily, in order to "send a clear message to President Ceauşescu that the U.S. government will not provide economic benefits to a nation which does not respect the basic human rights of its people."[126]

The Reagan administration held firm, in part because of Romania's strategic significance in the Cold War against the Soviet Union. In 1982, Reagan and the NSC had developed a National Security Decision Directive (NSDD) to guide U.S. relations with the Soviet Union and Eastern Europe, which it issued as NSDD 75 on January 17, 1983. This directive indicated that "the primary U.S. objective in Eastern Europe is to loosen Moscow's hold on the region while promoting the cause of human rights in individual East European countries."[127] Part of this strategy involved rewarding countries such as Romania that exercised foreign policy independence from the Soviet Union and other Warsaw Pact nations with normalized trade relations.[128] The NSC documents suggest that the Reagan administration believed this differentiation policy would compel compliance with human rights norms while improving U.S.-Eastern European relations and weakening the Warsaw Pact.[129] The reports of ongoing human rights abuses in Romania ensured that many legislators and members of the public remained skeptical of these claims.

In his annual messages to Congress in 1986 and 1987 on his decision to waive the emigration requirements of the Trade Act of 1974 in order to extend MFN status to Romania, Reagan sought to counteract the testimony of evangelical activists and sell the promise of his Eastern European strategy. He reassured Congress, "I share the strong concerns manifested among the public and in the Congress regarding the Romanian Government's restrictions on religious liberties," and detailed the suggestions that his administration had made to President Ceauşescu to address U.S. human rights concerns.[130] Reagan insisted that extending MFN served "to strengthen the extent of religious observance in Romania," and "facilitated American citizens' access to coreligionists in Romania as well as the flow of several million dollars' worth of material assistance to them each year."[131]

Yet testimony from Baptists, Pentecostals, and other evangelical Christians prompted some legislators to doubt the efficacy of trade leverage to produce substantive human rights improvements. As Philip H. Crane (R-IL) noted: "Romania is supposed to be making progress in human rights, thanks to our generous trade policy. However, Mr. Chairman, a regime that bulldozes churches, murders clergymen, and incarcerates individuals who are discovered transporting bibles in the trunk of a car is not making progress in human rights."[132] Frustration over the seemingly ceaseless reports of state brutality against Christians contributed to bipartisan support for congressional resolutions to suspend Romania's MFN status. Legislators frequently incorporated examples of religious persecution that evangelical witnesses shared with their committees and from their own personal visits to Romania and the Soviet Union. Drawing directly on the testimony of Collins and Havadtoy, Representative Siljander and Senator Christopher Dodd (D-CT) described the destruction of the twenty thousand Baptist World Alliance Bibles as particularly illustrative of Romanian disdain for freedom and human rights.[133] In addition to the proposed legislation, groups of congressmen sent letters to Romanian officials and President Ceauşescu warning that reports of such grievous acts of religious persecution jeopardized the renewal of MFN status.[134]

After years of acrimonious debate, both houses of Congress voted to suspend Romania's MFN status in 1987 as a result of ongoing human rights abuses.[135] In response, the Ceauşescu government renounced Romania's MFN status "as a protest against foreign 'interference' in its domestic affairs."[136] Reagan allowed the MFN waiver to expire on July 3, 1988.[137] Evangelical activists and church groups continued to monitor Romania, reporting on repression as well as on the stirrings of religious revival.[138] They also worked to expand their contacts with their coreligionists there. Members of the Church of God, for example, reconnected in 1989 with several Romanian ministers who had received their pastoral training at their School of Theology in Cleveland, Tennessee.[139] These connections ensured that U.S. Baptists and Pentecostals were well prepared to plant churches, evangelize, and distribute religious literature as soon as religious restrictions began to loosen in Romania after the Romanian Revolution and President Ceauşescu's execution in 1989.[140]

Religious Rights under Gorbachev

Social disaffection and a desire for change began bubbling up throughout the Soviet bloc in the 1980s as the Soviet Union grappled with a stagnant economy, a military quagmire in Afghanistan, and a crisis in Poland that threatened the entire Warsaw Pact.[141] The reverberations of the Helsinki Final Act and other international agreements on human rights contributed to the growth of civil society and dissent within the USSR and the Eastern bloc, compounding the challenges that Soviet leaders faced.[142] Soviet Baptists and Pentecostals participated in the dissident movement through samizdat publications and civil disobedience, advocating for reforms that would allow them to practice their faith freely.[143] After Leonid Brezhnev's death in 1982, his successor Yuri Andropov attempted to revitalize the moribund Soviet leadership, but by and large he continued his predecessor's policies. Konstantin Chernenko, who took power after Andropov died in early 1984, made similarly little headway in pulling the Soviet Union out of its torpor. Within hours of Chernenko's death in March 1985, the Central Committee elected Mikhail Gorbachev to serve as the new general secretary of the Communist Party. Gorbachev had risen to influence within the Politburo during Andropov's tenure, and his youth and new thinking seemed to promise a renewal of communism and the Soviet system.[144] Yet the reforms he implemented to save Soviet communism ultimately hastened its collapse.

In May 1985, Gorbachev intimated that he would initiate changes to overcome the corruption, economic inefficiencies, and moral decline he saw plaguing the Soviet Union. He brought in "new thinkers" to help reorient foreign policy, launched a campaign to combat alcoholism, and announced his new policy of perestroika to reform the economy and political system.[145] He also began to implement reforms to soften religious restrictions and reduce persecution in the Soviet Union.[146] Though modest and mostly focused on relations with the Russian Orthodox Church at first, these reforms gradually accelerated and expanded in scope after he announced his policy of glasnost in 1987.[147] In addition to approving the Russian Orthodox Church's plan to restore the Danilovskiy Monastery, which the Soviet state had only recently returned to the church, Gorbachev announced plans to draft new legislation to protect freedom of conscience in 1988.[148] He also met with the Holy Synod of the Church and endorsed proposals for the celebration of the millennium of Orthodox Christianity in Russia in June 1988.[149]

Some analysts suggested that this opening to the Orthodox Church signaled a realization among Soviet leaders that outright religious repression had failed and that a more conciliatory approach might allow them to better harness the power and influence of religion to reshape and democratize society.[150] Others viewed the moves cynically in light of ongoing repression against Pentecostals, unregistered Baptists, and sects such as the Hare Krishna, describing Gorbachev's reforms as a public relations effort rather than the first step toward fostering genuine religious toleration in the Soviet Union.[151] Influential legislators also expressed skepticism.[152] Reagan and Shultz, therefore, continued to push Gorbachev on human rights and religious freedom in their diplomatic exchanges.[153] Only in 1990 did the Soviet Union pass a new law granting religious freedom and declaring all faiths equal under the law.

Between 1986 and 1990, evangelicals in the United States observed developments in the Soviet Union with cautious optimism. During visits with the

AUCECB in the Soviet Union in 1986, U.S. church leaders built up networks with local Baptists and Pentecostals, exploring opportunities for evangelism and commenting positively on the "new and growing openness" to Christianity that they observed among the Soviet people.[154] In October 1988, the Baptist Joint Committee on Public Affairs, an international coalition of Baptist denominations working to promote religious liberty, issued a resolution commending Gorbachev and the Soviet Union for making "progress toward religious freedom."[155] The resolution cited evidence from U.S. ambassador Richard Schifter showing that Soviet leaders had begun to allow the importation of Bibles and Christian literature, and had reduced the arrest and incarceration rate of believers.[156] The group urged the Soviet Union to ratify legislation protecting religious freedom.[157] It also continued to monitor and publish reports on Soviet progress toward these goals.[158]

Unsure of how long the new period of openness would last, U.S. evangelical groups moved quickly to aid and connect with their brethren.[159] In 1988, the Baptist World Alliance took advantage of slackening restrictions by launching a campaign with the United Bible Societies to send hundreds of thousands of Bibles to believers in Russia and Eastern Europe.[160] The Assemblies of God, the largest Pentecostal denomination in the United States, celebrated the establishment of a legal Pentecostal Union in Russia by meeting with its leaders there and discussing how they could support church growth throughout the Soviet bloc.[161] They coordinated with these and other Russian Pentecostal leaders to distribute Bibles, create new ministries, and expand evangelistic radio programming in Russia.[162] Their actions reflected the powerful sense of connection that they felt with their brethren abroad and their desire to spread the gospel "to all nations," as commanded in the Bible.[163] They capitalized on the work of denominational foreign mission boards and evangelical NGOs, including the Slavic Gospel Association, Strategic Prayer for Communist Countries, and CSI, which had forged transnational bonds during the 1970s and 1980s.[164]

Project Christian Bridge

Perhaps Gorbachev and other reform-minded Soviet leaders took note of the power of these connections and of the potential influence of U.S. evangelical groups. Western believers had provided ongoing support to dissidents in the Soviet Union through letter-writing campaigns as well as radio broadcasts, bolstering the wave of Soviet human rights activism that followed the

Helsinki Accords.[165] This activism formed the foundation of a new civil society in the Soviet Union. As Geoffrey Hosking and other scholars of Russian history have argued, "The Soviet Union's acknowledgment of a complex of international juridical obligations, no matter how purely symbolic at first, aided the process of the formation of a civic consciousness inside the country, especially since foreign radio stations, broadcasting in Russian, spread information about these obligations and about Soviet authorities' violations of them."[166]

In his memoirs, Gorbachev credited the dissident movement with laying the groundwork for social and political reform in the USSR.[167] At the 28th Congress of the Communist Party of the Soviet Union in July 1990, he identified the emergence of civil society as a key factor in the transformation of the Soviet political system; with the revival of civic engagement, he noted, "genuine democracy is being established with free elections, a multi-party system and human rights."[168] This transformation had costs. By 1990, nearly every Soviet republic and all of the communist nations in East and Central Europe had peeled away and established independent governments.[169] Despite these challenges, Gorbachev remained committed to strengthening the Soviet Union through political and social reform. He reached out to Western NGOs, including some U.S. religious organizations, for advice on making the transition to democracy as well as for aid in fostering civil society in Russia.[170]

As part of this outreach effort, several members of the Supreme Soviet invited a group of evangelical Christian leaders from the United States to meet with Gorbachev in Moscow in September 1991.[171] In their letter to this ad hoc delegation, chairman of the Supreme Soviet Konstantin Lubenchenko and his compatriots praised Christian NGOs for their past work in "social development," expressing hope that by sharing their values and organizational experience, U.S. evangelical groups would help Russia to "implement moral ideas [and] . . . develop charitable funds and civil societies."[172] This overture ultimately led to the formation of Project Christian Bridge, an organization that facilitated transnational evangelical cooperation and democratization in the USSR during and after its collapse. Project Christian Bridge gave U.S. evangelicals unprecedented access to Soviet society, opening a window of opportunity to expand their evangelistic efforts and promote religious freedom during a period of rapid political and social change in the Soviet bloc.

Lubenchenko tapped Ukrainian émigré Mikhail Morgulis to organize the delegation of U.S. evangelicals.[173] After emigrating to the United States in the 1970s, Morgulis had founded the Slavic Gospel Press with the Whea-ton, Illinois-based Slavic Gospel Association in 1982.[174] During the 1980s, he had gained a valuable audience among Russian Christians by producing and broadcasting evangelical radio programs.[175] He thus had an international reputation as a Christian leader as well as deep personal ties to Russia and Ukraine. Morgulis reached out to a diverse group of U.S. evangelical leaders to draft a response to the Supreme Soviet's letter and to accompany him on the trip as part of what he termed "Project Christian Bridge." The del-egates included Billy Melvin, executive director of the National Association of Evangelicals, Kent Hill, executive director of the Institute on Religion and Democracy, Philip Yancey, editor-at-large of *Christianity Today*, Brandt Gustavson, executive director of the National Religious Broadcasters, Alex Leonovich, president of the Slavic Missionary Service, and Peter and Anita Deyneka of USSR ministries, among others.[176] These leaders and organiza-tions, some of the most powerful and well connected in the United States, operated as key nodes in the global evangelical network and, as Philip Yancey noted, each delegate came on the trip came eager to advance the shared goal of global evangelism.[177]

In Moscow, they met with Soviet leaders who were distraught over what they termed the "profound moral and spiritual vacuum" plaguing their crumbling empire.[178] The evangelicals, accustomed to viewing the Kremlin through the prism of over seventy years of Soviet religious persecution and state-sponsored atheism, reported their genuine surprise that members of the Supreme Soviet sought spiritual guidance from them.[179] Commenting on their consultations with committee chairmen and deputies of the Supreme Soviet, Yancey marveled that: "They looked on the United States, with all its problems, as a shining light of democracy; they saw the Christian church as the only hope for their demoralized citizens. The Soviet leaders voiced a fear of total collapse and anarchy unless their society could find a way to change at the core, and for this reason they had turned to us for help."[180] According to Yancey, this fear of collapse led the head of the Ministry of State Security to announce that "this meeting with you Christians tonight is more important for the long-term security of our nation than the meeting between our nations' presidents on eliminating nuclear weapons."[181] When the evangelicals visited the KGB, General Nikolai Stolyarov echoed these sentiments, going so far as to offer repentance for the agency's persecution of Christians.[182]

At the capstone meeting of the trip, Gorbachev expressed appreciation to the delegates for their offer of "spiritual and material aid" to the Soviet

Union. Yancey reported that when Gorbachev addressed the group, he stated that, "Christians are doing much better than our political leaders on the important questions facing us. We welcome your help, especially when it is accompanied by deeds. My favorite line in your letter is, 'Faith without deeds is dead.'"[183] As he had with other religious leaders, Gorbachev stressed his belief that the Soviet Union needed to instill morality among its people in order to reestablish a functioning society.[184] Following the meeting, Gorbachev had the Project Christian Bridge mission statement released to the press.[185]

This transformed the ad hoc delegation into a coordinated effort by U.S. evangelical organizations to promote religious freedom, Christian values, and democratic reform in the Commonwealth of Independent States (CIS), which formed after Gorbachev resigned as president and the Soviet Union dissolved itself in late December 1991.[186] The members of Project Christian Bridge, and many other U.S. evangelicals, viewed the dissolution of the Soviet Union as a tremendous opportunity to foster evangelism, strengthen relationships with their brethren, and rebuild religious culture in the region. Although the Russian Orthodox Church found these aims chauvinistic given the long history of Christianity in Russia, Russian officials, intellectuals, and business leaders welcomed the intervention of Christians from the United States.[187] As the editor-in-chief of *Pravda* told Yancey, "morality is the worst crisis, worse than the economic and political problems. Christian values may be the only thing to keep our country from falling apart."[188]

Eager to seize on this opening into formerly closed and repressive societies, Project Christian Bridge launched a multipronged effort to bring Christianity and moral values to bear on the post-Soviet states. Some members pledged to remain in Moscow to teach and set up long-term ministries.[189] The rest returned home, ready to call on the vast network of U.S. evangelical organizations to coordinate and expand their involvement with churches, parachurch organizations, and government officials in the former Soviet Union. In January 1992, the National Association of Evangelicals joined with the Evangelical Fellowship of Missions Agencies to hold a Consultation on the Commonwealth of Independent States, which drew participants from a wide range of evangelical denominations and parachurch organizations.[190] Together, the participants outlined a strategic vision aimed at imposing order and direction on the proliferation of mission projects that U.S. organizations had launched in the CIS. Although they could not decide on a definitive list of project priorities, most agreed they should focus evangelistic efforts on the "prime target areas" of the CIS educational systems, media, and military.[191]

Participants also stressed the need to gather and share data about their work in the former Soviet Union, which the NAE pledged to disseminate "to denominations and churches, and through the National Religious Broadcasters to their network of media contacts."[192] This would help build widespread grassroots evangelical support and funding for their efforts.

The Consultation on the Commonwealth of Independent States also established an important set of recommendations for evangelicals and evangelical NGOs working in the CIS. Chief among these, participants emphasized that NGOs must make long-term commitments to their mission field, listen to and learn from local leaders, encourage indigenous evangelism, and avoid U.S. or Western ethnocentrism.[193] Mark Elliott, director of the Institute for East-West Christian Studies at Wheaton College, expressed concern about U.S. evangelicals going on short-term missionary trips to the CIS, issuing an "exhortation against 'hit and run evangelism.'"[194] Instead, he called evangelicals to "tarry" and develop deep connections with brethren and the local culture.[195] He and others at the meeting called for cooperative and partnership-based models of evangelism to facilitate the establishment of "church planting/cell groups" to foster the lasting growth of local churches and organizations.[196] As one participant cautioned, they must "take Christ to Eastern Europe and the CIS, not American Christianity."[197]

The NAE publicized its efforts to coordinate aid to the former Soviet Union widely, and many evangelical groups seemed inclined to follow the basic parameters that the consultation set forth.[198] In 1992, the Church of God met with bishops and pastors from formerly unregistered and underground Pentecostal churches throughout the CIS to sign an "Agreement of Cooperation." This document pledged partnership and a long-term commitment to: "shared efforts of evangelism; building and opening of educational centers; creation of Sunday Schools; creation of centers for the distribution of humanitarian aid; starting and equipping new missions; sharing in the production of Christian literature; and engaging in cultural and spiritual exchanges between the churches."[199] The Church of God "Strike Force Team" worked closely with their partners in the CIS, not only to plant churches but also to ensure ongoing support and religious education for the converts they won at their crusades.[200]

As the consultation and the NAE worked to guide evangelistic activities in the CIS, Mikhail Morgulis and other evangelical leaders began to coordinate visits from Russian officials to the United States. In November 1992, General Stolyarov, whom Morgulis met during Project Christian Bridge's visit to the KGB, traveled to the United States to meet with government leaders, Christian businessmen, and churches. According to newspaper reports,

Stolyarov sought advice on how to instill Christian values among soldiers and officers in the Russian military.[201] Similarly, the Church of God "Agreement of Cooperation" with the unregistered Pentecostal churches of the CIS attracted the attention of prodemocratic Russian military officers, two of whom traveled to the Church of God headquarters in early 1993 seeking "assistance with the development of benevolence ministries, establishment of chaplaincy in the military and information concerning the use of law to ensure freedom of religion in Russia."[202]

Yet, despite the best intentions of U.S. evangelical organizations, the initial enthusiasm that citizens of the CIS felt for U.S. Christian intervention soon waned. In an article for *Christianity Today*, Anita Deyneka noted that when she and her husband established their ministry in Moscow in 1991, "most Russians I met believed that the West—especially America—represented democracy, economic progress, and prosperity."[203] By 1994, she observed "that fascination with the West is fading," as U.S. intervention had failed to bring democracy and social stability to the CIS.[204] Although Deyneka praised the work of U.S. and Russian Christian organizations for their role in stoking religious revival, the proliferation of missionaries and religious NGOs in the former Soviet Union prompted a major backlash from the Russian Orthodox Church. In 1993, the church began to press Parliament to amend the law guaranteeing freedom of conscience in order to control the number and activities of foreign religious groups in Russia.[205] Despite protests from U.S. religious groups, Congress, and President Bill Clinton, Russian president Boris Yeltsin signed a revised version of the legislation limiting religious freedoms into law in September 1997.[206] This law specifically targeted evangelical churches and parachurch organizations.

Ultimately, although U.S. evangelical engagement did contribute to the renewal of Christian culture in the former Soviet Union in the 1990s, it also spurred the reintroduction of state restrictions on religion. Nevertheless, U.S. evangelical groups have continued to send missionaries and to advocate for religious freedom in the CIS even into the present day. Their involvement in efforts to inculcate moral and democratic values in former Soviet societies—especially their commitment to promoting religious liberty—reflected above all else their deeply held and eschatologically based desire to advance global evangelism. Yet given the instability of post-Soviet society and the widespread public disillusionment with U.S.-led democratization and economic reform measures, evangelicals discovered that their window of opportunity to reshape religious culture in the CIS was both very narrow and hotly contested indeed.

Figure 8. Raisa Gorbachev, General Nikolai Stolyarov, Mikhail Morgulis of Project Christian Bridge, Anita Deyneka of the Slavic Gospel Association, and Mrs. Stolyarov at a February 1992 reception for the opening of the Gorbachev Foundation, which aims to foster civil society and democratic and moral values. Courtesy of Special Collections, Buswell Library.

Extending the Vision

The arc of evangelical engagement with the Soviet Union in the last decade of the Cold War demonstrates the range of strategies that conservative Christians employed to advance the cause of religious liberty and evangelism in repressive communist regimes. Congressional lobbying, letter-writing campaigns, petitions to the president as well as foreign ambassadors, media coverage and testimony from victimized believers, and organized visits with Soviet Baptist and Pentecostal congregations for sympathetic legislators all contributed to the sustained attention that the issue of religious repression received in the United States. The concern that these efforts generated, in turn, filtered into diplomatic exchanges between the United States and the Soviet Union. Reagan, Shultz, and their aides pled for religious freedom in the Soviet bloc—including the right to provide religious instruction to children and to evangelize.

Throughout the 1970s and 1980s, U.S. evangelicals built enduring links with members of underground churches and registered Baptists and Pentecostals in the Soviet Union. In addition to providing financial and spiritual succor to their suffering brethren, they publicized the plight of persecuted believers through international media. This attention emboldened Soviet Christians and contributed to their participation in the broader dissident movement. As one leader in the Church of God noted, despite the decades of repression in Eastern Europe and the USSR, "believers kept their faith alive. They established a vast network which provided spiritual guidance, personal contacts and information mostly unavailable from other sources. When the opportunity came for these Christian believers to assert themselves they did so with zeal and a faith in the rightness of their cause, giving the revolution in Eastern Europe a distinct religious flavor."[207] Evangelicals from the United States drew on this network to foster productive exchanges with their coreligionists. As opportunities for congregational visits, evangelism, and the importation of religious literature and other media expanded after Gorbachev's reforms, evangelicals (and many other religious groups) from the United States descended on the Soviet Union en masse.

These groups understood that the dramatic social and political transformations in the Soviet Union and Eastern Europe constituted an unprecedented opportunity to build the Kingdom of God on Earth. In 1991, Jerry Parsley, the director of Russian Evangelism Outreach for the Assemblies of God, remarked reverently on the flurry of evangelism in the CIS, noting, "I firmly believe that this is God's hour for Russia, and we join our brethren there in believing that we have been called for 'such a time as this.' We have before us perhaps the greatest opportunities for reaching the unreached in Church history."[208] The nature of evangelical engagement with post-Soviet societies in the CIS reveals that, rather than just simple anticommunism, the drive to spread the Good News throughout the world had inspired the years of activism on behalf of persecuted Soviet Christians. Human rights language, in turn, provided a powerful tool for attracting widespread support for this larger agenda. Committed to the task of world evangelism, conservative evangelical Christians in the United States used their vision for religious human rights to frame and guide their foreign policy engagement with a number of other nations throughout the world during Reagan's presidency. As with the former Soviet Union, their efforts wrought mixed results and unintended consequences.

Chapter 5

Supporting a "Brother in Christ" in Guatemala

On March 23, 1982, a group of young officers in the Guatemalan army staged a coup d'état at the National Palace in Guatemala City. After ordering the president, General Romeo Lucas García, to step down, the young officers announced their intention to replace him with a temporary military junta that would rule until Guatemala could hold free elections for a new president.[1] The officers named Brigadier General José Efraín Ríos Montt, General Horacio Maldonado Schaad, and Colonel Luis Gordillo Martínez as the leaders of the junta.[2] Not on active duty at the time of the coup, Ríos Montt learned of the decision from a radio broadcast calling him to the National Palace while he prepared for student-teacher meetings in his role as academic director at el Verbo ("The Church of the Word") Christian day school.[3] Prior to accepting the army's call, Ríos Montt asked for guidance from the elders of el Verbo, a neo-Pentecostal church that missionaries from the Eureka, California-based Gospel Outreach Church had founded in 1976 and continued to direct.

In an interview four days after the coup, U.S. missionary and el Verbo governing church elder Carlos Ramirez told reporters that following the young officers' call, he and the other elders had gathered "to lay hands on Efraín, to pray over him as the Bible teaches, and basically send him out from us with His blessings to the palace."[4] Through prayer with these church leaders, Ríos Montt came to believe that God had ordained him to lead the junta.[5] Within a few months, he had marginalized the two other junta members, and he declared himself president of Guatemala on June 5, 1982.[6] In public speeches and weekly radio and television sermonettes, Ríos Montt emphasized his certainty that "the Lord God, in his infinite wisdom, had given him the mission to save the people of Guatemala," a belief the elders of el Verbo nurtured.[7] As president, he pledged to bring Christian moral precepts to bear on the problems of the nation, and he called on the people and God to help him create a new Guatemala.[8]

Despite Ríos Montt's vows to end government corruption and rampant human rights abuses, thousands of leftist political activists, guerrillas, and Mayan civilians perished under his counterinsurgency program. Thousands more "disappeared." Over a million people fled the country. In August 1983, another group of army officers, frustrated by their lack of influence in policy decisions as well as by Ríos Montt's religious beliefs and ties to evangelical groups, led a coup to remove him from power. Although later regimes proved no less abusive, Guatemalans have termed the period in which Ríos Montt ruled *la violencia*, signifying it as a particularly brutal episode in the long and ruthless civil war that plagued Guatemala for thirty years.

Reports of ongoing human rights abuses complicated relations between the United States and Guatemala. In addition to laws that prohibited "military sales and assistance, development assistance, and favorable votes for certain multilateral loans" to countries guilty of a "consistent pattern of gross violations of internationally recognized human rights," the U.S. Congress also explicitly blocked military funding to Guatemala in 1977.[9] In early 1980, the U.S. ambassador to Guatemala asserted that these decisions had hindered U.S. communications with and influence over military leadership, and had failed to stem human rights violations.[10] During his presidential campaign, Ronald Reagan seized on such cases to criticize Jimmy Carter's approach to international relations, suggesting that Carter administration efforts to punish authoritarian regimes for violating human rights norms alienated otherwise pro-U.S. governments.[11] The Reagan administration, which viewed Guatemala as a key anticommunist ally in Central America and a potential regional counterweight against the influence of the Sandinistas in Nicaragua and the Farabundo Martí National Liberation Front in El Salvador, sought to reinstate military aid to Guatemala. Entrenched congressional resistance stemming from human rights concerns ensured that Reagan faced an uphill battle.

Support from U.S. and Guatemalan evangelicals for Ríos Montt and for the Reagan administration's efforts to extend military aid to Guatemala became significant factors shaping relations between the two countries. Ríos Montt's rhetoric and the evident sincerity of his religious beliefs captured the imagination of internationalist evangelical Christians in the United States. Seeing great potential to spread the gospel in Central America through Ríos Montt's Christian leadership, U.S. evangelicals and parachurch organizations aided his regime directly through public outreach, fundraising, and congressional lobbying. Despite mounting evidence that his campaign against Guatemala's "communist insurgency" involved the mass killing of indigenous Mayans, evangelical groups argued that the dictator's Christian faith would compel him to improve the country's human rights situation. That Ríos Montt appointed el Verbo elders to serve as his personal presidential advisers encouraged this belief, and highlighted the web of evangelical connections that influenced his policymaking. Neo-Pentecostal U.S. missionaries and their Guatemalan brethren played a key role in the Ríos Montt regime, shaping the dictator's discussions with the Reagan administration, factoring into his internal strategic planning, and guiding his understanding of his role as a Christian leader.

The intricate, overlapping web of influence that U.S. Christians wove—or found themselves woven into—in Guatemala in the early 1980s exemplified the transnational connectivity, shared evangelistic goals, and extensive reach of the global evangelical community. This chapter links the circumstances and socio-political implications of the proliferation of Pentecostal and neo-Pentecostal churches in Guatemala during the late 1970s with the theological and political beliefs that underpinned evangelical support for Ríos Montt in the United States in the 1980s. It argues that connections between evangelicals in the United States and in Guatemala influenced U.S. relations with the Ríos Montt regime and the response of the Guatemalan government to U.S. policies. This chapter also offers a unique contribution to our understanding of the political implications of global evangelicalism. It places evangelical involvement in the Ríos Montt regime in an international context as part of the larger crusade to evangelize the world and reveals how nonstate actors shaped U.S. relations with Central America in this period.[12]

Spiritual Aid for the Suffering

At just after 3 a.m. on February 4, 1976, a devastating 7.5 M_w earthquake struck Guatemala, radiating death and destruction throughout the country. Twenty-three thousand people perished, and more than seventy-six thousand suffered injuries.[13] The earthquake exacted a staggering economic toll, leaving over a million homeless, with large swaths of Guatemala City and other towns reduced to rubble and critical infrastructure destroyed.[14] Christian relief agencies and churches in the United States responded immediately, sending food, clothing, building supplies, and medical aid to help in the rescue and recovery efforts. The response from these groups proved so effective that within two weeks of the earthquake, the Ford administration's coordinator for disaster relief "urged persons wishing to help to contact church and private service organizations," rather than government agencies.[15] Although most Guatemalans were at least nominally Catholic at the time, evangelical Christian groups, including the National Association of Evangelicals' World Relief Commission, the Assemblies of God World Missions, and the Southern Baptist Foreign Mission Board, delivered substantial aid to their brethren and others suffering from the effects of the earthquake.[16] They also sent in missionaries. Ultimately, the extent and success of the evangelistic outreach that the earthquake triggered turned Guatemala into one of the most Protestant nations in Latin America, a transformation that had profound implications for Guatemalan society and politics.[17]

One week after the disaster, Billy Graham chartered a private plane from Mexico with Latin American evangelist Luis Palau to tour the most devastated areas and offer spiritual solace. The destruction and misery they witnessed overwhelmed them. During a meeting with Guatemalan president Kjell Eugenio Laugerud García, Graham stated that although the Billy Graham Evangelistic Association had sent in large shipments of food, medicine, and clothing, the aid provided to that point was insufficient to meet the tremendous need. He promised to send more.[18] Yet for Graham and other evangelicals concerned with helping Guatemala rebuild from the tragedy, material assistance alone would not suffice. They believed the nation needed Christian salvation as well. In a statement to the press, Graham declared that despite the devastation, the earthquake could serve a greater purpose and turn out to be a blessing, as the "tears shed by Guatemalans may be the way to reconciliation with God."[19] Urging the populace to accept that "peace can only be found in Jesus Christ," Graham made it clear that he saw the earthquake as a potential catalyst for mass conversion and, therefore, salvation.[20] Mission-minded evangelicals throughout the United States shared Graham's view. The disaster presented a tremendous opportunity for evangelical expansion, and they seized it.

The impulse to send spiritual as well as material aid to help those affected by the disaster reflected core evangelical beliefs about the relationship between evangelization and social action. Regardless of denomination, evangelicals shared a belief that they must engage in missionary work or evangelism to "make disciples of all nations," as Jesus commanded in his Great Commission to the eleven disciples at Galilee.[21] For premillennialist evangelicals such as Graham, this Great Commission figured prominently into their understanding of eschatology. Premillennialists believed that "Jesus Christ will return personally and visibly, in power and glory, to consummate his salvation and his judgment," as described in the books of Mark, Matthew, Hebrews, Revelation, and others.[22] They interpreted these scriptures as prophecy and trusted that, upon the fulfillment of biblical predictions, Christ would return to usher in the Kingdom of God on Earth.[23] World evangelization played a key role in those apocalyptic predictions, as many evangelicals read scriptures such as Matthew 24:14 ("And this good news of the kingdom will be proclaimed throughout the world, as a testimony to all nations; and then the end will come") and Mark 13:10 ("And the good news must first be proclaimed to all nations") as evidence that evangelism must precede the second coming.[24]

In an era fraught with debate over liberation theology and the embrace of a social justice rather than a missionary orientation within Catholicism and mainline Protestant denominations, evangelicals held fast to their commitment to global evangelism.[25] When religious leaders gathered in Lausanne, Switzerland in 1974 for the International Congress on World Evangelization (ICOWE), the place of social action in the hierarchy of Christian responsibility had emerged as a major point of debate. Many Western evangelicals viewed global efforts to spread the gospel as the most significant form of social action they could undertake as Christians.[26] At the congress, Fuller Theological Seminary professor Donald McGavran argued that "men have no greater needs than to be reconciled to their Father and to walk in the Light."[27] Though he acknowledged the pressing material needs that many faced throughout the world and welcomed Christian efforts to bring about change, McGavran pushed back against what he saw as the "drive to replace evangelism with social action."[28] He argued that salvation and church expansion provided the fundamental building blocks for "a righteous, peaceful society."[29] From this perspective, which informed evangelical disaster relief efforts in Guatemala after the earthquake as well as in crises elsewhere in the world, there could be no greater salvation for the suffering than salvation in Christ.[30]

In addition to the famous evangelists and major parachurch organizations that delivered assistance to Guatemala, missionaries from a number of small, independent evangelical churches fanned out into the cities and countryside to help the country rebuild and to plant churches. The rapid proliferation of these mostly neo-Pentecostal congregations reshaped not just the religious landscape of Guatemala, but the social and political culture as well. Sociologists and scholars of religion have argued that conversion to Protestantism and, in Latin America specifically, to Pentecostalism, facilitated social mobility among believers and modernization throughout the economy more broadly.[31] In Guatemala, this proved particularly true in the case of the many neo-Pentecostal congregations that sprang up in urban areas following the disaster.

Although the first Protestant missionaries had arrived in Guatemala in 1882, only about 7 percent of the population belonged to a Protestant or evangelical church prior to the 1976 earthquake.[32] As missionaries and evangelical NGOs streamed into Guatemala to aid the suffering populace, the rate of conversion increased exponentially. According to survey data that researchers at San Carlos University in Guatemala published in 1989, the Protestant population grew by 14 percent between 1976 and 1978, and by 42 percent between 1978 and 1982. By 1982, just over 22 percent of the population belonged to a Protestant church. The rate continued to increase throughout the 1980s and 1990s.[33] Pentecostal and neo-Pentecostal denominations accounted for a major share of this growth.

Missiologist Veronica Melander notes that not all of the Protestant expansion that followed in the wake of the earthquake originated from churches that U.S. missionaries planted *after* the disaster. Many long-established churches took the opportunity that the disaster presented to expand into new territory.[34] Immediately after the earthquake, the Assemblies of God, which had sent its first missionaries to Guatemala in 1934, shared optimistic reports from local evangelists about the potential for revival in the disaster-stricken country.[35] Throughout the following year, Assemblies of God missionaries launched 200 "Good News Crusades" in Guatemala as part of a campaign—nicknamed "Invasion '77"—to expand the reach of their denomination.[36] Alongside the crusade activities of larger denominations, many small evangelical churches established themselves in Guatemala City at this time, too. The diversity and range of evangelical expansion efforts made for a vibrant "marketplace" of religion, which helped to attract and retain new adherents.[37] These factors, along with the influx of funding from evangelicals in the United States postearthquake, contributed to the continuing spread of U.S.-style evangelical Protestantism in Guatemala.

The particularities of U.S. evangelical belief and worship practices ensured that this expansion wrought deep change in Guatemala, reshaping thousands of lives, coalescing with ongoing political change in the country, and solidifying transnational ties with evangelicals in the United States. People suffering from poverty and the destruction in Guatemala found neo-Pentecostalism attractive for both spiritual and material reasons. Theologian Néstor Medina suggests that in addition to the fact that the Protestant churches proved more efficient than Catholics at providing disaster relief, the message of Pentecostalism resonated with many Guatemalans in the aftermath of the earthquake.[38] Medina notes that the conversion rate continued to rise in Guatemala even as the inflow of aid tapered off, and as such he suggests: "Pentecostalism helped people rebuild their lives and make sense of their reality through apocalyptic lenses. The Pentecostal message of the imminent coming of the Lord, war, suffering, and earthquakes as signs of the end times contributed greatly to people flocking to Pentecostal churches. The eschatological message seemed to fit the social and political context."[39]

In addition to the apocalyptic overtones of the disaster itself, neo-Pentecostal churches took advantage of the rush of internal migration from rural villages to Guatemala City that the earthquake jumpstarted. According to historian Virginia Garrard-Burnett, evangelicals offered these rural immigrants food, shelter, and loans to help them establish themselves in the city—essential assistance that the Catholic Church and local government did not provide.[40] Evangelical churches "actively encouraged the economic improvement of their members by conflating notions of material and spiritual well-being."[41] In addition, the small prayer meetings, women's groups, and other associations that evangelical churches organized gave migrants a sense of community, which helped counterbalance the otherwise isolating experience of their new urban lives.[42]

The particular form of U.S. Pentecostal worship, with its emphasis on ecstatic expression and the experience of an "unmediated, personal relationship with God," drew immigrants in, yet it also blended with elements of indigenous spirituality that had persisted in rural villages.[43] This indigenization supplied a comforting familiarity for migrants and aided the vast expansion of neo-Pentecostal churches from the urban core to the rural highlands and beyond.[44] Although Pentecostalism spread quickly and became indigenized among rural Mayans, Pentecostal churches in the cities tended to retain an American character and bonds with counterparts in the United States, even as local leaders gradually took over from the original missionaries.[45] El Verbo, with its ties to the Gospel Outreach Church in California, typified this pattern of urban church growth and connectivity.

Gospel Outreach and Ríos Montt

Shortly after the earthquake struck Guatemala in 1976, Gospel Outreach Reverend Carlos Ramirez led a group of fifteen missionaries and six of their children from the California church to Guatemala City to assist in the reconstruction efforts and to spread the gospel.[46] Initially, they focused their efforts on helping local people rebuild their houses. Soon, however, they began to hold regular Bible study meetings in the homes of middle and upper-class residents of Guatemala City.[47] Ríos Montt joined one of these Bible study groups in 1979 at the urging of a fellow army officer. Ramirez and Jim DeGolyer, another U.S. Gospel Outreach pastor, led the group, which included future Ríos Montt advisers Francisco Bianchi and Alvaro Contreras.[48] Through these Bible study meetings, which involved prayer, close readings of scripture, and discussions of the challenges that each participant faced in their lives, Ríos Montt had a salvation experience and became a "born-again" Christian.[49]

Ríos Montt's receptivity to evangelicalism stemmed from personal setbacks linked to government corruption and the ongoing Guatemalan Civil War.[50] In 1974, after serving in the Guatemalan army for nearly thirty years, at various points as director of the Army's Escuela Politécnica, as brigadier general, and as Army chief of staff, he had run for president on the Christian Democratic ticket. He and his running mate won popular support and the majority of the votes on a platform of moderate reform. Yet rampant electoral fraud at the hands of the extreme right-wing Movimiento de Liberación Nacional (MLN) party denied him his victory. After the stolen election, the Guatemalan Minister of Defense assigned Ríos Montt to serve as a military attaché in Madrid, Spain in order to prevent him from posing a threat to Kjell Laugerud, whose triumph at the polls the MLN and sitting president General Carlos Manuel Arana Osorio had coordinated.[51] The loss of the presidency and forced exile left Ríos Montt embittered.[52]

Within Guatemala, widespread disaffection over the fraudulent election, coupled with the insufficiency of military reform programs, reignited the guerrilla movement.[53] In response, General Romeo Lucas García, whom Kjell Laugerud handpicked as his successor in 1978, intensified the repression against the guerrillas and indigenous groups, employing death squads to assassinate political enemies and massacring entire Mayan villages indiscriminately.[54] His government justified these depredations with Cold War ideology, linking the guerrillas with Cuban communism and characterizing guerrilla successes as progress toward totalitarianism and, therefore, an existential threat to the state.[55] The state violence further radicalized the populace and earned Guatemala international censure for human rights violations.

While the situation in Guatemala deteriorated, Ríos Montt grew increasingly frustrated with his life in exile. In 1977, the Escuela Politécnica that he had attended as a cadet and later led as its director invited him to attend the inauguration of its new facilities.[56] He used the invitation as a means to return home permanently, informing government officials that he would not resume his post in Madrid. The minister of defense placed him on inactive military status, and Ríos Montt retired to private life, where he nursed hopes that another opportunity to run for president would present itself.[57] Not long after, he began attending el Verbo prayer meetings.

In their recollections of Ríos Montt's conversion experience, church elders suggested that the general found relief from his bitterness over the lost election and exile in the evangelical teachings and lively spiritual community of el Verbo.[58] These fundamental Pentecostal elements hewed closely to those of the Gospel Outreach Church, which Ramirez had modeled el Verbo after in message, worship style, and mission when he established his ministry in Guatemala in 1976. Gospel Outreach had grown out of the Jesus Movement that swept the United States in the late 1960s and early 1970s, attracting disaffected youth who found the emotionality of Christian revivals, emphasis on the Holy Spirit, and simple, communal living an appealing alternative to mainstream culture.[59]

Jim Durkin, a California real estate agent and evangelical preacher, had founded Gospel Outreach after he began ministering to a small group of Jesus People who had rented one of his buildings for use as a "coffee house ministry."[60] The church grew rapidly as hundreds of people, including a young Carlos Ramirez, flocked to the Lighthouse Ranch and other properties that Durkin had acquired for the fledgling church.[61] There, according to Gospel Outreach materials, "many of them found the Lord Jesus Christ as their Savior and decided to stay."[62] The vision that Durkin articulated to his followers entailed three core evangelical tenets, drawn from scripture: "to preach the gospel to every creature," to "have the same unity with each other as the Lord Jesus had with His Father" in order to "effectively carry out God's work," and "to be individually conformed to the image of Christ."[63]

These deeply held evangelical beliefs about the necessity of Christian witness to fulfill the Great Commission motivated Durkin and the other leaders of Gospel Outreach to propagate their model of worship throughout the United States and the rest of the world. Within a decade of its founding, Gospel Outreach had established ministries in forty-four U.S., European, and Latin American cities—including el Verbo in Guatemala.[64] The promise of individual salvation, energetic worship, and tight-knit community that attracted Ríos Montt to the church brought a number of other local residents, including prominent business and political leaders, into the fold as well. By 1982, el Verbo boasted nearly 1,200 members, with an additional 450 children enrolled in the affiliated Christian day school.[65]

While el Verbo engaged in efforts to expand throughout the Guatemalan countryside and into other Latin American countries, it retained close ties with its parent church in California. The relationship extended beyond communications between the original Gospel Outreach missionaries and Gospel Outreach leaders, and a network of intellectual exchange between Guatemalan evangelical converts and their U.S. counterparts flourished. Indeed, in 1979, Ríos Montt visited Gospel Outreach in California with his wife and daughter, meeting with the founders and speaking at their church services.[66] Encouraging reciprocal bonds of kinship with members of its missionary churches, Gospel Outreach embraced a policy of global engagement aimed at building a cohesive community of believers that transcended national boundaries—a goal that many U.S. evangelicals shared.

As just one of the hundreds of similar Guatemalan evangelical churches, el Verbo stood out mostly for its relationship with Ríos Montt, yet the political connections and social mobility of its members also exemplified the socio-political realignment that emerged from evangelical expansion in Guatemala during this period. Core theological and political predilections led evangelical Protestants, particularly neo-Pentecostals such as the followers of el Verbo, into a de facto alliance with the right-leaning government of General Lucas. With their deep commitment to evangelism, rooted in eschatological imperatives as well as to their faith in the centrality of individual salvation, evangelicals in Guatemala and elsewhere tended to focus first on otherworldly, rather than worldly, matters. Ostensibly, this meant they avoided politics. In practice, however, it led them to support the status quo, at least tacitly. Like their evangelical counterparts in the United States, many Guatemalan evangelicals rigidly opposed communism. Communist ideology and objectives stood in direct opposition to evangelical ideology and objectives, as they posed a threat to evangelism and salvation through faith in Jesus Christ. As such, most evangelicals supported government efforts to quell the insurgency.[67]

The Lucas regime took notice of evangelical political sympathies and anticommunism and elevated evangelical Protestants over Catholics, whom the regime perceived as serving the interests of the political left. Due to their commitment to liberation theology and its "preferential option for the poor," Catholics tended to support the broad movement for social justice, which the Lucas regime believed Cuban communists led.[68] Consequently, the Guatemalan government sought to diminish their influence by assassinating outspoken priests and denouncing their followers for allegedly acting "as agents of a network of the enemies of Guatemala who operate from outside the country, in their vain proposals to turn us into the prey of totalitarianism."[69] This rhetoric turned Catholics into potential military targets and exacerbated existing tensions between Catholics and Protestants.[70]

When the growing frequency and ruthlessness of army massacres between 1980 and early 1982 led to increased public support for the guerrillas and greater solidarity among indigenous and leftist religious groups, the ruling regime looked to the rapidly expanding evangelical sects to shore up political support. By the time the campaign for the 1982 presidential election began, Protestants comprised nearly 20 percent of the Guatemalan population, a sizeable potential voting bloc. President Lucas's hand-selected successor, General Ángel Aníbal Guevara, courted them. He donated money to U.S. missionary churches and appeared at an evangelical revival held at the national soccer stadium, where he promised the fifty thousand people in attendance that he would give "special consideration to evangelicals in his administration" if elected.[71]

With the army overseeing the election, Lucas ensured Guevara's victory. When the other candidates and their supporters protested the blatant election fraud, the regime responded swiftly and violently to repress the dissent.[72] Yet Lucas could not stifle the seething anger that the Guatemalan people—including those serving in the military—felt over the election and the state of affairs within the country more broadly.[73] Within a few weeks, a cadre of young army officers staged the coup that removed Lucas from power and placed Ríos Montt at the head of the new ruling junta. Their demands made clear that they sought, above all else, to reinstate free and fair elections in Guatemala. After taking power, they announced that "the junta would govern for sixty days during which time it will supervise national elections and no military candidates would be permitted to stand for office."[74]

Bringing God to Government

Although the young officers did not realize that Ríos Montt had converted to evangelical Christianity when they asked him to head the junta, the soaring religious rhetoric that animated his first speech to the nation on the evening of March 23, 1982, made his new outlook apparent. Ríos Montt's proclamations after the coup, and in the months that followed, seemed to indicate to U.S. and Guatemalan evangelicals his intentions to improve life in his country and help fulfill the Great Commission by turning Guatemala to God. Dressed in military fatigues and flanked by the other junta leaders at his first press conference on the evening of the coup, Ríos Montt told the assembled reporters, "I am trusting God, my Lord and my King, to enlighten me because he is the only one who gives or takes away authority."[75]

Having thus expressed his belief that divine will had placed him in a position of power, he pledged to the people of Guatemala that "he and his two junta partners have a mission to revitalize the nation's moral values, extend more human rights, and cut down on corruption."[76] In keeping with evangelical doctrine concerning individual salvation, he stressed that each Guatemalan must work toward improving the country, noting that only "once there is peace in your heart . . . there will be peace in society."[77] He reiterated these themes in the weekly sermons he broadcast throughout Guatemala on Sundays, urging his countrymen to live according to Christian morality and to spread the gospel so that they could "share the joy of knowing God."[78]

For their part, many Guatemalans viewed the coup and the new ruling triumvirate cautiously. Despite his reputation as a political moderate and his outspoken identity as a "born-again" Christian, Ríos Montt was still a brigadier general in the army. The two other junta leaders, Maldonado Schaad and Gordillo Martínez, served in the army as a general and a colonel, respectively. The Washington Office on Latin America, a U.S.-based human rights NGO, and the Iglesia Guatemalteca en el Exilio (IGE), a Catholic group that aided Guatemalan refugees in Mexico, argued that although Guatemalans welcomed the end to urban violence and politically motivated killings in the cities that Ríos Montt effected after taking power, little else had changed.[79]

Those seeking reform in Guatemala suggested that even with Lucas gone, "The oppressive apparatus of the army is still in place and there is absolutely no indication that the Junta is about to introduce the far-reaching reforms that the country needs to remove the social, economic and political contradictions that condemn the vast majority of the population to a life of degradation and poverty."[80] Indeed, many Guatemalan Catholics railed against Ríos Montt's use of religious rhetoric.[81]

Decrying Ríos Montt as a false prophet, leftist Catholic and Christian organizations, including IGE, Comite Pro-Justicia y Paz de Guatemala, and Cristianos Revolucionarios "Vicente Menchú," cultivated a steady stream of opposition to the general.[82] Although Catholic leaders in Guatemala evinced concern about religious competition with evangelical churches such as Gospel Outreach, the primary driver of their hostility to Ríos Montt was their fear that he would continue the repressive policies of his predecessors, who associated Catholicism with the communist insurgency. A small proportion of U.S. evangelicals, including some missionaries as well as the staff of the evangelical left magazine *Sojourners*, spoke out against the Ríos Montt regime for these reasons as well.[83]

Nevertheless, Ríos Montt's rise to power inspired a dizzying sense of possibility among politically conservative evangelicals living in Guatemala and the United States, stirring tremendous excitement and expectation about his potential to further evangelical aims. Evangelicals took his statements of faith at face value, believing, earnestly, that God had chosen Ríos Montt to lead Guatemala in order to advance evangelism—which they saw as the only tenable solution to Guatemala's struggles.[84] Missionaries writing home to friends, family, and fellow church members in the United States declared Ríos Montt a "spirit-filled Christian" and a "born-again believer," calling on their coreligionists to pray that his ascension would win new souls to Christ.[85] In Gospel Outreach's newsletter *Radiance Monthly*, church founder Jim Durkin explained the significance of Ríos Montt's leadership from an evangelical perspective: "we believe that in Guatemala—through prayer and offensive spiritual warfare against the enemy—Satan and his prince (principality) have been toppled. I believe that if we continue in prayer there is tremendous opportunity in Guatemala to show the life and power of Jesus Christ. Justice, prosperity, and blessings can come to a hurting people who are crying out for help. Christ Jesus Himself is that help."[86] Standing in front of a map of Latin America on the Christian television program *The 700 Club* one week after the coup, Pat Robertson made a similar plea, intoning, "God we pray for Ríos Montt, your servant, Lord that you would cover him . . . Lord we thank you that your spirit is moving in Guatemala. And we pray right now, heavenly father, for this great nation in Jesus' holy name."[87]

U.S. evangelicals saw in Ríos Montt a divinely ordained opening for increased evangelism in the predominantly Catholic countries of Central America. They lavished him with financial support and provided access to political elites in the United States, inspiring his confidence that they would underwrite his policies. Indeed, he told U.S. ambassador to Guatemala Frederic Chapin on multiple occasions that he expected U.S. Christians would send him a billion dollars in development aid.[88] Though they never raised nearly this much money for the regime, U.S. evangelicals mobilized a variety of resources to help Ríos Montt do his part to usher in the Kingdom of God on Earth by creating a new Guatemala.

In this manner, the evangelicalism that flourished after the 1976 earthquake offered Ríos Montt a useful moral language for distinguishing himself from past regimes while also connecting him with new allies in the United States eager to aid him in his fight against the same "communist insurgents" whom his predecessors had targeted. These relationships moved to the fore as Ríos Montt developed strategies to reform his government, extract military aid from the United States, and defeat the insurgency.

Evangelical Connections

When Ríos Montt took power in March 1982, he looked to the leaders of his church for spiritual, personal, and professional guidance. He appointed el Verbo elders Francisco Bianchi and Alvaro Contreras executive secretary and secretary of public relations, respectively, vital positions that allowed them privileged access to him and significant policy influence. Referencing their participation in meetings with embassy staff, Ambassador Chapin noted, "it was evident not only at the dinner but at the meeting with the congressional staffers. . . . that the two young church leaders play an important role in molding President Rios Montt's views and policies."[89] Although Chapin bristled at their religious rambling, the general believed their appointments would help him instill morality in the government.[90]

Ríos Montt aspired to govern Guatemala with the Bible in mind. He shared the view of U.S. el Verbo pastor Jim DeGolyer, who noted, "there is an amazing amount of guidance that the Bible gives kings, heads of state, in how they should rule."[91] DeGolyer and the other el Verbo advisers shared relevant Bible verses with Ríos Montt on a regular basis. Ríos Montt utilized the teachings of DeGolyer and other el Verbo advisers in his speeches and sermonettes, mused on them in discussions with staffers and officials from the U.S. government and incorporated them into his domestic policies.[92] Soon after coming to power, he launched an anticorruption program that he named "Project David," in reference to the biblical King David of Israel, whom he regarded as a virtuous ruler.[93] As part of this program, he called on all government officials to pledge "No robo. No miento. No abuso," or "I do not steal. I do not lie. I do not abuse."[94] He also drew attention to his efforts to root out and prosecute corrupt officials.[95] Evangelicals celebrated this package of promised reforms. When a delegation of Gospel Outreach Church members visited the U.S. embassy in Guatemala on April 6, 1982, they assured the staff there that Ríos Montt would implement his program successfully and "human rights violations [would] all but disappear" under his leadership.[96]

U.S. evangelical magazines and newspapers praised the president for "Project David," offering it as concrete evidence of the sincerity of his promise to bring justice and biblical rule to his country.[97] Within Guatemala, the anticorruption measures and weekly sermonettes led to a rapid decline in crime, political repression, and death squad activity in urban centers.[98] According to Virginia Garrard-Burnett, these initiatives "contribut[ed] to urban residents' sense of personal safety and thus len[t] social support to the Ríos Montt regime, especially among the urban middle and upper classes."[99] Evangelicals, as well as the U.S. government, seized on these improvements as a sign that Ríos Montt intended to honor his pledge to promote human rights in Guatemala.[100]

Yet Guatemalans whom he regarded as subversive or as communist sympathizers, remained outside of his moral compass. During a postcoup press conference, Ríos Montt growled angrily that his enemies should lay down their arms immediately, as "anyone who is outside the law will be executed."[101] As the violence in the cities where the mostly *ladino* (nonindigenous) population resided declined in the first months of Ríos Montt's government, the Guatemalan army moved with devastating efficiency in the rural highlands, systematically killing guerrillas and Mayan civilians.[102] After offering the guerrillas a one month amnesty period in May, Ríos Montt launched Fusiles y Frijoles ("Rifles and Beans"), the first phase of his Victoria 82 counterinsurgency program, on June 20, 1982. Under this program, the government assessed each Guatemalan village to determine the loyalty of the residents, classing them white for "friendly," red for "enemy," or pink for those "of uncertain allegiance."[103] According to reports, those who supported the government received food, housing, and other forms of government largess;

Figure 9. Efraín Ríos Montt speaking, holding the Constitution of the Republic of Guatemala in his left hand. Guatemala City, ca. 1982. Photograph by Juan Rolando González Díaz, courtesy of Fototeca Guatemala, CIRMA.

those perceived as foes met with "whatever force [was] considered necessary."[104] The army occupied "red" villages, killed suspected guerrillas, and forcibly relocated any remaining residents to "strategic" villages.[105] After the pacification program took effect and the guerrilla forces started to retreat in September 1982, the army returned residents to the abandoned hamlets—rechristened "model villages"—and increased the use of civilian patrols to continue the fight against the insurgency.[106] Ríos Montt and his advisers discussed plans to invite U.S. evangelicals to Guatemala "as volunteers to reconstruct the Quiche, Huehuetenango, San Marcos, and other departments as the army beings to pacify them," assuring State Department officials that U.S. churches would fund these efforts.[107]

Although human rights watch groups raised concerns about Ríos Montt's military strategy, U.S. foreign policymakers and the Reagan administration cautiously embraced his leadership. They found his religiously infused rhetoric moderate in comparison to previous regimes and his commitment to fighting the "communist insurgency" encouraging.[108] But tensions between the two governments arose from congressional opposition to providing any military aid to Ríos Montt—specifically its refusal to sell his government the spare helicopter parts it needed to wage war against the guerrillas in the remote, mountainous regions of Guatemala.[109] In response to congressional intransigence, evangelicals in the United States and Guatemala facilitated direct meetings between the regime and U.S. government officials, and conducted a public relations campaign to counter the negative impressions that members of Congress and the U.S. public held about the troubled Central American nation.

In an effort to improve bilateral relations, evangelicals from the United States invited Francisco Bianchi to attend a meeting at the home of William O. Middendorf, the U.S. ambassador to the Organization of American States and a fellow believer, in June 1982.[110] They also invited Ambassador Chapin, Reagan cabinet members Edwin Meese and James Watt, evangelical leaders Pat Robertson and Jerry Falwell, Gospel Outreach member Bob Means, and a handful of other evangelicals.[111] At the dinner, they brainstormed ways for the U.S. government and evangelicals to help Ríos Montt. In addition to direct military aid, Pat Robertson proposed coordinating a "Christian relief strategy" with evangelicals in Guatemala. He suggested that aiding Guatemalan villagers, particularly those whom the army had relocated, with building materials, medical care, food, and other donated goods would buttress the counterinsurgency efforts and shore up support for the regime among people living in the rural highlands.[112] After the meeting, the participants worked with key players in the evangelical community and the government "to launch a national campaign to help Guatemala which will also counter misinformation about the government."[113] Bianchi and Alvaro Contreras networked with evangelical leaders in the United States, meeting privately with Jerry Falwell and Pat Robertson, building relationships with key members of the National Religious Broadcasters, and attending the 1982 Washington Rally for Jesus.[114]

As the evangelical network within the United States sprang into action, it marshaled supporters and funds from the religious, business, and political communities within which it operated. According to an article in *The Nation*, Pat Robertson proved particularly influential as a spokesman for Ríos Montt; his televised "appeals for prayers and financial support for the regime . . . resulted in a flood of letters to the White House demanding U.S. military aid for Guatemala."[115] Building on Robertson's momentum, el Verbo pastor Carlos Ramirez, who served as unofficial adviser to Ríos Montt, returned to the United States at the president's request to appeal directly to U.S. Christians.[116] Fundraising letters from his organization, Love Lift International, emphasized that supporting Ríos Montt's regime would hasten global evangelism, bring freedom to the Guatemalan people, and help defeat communism in the region.[117]

These promises resonated with U.S. evangelicals. In September, Ramirez met with a group of pastors in California to establish the Guatemalan Task Force, which worked as the U.S. "base of support" for his organization.[118] Members of this task force exclaimed that that "God is the Author of the tremendous changes taking place today in Guatemala," and affirmed their commitment "to support the spiritual revival and the peaceful socio-economic revolution that revival is bringing about," noting "the whole nation of Guatemala will benefit as a result."[119] They partnered with Youth with a Mission, a major missionary organization founded in 1960, to gather and deliver tools, medicine, clothing, food, and other supplies to the poor and displaced in Guatemala.[120] Pat Robertson joined in the efforts to raise money for Operation Love Lift. He informed viewers of *The 700 Club* that the donated materials would go to help indigenous refugees who had fled their villages to escape guerilla depredations; without support, Robertson alleged, communist forces would overrun Guatemala.[121] Congressman Jack Kemp endorsed these initiatives and similarly warned about the consequences of failing to provide Ríos Montt with aid.[122] Kemp's embrace of the cause and the language that he used to describe the issues at hand revealed that evangelical human rights activism both overlapped with and influenced conservative foreign policy aims and rhetoric.

By the end of 1982, evangelical efforts to encourage the Reagan administration to push Congress to extend military aid to Guatemala began to bear fruit. Evangelicals convinced Reagan, as well as key State and Defense

Department personnel, that Ríos Montt's policies were reducing human rights violations while also eroding the influence of the communist insurgents.[123] Ríos Montt and Reagan planned a meeting in Honduras for early December 1982 as the last stop on Reagan's tour of Latin America.[124]

During an NSC planning meeting prior to the trip, Secretary of State George Shultz had summed up the cautious optimism surrounding Ríos Montt that had developed within the administration, telling Reagan, "I have my fingers crossed on this one. We must make the effort to encourage movement toward democracy; they are doing better now than they have for a long time. But, don't throw your arms around him."[125] The NSC stressed to Reagan that Ríos Montt represented a significant break from past regimes. Reagan's advisers emphasized the importance of reassuring the Guatemalan leader that the United States supported him, yet they also instructed: "He must understand that the GOG [Government of Guatemala] image abroad is so bad that it is difficult for the democratic countries, including the United States, to convince their legislatures to appropriate assistance. We should encourage him to continue the human rights progress, which will help us in our effort to convince the Congress that the GOG and USG [U.S. government] share a common objective in defeating the guerrillas."[126] These recommendations underscore the efficacy of congressional human rights activism in constraining the Reagan administration's overtures to repressive authoritarian leaders in Central America.[127] Eager to counter communism in the region, especially in Nicaragua and El Salvador, Reagan and his advisers sought to overcome or work around this congressional resistance. In time, they began framing their support for anticommunist leaders as a strategy of "democracy promotion" that they argued would spread U.S. values and foster human rights.[128]

At the December 1982 meeting, Ríos Montt gave President Reagan an overview of his programs and reform efforts, emphasizing the progress his regime had made toward protecting human rights. Ríos Montt provided Reagan and Shultz with a folder of documents titled, "Este Gobierno Tiene el Compromiso de Cambiar" ("This Government Is Committed to Change"), which included descriptions of his government's policies as well as transcripts of his major speeches—all of which referenced his faith in God and its role in his efforts to create a new Guatemala.[129] After affirming the Guatemalan government's commitment to bringing "peace, reform, economic progress and democracy" to the country, Ríos Montt delved into the details of his Fusiles y Frijoles program and counterinsurgency strategy, casting both as positive steps toward providing for the poor.[130] He stated that he planned to use the spare helicopter parts he sought from the United States to engage in "humanitarian work such as airlifting food to Indian farmers who have fled from their homes for fear of violence by subversive forces, the transportation of brigades of doctors and social workers who provide services to refugees, and other comparable tasks."[131]

In this manner, Ríos Montt sought to persuade Reagan and Shultz of his desire to win their shared battle against communism. He repeated what he and his evangelical proponents in the United States had stressed for months: reports from international human rights organizations and the news media about massacres, kidnappings, torture, and the mass displacement of thousands of indigenous Guatemalans misrepresented the situation on the ground. The guerrillas committed these crimes, Ríos Montt argued, not the army.[132] Despite overwhelming evidence to the contrary, Reagan seemed to take the general at his word, calling him "a man of great integrity."[133] In reality, during the seventeen months that Ríos Montt led Guatemala, nearly eighty-six thousand people—mostly Maya—perished or disappeared at the hands of the army.[134] Military actions against Guatemalan villages turned over a million people into refugees.[135]

Figure 10. Ríos Montt and President Ronald Reagan in Honduras in December 1982, examining "This Government Is Committed to Change." © Bettman/Getty Images.

Influenced by Ríos Montt's evangelical faith, Reagan asserted that the Guatemalan government had "been getting a bum rap" from the liberal news media.[136] According to a news correspondent reporting on the meeting in Honduras, "one administration aide said the president was impressed by the intense, forceful style of the Guatemalan as well as Rios Montt's uncompromising faith in God."[137] After the meeting, Reagan expressed his desire to reinstate military aid to the regime, and over the ensuing months his administration worked assiduously to find ways to provide support to Ríos Montt.[138] National Security Adviser William P. Clark assured Jorge Serrano Elías, a neo-Pentecostal acolyte Ríos Montt had sent to the United States as his personal emissary, that the Reagan administration was "doing its best" to convince Congress to be more responsive to and positive about Guatemala.[139]

Evangelicals in the United States also pressured Congress and the administration to extend military aid to Guatemala. In the weeks before and after Reagan's meeting with Ríos Montt, letters from supportive evangelicals poured into Washington.[140] Many emphasized personal connections to Guatemala, referencing missionary work and independent travel there as religious leaders. They often parroted the messages about Ríos Montt that the evangelical press, Christian opinion leaders, and the regime itself put forth. One pastor writing to Reagan noted that he too lamented the "bum rap" he believed Ríos Montt had received in the U.S. press. Based on his conversations with Guatemalans in the rural highlands, he argued: "I believe his government is very humane, progressive and motivated by great integrity. I do hope you will be able to get the modest aid for Guatemala which has been requested. Their helicopter situation is critical, both for defense and evacuation of villages when the communists strike."[141]

One young woman sent an article about the situation in Guatemala that she had written for an evangelical newsletter to White House Chief of Staff James Baker, requesting that he pass it along to President Reagan.[142] After praising Ríos Montt for using his position to evangelize as well as for battling the guerrillas, whom she described as "Russian backed" and responsible "for killing innocent people," she called on fellow evangelicals to urge their congressional representatives to approve military aid.[143] Reagan responded to her letter and article, citing his trip to Honduras as he assured her that he "was impressed with [Ríos Montt's] sincerity in working for his people," and that his administration would do all it could to support the Guatemalan government.[144] Letters of this nature from rank-and-file evangelicals in the

United States to the president, cabinet members, and congressional representatives made manifest the power of the evangelical network to control and propagate its message and political objectives from the elite level to the grassroots.

Ríos Montt and his advisers, cognizant of the influence that this network had on evangelicals in the United States and, potentially, their elected representatives, invited a group of fifteen evangelical leaders to visit Guatemala in late December 1982. The group included Billy Melvin, executive director of the National Association of Evangelicals (NAE), Jerry Ballard, the director of the NAE's humanitarian organization World Relief, David Howard, executive director of the World Evangelical Fellowship, J. Philip Hogan, executive director of the Assemblies of God Division of Foreign Missions, and Christopher Moree, a representative from the World Missions Division of the Church of God, among others. The trip encapsulated the nature of Ríos Montt's relationship with evangelical Christians from the United States, and revealed the context in which those evangelicals understood the ongoing conflict in Central America, theologically and politically.

Ríos Montt's advisers choreographed the four-day trip with great care. On the first morning, the group visited the National Palace for a briefing with the president's cabinet members. J. Philip Hogan reported that Ríos Montt canceled one of his morning meetings in order to pray with them before the session: "Accordingly, he came in in a very humble fashion, began to praise the Lord and give glory to His name and tell about how real Jesus was to him and how he wanted to serve God and his country. Most everyone was completely taken off their feet to find him a bubbling over, hallelujah, praise God, shouting charismatic. There didn't seem to be anything superficial about it. He spoke in glowing terms of his relationship with the Lord."[145] Thus primed, the visitors listened attentively to the information they received about the military, political, and refugee situations confronting the Guatemalan government. Next, U.S. Ambassador Chapin spent over an hour and a half with the group, going "almost overboard in his endorsement of President Ríos and what he is doing in Guatemala."[146] Chapin spoke in particular about the improved human rights situation there, reassuring the evangelical representatives that Ríos Montt had ended all state-directed killings, and suggesting that any soldiers committing acts of violence had just "been a little slow to get the message."[147] He also emphasized the extent to which President Reagan supported Ríos Montt. In between these meetings with government officials, the visitors conversed with local missionaries and

Guatemalan evangelicals, all of whom emphasized their faith in the general and their sense that his "efforts have been blessed of God in helping to restore peace to their troubled country . . . and renewed vigor to the Evangelical community in Guatemala."[148]

The next day, the group boarded military helicopters and flew ninety miles north of the capitol to visit a refugee camp in a region occupied by the insurgency.[149] J. Philip Hogan described the camp in terms that revealed the ideological lens through which both he and his hosts understood Ríos Montt's rural pacification program. Declaring the conditions better than those he had observed in Southeast Asia and North Africa, Hogan stated that the camp contained "about 6,000 to 10,000 refugees who have, because of the scorched-earth policy of the communists, had to flee their little farms and villages for protection."[150] Once the government overcame the insurgency, the villagers could return to their land, he asserted.[151] Such accounts aimed explicitly to counter claims from human rights organizations and internal dissident groups that Ríos Montt's rural pacification program was a "scorched-earth policy."[152] The evangelical visitors took the Guatemalan government at its word though, rejecting other reports as liberal distortions of what they had observed during their visit. While at the refugee camp, Hogan and Moree both expressed delight to find a Church of God congregation, where they conversed and worshipped with their Pentecostal brethren.[153] In his memorandum to the Assemblies of God administration about the trip, Hogan expressed his desire to raise money through the World Relief Commission for these Guatemalan refugees to help them purchase livestock and farming equipment once the regime resettled them.[154]

On the final evening of the trip, Ríos Montt hosted a dinner at the palace for the evangelical visitors, where he "shared his Christian testimony and spoke informally about some of his hopes for Guatemala," before asking his guests to "pray for him and his government."[155] Upon their return to the United States, the participants published laudatory accounts and analyses of their visit in evangelical magazines. Moree urged readers of *Evangel*, the official Church of God magazine, to take the Guatemalan president "at face value," arguing that his regime had demonstrated "a great respect for human rights" while noting that "recently captured documents indicate that the guerrillas themselves believe they have been set back twenty-five years in their struggle because of the new attitude of this government, its representatives, and the armed forces."[156] Hogan praised Ríos Montt for fighting the "dangerous and growing insurgency," for establishing a state council that included Mayan representatives, and for speaking to the Guatemalan citizens about "his personal salvation and his aspirations that Guatemala be a peaceful, Christian land."[157] Other periodicals picked up and referenced these accounts, ensuring that they received wide distribution among believers in the United States.[158]

These accounts, in turn, worked their way into letters that trip participants and other evangelicals wrote to encourage their congressional representatives to approve military aid to Guatemala. Writing to Missouri congressman Gene Taylor, Hogan emphasized the threat that the "communist insurgents" posed to Ríos Montt's government. He referenced his personal conversations with soldiers, refugees, and local pastors who asserted that Ríos Montt had made great strides toward protecting human rights, stating that because this information originated from "the grass roots," he trusted in its veracity completely.[159] Hoping to provide additional evidence to encourage support for military aid and to counter negative press from human rights organizations, Taylor forwarded Hogan's letter to National Security Adviser William P. Clark, noting that, "because of recent newspaper accounts of the situation there, I thought that Mr. Hogan's evaluation would be of interest to you."[160] Clark agreed, thanking Taylor for the letter and disclosing that, "Mr. Hogan's account is very similar to others that we have received. There is sound evidence that supports the Administration's belief that Guatemalan President Rios Montt is getting a 'bum rap,' as the President said after having met with him in Honduras."[161]

Despite the best efforts of the Reagan administration and the evangelical community, however, congressional opposition to direct military aid to the regime persisted. Although Reagan and his advisers searched for ways to maneuver around Congress and provide military assistance without congressional approval, they failed to do so amid news of extrajudicial killings and the murder of several USAID-affiliated workers by Guatemalan soldiers.[162] Reagan and his congressional allies insisted that, despite these killings, the human rights picture in Guatemala was improving.[163] Congress continued to deny Foreign Military Sales (FMS) credits, citing extensive reports from human rights NGOs and international journalists about egregious abuses.[164] As such, offering the needed helicopter parts for cash rather than as a grant emerged as the best option. In early 1983, the Reagan administration announced its approval of FMS funding to Guatemala for purchase of helicopter spare parts in recognition of "the progress in human rights achieved by Ríos Montt since he came to power."[165]

Citing a lack of money to purchase the needed spare parts, Ríos Montt ignored the offer and looked to the U.S. evangelical network for more substantive support.[166] Gospel Outreach and other Christian benefactors provided assistance in acquiring military materiel, including the elusive spare helicopter parts, from private dealers in the United States as well as from Canada and Israel.[167] Love Lift International, the organization that el Verbo pastor Carlos Ramirez had founded in 1982 with support from U.S. evangelical leaders, coordinated and funded many of these purchases.[168]

U.S. evangelicals also lent direct aid to the rural pacification program, as Ríos Montt asserted they would at the outset of his rise to power. Gospel Outreach and el Verbo members worked alongside the army in establishing the "model villages" or strategic hamlets in the Guatemalan countryside.[169] Love Lift International played a key role in this effort, establishing the Fundación de Ayuda al Pueblo Indígena to provide funds, personnel, and administrative support to run the villages.[170] They discussed plans to construct villages, staff medical and dental facilities, and launch development projects including electrification and water systems in the Ixil Triangle—a region the Ríos Montt regime claimed was a hotbed of guerilla activity.[171] Assuming churches would continue to raise funds for this effort, some State Department officials found the strategy promising enough to promote it to others within the U.S. government.[172]

By Ríos Montt's own description, the planned model villages blended military strategy he learned at the School of the Americas with the "communitarian" Christian values of the Gospel Outreach Church.[173] Although newspaper reports detailed the dismal conditions in the villages, as well as the compulsory conscription of male refugees into civilian armies to fight the guerrillas, U.S. evangelicals claimed the model villages provided Christian charity, spiritual uplift, and a bulwark against communism.[174] As one press release noted, "food, shelter, clothing, and medicine are being provided to those in need; along with Army protection, training of civil patrol groups, and weapons to defend themselves."[175]

Ultimately, U.S. evangelical oversight of the model villages outlasted Ríos Montt's tenure in office. Gospel Outreach and Love Lift International continued their ministrations—with USAID funds—even after Óscar Humberto Mejía Victores removed Ríos Montt in the August 1983 coup.[176] The network linking U.S. and Guatemalan evangelicals proved resilient. Although evangelicals enjoyed a period of particular power and visibility during Ríos Montt's presidency, their involvement within and influence on Guatemalan society and politics persisted long after he stepped down.

Ousting "Dios" Montt

The evangelicalism that helped Ríos Montt gain and hold power in Guatemala in 1982 contributed to the unraveling of his presidency in 1983. Although coup rumors had plagued his government since he had declared himself president, they became quite real by June 1983.[177] Disgruntled members of the military and the major political parties, including original junta member Luis Gordillo Martínez and a former MLN vice president, complained on television about Ríos Montt's "religious fanaticism" and "use of the presidency as a pulpit to promote his evangelical Protestant beliefs."[178] Brigadier General Echeverría asked Ríos Montt to restore constitutional government and stop mixing religion with politics.[179] Army leaders expressed frustration about the power evangelical advisers Bianchi and Contreras exercised within the government.[180] Despite the simmering unrest, Ríos Montt refused to let his advisers resign.[181]

The State and Defense Departments expressed concern about the coup rumblings, reiterating their approval of Ríos Montt's counterinsurgency program, progress on human rights, and political moderation.[182] Defense Department experts estimated that the general could stay in power only with army backing; without this support, a coup was imminent.[183] These officials worried that if the army or a right-wing political faction ousted Ríos Montt, the regime that replaced him would be as oppressive, corrupt, and abusive as the one he had replaced in 1982.[184] The State Department had expressed similar concerns, indicating its belief in one memorandum that, "if he is overthrown, it is likely he will be replaced by a reactionary government whose repressive actions will play into the hands of the Marxist guerrillas."[185] These concerns proved prescient. On August 8, 1983, disgruntled senior army commanders overthrew Ríos Montt and placed Mejía in power, stating "that they acted to rid the country of a religious fanatic who has ignored the separation between church and state."[186] Soon after, reports of human rights abuses multiplied. The army returned openly to the practices of the Lucas regime, utilizing military death squads and political repression to control the countryside.[187]

After Mejía assumed control of the government, Ríos Montt retired to private life, spending much of his time working at el Verbo. He continued to nurture his contacts with evangelicals in the United States, attending the annual National Prayer Breakfast in Washington in 1985 and maintaining an ongoing correspondence with Douglas Coe of the Fellowship Foundation.[188] Ríos Montt also traveled within the United States to raise funds for Love Lift

International, speaking at evangelical churches throughout the country.[189] For these audiences, he emphasized the ongoing threat that communism posed to Central America, and reiterated his belief that he had made critical improvements for the people of Guatemala during his time in power. Indeed, he insisted throughout his 2013 trial for genocide and crimes against humanity that he had not ordered military violence against the Maya in 1982–83. The staggering evidence the prosecution presented at the trial belies these assertions.[190]

The support that Ríos Montt garnered from evangelical Christians in the United States illuminates a great deal about the religious and ideological beliefs that grounded evangelical understandings of human rights and anticommunism. U.S. evangelicals who visited Ríos Montt, el Verbo, and their brethren in Guatemala believed these individuals when they asserted that the guerrillas, not the army, committed the majority of the violence against the Guatemalan people. They trusted Ríos Montt when he argued that pacifying the countryside and removing the communist threat would bring justice, peace, and human dignity to poor villagers. These messages resonated with preexisting evangelical beliefs about communism as an existential threat not only to a nation, but to religious faith as well. When Guatemalan evangelicals claimed that under Ríos Montt, they could proselytize without fear of retaliation from the guerrillas, it reinforced deeply held hopes that evangelicals might achieve the Great Commission during their lifetimes.[191] Had U.S. evangelicals consulted the Mayan and Catholic refugees who fled across the border into Mexico to escape army violence, they might have heard a different, more realistic perspective on the situation. Instead, they and the Reagan administration backed Ríos Montt, aiding and abetting genocidal state violence in the process.

Evangelicals believed religious liberty—the freedom to evangelize—was *the* core human right because they saw salvation as the basis for human freedom and the truest cure for man's suffering. When Ríos Montt adopted the distinctive language and leadership style of their particular form of apocalyptic American Christianity, U.S. evangelicals thought they had found in the Central American leader the personification of their most deeply cherished objectives. Reagan, meanwhile, believed he had found a key ally in his fight against communism in Central America. Support for such a "Brother in Christ" flowed freely in response.

Chapter 6

The Challenge of South African Apartheid

In September 1981, the South African Mission to the United States in Chicago sent a confidential report to Brand Fourie, the director-general of the South African Department of Foreign Affairs and Information, describing the disposition of various U.S. church groups toward the Republic of South Africa (RSA). The report bemoaned the "anti-RSA activities" and attitudes of the National Council of Churches (NCC) and the leaders of most of the mainline Protestant denominations that made up its membership. According to the consulate official, these churches and parachurch organizations actively undermined the RSA by publicizing their negative views of the apartheid regime, distributing anti-apartheid films, and urging U.S. corporations to divest their interests in South Africa.[1] By contrast, the report praised the more supportive attitudes of U.S. evangelical churches, particularly the Southern Baptist Convention (SBC), highlighting the close ties the consulate had developed with the SBC Foreign Mission Board as well as with the Christian Broadcasting Network.[2] These relationships facilitated visits from U.S. evangelical groups to the RSA as well as the broadcast of sympathetic coverage of southern African affairs on Christian television programs, part of a larger effort to improve U.S. public opinion toward the RSA and U.S.-South African relations.[3]

The cozy relationship between the evangelical churches and the government of South Africa that the consulate official reported to Fourie belied the considerable diversity of opinion that U.S. evangelicals held about South Africa and its leadership. African American Christians formed a strong base of anti-apartheid activism. While some supported the moderate plan for corporate responsibility in South Africa that civil rights activist and Baptist preacher Leon Sullivan introduced with his "Sullivan Principles" in 1977, the majority sought stronger action, including stringent sanctions and divestment.[4] Though most white evangelicals in the United States claimed to abhor South African apartheid, their policy positions and the extent to which they supported South African leaders such as John Vorster and P. W. Botha varied, even within denominations. By 1985, the views of Southern and Independent Baptists, for example, ranged from the bombast of Rev. Jerry Falwell in his opposition to disinvestment and his vociferous denigration of South African anti-apartheid activists such as Rev. Desmond Tutu, to the SBC Christian Life Commission, which embraced some divestment and urged Southern Baptists to press their representatives to pass legislation that would challenge apartheid.[5]

Such policy differences notwithstanding, white U.S. evangelicals in the 1980s on the whole tended to support peaceful efforts to reform or dismantle apartheid, a stance that aligned them with the Reagan administration. Evangelical leaders embraced this gradualist position in an effort to combat two core threats to the spread of Christianity that they perceived in the unfolding conflict in South Africa. First, white evangelicals linked militant anti-apartheid activists with "Marxist" forces, both within and outside of the RSA, and feared that radical change would spur a communist takeover of what they considered the only Christian government in Africa.[6] At the same time, evangelicals understood apartheid as an affront to Christian teachings and recognized that the South African government needed to abolish the system.[7]

Through exchanges with their brethren in South Africa, as well as with U.S. missionaries, white evangelicals in the United States came to view apartheid as a hindrance to their efforts to achieve the Great Commission. Since many black and colored South Africans associated the white-led Christian churches with the racist and repressive power structure, white evangelicals feared that the apartheid regime dampened the appeal of Christianity throughout the continent and therefore thwarted evangelistic efforts.[8] Yet because white evangelicals advocated for peaceful, gradual reforms, most observers in the United States viewed them as apologists for (or, worse, active supporters of) apartheid.[9] Given their political power as part of the religious right, white evangelical engagement on this issue had significant policy implications.[10]

Few international issues in the 1980s garnered the attention of the American public with more force than South African apartheid. The brutal system of racial segregation and minority White rule that the RSA had enforced since 1948 horrified most Americans, as did the ferocity with which the South African government repressed internal opposition. In the 1950s, U.S. organizations such as the Council on African Affairs (established in 1942) and the American Committee on Africa (established in 1953) lent support and attention to anti-apartheid efforts in South Africa. Anti-apartheid activism in the United States waxed and waned through the 1970s, intensifying in response to moments of particular crisis in South Africa, such as the Sharpeville Massacre in 1960 and the Soweto uprising in 1976. In 1984, the movement exploded. A high-profile protest at the South African embassy on November 21, in concert with increased news coverage of escalating violence in the South African townships, contributed to wide-spread public concern. Graphic reports of escalating state violence against South African students, workers, and other anti-apartheid protestors, not to mention mass arrests and the banning of dissenting political organizations, spurred a dramatic revival of grassroots anti-apartheid activism in the United States.[11]

By 1985, this movement had amassed considerable political power. Liberal and progressive U.S. activists called on the Reagan administration to impose sanctions on the RSA and pressed U.S. corporations to divest their interests in the region. Mainline Protestant religious leaders and church groups in the United States and South Africa played a central role in this movement, particularly as their South African brethren Bishop Desmond Tutu and Reverend Allan Boesak gained international renown as anti-apartheid leaders.[12]

Many evangelical churches in the United States as well as in South Africa opposed the movement for sanctions and disinvestment, however, claiming such actions would hurt black South Africans and embolden groups such as the African National Congress (ANC), which they believed promoted violence and Marxism.[13] Anticipating that communist rule would threaten Christianity in South Africa, they sought political stability and opposed the ANC. Yet some also recognized that the apartheid regime's racism, violence, and human rights abuses made evangelism more difficult. In short, evangelicals found themselves divided over how to best combat apartheid—in part because of a perceived conflict between their missionary goals and foreign policy objectives.

This chapter details the range of evangelical responses to apartheid that evolved over the course of the 1970s and 1980s and examines the role that evangelicals played in national debates over U.S. relations with the apartheid government of South Africa. It pays particular attention to the networks that evangelical leaders built with their counterparts in South Africa in the 1970s and the manner in which these connections informed the policy opinions of conservative Christians in the United States. During this period, Pentecostals and Baptists built relationships with their denominational brethren as well as with moderate to conservative anticommunist South African leaders such as Bishop Isaac Mokoena, Bishop B. E. Lekganyane, and Chief Mangosuthu Buthelezi. Although anti-apartheid activists called the influence of such leaders into question, evangelicals and other political conservatives in the United States seized on the public statements and opinions that these men shared with them about their opposition to U.S. sanctions and disinvestment in the 1980s. U.S. evangelicals used this information to help shape conservative human rights discourse about the apartheid regime and to provide moral backing to Republican leaders who voted against sanctions. This chapter argues that although ultimately they lost their battle to stop congressional sanctions in 1985, white evangelicals served as influential allies of the Reagan administration's policies toward South Africa. It also reveals how U.S. evangelical views on apartheid and human rights in South Africa evolved, particularly after South African evangelicals began to play a more significant role in the Truth and Reconciliation process in the early 1990s.[14]

Illuminating the complexity of evangelical opinion about apartheid as well as the nature of evangelical engagement within South Africa expands our understanding of the sanctions debate and anti-apartheid movement in the United States. It also shows that as Christian interest groups developed an international network of believers with a shared religious ideology, they used that network and ideology to shape how U.S. policymakers discussed and understood U.S. relations with violent yet avowedly anticommunist regimes such as the RSA.

Evangelism in Apartheid South Africa

In November 1971, *Christianity Today* published a lengthy article by South African evangelist Michael Cassidy on apartheid and how Christians throughout the world could best encourage efforts to hasten its end. Cassidy, the white founder of the interdenominational, interracial evangelistic organization African Enterprise (AE), critiqued apartheid as "sinful" and "unscriptural" because "in its practical outworking it denies human dignity," a core principle of the Christian faith.[15] Despite the litany of injustices that he observed under apartheid, he expressed hope that growing opposition to the system among students, businesses, churches, and even some Afrikaner nationalists signaled positive change. He urged patience though, concerned that harsh Western restrictions would deter progress. Drawing on the common evangelical belief that spiritual salvation offered the principal means to ease man's suffering, he argued that Christians should work for change primarily through evangelism.[16] Bringing people to Christ, he believed, would transform their hearts. Citing scripture, Cassidy affirmed his commitment "to a ministry of reconciliation, to love, to dialogue, to contact, and to proclaiming the Christ of Calvary—a Christ who didn't take a Sten-gun or a Molotov cocktail but a Cross."[17] In the face of profound inequity, Cassidy preached peace, not justice. This emphasis on nonviolence and reconciliation resonated with evangelicals in both the United States and South Africa, becoming a familiar refrain in their policy recommendations through the 1980s and reflecting the ethos and language of evangelical human rights activism more generally.

The broad appeal of peaceful reconciliation aside, Cassidy represented a middle ground in South African evangelical opinion about how to confront the challenge of apartheid. Anthony Balcomb, a scholar of African religion, notes that evangelical views within the RSA on this issue varied by denomination as well as by race. Many white Charismatic Christians and black Pentecostals adopted essentially apolitical stances, resisting calls to involve themselves politically in the struggle against apartheid in the 1970s and early 1980s.[18] Evangelicals who hailed from politically and ecclesiastically conservative churches with predominately white memberships tended to support apartheid, citing as justification for their views the scriptural command in Romans 13 that Christians should submit to governing authorities.[19] On the opposite end of the spectrum, progressive evangelicals, including black Pentecostals such as Apostolic Faith Mission (AFM) leader Frank Chikane, supported the ANC in its political struggle against the RSA.[20] As noted earlier, U.S. evangelical writing on apartheid revealed a corresponding diversity of opinion along this same spectrum, though the majority of white evangelicals supported the peaceful reconciliation that Cassidy and other moderate pragmatists advocated.[21]

To some extent, this shared outlook reflected U.S. evangelical efforts to develop and maintain close ties with their South African counterparts. Several U.S. Pentecostal denominations had operated missions in Southern Africa since the early twentieth century, including the Apostolic Faith Mission, the Church of God, and the Assemblies of God.[22] During much of the twentieth century, these missions expanded through indigenous evangelism, though the revival of world evangelism that emerged from the Lausanne Movement brought an influx of new foreign missionaries to the region in the 1970s.[23] Similarly, the SBC cultivated a relationship with the Baptist Union of South Africa, an organization that English and German Baptists had founded in 1877. In addition to providing aid and personnel for evangelistic crusades, the SBC established its own missions in South Africa beginning in 1977.[24] These networking efforts, part of the larger drive for world evangelism that arose in the early 1970s, contributed to a rapid expansion of evangelical Christianity—particularly in its Charismatic and Pentecostal forms—throughout South Africa in subsequent decades.[25]

Yet apartheid complicated both the religious landscape and evangelistic efforts. Denominations such as the AFM had entirely white leadership, with separate church sections for black, colored, and Indian worshippers, which white leaders oversaw.[26] These divisions reflected national apartheid policies but made cross-cultural evangelism legally and politically challenging in the RSA.[27] At the International Congress on World Evangelization in 1974, the interracial delegation from South Africa debated extensively over whether bringing in foreign evangelists might encourage greater "cooperation" within the denominations and "aid South African Christianity in some of its racial dilemmas."[28] The black South African delegates expressed their deep frustration over racial segregation in the RSA and its churches to their white counterparts, noting that, among other issues, racism undermined the gospel message and evangelistic efforts.[29]

Although U.S. evangelical denominations and parachurch groups operated integrated ministries in South Africa and advocated that their coreligionists desegregate their churches, they did not push white church leaders especially hard on the issue, as they feared that they might alienate them.[30] Instead, U.S. evangelicals prioritized network building with South African Christians, eager to promote evangelism and peaceful reconciliation in the RSA as the means to advance their global missionary agenda.

Figure 11. Michael Cassidy, a South African evangelist who founded African Enterprise and sought to mobilize the church against apartheid. Courtesy of the Billy Graham Center Archives, Wheaton College, Wheaton, IL.

U.S.-led evangelistic outreach and church planting efforts, along with divinity school training, created sites of connection and exchange. Cassidy founded his influential ministry, AE, with financial and spiritual support from Fuller Theological Seminary in Pasadena, California, where he earned his Bachelor of Divinity in 1963.[31] During this time he also attended several Billy Graham crusades in England and the United States, which inspired him to launch a similar series of urban missions across the African continent.[32] As Cassidy and AE grew in influence, they functioned as important nodes in the larger network that linked like-minded evangelicals across the world with political and religious leaders in South Africa. So too did the South African Pentecostal preacher Ray McCauley, who attributed his conversion to Pentecostalism to the books and tapes that Kenneth Hagin Sr.'s ministry distributed in South Africa in the 1970s.[33] McCauley attended divinity school at the Rhema Bible Training Center in Broken Arrow, Oklahoma, where he forged life-long relationships with U.S. Pentecostal leaders Kenneth Hagin Jr., Arthur Blessit, and Kenneth Copeland.[34] Evangelicals also formed cross-cultural relationships through the work of U.S.-based parachurch organizations, such as World Vision, Youth with a Mission, Campus Crusade for Christ, Samaritan's Purse, and the Full Gospel Business Men's Fellowship International, all of which established or expanded their regional bases in South Africa in this period.[35]

Doug Coe, who headed the shadowy yet influential Washington, D.C.-based Fellowship Foundation, also worked tirelessly in the 1970s to cultivate connections between U.S. and South African leaders.[36] Shortly after Cassidy founded AE, Coe began corresponding with him regularly, laying the groundwork necessary to create Fellowship Foundation cores, or cell groups, in the RSA.[37] In his reports to Coe, Cassidy shared details on religious life under apartheid as well as on political developments throughout Southern Africa. In 1971, Cassidy observed a growing awareness amongst government leaders that "they cannot keep the apartheid lid on forever," but he expressed concern that even if the RSA reformed its system, changes might come too late to staunch public support for the ANC and the movement "towards black power rather than multi-racialism."[38] Cassidy predicted that "we cannot ride out the next 10 or 12 years without a very serious upheaval."[39] In response to this looming crisis, he began organizing church leaders to strategize on evangelism and reconciliation within the South African context.[40] For his part, Coe succeeded in building South African core groups in 1972 and 1973, connecting his religious contacts, most notably the Anglican reverend I. Ross M. Main and Cassidy, with political leaders including Chief

Leabua Jonathan of Lesotho, Chief Mangosuthu Buthelezi of Zululand, and several South African National Party members in Pretoria, Johannesburg, and Cape Town, South Africa.[41]

Although the Fellowship Foundation maintained that it operated as a nonpolitical organization concerned foremost with promoting global Christian leadership and spreading the gospel, the extant communications between Coe and the core leaders in South Africa hint at extensive, behind-the-scenes maneuvering on a range of political issues, including apartheid and RSA relations with other states in Southern Africa. As their first foray into the upper echelons of South African political leadership, Coe and Rev. Ross Main coordinated a meeting in Pretoria between eleven National Party leaders, including two cabinet ministers in Prime Minister B. J. Vorster's government, and Republican U.S. congressman (and Fellowship Foundation member) John R. Dellenback in late 1973. Main also set up meetings for Dellenback in Durban, South Africa with Chief Buthelezi and several other black leaders. In a letter to Dellenback penned shortly before the meeting, Main stated that he considered bringing these men together and into the Fellowship fold essential "if we are to be a force for reconciliation" in the region.[42] The confidential report from the meeting with the National Party members praised Dellenback for his handling of questions about how the Fellowship Foundation would address RSA racial policies. According to the report, Dellenback stated that "his job would be to encourage the men in Leadership. . . . to tackle their problems as God would have them do."[43] In his comments, Main asserted that the meeting had produced important government contacts for the foundation, including a positive nod from the prime minister.[44]

Although Washington Core leaders instructed Main to avoid discussing his group's work on "the South African racial issue" in his letters, Main's correspondence between 1973 and 1979 revealed the growing influence his core group exercised with government leaders in the RSA.[45] In 1975, Main reported that members of his cell had initiated meetings between high-level black and white leaders, though he declined to name the participants out of concern that their constituents would denounce them for their involvement.[46] After Coe invited Main and several South African politicians to the 1975 National Prayer Breakfast in the United States, Main claimed that the experience had led one conservative nationalist participant to reevaluate his positions—and discuss his new outlook with Afrikaner leaders.[47] By 1976, the South African core group had expanded considerably, with Parliament Member Graham McIntosh leading weekly prayer breakfasts with National and United Party members in the South African Parliament, Cabinet Member Piet Koornhof organizing prayer breakfasts for National Party members in Cape Town, and Chief Buthelezi participating in prayer breakfasts with black leaders in Durban.[48] Fellowship Foundation records indicate that the U.S. core provided financial support to facilitate Ross Main's networking activities with government officials in South Africa.[49]

The leaders of the Fellowship Foundation believed that bringing influential black and white South Africans together to pray and discuss the gospel would foster greater mutual understanding and racial reconciliation, as well as expand evangelicalism in the region. In a report on his visit to the South African National Prayer Breakfast in 1976, Washington Core member James Bell called attention to the sentiment that MP Graham McIntosh expressed at the event when he stated that, "although South Africa is bitterly divided, all Parties have a higher loyalty to Christ who can be the bridge between them all."[50] Bell noted that he saw in this statement the work of the various evangelical Fellowship groups his organization had established throughout the country by that time.[51] Ross Main echoed this sentiment in an op-ed he wrote for *The Natal Mercury*, in which he alluded to the Fellowship Foundation and its efforts to foster interracial cooperation in Christ.[52] Yet these tepid moves toward unity and "understanding" did not address fundamental questions of justice.

Two months after Bell sent his laudatory report to the Washington core, South African police forces opened fire on a group of unarmed students holding a protest in the township of Soweto against the discriminatory Bantu Education System. The shooting incited riots in Soweto that left between 176 and 600 people dead and four thousand wounded.[53] The violent repression of the Soweto Uprising and the demonstrations it inspired in other townships shocked the world. On June 19, 1976, three days after the Soweto shootings, the United Nations Security Council adopted a resolution that "strongly condemn[ed] the South African Government for its resort to massive violence against and killings of the African people."[54] Additionally, the Security Council reaffirmed an earlier resolution from 1963 that condemned apartheid as "a crime against the conscience and dignity of mankind," and a contributor to regional instability.[55]

The events in Soweto also generated anger among members of Congress, setting off a significant shift in U.S. relations with and attitudes toward South Africa. For most officials in the Nixon and Ford administrations, the issue of apartheid had occupied a relatively minor area of concern.[56] As a locus of Cold War tensions after the rise of Soviet-backed anticolonial

African nationalist movements in the mid-1960s, the region and its multi-plying guerilla conflicts in Angola, Namibia, Rhodesia, and Mozambique attracted the most attention from policymakers. Where President Lyndon Johnson had distanced the United States from the apartheid regime out of revulsion at its racist policies, Richard Nixon and Henry Kissinger opted to pull closer to South African leaders in an effort to counter the looming Soviet threat that they believed the liberation movements posed.[57] Although the small but growing anti-apartheid movement mounted pressure on the Nixon administration to use trade restrictions to compel South Africa to reform its system, political scientist Alex Thomson has argued that their efforts failed to gain traction in Congress before 1976.[58]

By contrast, Congress took up South African apartheid with some vigor after Soweto.[59] In addition to subjecting Kissinger to harsh questioning about his continued diplomatic interactions with South Africa's prime minister B. J. Vorster in 1976, Democratic legislators began to speak out against South Africa's Bantustan policy, calling on the Ford administration to reject the legitimacy of "independent" homelands such as Transkei.[60] Representative Stephen Solarz (D-NY), a freshman member of the House Foreign Affairs Committee and a staunch opponent of apartheid, argued that the home-lands policy would strip black South Africans of their national citizenship and further deprive them of human and civil rights. For the United States to do anything other than condemn the policy would be "incompatible with any notion of human dignity," he said.[61] Some of his other House colleagues echoed his sentiments, including Representative Cardiss Collins (D-IL), who asserted that if the United States failed to take a strong stand against the apartheid regime, "racism will continue to crush human dignity in that region of the world."[62]

Jimmy Carter, who took office in 1977, shared these concerns and pledged to promote human rights in his foreign policy. Furthermore, as the South African regime tightened its policies and ramped up repres-sion against its domestic anti-apartheid opponents, the Carter adminis-tration signed on to a mandatory United Nations arms embargo against the RSA in early November 1977 and issued increasingly condemnatory statements about apartheid.[63] Still, historians have described the Carter administration's policies toward South Africa as "cautious" and gradual-ist.[64] Despite employing harsher rhetoric than did his predecessors, Carter proved unwilling to impose sanctions on the RSA, believing instead that U.S. corporate expansion in South Africa would push the regime to reform apartheid.[65]

U.S. evangelicals did not play a role in congressional hearings on South Africa during the Carter administration; instead, after Soweto they redoubled their efforts to build relationships with evangelicals in the RSA, reaffirming their commitment to evangelism and peaceful reconciliation. Billy Graham, who rejected apartheid unequivocally and refused to preach in South Africa until after the state desegregated the venues where he could hold crusades, stated in an interview in Nairobi, Kenya, that he opposed violence and "'hope[d] the people of Southern Africa will be able to solve their problems in a peace-like way, without fighting.'"[66] Graham called on Christians to use their "'moral influence'" to bring about change, both in government and in the attitudes of denominations that supported apartheid, such as the Dutch Reformed Church.[67]

The leaders of the Church of God similarly emphasized nonviolence and Christian salvation as the way forward in South Africa. When they visited the region in 1978 to attend an evangelistic conference and preach with their brethren in integrated Full Gospel Church of God services, they also met with South African minister of foreign affairs Pik Botha. They reported that they prayed with Botha after he shared his views on governance and the escalating racial conflict in the RSA.[68] The church officials recounted with satisfaction that Botha informed them that "the church is one of the most important channels from which help can come to Southern Africa with its problems," a belief they shared.[69] Doug Coe, meanwhile, continued to invite South African leaders such as Buthelezi and Koornhof, who advocated for peaceful and nonrevolutionary change, to the United States to discuss South African affairs with members of Congress.[70] Thus despite the devastating violence that the apartheid regime inflicted on its black citizens in Soweto and the other townships, U.S. evangelicals continued to push for policies that supported gradualism and peaceful reconciliation in their private conversations with U.S. legislators in the late 1970s.

UN censure, increased diplomatic pressure from the Carter administration, and growing international isolation failed to have much of an effect on the Nationalist government in South Africa, yet Soweto did mark a turning point in South African politics. Both Prime Minister Vorster and his successor P. W. Botha, who took power in 1978, implemented some systemic reforms by easing petty apartheid.[71] On more than one occasion in 1979, Botha warned his party "'we must adapt or die,'" noting that violent revolution "'can only be averted if the Government looks at the interests of all population groups and not just the whites.'"[72] Still, the reforms he put in place aimed primarily at reducing racial tensions in order to allow white

Afrikaners to maintain their political control and racial privilege, rather than offering meaningful steps toward ending apartheid.[73] Furthermore, Botha balanced the reforms with increased repression of opposition groups. He rejected calls for an end to the homelands system and the implementation of a "one man, one vote" policy for electing governing officials.[74]

Although many black South Africans viewed these reforms as disappointing and superficial, some South African evangelicals—and their U.S. evangelical counterparts—saw room for hope, at least initially. Ross Main wrote several detailed letters to Doug Coe and James Bell of the Fellowship Foundation that described the changes in government leadership and shifts in policy he observed between 1977 and 1978. Though he expressed disappointment that a conservative National Party member had received a cabinet appointment instead of Fellowship Core member Piet Koornhof, Main opined that some of the proposed reforms represented "a revolution in Nationalist policy."[75] James Bell forwarded one of Main's letters to Representative Don Bonker, former senator John Dellenback, J. Douglas Holladay, and several other members of the Fellowship Foundation's "South African Prayer Group," praising its contents as "heartwarming."[76] The high-level contacts that Main had developed made his commentary invaluable to congressional policymakers, particularly those involved with the Fellowship Foundation, as they provided direct insight into the reactions of RSA leaders to international pressure (and evangelistic influence).

U.S. missionaries in South Africa also reported about the changes they witnessed in South Africa to their denominational leaders. Southern Baptist missionary workers at the newly established Baptist Mission in South Africa praised the reform efforts that they observed in the RSA in 1978, noting Botha's openness to peaceful change and a revised constitution.[77] These firsthand accounts from missionaries and local brethren offered evangelical leaders back in the United States vital information that shaped their perceptions of the South African government, and also demonstrated the extent to which evangelical networking expanded beyond the purely spiritual realm.

South African evangelicals developed a range of responses to Soweto and the reforms that followed, sharing information about their initiatives with and seeking support from evangelicals in the United States. Although many Pentecostals and Charismatics continued to promote spiritual rather than political change, even some white church leaders in those denominations began to show some empathy for the injustices that their black, colored, and Indian brethren faced. A report from an interracial conference of Charismatic leaders claimed that Pentecostal church members, including the influential Assemblies of God pastor Nicholas Bhengu, "have been meeting racial issues and facing them as never before," through their evangelistic activities.[78] With specific reference to the events in Soweto, the report continued by noting that, "above all, recent events in the townships and campuses, together with hard pressures upon black Christians, give the final blow to any illusion that you can be renewed in the Spirit and at the same time ignore your fellow man of another race and his problems."[79] The inherent violence and repression of apartheid hindered Christian witness.

Cassidy and AE drew on the transnational evangelistic network to launch the South African Christian Leadership Assembly (SACLA) in 1979, bringing together church leaders from every race and denomination "'to save the day in South Africa'" through Christian witness.[80] Moving into the political realm while remaining attentive to the imperative for global evangelism, Cassidy believed that SACLA would offer a "non-political" space where Christians could work through South Africa's political challenges and provide "the moral and spiritual dynamic" necessary to achieve racial reconciliation and reform apartheid without jeopardizing the safety of any groups.[81] Chief Buthelezi and Afrikaner cabinet minister Piet Koornhof presented together at the first SACLA conference, and the openness of their working relationship—and the fact that they referred to each other, publicly, as "brothers in Christ"—had a ripple effect on South African politics.[82] SACLA gained considerable traction in the 1980s and played an important role in dismantling apartheid in the early 1990s. Yet the ecumenicism of SACLA sparked a backlash from far-right, fundamentalist evangelical groups such as the Gospel Defence League and the Christian League of Southern Africa, which railed against SACLA's efforts to bring about political change.[83]

Though limited in scope, the diversity of South African evangelical responses to Soweto and the violence that followed influenced white U.S. evangelical thinking about the nature of the religious, political, and social cleavages that plagued the RSA. U.S. evangelical leaders and their South African counterparts spent the 1970s creating a thriving evangelistic network with each other, eager to expand the reach of evangelicalism throughout the region. Although not unconcerned with apartheid, they remained mostly on the sidelines of the anti-apartheid movements developing in their respective countries. Their belief in individual salvation and the priority of global evangelism, coupled with their concern that Soviet-backed liberation movements would bring violence and the spread of communism in Southern Africa, ensured that their efforts remained focused on fostering reconciliation and changing individual hearts. As the political struggle in the RSA escalated in the mid-1980s, however, many South African evangelicals began to see the deficiency and inefficacy of this approach.[84] At the same time, U.S. evangelicals began to get involved in the national debate about apartheid unfolding in the United States. Moreover, the connections that evangelicals had established in the 1970s with important political figures in South Africa, including Chief Buthelezi and P. W. Botha, grew increasingly consequential for U.S.-South African relations during the Reagan administration.

Constructive Engagement

On January 4, 1981, just weeks before Ronald Reagan took the oath of office for his first term as president, the CIA released an assessment of the political conditions in South Africa and their implications for U.S. national security and regional interests. The report noted that the slow pace of Prime Minister P. W. Botha's reforms had contributed to a sense among many black, colored, and Indian South Africans that the Afrikaner government sought above all else to hold onto power, not to change the system in any meaningful way. According to the evaluation, even U.S. ally and proponent of peaceful reconciliation Chief Buthelezi had grown disillusioned with the Botha government; in the absence of "acceptable reforms," the CIA feared that many of Buthelezi's supporters might turn to more radical leaders.[85] The CIA anticipated rising racial tensions and urban unrest, with a harsh consequent crackdown by South African authorities.[86] It also predicted that "black insurgent groups, primarily the African National Congress (ANC), which is backed by the Soviets, will continue to pull off spectacular terrorist operations" in response to government repression.[87] The CIA maintained that the need to uphold "American principles as well as U.S. objectives in preventing racial instability in South Africa from jeopardizing U.S. economic and strategic interests there and from creating openings for the Soviets throughout the region" meant that the United States had to take appropriate action to encourage the South African government to make substantive reforms.[88]

Upon taking office, the Reagan administration launched a policy of "constructive engagement" to guide U.S.-South African relations. In statements before and during his presidential campaign, Reagan had criticized the Carter administration's approach to Southern Africa. Though he claimed that he did not condone apartheid in the RSA, Reagan argued that Carter's focus on human rights distracted policymakers from the real threat to U.S. interests in the region: Soviet expansionism.[89] The team that Reagan assembled during his campaign to advise him on African affairs included Jeane Kirkpatrick, Ernest Lefever, and Chester Crocker, all of whom shared his negative assessment of Carter's policies and his belief that the United States should back friendly authoritarian regimes in order to thwart the global spread of totalitarianism.[90]

Crocker, who served as assistant secretary of state for African Affairs throughout Reagan's presidency, outlined the contours of the constructive engagement policy in a 1980 article for *Foreign Affairs*. Noting that the United States could neither endorse the racist system of apartheid nor entirely disengage from South Africa in protest, he argued that the best approach for encouraging change would balance diplomatic pressure with support for even modest improvements.[91] Placing the need for reform within the context of the Cold War rivalry with the Soviet Union, Crocker asserted, "the real choice we will face in southern Africa in the 1980s concerns our readiness to compete with our global adversary in the politics of a changing region whose future depends on those who participate in shaping it."[92] With this in mind, he stated that he viewed Prime Minister Botha as a reformer, a modernizer, and a leader committed to implementing the necessary changes, someone whom the Reagan administration could work with effectively to achieve a mutually beneficial political transformation in South Africa.[93] He also ruled out sanctions as inimical to this goal.[94] In Reagan's first term, the White House adopted Crocker's recommendations, drawing closer to the South African regime to encourage reform and discourage the spread of communism.[95]

Anti-apartheid activists in South Africa, most notably the Anglican Secretary-General of the South African Council of Churches (SACC) bishop Desmond Tutu, observed this shift in policy with considerable alarm.[96] In March 1981, Tutu traveled to the United States to meet with Chester Crocker, among others, and convey his concern about constructive engagement.[97] He made little headway with Crocker but received favorable coverage in the international press. A towering figure in the anti-apartheid movement, Tutu promoted nonviolent resistance to the regime and supported economic sanctions as an appropriate lever to induce reform.[98] He argued that racial injustice, rather than Soviet expansion, posed the most serious threat to South Africa; without reform, Tutu believed that disaffected black South Africans would turn to violent protest and communism.[99] The bishop relied on his international travels and contacts to spread awareness about the ongoing injustices in South Africa and to raise money to support imprisoned activists.[100] He built connections with mainline Protestants, liberal leaders, and the growing anti-apartheid movement in the United States and Europe.[101]

With Tutu at the helm, the SACC, an ecumenical organization linked to the World Council of Churches (WCC) that united mainline Protestant denominations in South Africa, became a key activist group and a thorn in the side of the apartheid government. Tutu met with Prime Minister Botha and representatives of the National Party (including Fellowship Core member Piet Koornhof) in 1980 and 1981. In their meetings, he and other leaders of the SACC pressed the government to end the homelands policy, stop forcible population removals, and abolish discriminatory legislation such as the pass laws.[102] Botha and the National Party viewed Tutu and the SACC with deep suspicion though, believing that they supported the ANC and other revolutionary communist forces arrayed against the government.[103] When Bishop Tutu made negative public statements concerning the slow pace of reform in South Africa and began to advocate for more confrontational (though still nonviolent) tactics, Botha cut off future meetings.[104] He also rescinded Tutu's passport to prevent the bishop from meeting with anti-apartheid activists abroad and launched a Justice Department inquiry into the SACC's finances in November 1981.[105]

This investigation, known as the Eloff Commission of Inquiry into the South African Council of Churches, exploited the heightened fear of violent revolution and communism in an effort to undermine the anti-apartheid leadership of Bishop Tutu and the South African Council of Churches. During the two-year inquiry, a panel of five commissioners combed through thousands of pages of financial statements and solicited testimony from hundreds of witnesses, seeking to build a case that would prove that foreign entities intent on spreading communism in South Africa funded and controlled the SACC.[106] Botha hoped that such a finding would enable the government to rule the SACC an "affected organization" and bar it from receiving foreign aid, minimizing its ability to engage in effective activism.[107]

As part of this effort, the Eloff Commission collected extensive testimonials from South African and U.S. fundamentalists and some conservative Pentecostals, all of whom claimed that the SACC and the WCC had close ties to communism and supported "terrorist" groups such as the ANC and the South West Africa People's Organization (SWAPO).[108] In one representative example, a leader of the Gospel Defence League lamented that the SACC directed its foreign funding to revolutionary movements. In one of several letters to the commission, Dorothea Scarborough claimed that "by allowing this massive transfer of funds from enemy sources overseas, we are permitting our assassins to prepare for our demise under our very eyes."[109] Likewise, J. H. Martin of the Zion Christian Church and Bishop Mokoena of the African Independent Churches both lambasted the SACC for claiming to represent all South African Christians while calling for international sanctions against the RSA and lending support to the ANC and SWAPO, actions these conservative Christian leaders explicitly opposed.[110] Several right-wing fundamentalist and evangelical organizations that the Botha government funded covertly to smear the SACC and Desmond Tutu in the late 1970s, including the Christian League of South Africa, also submitted censorious statements.[111] Although these groups represented the radical fringes of evangelicalism in South Africa and the United States, the commission solicited their (dubious) testimony because the Afrikaner commissioners recognized that they were among the only religious organizations in the country that pledged unquestioning fealty to the government. Their zeal to discredit Tutu underscored the fact that evangelical views on apartheid ranged widely, but also revealed the challenges that more moderate evangelicals faced: when far-right evangelicals embraced apartheid, it tarnished the faith and hindered evangelism, yet many moderates in this period feared that rapid political change would bring violence and communism.

The Eloff Commission provoked an immediate and heated response from the international community, which saw the investigation as evidence that the Botha regime did not intend to end apartheid or Afrikaner rule. The U.S. House Committee on Foreign Affairs submitted a letter to South Africa's minister of justice H. J. Coetsee condemning the RSA for its unscrupulous attack on Desmond Tutu. The committee reminded Coetsee and the commissioners that: "At a moment when the U.S. Government and many other nations are seeking evidence of a commitment to fundamental moral and social changes in South Africa, the Eloff Commission is looking for evidence of 'subversion' in the well-known peaceful activities of Bishop Tutu and the Council of Churches. The public spectacle being conducted by the Commission goes far beyond any legitimate concern with past bookkeeping practices of the Council."[112] The committee argued that the investigation "calls into question your Government's stated interest to initiate meaningful racial reform and which makes our own Government's policy efforts to help promote peaceful change more difficult to achieve."[113] Even the Institute on Religion and Democracy expressed dismay with the Eloff Commission. After condemning the inquiry in a public statement in 1982, the conservative Christian think tank called on "the Christian Churches in the United States

[to] renew their efforts to press the South African leadership to take significant steps toward full racial integration, political democracy, and elementary economic justice," even as it reproached the WCC for supporting the ANC and SWAPO.[114]

However, the RSA refused to disband the inquiry, which dragged on for two years before concluding that the SACC did not operate as an "instrument of foreign organizations."[115] Although the commission did divert the SACC's time and resources away from the anti-apartheid struggle, as Botha and other National Party leaders had hoped, the attack on Tutu combined with other repressive government actions emboldened broader resistance within South Africa. Furthermore, Botha's intransigence undermined U.S. public support for the Reagan administration's policy of constructive engagement, setting the stage for a major showdown between Reagan and Congress.

Battling Sanctions and Disinvestment

In 1983, the South African Parliament introduced a bill to implement a new constitution that would grant the vote and limited self-rule to colored and Indian citizens—but not the black majority. The proposed constitution expanded the power of the executive and created a racially segregated Tricameral Parliament, with a white House of Assembly and a much smaller House of Representatives and House of Delegates for colored and Indian members respectively. Each chamber had power over its "own affairs," which the constitution defined as matters related to "the maintenance of its identity and the upholding and furtherance of its way of life, culture, traditions and customs," such as education, housing, and welfare.[116] Since the white House of Assembly had far more representatives than the other two houses combined, it retained control over "general interest" issues, such as foreign relations, on which all three chambers voted. Botha and the National Party championed the proposal as evidence of progress and reform but outside observers and black leaders noted the obvious: the new Parliament "[would] be weighted in favor of whites and so [would] ensure white supremacy in practice."[117]

The proposal set off a firestorm of debate in South Africa. Even though the white minority would continue to hold all of the effective political power under the new constitution, an apoplectic far right claimed that "if the national referendum passes . . . 'Whites will have to pay the piper and integration will follow.'"[118] Liberals, meanwhile, slammed the proposal because it failed to grant representation to black South Africans and demonstrated that Botha planned to continue the homelands policy rather than pursue reforms toward a unified state with black majority rule.[119] Despite the dissatisfaction of the far right and the left, white South Africans voted to approve the new constitution on November 2, 1983, which passed with 66 percent of the vote.[120] A jubilant Botha announced that the RSA would enact the new constitution in 1984. Moderate leader and Western ally Chief Buthelezi commented on the outcome with a deep sense of foreboding, warning that "White South Africans have cast me and 22 million of my fellow (black) South Africans into the terrible politics of despair and anger."[121]

Buthelezi's fears materialized in 1984 as the implementation of the new constitution and ongoing black frustration with the injustice in South Africa erupted. Intermittent at first, the unrest grew near constant by the end of 1984.[122] Reports of riots, police violence, and numerous killings of demonstrators as well as labor leaders filtered into U.S. newspapers, reigniting U.S. public concern about apartheid. That the United States government seemed inclined to continue backing the apartheid regime in a time of escalating repression and diminishing evidence of real change lent credence to mounting anti-apartheid activist attacks on the Reagan administration for its warm relations with the RSA. Scholars such as Alex Thomson note that Reagan and Crocker's policy of constructive engagement stipulated U.S. support for South African progress and, with "very little else to praise concerning Pretoria's behavior," this compelled the State Department and Reagan administration to laud the constitutional reforms.[123] Reagan's stance on the new constitution disappointed allies in South Africa and infuriated many members of Congress.[124] In South Africa, President Botha responded to the unrest in the townships, much of it coordinated by the ANC, by declaring a state of emergency in July 1985 that amounted to a dramatic expansion of police powers and a vicious crackdown on dissent.[125]

These developments invigorated a growing movement in the United States to impose diplomatic sanctions and encourage corporate divestment from South Africa, policies that the Reagan administration—not to mention many U.S. and South African evangelicals—opposed.[126] By late 1984, Reagan faced congressional dissension not just from his Democratic opponents, but also from within his own party. On December 4, a group of thirty-five Republican representatives sent a letter to South African Ambassador Brand Fourie demanding: "an immediate end to the violence in South Africa accompanied by a demonstrated sense of urgency about ending apartheid. If such actions are not forthcoming, we are prepared to recommend that the

U.S. Government take the following two steps: One, curtail new American investment in South Africa unless certain economic and civil rights guarantees for all persons are in place; two, organize international diplomatic and economic sanctions against South Africa."[127]

As congressional efforts to enact strong anti-apartheid measures gathered steam, the Reagan administration scrambled to defend its constructive engagement policy and stave off the passage of comprehensive sanctions legislation, which the House and Senate introduced in 1985.[128] NSC memoranda indicate that the Reagan administration viewed these congressional actions as a significant threat to U.S. policy in Southern Africa. According to the NSC, the proposed legislation contributed to deteriorating U.S.-South African relations that jeopardized U.S. efforts to roll back Soviet gains in the region and resolve the conflicts in Angola, Namibia, and Mozambique.[129] Cognizant that the anti-apartheid sanctions movement had gained the upper hand because it enjoyed broad support from the American people, the Reagan administration embarked on a coordinated public relations campaign to oppose the sanctions bill and promote his constructive engagement policy.

U.S. evangelical leaders played a crucial role in this public diplomacy campaign, the contours of which the NSC established in a National Security Decision Directive (NSDD) on U.S. policy toward South Africa that the Reagan administration put in place in 1985. NSDD 187 noted that the combination of Soviet encroachment in Southern Africa, violent unrest in the RSA stemming from apartheid, and vocal public and congressional disapproval of the Reagan administration's policies made it "now necessary to re-emphasize the broad objectives of U.S. political strategy toward South Africa."[130] After enumerating these aims, listing "use U.S. influence to promote peaceful change away from apartheid" first before moving on to the need to curb revolutionary violence and promote "peace and coexistence" between South Africa and its neighboring states, NSDD 187 offered a broad plan for winning over the U.S. and South African publics.[131] In addition to new efforts to reach out to black South African leaders, the White House would begin working with nongovernmental groups—specifically religious groups—to "help strengthen the democratic forces in South Africa."[132] This included outreach within the United States to build opposition to the sanction and divestment movement sweeping through Congress and to quash the public perception that the Reagan administration and State Department were "lazy apologists for apartheid."[133]

Shortly after Reagan signed NSDD 187, the White House appointed Fellowship Foundation member J. Douglas Holladay as director of the Office of Public Diplomacy for South Africa and started a new Advisory Committee on South Africa.[134] Through his previous role as director of the Office of Public Liaison, Holladay had already done some work to promote Reagan's policies on South Africa, such as coordinating and participating in meetings on U.S.-South African diplomacy between members of Congress, Assistant Secretary of State for African Affairs Chester Crocker, and Doug Coe.[135] He had also arranged for the vice president to brief Fellowship Foundation members, including South African Core member Rev. I. Ross Main and several evangelical ministers, about U.S. relations with South Africa.[136] In bringing these men together, Holladay helped thicken the web of connections that linked evangelicals and government officials in the United States and South Africa while sharing key information that they could use to build up grassroots support for constructive engagement policies.

With his new position heading the Office of Public Diplomacy for South Africa and the looming threat that Congress would pass a comprehensive sanctions bill, Holladay initiated a multipronged public outreach effort to recapture the "moral advantage" in the debate.[137] In order to convince the public, U.S. allies in Europe, and black South Africans that the Reagan administration had committed itself to "using whatever leverage and influence that we possess to create a more just and open society in South Africa," and to channel anti-apartheid sentiments in a manner more amenable to Reagan's policy aims, Holladay began tapping allies and building connections with church, media, labor, and civil rights groups.[138] He identified evangelical television and print media, along with church leaders, as a group of "domestic allies capable of generating support" for the president.[139] He also dedicated considerable space in his strategy paper to discussing the central role that religion played in the South African conflict, noting the necessity of overcoming the negative perceptions that many mainline and Catholic clergy in South Africa as well as the United States held about the president's policies.[140]

As part of this campaign, the White House and the State Department began to reach out to and cultivate relationships with black political and church leaders in South Africa. Reagan had already established a rapport with Chief Buthelezi, who opposed sanctions because he believed that "the total isolation of South Africa [through a sanctions regime] would favour those who aim to bring about change by violent means and to establish a socialist or even communist state."[141] The chief praised Reagan for providing humanitarian aid to black South African organizations and for standing against sanctions, but also encouraged the president to push P. W. Botha to free Nelson Mandela and other imprisoned anti-apartheid activists.[142] Several

South African evangelical ministers that Reagan established contact with issued supportive statements about constructive engagement in the press and correspondence with the president, including Bishop B. E. Lekganyane of the Zion Christian Church and Bishop Isaac Mokoena of the African Independent Churches.[143] The administration also attempted to build relationships with leaders who did not already back Reagan's policy objectives. In late 1985, for example, the Public Affairs office organized U.S. outreach to Soweto community leaders, activist and Anglican reverend Allan Boesak, and other anti-apartheid advocates in South Africa. It also built public relations opportunities into official humanitarian initiatives, such as arranging a speaking event after the U.S. embassy, evangelical humanitarian organization World Vision, and Oxfam collaborated to renovate a medical clinic.[144] For the most part, though, these overtures came too late and amounted to too little to persuade black South African leaders that the United States had their interests at heart, especially after years of the Reagan administration dealing almost exclusively with white government officials.

Holladay attempted to sway the opinions of mainline Protestant clergy toward supporting the president through official briefings with Chester Crocker and Secretary of State George Shultz but found far more success in mobilizing evangelical leaders than in his efforts to change the minds of some of Reagan's staunchest opponents.[145] When the House of Representatives introduced the Comprehensive Anti-Apartheid Act (CAAA) in May 1986, Holladay and the Office of Public Affairs ramped up their outreach to evangelicals and other administration allies.[146] To build evangelical momentum for the president's policies, Holladay invited hundreds of church leaders to attend a special State Department conference with Secretary of State Shultz.[147] This briefing proved extremely effective. In one account, which gushed about how the appointment of Christians to State Department posts had created an inspiring transformation in the agency, Assemblies of God Missions director J. Philip Hogan praised the organizers of a session on "Spiritual Forces that Need to be Brought to Bear on South Africa," for framing the discussion around "'the power of reconciliation in the Gospel.'"[148] In Hogan's retelling of the event, Shultz said "he was appealing to the Christian community in the United States to pray" for reconciliation in South Africa.[149] Many evangelical participants left the briefing impressed with Shultz's strong assertion that apartheid must end and his thorough review of the strategic significance of South Africa, its resources, and the ever-present communist threat.[150] Some incorporated information that they learned from Shultz and other speakers into articles on U.S.-South African relations.[151]

Figure 12. President Reagan meeting with South African Zulu leader Chief Mangosuthu Buthelezi at the White House in February 1985. Courtesy of the Ronald Reagan Library.

Except for a small number of more progressive Southern Baptists, most rank-and-file U.S. evangelicals did not need Holladay or the State Department to convince them to oppose sanctions and disinvestment, though.[152] Throughout 1984 and 1985, Jerry Falwell, Pat Robertson, and other well-known evangelists had publicized their support for the Reagan administration's approach to South Africa widely through their popular television programs and newsletters. In one particularly inflammatory television appearance, Falwell rejected the legitimacy of anti-apartheid leaders Desmond Tutu, Allan Boesak, and Nelson Mandela, declaring Chief Buthelezi, Bishop Mokoena, and Bishop Lekganyane "'the real spokesmen for black South Africa.'"[153] Aligning himself with Reagan administration policies and claiming that he opposed apartheid, Falwell asserted that "'the best way to deal with South Africa is in a gradual and coercive effort that brings about the elimination of apartheid without creating violence and bloodshed in the land, and without giving the Marxists a toehold.'"[154] He and other evangelicals also contended that black South Africans would bear the brunt of the economic dislocation that sanctions and disinvestment would bring.[155] Here they parroted claims from Buthelezi and Mokoena that anti-apartheid activists (and even some members of the Reagan administration) hotly contested.[156]

Eager to find evidence of South African support for what they described as a "peaceful," Christian solution to the problem of apartheid, major evangelical denominational and parachurch leaders took "fact-finding" trips to South Africa in 1985. There they met with like-minded Pentecostal, Baptist, and nondenominational brethren and heard firsthand from them about why they opposed U.S. sanctions, feared revolutionary violence, and worried about the expansion of communism in their country.[157] The National Religious Broadcasters and others filmed these interactions and produced video segments to run on evangelical television programs back in the United States to bolster support for Reagan's policies.[158]

Despite these efforts, Congress passed an amended CAAA on September 12, 1986. Two weeks later, President Reagan vetoed the bill. In his message to Congress, he stated that his administration abhorred apartheid and viewed the system as "an affront to human rights and human dignity," but claimed that the CAAA sanctions would harm black South Africans.[159] He proposed a new executive order in its place. In advance of Reagan's announcement, the Office of Public Affairs began a frenzied effort to muster enough support in Congress to sustain the veto. Holladay called on Falwell, Robertson, and other grassroots evangelical supporters to lobby their representatives to vote against the bill. Roberts and Falwell both featured interviews with Buthelezi on their respective television shows, distributed a Christian Broadcast Network report about the terrorist activities of the ANC, and set up a phone bank to help viewers call their congressmen.[160] Other evangelical media executives ran announcements about the impending vote on thousands of Christian radio stations.[161] On the day of the vote to override the veto, the Christian Broadcast Network aired a special on South Africa and Pat Robertson appeared on the Phil Donahue Show to discuss his opposition to the CAAA.[162] Falwell lobbied some senators directly, with several Zulu supporters in tow. Neither the SBC nor the National Association of Evangelicals (NAE) could offer official statements—the SBC because deep disagreements on the issue had divided its membership and the NAE because it had yet to issue a resolution on sanctions—but their directors both expressed support to White House officials.[163]

In the end, the strenuous lobbying efforts failed. Congress overrode Reagan's veto, and the CAAA became law on October 2, 1986.[164] In his statement on the CAAA, Reagan asserted that: "America—and that means all of us—opposes apartheid, a malevolent and archaic system totally alien to our ideals. The debate, which culminated in today's vote, was not whether or not to oppose apartheid but, instead, how best to oppose it and how best to bring freedom to that troubled country."[165] That he felt the need to reiterate his opposition to apartheid demonstrated the extent to which the policy of constructive engagement had failed in the court of public opinion. Indeed, as scholar Joanne E. Davies has noted, the public diplomacy campaign had not had a chance of succeeding given that, without any substantive reforms from the Botha government to speak of, constructive engagement struck most observers as "appeasement of Pretoria" rather than a policy that compelled action to end apartheid.[166] The energy that Jerry Falwell, Pat Robertson, and other prominent evangelicals poured into fighting the CAAA led many commenters to conclude that they and their followers supported white rule in South Africa, their protestations to the contrary notwithstanding.[167]

The Unraveling of Apartheid

After Congress passed the CAAA, the issue of apartheid and U.S.-South African relations largely faded from the U.S. consciousness.[168] The Reagan administration insisted the sanctions had damaged the South African economy, contributed to increased political repression, led to high unemployment among black South Africans, and failed to bring an end to apartheid, yet, for the most part, abided by the law.[169] Furthermore, despite ever-increasing violence in the RSA, the administration received far less pushback on U.S.-South African relations from Congress after 1986.[170] The constructive engagement policy remained in place through the end of the Reagan administration, and some scholars have suggested that the CAAA sanctions reinvigorated it, making it more flexible and effective.[171]

U.S. evangelicals, especially those with long-standing relationships with South African brethren, remained actively engaged with the events playing out in the RSA. Many expressed concern about the ongoing unrest and the political challenges that the country faced. In an annual report to the SBC Foreign Mission Board, the Baptist Mission in South Africa noted: "Sanctions against the country are felt by all, if not economically then certainly emotionally. The country is becoming more and more isolated from the rest of the world . . . but, as in nearly all times of unrest and uncertainty, there is a greater openness of the people to the moving of the Holy Spirit."[172] One year later, the Baptist Mission lamented that the unrest and "stress" from the sanctions had limited missionary access, and therefore the spread of the gospel, in some parts of the country.[173] The Fellowship Foundation continued to nurture its connections with South African Christians and to attempt to foster "the spirit of reconciliation" in their country.[174] The information that missionaries and South African evangelical leaders such as Cassidy reported back belied the lack of international news coverage on events in the RSA.[175] As one missionary couple reported, "the State of Emergency declared in June 1986 still continues with a very powerful Army and Police Force 'maintaining' their concept of order. The blackout of most unrest-related news continues."[176]

In the face of the turmoil, evangelicals in South Africa began to speak out more decisively against apartheid. The state of emergency spurred one group of "concerned evangelicals" to reflect on their faith and offer a statement critiquing apartheid—and the prevailing evangelical responses to it—in 1986. *Evangelical Witness in South Africa: A Critique of Evangelical Theology and Practice by South African Evangelicals* argued that the state violence and repression hindered missionary campaigns and prevented them from fulfilling their scriptural mandate to evangelize.[177] The Concerned Evangelicals rejected the anticommunist rhetoric of the National Party and many South African evangelicals, noting, "in South Africa we hear more and more that 'no price is too high to pay for our religious liberty.' . . . The fact is that genocide is too high a price, and no one, not even evangelicals, not even for the highest ideals, have the right to take measures that might destroy millions of innocent noncombatants."[178] Furthermore, unlike the early statements of Cassidy and AE, the Concerned Evangelicals called for justice for the South African people, as well as for reconciliation.[179] Even some Pentecostal groups, most of which had formerly maintained an apolitical stance, began to organize politically against the apartheid regime—in 1988, a group called the Relevant Pentecostal Witness formed to battle racism within South Africa and the Pentecostal church.[180]

Still, as late as 1988 and 1989, many Pentecostal and Charismatic churches in the United States and South Africa remained wary of using political means to attack apartheid, preferring to foster change by sharing the gospel. Ray McCauley, the pastor of Rhema Church in Johannesburg, believed that "the primary commission of the Church is to change individual hearts first, then individuals will change government and social systems."[181] During the 1980s, McCauley and other Pentecostal and Charismatic preachers had gained wide renown for building large, racially integrated congregations in South Africa.[182] An anthropologist studying the Charismatic movement there found that the integrated worship services at these churches helped to transform the racial interactions of the congregants, nurturing interracial friendships and encouraging more "'enlightened'" attitudes.[183] So, too, did initiatives such as integrated Christian day schools and the "Joweto Project," which held interracial prayer meetings in Johannesburg as well as in the townships.[184] Some pastors insisted that these activities had garnered the wrath of the Botha government, which allegedly attempted to shut down the schools and discredit the churches.[185] At the same time, the Concerned Evangelicals and other Pentecostal activist organizations called on these churches to do more, urging them to get involved in the political struggle.[186]

These tensions and developments within the South African evangelical churches spurred a gradual change in how some U.S. evangelicals thought about their approach to the challenge of apartheid. For example, the SBC news agency reported extensively on the involvement of South African Baptists in the Christian anti-apartheid organization Koinonia, which initially promoted peaceful reconciliation to hasten the end of apartheid.[187] By 1990, Koinonia members engaged in acts of civil disobedience and asserted "the need for both prayer and action to effect change," a message that some Southern Baptists in the United States also began to embrace.[188] At a leadership convention for young evangelicals that the Lausanne Committee for World Evangelization organized in Washington, D.C., in 1988, Caesar Molebatsi of the Youth Alive ministry in Soweto urged those in attendance to join in the fight against oppression, explicitly linking social action with evangelism.[189] He expanded on this message in 1989 at the second International Congress on World Evangelization, noting that by remaining silent on injustice in South Africa, evangelical churches there had become de facto oppressors, undermining evangelism as well as the integrity of the faith.[190] Southern Baptist missionaries echoed Molebatsi's assertions, expressing their concern that working with racially segregated churches in South Africa served to "enforc[e] apartheid."[191] When a trustee of the Southern Baptist Convention's Christian Life Commission remarked in 1988 that apartheid "doesn't exist anymore and was beneficial when it did," the rest of the commission members swiftly and publicly denounced his comments.[192] The executive director of the commission then called on the SBC to recommit itself to the elimination of "racism and racist structures," including South African apartheid.[193] Although this did not take the form of overt political action, the SBC did begin to press its South African counterparts to integrate.[194] These internal conversations signaled an evolution in U.S. evangelical perceptions of injustice and human rights abuses in South Africa—and in their views on how to address them.

In February 1989, P. W. Botha resigned after having a stroke and F. W. de Klerk assumed the presidency of South Africa. De Klerk introduced sweeping reforms, unbanning political groups such as the ANC and pledging to release Nelson Mandela from prison. Despite an uproar from the far right and continued unrest among black South Africans, negotiations between the ANC and the de Klerk government to dismantle apartheid began on May 4, 1990, and continued through 1993.[195] After Nelson Mandela's release from prison in 1991, the United States lifted the CAAA sanctions. Mandela later won the presidency in the democratic elections that South Africa held on April 27, 1994.

As the efforts toward political reconciliation unfolded, haltingly but steadily, between 1991 and 1993, South African evangelicals also engaged in the process of reconciliation. The Church of God and the Assemblies of God in South Africa reintegrated, creating unified churches.[196] At the behest of President de Klerk, representatives from eighty-five churches in South Africa met in November 1990 for a conference in Rustenburg, Transvaal to aid in the negotiation and reconciliation necessary to end apartheid.[197] During the Rustenburg conference, Ray McCauley of Rhema Church and other evangelical leaders repented for their apoliticism in the face of injustice, and the Rustenburg Declaration that the group issued called for the repeal of all apartheid laws and the development of a new system based on justice.[198] In May 1991, Desmond Tutu, Michael Cassidy, Ray McCauley, Frank Chikane of the Apostolic Faith Mission, and other participants from the conference formed the Rustenburg Church Leaders' Committee. This group worked behind the scenes to negotiate South Africa's National Peace Accord, which helped to bring together the competing political groups and fostered negotiation.[199] In his memoirs, Cassidy noted that the National Peace Accord proved crucial in preventing simmering tensions from erupting into widespread violence in the years leading up to the 1994 elections.[200]

The SBC missionaries in South Africa praised the outcome of the 1994 election, and declared the peaceful transition as a "true *miracle* from God."[201] In the wake of sporadic, violent unrest prior to the election, the Southern Baptist Mission in Southern Africa hailed the renewed possibilities for evangelism that post-apartheid South Africa offered, informing the mission board that "we believe that many doors will begin to open, especially in the townships, that had previously been closed to sharing the Gospel. We are targeting these areas for significant missionary involvement."[202] Thus while the reconciliation process had required South African evangelicals to confront fundamental questions about justice and the role of social action in their faith, U.S. evangelicals continued to embrace a narrower understanding of human rights as they defined their mission for the global church and their foreign policy agenda.

Building the Kingdom

The evangelistic mission, rather than the pursuit of social justice, defined U.S. evangelical engagement with South Africa between 1970 and 1994. To the extent that white evangelicals embraced efforts to end the brutal apartheid regime during these years, they did so within the confines of their mission and the ideological context of the Cold War. Nevertheless, and in spite of reductive treatments of the evangelical response to apartheid during the Reagan years that focus exclusively on Jerry Falwell and Pat Robertson, evangelicals evinced relatively diverse views about how to best confront apartheid. Rather than simply acting as apologists for the racist white minority government in Pretoria (though some did act in this way), most Pentecostals, Southern Baptists, and other evangelical leaders called for apartheid's end and promoted peaceful reconciliation in South Africa. Their desire for reconciliation could not substitute for the South African peoples' demand for justice, however. Some of their counterparts in South Africa, notably Cassidy, came to embrace the need for justice as well as for reconciliation and salvation. Most white U.S. evangelicals remained attuned solely to their global evangelistic mission.

Yet the networks that U.S. church groups developed with South African Christians and leaders proved deep and enduring. They also created significant political openings. The access that evangelical organizations gained to the highest echelons of power in South Africa—and the United States—through their evangelistic networks allowed them to promote their objectives for a resolution in South Africa that would end apartheid without allowing totalitarianism, a system they believed posed an existential threat to evangelism, to take root. U.S. evangelicals may not have swayed congressional opinion on sanctions or disinvestment, but they played a role in the unfolding drama as they worked to build the kingdom.

Conclusion

Evangelical Foreign Policy Activism Ascendant

Human rights are not the invention of twentieth century politics, but are as old as the human race itself. They flow, in our belief, from the conviction that humanity was created in the image of God. . . . Evangelicals, convinced of this and committed to the inspired, authoritative Scriptures, know that the Word of God calls them to pray, speak and act on behalf of persons whose rights are violated by abusive regimes whether on the right or left.

—Robert P. Dugan Jr., testimony before the Senate Committee on Foreign Relations, 1981

With the collapse of the Soviet Union in 1991, the end of South African apartheid in 1994, and the gradual democratization of Guatemala and other countries in Latin America throughout the 1990s, the battles over human rights in some of the most repressive regimes of the previous thirty years seemed won. Yet as the Cold War order receded, ethnic and religious tensions exploded in parts of Africa, the Balkans, the Middle East, and Asia. New human rights abusers emerged. Reports of state repression and violence against evangelicals and other minority Christian populations multiplied.[1] Perceiving an increase in religious persecution abroad beginning around 1994, evangelical Christians in the United States continued their foreign policy advocacy throughout the Bill Clinton and George W. Bush administrations just as they had in earlier decades: by testifying in Congress, appealing to the White House, and mobilizing the grassroots in support of the suffering church.[2]

By the mid-1990s, U.S. evangelicals had a well-developed set of foreign policy objectives that blended their spiritual and political beliefs, skillful lobbyists to promote their interests in Congress, and a strong network linking them with their coreligionists throughout the world. Evangelical foreign policy activism and political influence contributed to the passage of legislation such as the International Religious Freedom Act in 1998 and the Sudan Peace Act in 2002. These achievements inspired some scholars and contemporary observers to proclaim that evangelicals and their allies from other faith traditions represented "a new human rights constituency."[3] Yet evangelical lobbying power on human rights issues did not materialize from a vacuum. Rather, it grew out of the political advocacy and overseas outreach that evangelicals had engaged in since the early 1970s.

Four developments contributed to the emergence of an evangelical foreign policy lobby in the 1970s with a focus on human rights and related issues, such as international trade relations and military aid. First, evangelicals built a global network on the basis of their shared desire to spread the Christian Gospel to everyone in the world. Second, as this network grew more robust, evangelicals in the United States became increasingly attuned to global affairs and policy issues that affected their brethren and missionaries overseas. Third, this internationalist outlook, combined with the growing domestic political power of the religious right, led evangelicals to exhort Congress, the president, and the State Department to implement policies that promoted religious freedom and Christian values abroad. Finally, evangelical lobbyists incorporated the language of universal human rights into their appeals for religious freedom in order to build support for their policy recommendations.

In the late 1960s, evangelical leaders such as Billy Graham and theologians such as John Stott, Donald McGavran, and Ralph Winter concluded that liberal Protestant critiques of missionary work as imperialism threatened the evangelistic mission of the global Christian church. At the same time, evangelical churches flourished in Latin America, Asia, and Africa, in part through the expansion of evangelical overseas missionary work and in part through increased indigenous evangelism in these regions. Although evangelicals in other areas of the world adapted their religious practice to suit local customs and needs, they held the same core beliefs as their Western counterparts did about salvation through Jesus Christ, the authority of the

Bible, and the responsibility to evangelize others. Eager to bring together evangelicals from around the world to achieve the Great Commission—the evangelization of all nations that Jesus commanded of his disciples in the Book of Matthew—Billy Graham organized the International Congress on World Evangelization (ICOWE) in Lausanne, Switzerland, in 1974.[4]

There, evangelicals from 150 countries discussed the future of world missions and how they could best spread the gospel to the billions of men, women, and children who had never before heard it. At the congress, many African, Asian, and Latin American Christians maintained that evangelicals should prioritize the promotion of social justice among the poor and oppressed. Many Western evangelicals resisted such calls, insisting that evangelism offered the promise of eternal salvation to those who suffered from earthly injustices and poverty.[5] At the end of the congress, the participants signed a statement of principles that affirmed the primacy of evangelism above all else, with social action playing only a supportive role toward that chief aim.

The ICOWE succeeded in launching a multifaceted global network of evangelical Christians, all of whom shared a commitment to world evangelism. The Lausanne Movement, which arose directly from the congress, supported foreign missions as well as indigenous evangelism. Members of the movement developed strong relationships with each other as they collaborated on missionary and evangelistic strategies at regional conferences in the 1970s and 1980s, as well as at the two major follow-up ICOWE gatherings in Manila in 1989 and in Cape Town in 2010. The movement also brought greater support and attention to a range of new evangelistic strategies, including radio, television, and internet evangelism, which help connect indigenous evangelicals with their brethren in the United States and provided them with resources to build local churches and followings in their home countries.

Expanded missionary outreach and support for indigenous leaders who sought to launch their own local evangelistic campaigns helped the ICOWE and the Lausanne Movement inspire individual evangelical churches and denominations to strengthen their connections with their followers in other countries. The missionary work of the Eureka, California-based Gospel Outreach Church in Guatemala reflects this impulse. U.S. missionaries planted churches and provided humanitarian aid in Guatemala City after a massive earthquake ravaged the area in 1976. As these churches grew by leaps and bounds, the original Gospel Outreach missionaries cultivated local pastors to take on leadership roles. These local church leaders and the U.S.

missionaries continued to evangelize in Guatemala and elsewhere in Latin America, but also maintained close ties with Gospel Outreach Church in the United States. The enduring connections that they built contributed to the vast expansion of evangelicalism (especially in its Pentecostal and Charismatic forms) throughout Guatemala. Large evangelical denominations, such as the Church of God, the Assemblies of God, and the Southern Baptist Convention, undertook similar efforts to expand their reach into Latin America, Asia, and Africa.

The drive for world evangelism also encouraged nondenominational evangelical organizations to adopt expressly internationalist agendas. The Fellowship Foundation built an evangelistic network that linked elites in government and business throughout the world on the basis of Christian fellowship and the desire to spread the gospel. Fellowship Foundation members established contacts in every country from Afghanistan to Zimbabwe, and not only hosted ambassadors and other leaders on visits to the United States, but also worked to form local "cell" groups in as many countries as possible, including Brazil, Indonesia, and South Africa.[6] The leaders of these local groups cultivated additional cells in their home countries, multiplying the Fellowship Foundation's global reach and political influence.

Evangelicals in the United States published articles about the ICOWE and other international evangelistic conferences in their magazines and newsletters, shared reports from missionaries about their experiences abroad, and urged their congregations to raise money to support churches in other parts of the world. They also urged believers to support the development of shortwave radio stations, publishing outfits, and evangelistic television programming. When natural disasters or humanitarian crises erupted, as in Guatemala in 1976, evangelical churches and parachurch organizations moved in quickly to provide spiritual and material assistance to their brethren, garnering new followers in the process. As evangelicalism itself expanded internationally during the 1970s and 1980s, these efforts connected evangelicals in the United States with their coreligionists in other countries.

In addition to facilitating evangelism, these networks kept U.S. Christians informed about the struggles that their brethren and missionaries faced in other parts of the world. The detailed accounts that evangelicals gathered and shared about the detention, harassment, and torture of Baptists and Pentecostals in Soviet bloc countries kindled evangelical concern, as did their warnings about the threat that communist expansion posed to democracy and Christianity in Guatemala and South Africa. Letters poured in to radio stations, evangelical human rights organizations, and well-known evangelists that made clear that persecution was escalating, but also that evangelistic connections provided suffering believers with spiritual as well as tangible support by shining a light and bringing international pressure to bear on repressive regimes.

Evangelicals translated this concern into political action during the Jimmy Carter and Gerald Ford administrations. Inspired by the effectiveness of U.S. Jewish organizing on behalf of the persecuted Soviet Jewry, evangelical leaders in the United States formed nongovernmental and parachurch organizations dedicated to fighting religious repression abroad. Representatives from these groups began testifying more often in Congress about the persecution that Christians faced in communist countries in the USSR and Eastern Europe. They recommended that the U.S. government suspend most favored nation trading status with states that restricted religious freedom. Rather than seek emigration rights for persecuted Christians to leave their repressive homelands, evangelical activists articulated a vision for universal religious liberty. They wanted their coreligionists to practice and propagate their faith freely throughout the world. In the 1980s and 1990s, evangelical leaders and organizations such as Christian Solidarity International advocated successfully in behalf of the Siberian Seven in the Soviet Union and persecuted Christians in Romania. Their congressional testimony and letters to policymakers contributed to the passage of legislation that restricted foreign trade and their remonstrations about religious persecution informed diplomatic exchanges. Evangelicals capitalized on the extensive influence that the religious right had cultivated in the United States and benefitted from the rhetorical support of the Reagan administration.

When evangelicals identified foreign leaders whom they believed would thwart the advance of communism and respect religious liberty, they rallied to their support. In the case of Guatemala in 1982–83, they campaigned to convince the U.S. Congress to grant military funding to evangelical dictator Ríos Montt. When the results of this effort proved disappointing, evangelicals in the United States raised funds on their own to provide the Guatemalan regime with the supplies and manpower it needed to fight the communist insurgency and pacify the countryside. Similarly, evangelicals in the United States played a significant role in supporting Reagan administration efforts to stop the passage of legislation that would impose sanctions on the apartheid government of South Africa in 1985–86. Many U.S. evangelicals feared that sanctions would hasten the spread of communism in Southern Africa by emboldening the African National Congress and other allegedly Marxist forces, leading to violence and endangering Christians rather than bringing a peaceful end to apartheid. This activism had far-reaching effects, in some cases helping to sustain repressive governments abroad.

In addition to mobilizing substantial political support in the United States for policies that protected religious liberty and promoted global Christianity, evangelical leaders also influenced society and politics in other countries. In the Soviet Union, radio evangelism, clandestine support for unregistered churches, and international campaigns to raise awareness about persecuted Christians helped to bolster the Baptist and Pentecostal movements. When the Soviet Union unraveled, Mikhail Gorbachev invited evangelical leaders from the United States to aid the post-Soviet states in their democratic transition. The strength of U.S. and Soviet evangelical organizing contributed to the passage of stronger religious freedom laws in Russia and other countries in the region, even though the subsequent explosion of evangelism from foreign religious groups ultimately undermined this achievement. Likewise, in Guatemala, U.S. evangelical missionary work helped turn that nation into one of the most Protestant countries in predominantly Catholic Latin America. Despite their involvement in Ríos Montt's strategic hamlets program and their support of his genocidal campaigns against the insurgency, neo-Pentecostals have continued to hold office in Guatemala in the decades since his ouster. And, in South Africa, notwithstanding decades of relative indifference to apartheid, evangelicals played an important, behind-the-scenes role in negotiating the National Peace Accord and in the reconciliation process that followed the peaceful transition to representative democracy.

As evangelicals built their global network, developed organized interest groups, and became accomplished political lobbyists, they employed the language of universal human rights. They often quoted from and referred to the 1948 UN Universal Declaration of Human Rights (UDHR) and the 1975 Helsinki Final Act in their congressional testimony and in their official statements on global religious liberty.[7] Later, they harnessed the language that animated the UDHR and other international documents, and emphasized that the core principles undergirding human rights stemmed from the Bible and from the belief that each human being reflected God's glory.[8] This evangelical vision differed substantially from that of liberal and secular human rights organizations, as it focused on the freedom of conscience above all other basic rights and argued that human rights originated from God, rather than from the state.

The emphasis on religious liberty and the divine origin of human rights defined evangelical human rights activism. Consequently, evangelicals sometimes supported repressive authoritarian regimes as well as opposed totalitarian governments. In the Lausanne Covenant in 1974, they affirmed their commitment to fighting for religious freedom and assigned priority to evangelism over social action.[9] Although liberal human rights groups emphasized the need for social and economic justice and railed against the brutality of authoritarian dictators fighting against "communist" insurgents, evangelicals believed that totalitarian powers that denied their citizens the right to practice their religion posed the greatest threat to human freedom. They did not deny the importance of feeding the hungry, tending the sick, and combating oppression, but they insisted that by sharing the word of God they offered humanity the surest route to salvation. For evangelicals, salvation in Christ promised eternal life—and eternal freedom from sin and pain.[10] As a result, they could embrace leaders such as Ríos Montt as stalwarts in the crusade for world evangelization. In their view, defeating communism ensured universal religious freedom; universal religious freedom provided the cornerstone for all other human rights.

While evangelical human rights organizations expanded and developed closer working relationships with nonevangelical religious and secular groups in the 1990s to 2000s, they built on two decades of previous advocacy work. Although some evangelical scholars downplay the cohesiveness and consequences of evangelical foreign policy engagement between 1969 and 1994, evangelical interest groups and NGOs shaped foreign relations in a number of key regions throughout the world in the last decades of the Cold War.[11] In the decades since, global evangelism, foreign policy lobbying, and the promotion of international religious freedom has had, and continues to have, cascading effects on the lives of people throughout the world.

Examining evangelical lobbying through the lens of foreign missionary work and the international human rights movement reveals previously unexplored dimensions of U.S. foreign relations in the late twentieth century. The work of diplomatic historians such as Andrew Preston, William Inboden, and Jonathan Herzog makes clear that religious beliefs and people of faith have influenced foreign policy in a variety of ways, from shaping Americans' perceptions of foreign threats and setting the parameters of acceptable policy responses to inspiring the sense that the United States has a providential mission to spread its founding principles.[12] Incorporating the rapid global expansion of evangelicalism and the rise of faith-based interest group lobbying in the 1970s into the story uncovers the spiritual motivations that transformed the landscape of religious foreign policy engagement at the end of the Cold War. In a world that has grown both increasingly globalized and, paradoxically, increasingly localized, the transnational ties and indigenous relationships that evangelicals built served as key vectors for sharing information about a wide range of political issues. This allowed evangelicals to mobilize their followers as never before to confront the challenges that the church faced as it worked to fulfill the Great Commission and hasten the coming of the Kingdom of God.

Shared religious identity connected U.S. evangelicals with fellow believers from all corners of the earth, offering common spiritual meaning amid tremendous cultural differences. Evangelicals felt a deep sense of belonging to a global mission, believing that they had an obligation to protect their brethren as they worked to spread the gospel to all. Their faith inspired their political activism and grassroots organizing amid the shifting social and political sands of the late twentieth century. Their impact on U.S. foreign relations is a testament to the power of religiously inspired individuals, united in common cause, to shape national politics as well as the international order.

Notes

Introduction

1. Carl F. H. Henry, "Why 'Christianity Today'?," *Christianity Today* 1, no. 1 (October 15, 1956): 21.

2. Carl F. H. Henry, "The Fragility of Freedom in the West," *Christianity Today* 1, no. 1 (October 15, 1956): 8–9.

3. Ibid.

4. Ibid., 10–11.

5. Mark A. Noll, "The Truth from the Evangelical Viewpoint: What 'Christianity Today' Meant to the Movement 50 Years Ago," *Christianity Today* (September 29, 2006), https://www.christianitytoday.com/ct/2006/october/17.46.html (accessed February 26, 2018).

6. Ibid.

7. Billy Graham, "Biblical Authority in Evangelism," *Christianity Today* 1, no. 1 (October 15, 1956): 6.

8. Keys, *Reclaiming American Virtue*, 47, 7, 33–34.

9. National Association of Evangelicals, "Human Rights," Policy Resolution (1956), https://www.nae.net/human-rights/.

10. Keys, *Reclaiming*, 47. Keys suggests that after the protests of the 1960s and the disaster of the Vietnam War, Americans seized on international human rights as a means of putting these traumas behind them and "searching for foreign rather than homegrown monsters to slay." Although U.S. policymakers including presidents Franklin Roosevelt and Harry Truman, understood and promoted "human rights" within an international context through the Atlantic Charter, the relevant United Nations documents, and the Truman Doctrine during

the "first" modern human rights moment after World War II, nevertheless, Keys's point about the internationalization of the concept of human rights in U.S. public opinion (rather than policymaker opinion) in the 1970s stands. Samuel Moyn has noted that the first human rights moment in the 1940s passed quickly as the world powers shifted their focus to the exigencies of the Cold War. The transformation in public understanding that Keys describes in her book had significant implications for the birth of the "second" human rights moment and the transnational human rights activism that emerged in the 1970s. See Moyn, *The Last Utopia*; Mazower, "The Strange Triumph of Human Rights, 1933–1950"; Borgwardt, *A New Deal for the World*.

11. Mk. 16:15 (New Revised Standard Version [NRSV]); Mt. 28:19 (NRSV), "the great commission."

12. This oft cited number—the two billion unreached—remained essentially unchanged from the 1950s to the present. Elmo Scoggin, "Israel, the Open Door," Southern Baptist Convention press release (May 19, 1955), http://media.sbhla.org.s3.amazonaws.com/656,19-May-1955.pdf; Donald McGavran, "Will Uppsala Betray the 2 Billion?," *Church Growth Bulletin* 4/5 (May 1968): 292–97.

13. A number of scholars in religious studies, theology, and the sociology of religion have linked the era of globalization that began in the 1970s with the rapid expansion of evangelical Christianity throughout the world, and more specifically throughout the Global South. These scholars describe how the economic and cultural changes of the 1970s contributed to the spread of evangelicalism, but also note that evangelicalism itself served as a conduit or force for change within the societies through which it spread. Evangelicals themselves believed that the social changes that globalization brought created openings for evangelism among the poor and recently displaced people. See Jenkins, *The Next Christendom*; Wuthnow, *Boundless Faith*; Berger, "Four Faces of Global Culture," *National Interest* 49 (Fall 1997); Berger, "Introduction: The Cultural Dynamics of Globalization," in *Many Globalizations*, ed. Berger and Huntington, 6, 8; Hunter and Yates, "In the Vanguard of Globalization," in *Many Globalizations*, 323–58; Cox, *Fire from Heaven*; Poewe, *Charismatic Christianity as a Global Culture*.

14. The scholarly literature on the rise of the religious right is extensive. Key works include Martin, *With God On Our Side*; McGirr, *Suburban Warriors*; Williams, *God's Own Party*; Dochuk, *From Bible Belt to Sunbelt*; Schäfer, *Countercultural Conservatives*; Balmer, *Thy Kingdom*; D. G. Hart, "Mainstream Protestantism, 'Conservative' Religion, and Civil Society," in *Religion Returns to the Public Square*, ed. Heclo and McClay, 195–225; Diamond, *Spiritual Warfare*; Diamond, *Not by Politics Alone*; Hunter, *Culture Wars*; Clyde Wilcox, "Laying up Treasures in Washington and in Heaven," 23–29.

15. In this way, evangelical views were in line with those of other conservative and neo-conservative human rights advocates, who similarly opted to focus on civil and political rights (especially in totalitarian regimes). Barbara Keys provides an overview of the distinctions between liberal and conservative perspectives on human rights in her monograph, *Reclaiming American Virtue*, though she does not discuss evangelical Christian contributions to the development of conservative human rights ideals. Keys, *Reclaiming*, 4–13. For other work on the origins of conservative human rights perspectives, see Duranti, *The Conservative Human Rights Revolution*; Moyn, *Christian Human Rights*.

16. "A Summons to Justice: Interview with Carl H. F. Henry," *Christianity Today* 36, no. 8 (July 20, 1992): 40.

17. George Weigel, "Why Cable TV Is Not a Human Right," *Christianity Today* 36, no. 8 (July 20, 1992): 33.

18. After several decades of dormancy following the UN's adoption of the Universal Declaration of Human Rights in 1948, the human rights movement experienced a rebirth in the

1970s. Yet the lack of agreement over the meaning of human rights—and how the international community should protect those rights—created an opening for a wide range of perspectives to gain a hearing from legislators, policymakers, and the public. These differing views led to debates over how the United States should incorporate human rights concerns into the matrix of factors that guided its foreign policy decision making. In the process, leaders adopted aspects of the policies that these diverse groups proposed and, gradually, each successive presidential administration developed its own human rights policy. Both liberal and conservative notions of human rights informed U.S. foreign policy decisions during the Reagan administration and beyond. On the dynamics of the "second human rights moment" that emerged in the 1970s, see Keys, *Reclaiming*; Eckel and Moyn, *The Breakthrough: Human Rights in the 1970s*; Moyn, *The Last Utopia*; Iriye, Goedde, and Hitchcock, *The Human Rights Revolution*; Morgan, "The Seventies and the Rebirth of Human Rights," in *The Shock of the Global*, ed. Ferguson, Maier, Manela, and Sargent, 237–50; Snyder, *Human Rights Activism and the End of the Cold War*; Cmiel, "The Emergence of Human Rights Politics in the United States," 1231–50; Cmiel, "The Recent History of Human Rights," 117–35; Bon Tempo, "From the Center-Right: Freedom House and Human Rights in the 1970s and 1980s," in *The Human Rights Revolution*, ed. Iriye, Goedde, and Hitchcock, 223–44; Bon Tempo, "Human Rights and the U.S. Republican Party in the Late 1970s," in *The Breakthrough*, ed. Moyn and Eckel, 146–65. On the role of human rights concerns in shaping U.S. foreign policymaking, see Peck, *Ideal Illusions*; Barbara Keys, "Congress, Kissinger, and the Origins of Human Rights Diplomacy," 823–52; Sikkink, *Mixed Signals*.

19. National Association of Evangelicals, "1996 Statement of Conscience Concerning Worldwide Religious Persecution," Policy Resolution (1996), https://www.nae.net/worldwide-religious-persecution.

20. Ibid.

21. The act passed 375 to 41 in the House and 98 to 0 with 2 not voting in the Senate. It established the Office of International Religious Freedom at the State Department as well as an independent Commission on International Religious Freedom and a special adviser to the National Security Council. *International Religious Freedom Act of 1998*, Public Law 105-292 (October 27, 1998), https://www.congress.gov/105/plaws/publ292/PLAW-105publ292.pdf.

22. A number of scholars have focused attention on evangelical involvement in passing human rights legislation during the Clinton administration. Among many others, Allen Hertzke has written extensively on the International Religious Freedom Act and evangelical engagement with human rights issues, particularly those that pertain to Christian witness and religious life in repressive regimes. Though Hertzke offers a brief overview of earlier evangelical organizing on human rights issues in the introduction of his 2004 monograph *Freeing God's Children*, he focuses almost exclusively on advocacy during the 1990s. On the whole, scholarship on evangelical human rights lobbying has tended to follow suit by focusing on this later time period. See Hertzke, *Freeing God's Children*; Hertzke, "Evangelicals and International Engagement," in *Public Faith: Evangelicals and Civic Engagement*, ed. Cromartie, 215–35; Farr, "America's International Religious Freedom Policy," in *Rethinking Religion and World Affairs*, ed. Shah, Stepan, and Toft, 262–78; Nichols, "Evangelicals and Human Rights: The Continuing Ambivalence of Evangelical Christians' Support for Human Rights," 629–62; McAlister, "The Persecuted Body: Evangelical Internationalism, Islam, and the Politics of Fear," in *Facing Fear*, ed. Laffan and Weiss, 134, 150–56; Wuthnow, *Boundless Faith*, 214–15; Amstutz, *Evangelicals and American Foreign Policy*, 38–39, 75, 147–48; Castelli, "Praying for the Persecuted Church: US Christian Activism in the Global Arena," 321–51.

23. "A Summons to Justice," 40.

24. Ibid.

25. Focusing on evangelical Christians as foreign policy actors also distinguishes this book from David Hollinger's *Protestants Abroad*, which examines liberal Protestant missionaries and their influence on U.S. culture. In the 1960s and 1970s, evangelicals began to supplant liberal Protestants in the mission fields as the latter grew more concerned about avoiding cultural chauvinism and sought to cultivate a strong social justice ethos. See Hollinger, *Protestants Abroad*.

26. The diversity of evangelicalism—and thus the challenge of offering a cohesive definition of what evangelicalism is and which groups count as evangelical—is oft remarked on in the religious studies, theological, historical, and sociological literature. Evangelicalism encompasses a wide array of denominations, nondenominational churches, and subcultures, including but not limited to Pentecostals, Charismatics, Baptists, Anabaptists, Seventh-Day Adventists, fundamentalists, and neo-evangelicals. For key works on U.S. evangelicalism, see Marsden, *Understanding Fundamentalism and Evangelicalism*; Marsden, "The Evangelical Denomination," in *Piety and Politics*, ed. Neuhaus and Cromartie; Balmer, *Blessed Assurance*; Noll, *American Evangelical Christianity*; Noll, *Protestants in America*; Smith, *American Evangelicalism: Embattled and Thriving*; Miller, *The Age of Evangelicalism*; Hutchinson and Wolffe, *A Short History of Global Evangelicalism*.

27. Grenz, *Renewing the Center*, 187; Smith, "The Evangelical Kaleidoscope and the Call to Christian Unity," 125–40.

28. Marsden, *Understanding*, 2; Marsden, "The Evangelical Denomination," 60.

29. Shibley, "Contemporary Evangelicals: Born-Again and World Affirming," 69. Others have put forth more involved definitions. Scholars often cite David Bebbington's four-part definition as the standard. He states that evangelical belief consists of Biblicism (the affirmation of biblical authority), conversionism (the necessity of a personal salvation experience), crucicentrism (the centrality of Christ's crucifixion and atonement to individual salvation), and activism (the obligation to evangelize). Bebbington, *Evangelicalism in Modern Britain*, 2–17. See also Marsden, *Understanding*; Noll, *The Rise of Evangelicalism*; Berggren and Rae, "Jimmy Carter and George W. Bush: Faith, Foreign Policy, and an Evangelical Presidential Style," 611–12; National Association of Evangelicals, "What Is an Evangelical?," http://www.nae.net/church-and-faith-partners/what-is-an-evangelical (accessed November 30, 2014).

30. Scholars have commented on how the syncretism of evangelical expression has contributed to its expansion throughout the United States and abroad. Syncretism, in this case, refers to the capacity of evangelical beliefs or practices to blend with other (often local or indigenous) beliefs or practices, rendering evangelicalism more familiar and legible in other cultural contexts. Nathan Hatch suggests that during the First Great Awakening, the adaptable nature of the evangelical faith, coupled with the "nonrestrictive" culture of early America, "accelerated the process of Christianization within American popular culture, allowing indigenous expressions of faith to take hold among ordinary people, white and black." Individual, ordinary evangelicals molded the religion to suit their needs and then propagated it widely. Similarly, Harvey Cox attributes the global reach of evangelicalism (specifically Pentecostalism) to its highly syncretic nature. He argues that Charismatic evangelicalism taps into a "primal spirituality" intrinsic to all cultures. According to Cox, the "potent combination of biblical imagery and ecstatic worship unlocked existing, but often repressed religious patterns, enabling Pentecostalism to root itself in almost any culture. Not only did missionaries travel all over the globe . . . but wherever they went, the people who heard them seemed to make the message their own and fan out again." Hatch, *The Democratization of American Christianity*, 9; Cox, *Fire From Heaven*, 81, 101–2.

31. In some respects, evangelicalism in the United States matured in tandem with the state itself, reflecting and supporting republican principles as well as democratic ideals. For example,

Nathan Hatch draws important connections between the individualism of evangelicalism and democratic values in the United States by highlighting the self-governing organization structures of evangelical churches as well as the emphasis on the ability of ordinary individuals to interpret the Bible for themselves. Hatch, *Democratization*, 10–13. For other works on early evangelicalism and U.S. culture, see Noll, *Rise*; Wacker, *Heaven Below*; Heyrman, *Southern Cross*; Preston, *Sword of the Spirit*; *Shield of Faith*, 11–13, 92–101; Lynerd, *Republican Theology*. On evangelicalism and U.S. culture (and politics) in the modern era, see Miller, *Age of Evangelicalism*; Boyer, *When Time Shall Be No More*; Finke and Stark, *The Churching of America, 1776–2005*; Martin, *With God on Our Side*; Walter Russell Mead, "God's Country?" See also Woodberry, "The Missionary Roots of Liberal Democracy," 244–74.

32. Kidd argues that the intrinsic evangelical commitment to the "individual right of conscience" led early U.S. evangelicals to become some of the most ardent advocates for religious liberty, the rights of religious dissenters, and religious disestablishment. In this manner, he suggests, the revivals of the Second Great Awakening "helped align many former [evangelical] radicals with the developing Patriot movement." Kidd, *The Great Awakening*, 287.

33. Ibid., 302, 323; Hutchinson and Wolffe, *Global Evangelicalism*, 70–75; Noll, *America's God*, 182–85, 197–98; Marty, *Protestantism in the United States*; Abzug, *Cosmos Crumbling*. Furthermore, as the Institute for the Study of American Evangelicals (ISAE) notes, "By the 1820s evangelical Protestantism was by far the dominant expression of Christianity in the overwhelmingly Protestant United States." Larry Eskridge, "Defining Evangelicalism," ISAE (2006), http://web. archive.org/web/20150218035525/http://wheaton.edu/ISAE/Defining-Evangelicalism (accessed December 20, 2014).

34. Such as the Fundamentalist-Modernist Controversy of the early twentieth century, which pitted those committed to protecting the "fundamentals" of Christian doctrine, including the inerrancy and literalism of the Bible, against those advocating for more liberal interpretations of the Bible as well as acceptance of cultural modernity. According to Walter Russell Meade, this controversy split U.S. Protestantism into three strands, with evangelicals representing a third way between fundamentalism and liberalism. Accordingly, though evangelicals and fundamentalists shared essentially the same theological beliefs, evangelicals continued to engage with the wider world, while separatist fundamentalists tended to retreat inward. Meade, "God's Country?"

35. Eskridge, "Defining the Term in Contemporary Times," ISAE (2006), http://web.archive. org/web/20150218035525/http://wheaton.edu/ISAE/Defining-Evangelicalism/Defining-the-Term. See also Meade, "God's Country?" That said, although most modern evangelicals are not fundamentalists, many fundamentalists do consider themselves evangelical; many scholars, including George Marsden, consider fundamentalism a strand of evangelicalism, much as they consider Pentecostalism part of evangelicalism.

36. Ibid. This inclination grew more pronounced among fundamentalists after the torrent of ridicule their beliefs suffered in the media during the 1925 Scopes Trial.

37. Ibid.

38. This is not to say that other religious movements, such as Mormonism, did not engage in global evangelism during the period under study, but for doctrinal reasons these groups do not fall under the category of evangelical, did not consistently align themselves with the evangelical Protestant foreign policy agenda, and did not exercise the political power that evangelical Christians did beginning in the late 1970s. As such, they fall outside the bounds of this particular study.

39. Jenkins, Shaw, and Robert argue that owing in part to decolonization and in part to the expansion of Pentecostalism, the locus of Christianity has shifted to the Global South in recent decades. Wuthnow debates the significance of this shift southward by arguing that U.S. churches

and evangelical culture retain an outsize influence on these local churches. Still, he emphasizes that globalization has fostered linkages between evangelical Christians in the United States and their southern counterparts that have facilitated the export of U.S.-style evangelicalism abroad. Jenkins, *The Next Christendom*; Shaw, *Global Awakening*; Dana L. Robert, "Shifting Southward: Global Christianity Since 1945," *International Bulletin of Missionary Research* 24, no. 2 (April 2000): 50–58; Wuthnow, *Boundless Faith*.

40. Pierson, "The Rise of Christian Mission and Relief Agencies," in *The Influence of Faith*, ed. Abrams, 169.

41. Hollinger, *After Cloven Tongues of Fire*, 72; Dow, "Romance in a Marriage of Convenience: The Missionary Factor in Early Cold War U.S.-Ethiopian Relations, 1941–1960," 861, fn. 8; Mead, *Special Providence*, 142; Hutchison, *Errand to the World*, 193.

42. This was true of missionaries in the nineteenth as well as the twentieth century. See Preston, *Sword*, 191; Reed, *The Missionary Mind and American East Asia Policy, 1911–1915*, 126; Amstutz, *Evangelicals*, 66.

43. Preston, *Sword*, 190–91.

44. Preston suggests that evangelical internationalism emerged out of the worldwide social and political upheavals of the 1960s. He argues that with the world in turmoil, evangelicals sought to deal with the realities of globalization by hearkening to traditional values. Accordingly, "the evangelical worldview . . . was based on what appeared to be a series of internal contradictions that made perfect sense to its adherents: peace through strength, universal nationalism, the promotion of both local autonomy and globalization, and saving the world despite the imminence of end times. Most paradoxically of all, evangelical internationalism combined a fierce traditionalism with a subtle recognition that circumstances had changed forever." McAlister uses "evangelical internationalism" more specifically to mean the international outreach efforts of individual evangelicals as well as evangelical NGOs in the form of humanitarian interventions as well as foreign policy advocacy for Christians living in troubled parts of the world. Preston, "Evangelical Internationalism: A Conservative Worldview for the Age of Globalization," in *The Right Side of the Sixties*, ed. Gifford and Williams, 223; McAlister, "The Persecuted Body"; McAlister, "What Is Your Heart For? Affect and Internationalism in the Evangelical Public Sphere," 870–95.

45. In describing the diverse and often uncoordinated evangelical organizing efforts around foreign policy issues as an example of political lobbying, I rely on the scholarship of Daniel Hofrenning, Kay Lehman Schlozman, and John Tierney, among others. In their work on political organizing Schlozman and Tierney employ the useful category of "organized interests" rather than "interest groups" in order to capture the broad range of political activity that occurs both within and outside of specific membership or activist organizations. In his book on religious lobbying, Daniel Hofrenning adapts this term by classifying politically active religious groups and individuals as "organized religious interests" in order to encompass "membership organizations, coalitions of membership organizations, and large denominations," as well as educational think tanks. This book similarly uses the notion of organized interests broadly, surveying the congressional and presidential lobbying efforts of large membership organizations such as the NAE, activist organizations such as Christian Response International, religious denominations such as the Southern Baptist Convention, and individual leaders such as Billy Graham. Much like Allen Hertzke, I also examine the work of professional evangelical lobbyists based in Washington, D.C. See Schlozman and Tierney, *Organized Interests and American Democracy*; Hofrenning, *In Washington but Not of It*, 21–22; Hertzke, *Representing God in Washington*; Schlozman, Verba, and Brady, *The Unheavenly Chorus*, 320–21; Weber and Stanley, "The Power and Performance of Religious Interest Groups," 28.

46. This basic supposition grounds my argument from a theological as well as an ideological standpoint. Here, I build off of (but diverge from) the work of Joel Nichols and Allen Hertzke, which links the evangelical commitment to fulfilling the Great Commission with support for international religious freedom during the 1990s. As Nichols notes, "Because of evangelicals' emphasis on the Great Commission and the attendant emphasis on conversion as cognitive assent, evangelicals have a particular need to be able to speak freely and persuade others of the truth of their religion. Any persecution of coreligionists necessarily stifles the opportunities for such evangelism (by suppressing both the co-religionists' right to share their faith and the potential recipients' right to hear) that is core to evangelical theology." This book diverges from Nichols and Hertzke in providing a different periodization of evangelical engagement with human rights issues as well as an argument for the existence of an evangelical human rights vision separate from one based solely on Western or Enlightenment-era ideals. Nichols, "Evangelicals and Human Rights," 630; Hertzke, *Freeing*. See also Ferrari, "Proselytism and Human Rights," in *Christianity and Human Rights*, ed. Witte and Alexander, 258.

47. There is an extensive body of literature on religion in the domestic and foreign affairs of the early republic, but scholars had, until recently, largely neglected to account for the persistence of this connection between foreign policy and religious rhetoric, values, and interest groups in the modern United States. Part of this lies in the inherent methodological challenges of using religion as a means for analyzing or understanding foreign policymaking. For articles that discuss the pitfalls and potential rewards of incorporating religion in the study of diplomatic history, see Ribuffo, "Religion and American Foreign Policy: The Story of a Complex Relationship," 36–51; Hill, "Religion as a Category of Diplomatic Analysis," 633–40; Preston, "Bridging the Gap between the Sacred and the Secular in the History of American Foreign Relations," 783–812.

48. See, for example, Preston, *Sword*, 4–13; McAlister, *Epic Encounters*; Settje, *Lutherans and the Longest War*; Gunn, *Spiritual Weapons*; Inboden, *Religion and American Foreign Policy*; Herzog, *The Spiritual-Industrial Complex*; Rotter, "Christians, Muslims, and Hindus: Religion and U.S.-South Asian Relations, 1947–1954," 593–613; Thomas, *The Global Resurgence of Religion and the Transformation of International Relations*; Martin, "The Christian Right and American Foreign Policy," 66–80.

1. A Global Shift in Missionary Christianity

1. Billy Graham, "Why Lausanne?," *Christianity Today* (September 13, 1974): 4–5.

2. Ibid., 4.

3. Tizon, *Transformation after Lausanne*: 54–58; Robert, "The Great Commission in an Age of Globalization," in *The Antioch Agenda*, ed. Jeyaraj, Pazmino, and Petersen, 6–7. The debate over this crisis of missions raged throughout the 1960s and 1970s in academic journals and Christian periodicals, as well as at major interdenominational conferences. For one key exchange between an ecumenical author (Linnenbrink) and two evangelical leaders (Lindsell and McGavran), see Günter Linnenbrink, "Witness and Service in the Mission of the Church," *International Review of Mission* 54, no. 216 (October 1, 1965): 428–36; Harold Lindsell, "A Rejoinder," *International Review of Mission* 54, no. 216 (October 1, 1965): 437–40; Donald McGavran, "Wrong Strategy: The Real Crisis in Missions," *International Review of Mission* 54, no. 216 (October 1, 1965): 451–61. See also Kaj Baago, "The Post-Colonial Crisis of Missions," *International Review of Missions* 55, no. 219 (July 1, 1966): 322–32; Ian Henderson Douglas and

John Braisted Carman, "'Post-Colonial Crisis of Missions' Comments," *International Review of Mission* 55, no. 220 (October 1, 1966): 483–89.

4. Harold Lindsell, "Lausanne 74: An Appraisal," *Christianity Today* (September 13, 1974), 21; Billy Graham, "My Hope for the World Congress on Evangelism," Congress Bulletin (November 1966), Collection 459 Records of the Fellowship Foundation, Box 490, Folder 19, Billy Graham Center Archives (hereafter BGCA), Wheaton, IL.

5. Donald McGavran, "A. Criticism of the WCC Working Draft on Mission 1. Will Uppsala Betray the Two Billion?," reprinted in McGavran, *Eye of the Storm*, 233. Originally published in *Church Growth Bulletin*, Special Uppsala Issue, May 1968.

6. John Stott, "C. Defense and Further Debate 3. Does Section Two Provide Sufficient Emphasis on World Evangelism?," reprinted in McGavran, *Eye of the Storm*, 266–68.

7. Donald McGavran, "C. Defense and Further Debate 5. Uppsala's 'Program for Mission' and Church Growth," 275, reprinted in McGavran, *Eye of the Storm*, 273–79.

8. Stott, "Defense," 268.

9. Finke and Stark, *The Churching of America*, 246; Jenkins, *The Next Christendom*, 51.

10. Robert, "Shifting Southward: Global Christianity since 1945," 53.

11. Ibid.

12. Finke and Stark, *Churching*, 246; "The Missionary Retreat," *Christianity Today* 26, no. 2 (November 19, 1971): 26.

13. Cox, *Fire from Heaven*, 78; Robeck, *The Azusa Street Mission & Revival*, 280.

14. "The Missionary Retreat," 26; Bühlmann, *The Coming of the Third Church*, 22. Bühlmann first published this book in German in 1974.

15. Graham, *Just as I Am*, 561. Graham noted that "a beginning had been made in 1951 with the founding of the World Evangelical Fellowship. Its membership was limited, however; and many evangelicals, particularly in the traditional mainline churches, were not associated with it."

16. Ibid., 561–67.

17. William F. Willoughby, "The New Evangelical Surge," *Christianity Today* 25, no. 17 (May 21, 1971): 41; William F. Willoughby, "The NAE: New Marching Orders?," *Christianity Today* 25, no. 16 (May 7, 1971): 37.

18. On the significance of the ICOWE to these developments from the evangelical perspective, see Beuttler, "Evangelical Missions in Modern America," in *The Great Commission*, ed. Klauber and Manetsch, 126–27.

19. The literature on evangelical internationalism in the late twentieth century is still in its formative stage. It comes in marked contrast to the prevailing literature on how conservative U.S. political and religious groups engaged with globalization during this period, which tends to assume that conservative Christians operated with a traditionalist and isolationist mind-set. Here the distinctions between fundamentalist and evangelical Christians become particularly important; though both groups espoused a conservative ideology—hence the tendency to lump them together in popular discourse—evangelicalism had, by its very nature, an outward-looking focus. Andrew Preston describes this evangelical internationalism as "a conservative belief that global engagement was unavoidable, even desirable, but that it must unfold on American terms and without compromising American values," based on "peace through strength, universal nationalism, the promotion of both local autonomy and globalization, and [the necessity of] saving the world despite the imminence of end times." He contrasts this outlook with that of fundamentalist Christians, who retained an entrenched isolationism throughout the 1960s. See Preston, "Evangelical Internationalism," in *The Right Side of the Sixties*, ed. Gifford and Williams, 223, 235. For other works on evangelical internationalism, see McAlister, "What Is

Your Heart For?," 870–95; Swartz, "Embodying the Global Soul," 887–901; King, "The New Internationalists," 922–49.

20. "Evangelism Meeting Set, Graham Says," *Washington Post* (August 26, 1972): B11.

21. Billy Graham, "The Twentieth Century: Advance or Retreat?," International Congress on World Evangelization Feature Press Pack, Collection 345 BGEA: Media Office Records, Box 64, Folder 64–11, BGCA.

22. Russell Chandler, "World Evangelization in Vogue, Five Diverse Congresses Planned," *Los Angeles Times* (July 6, 1974): 22; John Dart, "Thousands Jam Explo 74 in Seoul Despite Political Storm Clouds," *Los Angeles Times* (August 17, 1974): 25.

23. Russell Chandler, "3 Offer Plans to Spread Gospel for Study at World Congress," *Los Angeles Times* (February 16, 1974): A27. Chandler also noted in this article, "evangelicals traditionally have been wary of groups that would commit them to organic unity," which made the stated intentions of the ICOWE to create a global evangelical network all the more unusual and noteworthy.

24. "Evangelism to Meet World Needs," *Chicago Defender* (August 4, 1973): 25; Chandler, "3 Offer," A27.

25. Preston, *Sword of the Spirit, Shield of Faith*, 191.

26. Ibid. For this reason, historians have argued that Christianity played a key role in laying the foundation for modern empires, including "informal" empires such as that of the United States. The literature on mission and empire in the modern era is massive, with particularly rich scholarship on Christianity and colonialism in the British and Spanish empires. A brief selection includes Comaroff and Comaroff, *Of Revelation and Revolution*, Volume 1; Porter, *Religion versus Empire?*; Muldoon, *The Americas in the Spanish World Order*. For Christianity, U.S. imperialism, and cultural exchange in the late nineteenth and early twentieth centuries, see Hutchison, *Errand to the World*; Reed, *The Missionary Mind and American East Asia Policy*; Walls, *The Cross-Cultural Process in Christian History*; Dunch, "Beyond Cultural Imperialism," 301–25; Harris, "Cultural Imperialism and American Protestant Missionaries," 309–38; Schlesinger, "The Missionary Enterprise and Theories of Imperialism," in *The Missionary Enterprise in China and America*, ed. Fairbank, 336–73.

27. Mt. 28:16–20 (New Revised Standard Version), "the great commission." See also Mt. 24:14; Mk. 13:10, 16:15.

28. "The Lausanne Covenant," in *Let the Earth Hear His Voice: International Congress on World Evangelization, Lausanne, Switzerland Official Reference Volume*, ed. J. D. Douglas (Minneapolis, MN: World Wide Publications, 1975), 8–9; Wilmore, *Last Things First*, 47–48; see also Mt. 24; Mk. 13:10; Heb. 9:28; Rev. 20:7–10 and 21:1–5.

29. Mk. 13:10 and 13:26; "The Lausanne Covenant," 9; Mt. 28:16–20 describes the Great Commission.

30. The term "two-thirds world" came into evangelical parlance in the mid-1970s partly because of this extraordinary population growth; rather than referring to the combined regions of Africa, Asia, and Latin America region as the "Third World," Christians used "two-thirds world" to denote the proportion of the global population in these regions, as well as the proportion of those in the world living in poverty.

31. David Barrett, "AD 2000: 350 Million Christians in Africa," *International Review of Mission* 59, no. 233 (January 1970): 49. Barrett's projections were not far off. Though the studies are not directly comparable, a Pew Foundation study on Global Christianity showed that in 2010, the Global North had a population of approximately 856 million Christians while the Global South had about 1.3 billion. Pew Forum on Religion & Public Life, "Global Christianity: A Report on the Size and Distribution of the World's Christian Population," 14.

32. Barrett, "AD 2000," 50.

33. Missiologists and theologians of all stripes cited Barrett's study in statements on the future of world missions. See R. Pierce Beaver, "Christian Mission, a Look into the Future," *Concordia Theological Monthly* 42, no. 6 (June 1, 1971): 350; Donald McGavran, "Great Debate in Missions," *Calvin Theological Journal* 5, no. 2 (November 1, 1970): 176–77.

34. Willoughby, "Evangelical Surge," 40.

35. Billy Graham, Congress on World Evangelism Planning Committee, "The World Congress on Evangelism 1971–1972," meeting minutes (February 6–7, 1970), Washington, D.C., Collection 345 BGEA: Media Office Records, Box 63, Folder 63–10, BGCA.

36. Graham, *Just as I Am*, 568; BGCA, "International Congress on World Evangelization— Collection 53," http://www.wheaton.edu/bgc/archives/GUIDES/053.htm#3 (accessed November 21, 2010).

37. Billy Graham, "Let the Earth Hear His Voice," in *Let the Earth Hear His Voice*, 16–17.

38. Congress on World Evangelism Planning Committee, "The World Congress on Evangelism 1971–1972," meeting minutes (February 7, 1970), Washington, D.C., Collection 345 BGEA: Media Office Records, Box 63, Folder 63-10, BGCA. These planning committee discussions reflected the growing interest and concern that U.S. and European evangelicals evinced as they observed the changes in the two-thirds world. Some believed that if they did not find a way to partner effectively with African, Asian, and Latin American churches, their ability to participate in the evangelistic mission of the church might wither away. See also W. Dayton Roberts, "Looking Beyond Lausanne," June 14, 1973, Collection 338 Records of the World Evangelical Fellowship, Box 4, Folder 3, BGCA.

39. Chapman, "Evangelical International Relations in the Post-Colonial World," 357.

40. Chandler, "3 Offer," A27.

41. Graham, *Just as I Am*, 569.

42. Arthur Matthews, "To Pray, to Plan . . . to Work Together," International Congress on World Evangelization Press Release (August 15, 1974), 3. Collection 345 BGEA: Media Office Records, Box 65, Folder 65-9, BGCA.

43. Paul Little, "Looking Ahead to Lausanne," *Christianity Today* 28, no. 4 (November 23, 1973): 6.

44. Tizon, *Transformation*, 37.

45. Little, "Looking Ahead," 6.

46. Ibid.

47. Record of Discussion Meeting Relative to Explo '74 NRB (Ben Armstrong), Campus Crusade for Christ, April 8, 1974, Collection 309 Records of the National Religious Broadcasters, Box 72, Folder 2, BGCA.

48. Graham, *Just as I Am*, 571.

49. Matthews, "To Pray, to Plan."

50. A committee consisting of John Stott, Samuel Escobar, and Hudson Armerding presented a revised version at the congress. Stott, *Making Christ Known*, 5.

51. Congress Research Committee, *World Congress Country Profiles* (Monrovia, CA: Missions Advanced Research & Communication Center, 1974); "Evangelistic Strategy Papers and Reports," in *Let the Earth Hear His Voice*, 483–982; "Geographical Reports," in *Let the Earth Hear His Voice*, 1318–461.

52. Graham, "Why Lausanne?," 22.

53. Ibid., 26.

54. Ibid., 34.

55. Ibid., 28.

56. Graham, "Why Lausanne?," 30.

57. David J. Cho, "Missions Structures," in *Let the Earth Hear His Voice*, 501. See also David J. Cho, "My Pilgrimage in Mission," last modified September 10, 2010, http://davidcho.org/archives/282.

58. Ernest W. Oliver, "Missions Strategy," in *Let the Earth Hear His Voice*, 494; S. O. Odunaike, "Inter-Mission Relationships," in *Let the Earth Hear His Voice*, 522.

59. "The Lausanne Covenant," 5.

60. C. René Padilla, "Evangelism and the World," in *Let the Earth Hear His Voice*, 125.

61. Ibid.

62. Ibid.

63. Ibid.

64. Padilla, "Evangelism," 121.

65. Ibid., 126, 139.

66. Ibid., 121.

67. Though not mentioned explicitly in the congress papers, the influence of theological movements in Latin America, such as Gustavo Gutiérrez's Liberation Theology, which called on Christians to join in God's efforts to end injustice in the world, and the Medellín Conference of 1968, which emphasized the integral role that promoting justice and peace played in the Christian mission, provide a crucial backdrop to the ideas that Padilla discussed.

68. Padilla, "Evangelism," 136.

69. C. René Padilla, interview by Paul Ericksen, March 12, 1987, Collection 361 Carlos Rene Padilla, T3 Transcript, BGCA, https://www2.wheaton.edu/bgc/archives/trans/361T03.htm (accessed November 18, 2010).

70. Padilla, "Evangelism," 136; Padilla, Interview, March 12, 1987.

71. Donald McGavran, "The Dimensions of World Evangelization," in *Let the Earth Hear His Voice*, 94–95.

72. Ibid., 96.

73. Ibid., 99–100.

74. Ibid., 106–7.

75. McGavran, "Dimensions," 106, 111

76. Ibid., 109.

77. Ralph Winter, "The Highest Priority: Cross-Cultural Evangelism," in *Let the Earth Hear His Voice*, 213, 232. In this formulation, Winter included Catholics among the nominal Christians and defined the unreached as Muslims, Hindus, Buddhists, and so on who did not reside near any Christians.

78. Ibid., 214–16, 220.

79. Jacob Loewen, "Response to Dr. Ralph D. Winter's Paper," in *Let the Earth Hear His Voice*, 247. Loewen cited Acts 1:8 as biblical evidence for near-neighbor evangelism.

80. Ibid., 250.

81. Ibid., 250–51.

82. Winter, "The Highest Priority," 227–29.

83. Ibid., 228.

84. "The Lausanne Covenant," 1–9. The text of the covenant is available at http://www.lausanne.org/covenant

85. Ibid., 6–7.

86. Stott, "1974: The Lausanne Covenant, with an Exposition and Commentary," in *Making Christ Known*, ed. Stott, 36, 42.

87. Samuel Escobar, "Evangelism and Man's Search for Freedom, Justice and Fulfillment," in *Let the Earth Hear His Voice*, 304.

88. "The Lausanne Covenant," 4–5.

89. Russell Chandler, "Alternative Style of Faith Pledged by New Evangelical Fellowship," *Los Angeles Times* (July 26, 1974): A14.

90. Lindsell, "Lausanne," 26.

91. Graham, *Just as I Am*, 573.

92. Ibid.

93. Over 90 percent of the participants voted to establish some means for continuing the discussions begun at the congress and 72 percent supported the creation of a continuation committee to organize future conferences. Stott, *Making*, xv.

94. Lausanne Continuation Committee, "'Forward from Lausanne' Draft of a Statement on the Future Plans of the Lausanne Committee," Appendix IX of the Lausanne Continuation Committee (January 20–23, 1975), BGCA, https://www2.wheaton.edu/bgc/archives/docs/Lausanne/704/app09a.htm (accessed October 6, 2010).

95. Lausanne Continuation Committee, "Minutes of the Lausanne Continuation Committee" (January 23, 1975), BGCA, https://www2.wheaton.edu/bgc/archives/docs/Lausanne/704/min08.htm (accessed October 6, 2010), 8, 15; Lausanne Continuation Committee, "Minutes of the Lausanne Continuation Committee" (January 22, 1975), BGCA, https://www2.wheaton.edu/bgc/archives/docs/Lausanne/704/min07.htm (accessed October 6, 2010), 7; Graham, *Just as I Am*, 573.

96. Lausanne Continuation Committee, "Minutes of the Lausanne Continuation Committee" (January 21, 1975), BGCA, https://www2.wheaton.edu/bgc/archives/docs/Lausanne/704/min02.htm (accessed October 6, 2010), 2.

97. Stott, *Making*, xvi, xviii–xx.

98. Gottfried Osei-Mensah, "The World Evangelical Fellowship," August 24, 1977, Collection 338 Records of the World Evangelical Fellowship, Box 4, Folder 3, BGCA.

99. The Consultation on World Evangelization, "The Thailand Statement," June 16–27, 1980, reprinted in Stott, *Making*, 162; "Lausanne Occasional Paper 24," reprinted in Stott, *Making*, 164.

100. G. B. K. Owusu, "Ghana Participants at Lausanne Congress Plan Mammoth Gospel Crusade," *Christian Messenger: Ghana's Oldest Christian Paper* IV, no. 8 (August 1974), Collection 345 Records of the Media Office, Box 65, Folder: ICOWE Miscellaneous, BGCA.

101. Russell Chandler, "World Evangelism Group Tallies Results," *Los Angeles Times* (June 4, 1977), A29. Leaders from the Global South planned and participated in more than half of the Lausanne-affiliated evangelical gatherings that occurred between the 1974 ICOWE and 1989 Congress in Manila.

102. Although all evangelical denominations embrace the core beliefs discussed in the introduction, their practices and governing structures differ. These variations are complex and beyond the scope of this book. As a brief example, where Presbyterians baptize infants with a sprinkling or pouring of water, Baptists fully immerse professing believers (generally adults) in water; where Pentecostals believe the Holy Spirit bestows miraculous gifts such as speaking in tongues on present-day believers, most Baptists do not believe this happens in the present time.

103. Chandler, "Alternative," A15.

104. W. E. Johnson, "Maintaining Spiritual Identity in the Midst of Fast Growth," *Evangel* 59, no. 43 (January 12, 1970): 12.

105. Southern Baptist Foreign Mission Board, "Report of Findings Committee, Consultation on Foreign Missions, Foreign Mission Board, Southern Baptist Convention, Miami Beach, FL (June 4–8, 1975)," 4, Southern Baptist Convention Foreign Mission Board Historical Files AR 551-8, Box 2, Folder 23, Southern Baptist Historical Library and Archives, Nashville, TN (hereafter

SBHLA); Southern Baptist Foreign Mission Board, "Foreign Missions Looks toward 2000 A.D.," January 13, 1976, John David Hughey Papers, AR 711, Box 6, Folder 1, SBHLA.

106. Winston Crawley, "Report to the Board, SUBJECT: 'Moratorium,' (November 1977)," John David Hughey Papers, AR 711, Box 6, Folder 1, SBHLA.

107. Ibid, 3.

108. Southern Baptist Foreign Mission Board, "SUBJECT: Indigenous Church Strength (March 1979)," John David Hughey Papers, AR 711, Box 6, Folder 1, SBHLA.

109. Neigel Scarborough, "A Strategy for the Indigenous Church," *Evangel* 59, no. 43 (January 12, 1970): 13. Some of this desire to establish indigenous churches stemmed from geopolitical concerns. As W. E. Johnson noted, "The ultimate goal of the Church of God is to train and prepare people of other cultures and other lands in the true doctrines of the Church of God so that when nationalism or any other circumstances has driven Americans out of their countries they can carry on the work of the church; and that day will come if the Lord tarries." Johnson, "Maintaining Spiritual Identity," 12. See also Bühlmann, *Third Church*, 48–49.

110. S. E. Arnold, "Ghana: A Need to Harness Indigenous Talent," *Evangel* 59, no. 43 (January 12, 1970): 23–24; T. R. Morse, "West Indies: Placing Nationals in Strategic Positions," *Evangel* 59, no. 43 (January 12, 1970): 24; Lovell R. Cary, "Asia: Mobilizing the Asian Church for Evangelism," *Evangel* 59, no. 43 (January 12, 1970): 24–25.

111. Johnson, "Maintaining Spiritual Identity," 11; Southern Baptist Foreign Mission Board, "Report of Findings," 9.

112. Southern Baptist Foreign Mission Board, "Foreign Missions," 41.

113. Ibid., 4. This is a reference to Mk. 12:28–32, in which Jesus proclaims that the greatest commandment is to "love the Lord your God with all your heart, and with all your soul, and with all your mind, and with all your strength," and that the second greatest commandment is to "love your neighbor as yourself."

114. Southern Baptist Foreign Mission Board, "Foreign Missions," 25.

115. Ibid. The report noted this explicitly, describing SBC programs for "Hunger Relief and Disaster Response" as *"consistent* with the biblical imperative of the Great Commission," and *"complementary* and *supportive* of our role in evangelism and church development." Southern Baptist Foreign Mission Board, "Foreign Missions," 27.

116. Ibid. Pentecostal denominations embarked on similar programs for disaster relief, with similar evangelistic motivations and with a similar outcome of fostering greater connectivity between Pentecostals throughout the world. Like the Southern Baptists, the Church of God viewed this work as a form of Christian witness, or "love in action." See, for example, T. L. Forester, "Love Shows," *Save Our World* 15, no. 2 (Summer 1976): 3.

117. Armstrong, *The Electric Church*, 63, 77–78, 103. Armstrong held leadership roles as Director of Trans World Radio and as Executive Director of the National Religious Broadcasters, where he worked from 1966 to 1989.

118. Wagner, "'Full Gospel' Radio: Revivaltime and the Pentecostal Uses of Mass Media, 1950–1979," 107–22; "History Highlights of the Assemblies of God Radio-TV Department, 1945–1987," Flower Pentecostal Heritage Center, Assemblies of God, Springfield, MO (hereafter FPHC); John Seregrow to George M. Flattery, December 4, 1973, Folder: Russia (1970–1979), Assemblies of God World Missions Archives, FPHC.

119. Southern Baptist Foreign Mission Board, "Foreign Missions," 16.

120. Ibid., 17.

121. Armstrong, *Electric*, 177.

122. Gordon Conwell Theological Seminary Center for the Study of Global Christianity, "Christianity in Its Global Context, 1970–2020: Society, Religion, and Mission" (June 2013): 16–19.

123. For a sampling of the extensive media coverage on these churches and movements in mainstream newspapers, see Leslie Berkman, "The Church That Chuck Built," *Los Angeles Times* (May 6, 1973): OC1; Mary Barber, "Protestant Church Feels Impact of Evangelic Tide," *Los Angeles Times* (August 24, 1975): SE1; Kenneth F. Bunting, "Christian Movement Reaches Millions on Air Waves," *Los Angeles Times* (January 7, 1979): B1; Louis Cassel, "The Jesus People," *Chicago Daily Defender* (March 27, 1971): 36; David Fortney, "The Jesus People: Their Now Crusade Gains Followers," *Chicago Tribune* (July 4, 1971): 1; Russell Chandler, "Jesus Movement Still Going Strong," *Los Angeles Times* (December 13, 1975): 34. For coverage in religious publications, see Russell Chandler, "Top '71 Religious News: World Revival," *Christianity Today* 16, no. 7 (January 7, 1972): 40–41; "The Jesus Movement: 'An Uncommon Morning Freshness,'" *Evangel* 61, no. 12 (August 23, 1971): 31.

124. Given the secrecy of the Fellowship Foundation's operations, scholarship on its activities is quite thin. In 2003, the foundation restricted access to its archives, closing all files less than twenty-five years old. For background on the Fellowship Foundation, see Sharlet, *The Family: The Secret Fundamentalism at the Heart of American Power*; Lindsay, "Is the National Prayer Breakfast Surrounded by a 'Christian Mafia'?," 390–419; Lindsay, "Organizational Liminality and Interstitial Creativity," 163–84; "Records of the Fellowship Foundation—Collection 459," BGCA, http://www2.wheaton.edu/bgc/archives/GUIDES/459.htm.

125. The foundation went by various names over the course of its early history, including the National Committee for Christian Leadership, International Christian Leadership, and the International Council for Christian Leadership. Vereides incorporated the Fellowship Foundation in 1945 so as to allow for the collection of donations, and in 1972, the board officially changed the name of the organization to the Fellowship Foundation. Members of the Fellowship Foundation often referred to it simply as "the family." Fellowship member Rev. Richard C. Halverson— board chairman of World Vision, senior pastor of Fourth Presbyterian Church, and later Senate chaplain—worked closely with Doug Coe and played an important role in coordinating the Senate and House prayer meetings and the National Prayer Breakfast. See "Records of the Fellowship Foundation," BGCA.

126. The concept of the (nondenominational) prayer meetings "was to bring together civic and business leaders informally to share a meal, study the Bible and develop relationships of trust and support and to promote Christian principles." See "Records of the Fellowship Foundation," BGCA. At the request of the Nixon administration, the foundation changed the name of the Presidential Prayer Breakfast to the National Prayer Breakfast in 1970. Memo, Dwight L. Chapin to H. R. Haldeman, "The Presidential Prayer Breakfast," November 23, 1970, Folder RM2 Prayers—Prayer Periods [1-69/12-70] 2 of 2, Box 3, White House Central Files Subject Files RM Religious Matters, Richard Nixon Presidential Library and Museum, Yorba Linda, CA.

127. Fellowship Foundation, Inc., "The Idea in Brief," December 1, 1968, Collection 459 Records of the Fellowship Foundation, Box 548, Folder 8, BGCA; Douglas Coe to George E. Swanson, August 9, 1965, Collection 459 Records of the Fellowship Foundation, Box 254, Folder 26, BGCA.

128. Fellowship Foundation, Inc., "The Idea in Brief," January 11, 1972, Collection 459 Records of the Fellowship Foundation, Box 548, Folder 8, BGCA.

129. "Fellowship Foundation By-Laws, Revised to February 4, 1970," Collection 459 Records of the Fellowship Foundation, Box 541, Folder 14, BGCA.

130. Minutes, Congressional Core Meeting #1, n.d. [ca. 1972–73], Collection 459 Records of the Fellowship Foundation, Box 378, Folder 9, BGCA.

131. Harold H. Hughes to H. F. Oppenheimer, November 13, 1973, Collection 459 Records of the Fellowship Foundation, Box 254, Folder 26, BGCA.

132. Ibid.

133. Rev. I. R. M. Main to Louis C. Kramp, December 5, 1973, Collection 459 Records of the Fellowship Foundation, Box 254, Folder 26, BGCA.

134. Enclosure, Rev. I. R. Main to Louis C. Kramp, December 5, 1973, "Visit of John Dellenback and Dick Hightower to South Africa and Botswana, November 20–24, 1973," Collection 459 Records of the Fellowship Foundation, Box 254, Folder 26, BGCA.

135. Ibid., 5.

136. Ibid., 6.

137. See Collection 459 Records of the Fellowship Foundation, Boxes 176–266 at the BGCA for the voluminous correspondence between members of the Washington Core and their contacts in other countries.

138. Harold Hughes to Yakov Aleksandrovich Malik, April 18, 1974, Collection 459 Records of the Fellowship Foundation, Box 263, Folder 59, BGCA.

139. Douglas Coe to Yakov Aleksandrovich Malik, December 20, 1974, Collection 459 Records of the Fellowship Foundation, Box 263, Folder 59, BGCA.

140. Memorandum, Douglas Coe to Richard Nixon, "Briefing on men in positions of responsibility, in various nations throughout the world, who are interested in strengthening the ties of friendship on a spiritual basis, and who are giving leadership in their own countries in groups similar to the U.S. Senate and House of Representatives Prayer groups," n.d. [ca. 1972–1974], Collection 459 Records of the Fellowship Foundation, Box 444, Folder 1, BGCA.

141. "Statements Concerning Effective Communications with the Worldwide Family," Collection 459 Records of the Fellowship Foundation, Box 513, Folder 1, BGCA.

142. Ibid., 2.

143. Ibid., 4.

144. Graham, "Why Lausanne?," 5.

145. Mt. 24: 13–14 (NSRV).

146. That said, many evangelicals also believed that Jesus might return at any time, whether or not they had completed the evangelistic task set forth in the Great Commission. Regardless of this difference of interpretation, they shared in the common evangelical conviction that they must work toward world evangelization as swiftly as possible.

2. The Communications Revolution and Evangelical Internationalism

1. John Fear, "Strategy Report Mass Media," in *Let the Earth Hear His Voice*, 598.

2. Ibid., 600. For recent work on U.S. evangelicals as early adopters of media and technology for use in proselytizing, see Stoneman, "Global Radio Broadcasting and the Dynamics of American Evangelicalism," 1139–70; Stoneman, "Preparing the Soil for Global Revival: Station HCJB's Radio Circle, 1949–1959," 114–55; Sutton, *Aimee Semple McPherson and the Resurrection of Christian America*; Wagner, "'Full Gospel Radio,' Revivaltime and the Pentecostal Uses of Mass Media, 1950–1979," 107–22.

3. Phillip Butler, "Evangelism and the Media: A Theological Basis for Action," in *Let the Earth Hear His Voice*, 531.

4. Fear, "Strategy," 600.

5. Phillip Butler, "Mass Communications Report," in *Let the Earth Hear His Voice*, 1311.

6. Ibid.

7. Much of the literature on media and evangelism focuses on domestic audiences, examining phenomena such as televangelism or direct mail marketing. For works that consider the international dimensions of media and communications technology in the expansion of global evangelicalism, see Coleman, *The Globalisation of Charismatic Christianity*; Robert, *Christian Mission*; Wuthnow, *Boundless Faith*; Stoneman, "Global Radio."

8. Erickson, *Religious Radio and Television in the United States*, 1–2; Lochte, *Christian Radio*, 25–26.

9. Armstrong, *The Electric Church*, 63–80.

10. Ibid., 63.

11. Neely, *Come Up to This Mountain*, 86–87; Jones, "As It Was Then—Christmas Day 1931," 1, 4.

12. Alan Riding, "From High in the Andes, Bible's Message Carries Far," *New York Times* (May 23, 1984); The Billy Graham Center Archives, "Papers of Clarence Wesley Jones," http://www2.wheaton.edu/bgc/archives/GUIDES/349.htm; Stoneman, "Preparing the Soil," 125–26. Stoneman notes that HCJB succeeded as an evangelistic tool in Ecuador despite tremendous resistance from the local Catholic hierarchy due to the station's careful collaboration with the Ecuadoran government as well as a concerted effort to expand radio set ownership throughout the country (133–48).

13. World Radio Missionary Fellowship, Inc., *Call of the Andes* 24, no. 2 (August 1967): 2, SC-113 National Association of Evangelicals (hereafter NAE) Records, 1941–2000, Box 93, Folder 40: Missions Situation: Radio, Wheaton College Special Collections, Buswell Library, Wheaton College, IL (hereafter WCSC).

14. Far East Broadcasting Company, Inc., *Which Part Will YOU Share?* brochure (ca. 1967), SC-113 NAE Records, 1941–2000, Box 93, Folder 40: Missions Situation: Radio, WCSC.

15. Ibid.

16. Caribbean Grace Broadcasters, *All Systems Are GO for WCGB*, brochure (ca. 1967), SC-113 NAE Records, 1941–2000, Box 93, Folder 40: Missions Situation: Radio, WCSC.

17. Missionary Electronics, Inc., *Multiplied Outreach—That All Might Hear of Him through Large Scale Production of the TP-3 Portable Preacher Unit* (1962), Collection 165 Evangelical Foreign Missions Association (hereafter EFMA), Box 73, Folder 16: Missionary Electronics; 1962, 1970, The Billy Graham Center Archives, Wheaton, IL (hereafter BGCA).

18. Ibid. Since its founding in Los Angeles in 1937, Gospel Recordings missionaries have sought to translate and record Bible stories in every language spoken on earth. They return to each mission field to distribute these recordings and, where necessary, hand-operated cardboard record players. See Global Recordings Network, "The History of GRN," http://globalrecordings.net/en/history (accessed October 15, 2017); Horne, *The Tailenders*.

19. FEBC, *Which Part*.

20. Mission Projects Fellowship, Inc., *Project: Progress Report* no. 5 (January 1968); Mission Projects Fellowship, Inc., *Project: Progress Report* no. 87 (April 1975): 4, Collection 165 EFMA, Box 73, Folder 1: Mission Projects Fellowship, Inc. 1968–1975, BGCA.

21. George N. Patterson, "The Communications Revolution and the Christian Gospel," *Christianity Today* (November 22, 1968): 158.

22. Ibid., 155.

23. Ibid., 157.

24. Ibid., 156.

25. George N. Patterson, "The Communications Revolution and the Christian," unpublished manuscript (1968): 16, Collection 165 EFMA, Box 97, Folder 13: Christian Communications Council, BGCA.

26. Patterson, "Communications Revolution," 156.

27. Robert De Moss to Dr. Clyde Taylor and Reverend Wade Coggins, October 11, 1968 and James L. Johnson "Communications Seminar Background Statement for Exploratory Talks on Communications Commission (November 27, 1968), Collection 165 EFMA, Box 65, Folder 41: Christian Communications Council: 1968–1972, BGCA.

28. Jerry Ballard, "Summary Report: Communications Commission Discussion," memorandum (November 27, 1968), Collection 165 EFMA, Box 65, Folder 41: Christian Communications Council: 1968–1972, BGCA.

29. Norman B. Rohrer, "Shakedown for Communicators' Council," *EP News Service* (June 7, 1969), Collection 165 EFMA, Box 65, Folder 41: Christian Communications Council: 1968–1972, BGCA.

30. James L. Johnson to Wade Coggins, July 12, 1972, Collection 165 EFMA, Box 65, Folder 41: Christian Communications Council: 1968–1972, BGCA.

31. "The Christian Communications Council Statement of Purpose—Out of Its Founding in 1971," attachment, James L. Johnson to Ben Armstrong, November 26, 1976, Collection 309 National Religious Broadcasters, Box 86, Folder 5: WEF—Christian Communications Council 1970–1978, BGCA.

32. Clyde Taylor, "Formation of an International Religious Communications Commission," memorandum (February 1, 1974), Collection 309 National Religious Broadcasters, Box 86, Folder 2: WEF 1973–1980, BGCA.

33. Ibid.

34. "A New Beginning," *WEF Communications Report* 1, no. 1 (Summer 1976): 1, 4.

35. Ibid., 1.

36. ICOWE Communications Section Task Force, ca. September 1974, Collection 309 National Religious Broadcasters, Box 86, Folder 2: WEF 1973–1980, BGCA.

37. Phillip Butler to James Johnson, September, 20 1974, Collection 309 National Religious Broadcasters, Box 86, Folder 2: WEF 1973–1980, BGCA.

38. Waldron Scott, "Notes on a Proposed International Conference of Evangelical Communicators," October 13, 1976, Collection 309 National Religious Broadcasters, Box 94, Folder 6: WEF Congress on World Communication, BGCA.

39. Ibid.

40. Lee W. Baas to Ben Armstrong, May 13, 1976, Collection 309 National Religious Broadcasters, Box 94, Folder 6: WEF Congress on World Communication, BGCA; Reverend N. Etuk to Ben Armstrong, August 30, 1976, Collection 309 National Religious Broadcasters, Box 94, Folder 7: WEF Correspondence; 1976–1979, BGCA.

41. Theodore Hsueh to James Johnson, October 18, 1976, Collection 309 National Religious Broadcasters, Box 94, Folder 7: WEF Congress on World Communication, BGCA.

42. Even though, in practice, U.S. evangelists still tended to preach a culturally specific, Americanized gospel.

43. Butler, "Evangelism," 526.

44. Ibid., 527.

45. Ibid.; Eph. 5:16–17 (NRSV); Col. 4:5 (NRSV).

46. Butler, "Evangelism," 527.

47. Ibid. See also Luke 14:28–30 (NRSV): "For which of you, intending to build a tower, does not first sit down and estimate the cost, to see whether he has enough to complete it? Otherwise, when he has laid a foundation and is not able to finish, all who see it will begin to ridicule him, saying, 'This fellow began to build and was not able to finish.'"

48. Butler, "Evangelism," 527.

49. Ibid.

50. See, for example, Menkir Esayas, "Communications Research," in *Let the Earth Hear His Voice*, 549–60.

51. Butler, "Evangelism," 528; I Corinthians 3:6 (NRSV): "I planted, Apollos watered, but God gave the growth."

52. Butler, "Evangelism," 528.

53. David Chao and Philip Butler, "Radio and Evangelism," in *Let the Earth Hear His Voice*, 563.

54. James F. Engel, "The Audience for Christian Communication," in *Let the Earth Hear His Voice*, 533–39.

55. Engel, *Contemporary Christian Communications*, 134.; 1 Cor. 3 (NRSV).

56. Engel, *Contemporary*, 132–33.

57. Ibid., 134.

58. Ibid.

59. See, for example, Timothy Yu, "Coordination of Christian Media Forces: Winning the Global Battle of Evangelization," in *Let the Earth Hear His Voice*, 540–48; Chao and Butler, "Radio and Evangelism," 561–66.

60. Engel, *Contemporary*, 154.

61. Ibid., 272.

62. Ibid., 275.

63. Ibid.

64. Engstrom, *What in the World Is God Doing?*, 89–95.

65. Edward R. Dayton and John A. Klebe, "Newest Tool for Missions," *World Vision Magazine* (October 1966): 10–11; Missions Advanced Research and Communications Center, *Unreached Peoples: A Preliminary Compilation* (Monrovia, CA: MARC, 1973).

66. In 1978, his title changed to executive director, a position he held until his retirement in 1989. The NRB is an association of Christian radio, television, and digital media broadcasters. Founded in 1944 by the NAE, it sets standards for religious stations and programming, lobbies on political issues of interest to its members, and serves as a clearinghouse for information on religious broadcasting.

67. Armstrong, *Electric*, 9.

68. Ibid., 167.

69. Ibid., 171; *WEF Communications Report* 3, no. 6 (October 1979): 3.

70. Armstrong, *Electric*, 172; "And this good news of the kingdom will be proclaimed throughout the world, as a testimony to all the nations; and then the end will come," Matthew 24:14 (NRSV).

71. Armstrong, *Electric*, 172.

72. Ibid., 173.

73. Ibid., 173–75.

74. WEFCC, Minutes of the Meetings of the World Evangelical Fellowship Communications Commission at the Foreign Missions Club, London (March 21–24 1980), Collection 309 National Religious Broadcasters, 1944– Records; 1922 (1969–1989) 1991, Box 86, Folder 2: WEF 1973–1980, BGCA.

75. Ibid., 1, 4–7, 9.

76. Ibid., M-3.

77. Ibid., 9–10.

78. WEFCC, Minutes, 18–19. Myrna Grant, a member of the Wheaton College communications department, Gladys Jasper, of Evangelical Literature Overseas, and David Adams, of Trans World Radio, rounded out the committee.

79. Ibid., T-5, M-3.

80. Ibid., T-7–T-8.

81. Ibid., M-4.

82. Stoneman, "Preparing the Soil," 154–55. In the case of communist nations, it tended to further the spread of Baptist and Pentecostal denominations despite resistance from the Russian Orthodox church and other denominations. For contemporary commentary on this phenomenon, see Sawatsky, *Soviet Evangelicals since World War II*, 258, 383.

83. Ibid.

84. Slavic Gospel Association, *Radio to Russia* newsletter (n.d., ca. 1982–84), SC-53 Institute of Soviet and East European Studies (hereafter ISEES) Collection, 1974–1993, Box 38, Folder 14, WCSC.

85. Rohrer and Deyneka, *Peter Dynamite 'Twice Born Russian'*, 149.

86. Slavic Gospel Association, Information Sheet: Radio Ministries in Eastern Europe (February 2, 1977), SC-53 ISEES Collection, Box 38, Folder 14, WCSC.

87. Thomas Kent, "Religion Thrives Underground in Russia," *St. Petersburg Times* (April 16, 1977): 5-D.

88. Ibid.

89. Ibid.

90. Word to Russia, "Second Underground Printing Press Discovered Near the Black Sea," *Word to Russia: Reports from Russia* (March 1977), SC-53 ISEES Collection, Box 38, Folder 2, WCSC.

91. Sawatsky, *Soviet Evangelicals*, 383.

92. Word to Russia, "Second Underground," 1.

93. Eastern European Mission, "United with Us," *Gospel Call* (September–October 1982), 14, SC-79, Intercessors for the Suffering Church Collection, Box 2, Folder 15, WCSC.

94. Robert H. Bowman, FEBC fundraising letter (September 1975), Collection 059 Far East Broadcasting, Inc, 1947–1979, Box 1, Folder 4, BGCA.

95. Ibid; Robert H. Bowman, FEBC fundraising letter (February 1979), Collection 059 Far East Broadcasting, Inc, 1947–1979, Box 1, Folder 4, BGCA.

96. "Christian Radio Broadcast Reaches All Strata of Soviet Life," *East/West News Service* (January 1, 1981), SC-53 ISEES Collection, Box 38, Folder 142, WCSC.

97. Rohrer and Deyneka, *Peter Dynamite*, 149.

98. Ibid.

99. Interview with Peter Deyneka, Jr., 9/23/[1975], SC-53 ISEES Collection, Box 38, Folder 14, WCSC.

100. Slavic Gospel Association, "Russian Radio Audience Survey Analysis and Tabulation" (July 1981), SC-53 ISEES Collection, Box 38, Folder 14, WCSC.

101. Rohrer and Deyneka, *Peter Dynamite*, 149.

102. "Under the Cloak of Religion," *Omsk Truth* (July 9, 1978), translated from the Russian by ISEES, SC-53 ISEES Collection, Box 38, Folder 5, WCSC.

103. Peter Deyneka, Jr., "The Need for the Development and Improvement of Russian Radio Programming," SGA memorandum (October 1976), SC-53 ISEES Collection, Box 38, Folder 14, WCSC.

104. A. Belov and A. Shilkin, "Antisovietism in the Western Religious Radio Propaganda" (ca. 1976), translated by ISEES, SC-53 ISEES Collection, Box 38, Folder 14, WCSC.

105. Stephen Constant, "Russia Hits at Religious Broadcasts," *Daily Telegraph* (London) (January 5, 1973), 4.

106. V. Mararitsa, "Tomorrow We Put Out to Sea," *Komsomolskaya Pravda* (March 11, 1982), translated by ISEES, SC-53 ISEES Collection, Box 38, Folder 5, WCSC.

107. "Book is Source for Three FEBA Series," *WEF Communications Report* 3, no. 6 (October 1979): 1.

108. "New Christian Radio Station Goes on Air in Holy Land," *WEF Communications Report* 3, no. 6 (October 1979): 1.

109. Ibid. Otis suggested that he wanted to focus on Isaiah in particular because he believed it "infers a role for Lebanon in opening the spiritual eyes of Israel" (4), indicating that he saw radio broadcasting in the region through the prism of his eschatological beliefs about the role of Israel in the end times prophesied in Revelation.

110. "New Christian Radio Station," 4.

111. William Claiborne and Jonathan C. Randal, "U.S. Christians Beam Religion, Politics Into Troubled Air of Southern Lebanon," *Washington Post* (March 18, 1981): A14.

112. "New Christian Radio Station," 4.

113. Claiborne and Randal, "U.S. Christians," A14.

114. Ibid.

115. Ibid.

116. Ihsan A. Hijazi, "5 Reported Dead in a Lebanon Raid," *New York Times* (October 18, 1985): A12.

117. Robertson set up his television station in Lebanon alongside Otis in June 1979. See "Media Pioneer," The Official Site of Pat Robertson, accessed January 8, 2018, http://www. patrobertson.com/mediapioneer/; Leighton Ford to Pat Robertson (June 24, 1983), Collection 253 BGEA: International Conference for Itinerant Evangelists, Box 40, Folder 3, BGCA.

118. "ECWA Plans Training Project for Christian TV in Nigeria," *WEF Communications Report* 3, no. 6 (October 1979): 3.

119. Ibid.

120. Dave Adams, "Development of Trans World Radio Ministry in Africa," memorandum (September 20, 1980), Collection 309 National Religious Broadcasters, Box 86, Folder 2, BGCA.

121. "ACTION Seeks News on AV Materials," *Action: World Association for Christian Communication Newsletter,* no. 14 (November 1976): 5.

122. "MAF and Micro Computers Report" (February 1980): 1–3, Collection 136 Mission Aviation Fellowship, Box 123, Folder 6, BGCA.

123. Dottie Krempl, "Prayer Partners," letter (July–August 1983), SC-79 Intercessors for the Suffering Church Collection, Box 7, Folder 3, WCSC; Bob Hosker to Mary Ann Gilbert (April 2, 1984), SC-79 Intercessors for the Suffering Church Collection, Box 1, Folder 21, WCSC. Bulletin board systems were precursors to the modern internet.

3. Religious Freedom and the New Evangelical Foreign Policy Lobby

1. "Year of the Evangelicals," *Newsweek* (October 25, 1976): cover, 3. *Newsweek* made this declaration in part based on Gallup polling that indicated that one-third of all Americans described themselves as "born-again" Christians. Kenneth L. Woodward, John Barnes, and Laurie Lisle, "Born Again!" *Newsweek* (October 25, 1976): 68.

2. Woodward, Barnes, and Lisle, "Born Again!" 68.

3. Ibid. Ford was Episcopalian and thus a member of a mainline rather than evangelical Protestant church, yet this article noted that he described and presented himself as an evangelical, at least during the election.

4. Evangelicals constituted an important population within the religious right, which also included fundamentalist Christians as well as conservative Catholics and other Protestant groups. The scholarly literature on the rise of the religious right is extensive. Key works include Martin, *With God on Our Side*; McGirr, *Suburban Warriors*; Williams, *God's Own Party*; Dochuk, *From Bible Belt to Sunbelt*; Schäfer, *Countercultural Conservatives*; Balmer, *Thy Kingdom Come*; Hart, "Mainstream Protestantism, 'Conservative' Religion, and Civil Society," in *Religion Returns to the Public Square*, ed. Heclo and McClay, 195–225; Diamond, *Not by Politics Alone* and *Spiritual Warfare*; Hunter, *Culture Wars*.

5. Ibid. *Engel v. Vitale* (1962) outlawed prayer in public schools, *Griswold v. Connecticut* (1965) legalized birth control, *Green v. Connally* (1971) ruled that private schools that violated federal antidiscrimination laws would lose their tax-exempt status, and *Roe v. Wade* (1973) legalized abortion. Randall Balmer has argued that *Green v. Connally* served as the initial catalyst for evangelical and fundamentalist domestic political organizing (as it affected Christian schools such as Bob Jones University), and only later in the 1970s did these groups join with Catholics to protest abortion rights and restrictions on prayer in schools. Catholics led the initial charge against birth control and abortion rights, beginning in the early 1960s. Balmer, *Thy Kingdom*, 13–14; Critchlow, *Phyllis Schlafly and Grassroots Conservatism*, 263–67.

6. This recent scholarship challenges conventional accounts that suggested that conservative Christians retreated entirely from political involvement after the Scopes Trial of 1925 and did not reemerge until the 1970s. Indeed, Williams provides evidence that threats to religious broadcasting in the 1930s and 1940s led to the foundation of two major evangelical lobbying groups based in Washington, D.C.: the NAE (founded in 1942) and the National Religious Broadcasters (founded in 1944), both of which quickly branched out from concern about broadcasting rights into other areas of evangelical policy advocacy. This interpretation provides a more nuanced understanding of the longer history of conservative Christian political engagement. Still, the vast majority of scholars, Williams included, note that a key shift occurred during the 1970s—a shift that rendered evangelical organizing effective and connected evangelicals much more closely with the Republican Party. See Williams, *God's Own Party*, 16–17. For traditional accounts from scholars as well as from evangelicals and fundamentalist leaders that suggest that conservative Christians eschewed political involvement after 1925, see Fox, "Experience and Explanation in Twentieth-Century American Religious History," in *New Directions in American Religious History*, ed. Stout and Hart; Carpenter, *Revive Us*; Robert D. Linder, "Fifty Years after Scopes: Lessons to Learn, a Heritage to Reclaim," *Christianity Today* 19 (July 18, 1975): 1010, 1012; Falwell, Dobson, and Hinson, *The Fundamentalist Phenomenon*. Recent work that calls this interpretation into question includes Edwards, "Rethinking the Failure of Fundamentalist Political Antievolutionism after 1925," 89–90; Williams, *God's Own Party*; Amstutz, *Evangelicals and American Foreign Policy*, 136; Lahr, *Millennial Dreams and Apocalyptic Nightmares*, 13–14.

7. It is notoriously difficult to track the precise proportion of the population that identified as evangelical at any given point in U.S. history, in part due to survey methodology and how individuals self-identified. When Gallup first began asking survey-takers if they described themselves "as a 'born-again' or evangelical" Christian in 1976, approximately 35 percent answered "yes." Although having a born-again experience is a core part of the evangelical identity, it is not the only defining aspect; as such this number might include individuals who did not embrace other aspects of the evangelical identity while excluding others who might, with a differently worded survey, have included themselves. One report in *Christianity Today* on the evangelical population throughout the twentieth century relied on survey data from the General Social Survey (GSS), which placed the evangelical population at 17.1 percent in 1972. Given the difference of survey methodology though, the GSS and Gallup surveys are not directly

comparable. Nevertheless, there was a perception at the time that the proportion of Americans who identified as evangelical was growing during this decade. See Albert L. Winseman, "'Born-Agains' Wield Political, Economic Influence," *Gallup News* (April 13, 2004), http://news.gallup.com/poll/11269/bornagains-wield-political-economic-influence.aspx; Ed Stetzer, "The State of the Church in America: When the Numbers Point to a New Reality, Part 2," *Christianity Today* (September 14, 2016), https://www.christianitytoday.com/edstetzer/2016/september/state-of-church-in-america-when-numbers-point-to-new-realit.html

8. Prior to this point, evangelicals had not linked themselves as a group exclusively with either party; indeed many white evangelicals in the South identified as Southern Democrats. Williams, *God's Own Party*, 2–3, 12, 14, 20, 36. In addition, even with the rise of the religious right and the important role that evangelicals played in the conservative movement, not all evangelicals identified with conservative political aims.

9. Lahr, *Millennial Dreams*; Inboden, *Religion and American Foreign Policy, 1945–1960*; Preston, *Sword of the Spirit, Shield of Faith*, 421–22, 444; Gunn, *Spiritual Weapons*; Diamond, *Spiritual Warfare*, 155–200; Williams, *God's Own Party*, 83, 166–67; Martin, "With God on Their Side: Religion and U.S. Foreign Policy," in *Religion Returns to the Public Square*, ed. Heclo and McClay, 336; Hofrenning, *In Washington but Not of It*, 45.

10. Amstutz, *Evangelicals*; Wuthnow, *Boundless Faith*; Castelli, "Praying for the Persecuted Church," 321–51; Hertzke, *Freeing God's Children*.

11. "The Lausanne Covenant," 8; "Evangelism Where There Is Government Hostility Report," in *Let the Earth Hear His Voice*, 955–57.

12. "The Lausanne Covenant," 8.

13. Ibid. See also UN General Assembly, *Universal Declaration of Human Rights*, Article 18 (December 10, 1948), http://www.un.org/en/documents/udhr/.

14. This stands in contrast to more recent understandings of the term "religious freedom." Elizabeth Hurd has argued that for advocates for international religious freedom in the twenty-first century, "belief is understood to be the central and defining feature of religiosity," with practice as another, less important consideration. For these advocates, "'believing' is taken as the universal defining characteristic of what it means to be religious, and the right to believe as the essence of what it means to be free." For the evangelicals of the 1970s though, belief was not the sole factor. As I demonstrate in this book, the desire for all evangelicals to be able to evangelize freely provided the foundation for their activism and understanding of religious liberty and their definition of international religious freedom as they began lobbying Congress on this issue. Hurd, "Believing in Religious Freedom," in *Politics of Religious Freedom*, ed. Sullivan, Hurd, Mahmood, and Danchin, 45–46.

15. McAlister, "The Persecuted Body," 139.

16. Ibid., 140; Wurmbrand, *Communist Exploitation of Religion*; George W. Cornell, "Minister Keeps Track of Communist Repression," *Bulletin* (Bend, OR) (January 10, 1976): 5. See also Preston, *Sword*, 565.

17. John Rutledge, "West Ignores Plight of Russian Baptists," *Baptist Standard* (September 17, 1975): 13 [Religious Dissidents—Rumania and U.S.S.R.], 3/77–4/77 [O/A 4461] folder, Box 98, Office of Public Liaison, Jane Wales Subject Files, Jimmy Carter Presidential Library, Atlanta, GA (hereafter JCPL); Christian Rescue Effort for the Emancipation of Dissidents, "CREED: Its Origins and Purposes," Folder 10 Congressional Legislative File—Subject File—CREED General, 1980–1984, Box 127, Jack Kemp Papers (hereafter JKP), Manuscript Division, Library of Congress, Washington, D.C.

18. Garthoff, *Détente and Confrontation*, 25–36; Litwak, *Détente and the Nixon Doctrine*, 82; Nelson, *The Making of Détente*, 71, 54–55; Hanhimäki, *The Flawed Architect*, 381.

19. Dallek, *Nixon and Kissinger*, 269; Litwak, *Détente*, 92; Nelson, *The Making of Détente*, 148, 171; Hanhimäki, *The Flawed Architect*, 381; Suri, *Henry Kissinger and the American*, 244.

20. See, for example, Nelson, *The Making of Détente*, 149; Hanhimäki, *Kissinger*, 342; Stern, *Water's Edge*; Kochavi, "Insights Abandoned, Flexibility Lost: Kissinger, Soviet Jewish Emigration, and the Demise of Détente," 550–72; Feingold, *"Silent No More": Saving the Jews of Russia, The American Jewish Effort*.

21. Stern, *Water's Edge*, 18; Kochavi, "Insights," 515; Kaufman, *Henry M. Jackson*, 280.

22. Members of the American Jewish Council, the American Jewish Congress, the Jewish Defense League, the American Israel Public Affairs Committee, and others organized demonstrations and letter-writing campaigns to support Soviet Jewry and the Jackson-Vanik amendment. See, for example, American Jewish Congress, "Executive Director's Report," 15; Friedman, "Intergroup Relations and Tensions in the United States," 115–16; Irving Spiegal, "Reform Jews Here Reject Nixon Policy on Exit Tax," *New York Times* (May 1, 1973), 5.

23. One congressman reported that the mail volume on the Jackson-Vanik amendment and the plight of the Soviet Jewry "is second only to that on Watergate." Marilyn Berger, "Move to Ease Tariffs on Soviets Stirring Liberal Storm," *Washington Post* (September 20, 1973), A28.

24. "Sec. 402. Freedom of Emigration in East-West Trade," Trade Act of 1974, HR 10710, 93rd Cong., 2nd sess., *Congressional Record* 120 (Washington, DC: U.S. Government Printing Office, 1974). President Ford signed the act into law on January 3, 1975.

25. Feingold, *"Silent,"* 115; Stern, *Water's Edge*, 21; Lazarowitz, "Senator Jacob K. Javits and Soviet Jewish Emigration," 21.

26. "No Memo for Brezhnev," *Christianity Today* (June 22, 1973): 23–24.

27. For example, the Baptist World Alliance discussed persecution and the human rights of Christians throughout the world extensively at their quinquennial congresses between 1955 and 2005, yet the audience for their proceedings, papers, and resolutions remained the Baptist, rather than the general, public. Charles W. Deweese, "International Baptist Perspectives on Human Rights," *Baptist History and Heritage* 43 no. 2 (Spring 2008): 60–69. For a typical letter from a Christian suffering from persecution in the Soviet bloc shared among members of a U.S. evangelical organization, see Ed Mainland to Clifton J. Robinson, February 5, 1972, Collection 459 Records of the Fellowship Foundation, Box 252, Folder 57, Russia 1972, Billy Graham Center Archives, Wheaton, IL. Examples of published accounts of persecution include Voronaeff, *Pastor Paul Voronaeff's*; Wurmbrand, *Tortured for Christ*; Bourdeaux, *Faith on Trial in Russia*; Harris, *Christian Prisoners in Russia*.

28. Jesus to the Communist World, *Baptists! Thousands of Your Brethren Are in Red Prisons!*

29. Prayer requests continued to form an important part of evangelical advocacy efforts throughout the period under study. Ralph Covell, "Evangelicals and Totalitarian Governments," paper presented at the Second Consultation on Theology and Mission, Trinity Evangelical Divinity School, School of World Mission and Evangelism, March 19–22, 1979, Box 70, J. H. Walker Jr., Folder: Miscellaneous Papers, Dixon Pentecostal Research Center, Cleveland, TN; Rutledge, "West Ignores Plight of Russian Baptists," 13.

30. Rutledge, "West Ignores Plight of Russian Baptists," 13; "Hotline from Europe: Aida Skripnikova Arrested Again!" *Underground Evangelism* 17, no. 9 (November 1976): 14, folder "20-0 Underground Evangelism 1976–77 63/5/1," ID: 30515, FPHC; Frank Grizzard, Prayer & Action Committee letter, ca. 1982, folder "20-10 Russian Pentecostals Clip File: 1982," ID: 94735 51/6/3, FPHC.

31. Covell, "Evangelicals," 13, 18.

32. Cerillo and Dempster, *Salt and Light*, 64. Cerillo and Dempster note that many of these left-leaning evangelicals were influential academics and/or theologians. That said, they also note

that the majority of evangelicals, especially rank-and-file believers, espoused conservative political views (24–25, 64).

33. In addition to basic political differences, Protestant sects in general remained divided along regional, racial, and denominational/theological lines. Williams, *God's Own Party*, 4–5; Marsden, *The Twilight of the American Enlightenment*, 108, 138.

34. Sutton, *American Apocalypse*, 352.

35. Williams, *God's Own Party*, 3; Marsden, *Twilight*, 128–29, 138–39.

36. Cerillo and Dempster, *Salt*, 64. The authors remark that most conservative evangelicals, such as Billy Graham, supported Nixon in the 1968 and 1972 elections; liberal evangelicals, unsurprisingly, tended to support democratic candidates. This picture of a politically diverse evangelical population in 1968 helps contextualize their later mobilization as a reliably conservative voting bloc (with the caveat that the evangelical left never entirely disappeared and, as such, evangelicals at no point held monolithic political views). On Billy Graham and his support for Nixon in the 1968 election, see Edward B. Fiske, "The Closest Thing To A White House Chaplain: Billy Graham," *New York Times* (June 8, 1969): SM27.

37. Documents from the Nixon administration reveal that the president and his advisers viewed connections with evangelical groups such as the Southern Baptists and the Baptist World Alliance as "good politics"—a way to cultivate support among voters. This cultivation of support did not extend to policy influence however. The administration ignored suggestions from evangelicals inside and outside of the government about the role that evangelical missionaries could play in shaping U.S. relations abroad. See Memo, George T. Bell to Connie Stewart, June 17, 1970, folder Southern Baptist Convention [3 of 4], Box 108, White House Special Files: Staff Member and Office Files: Subject Files: Charles W. Colson, Richard Nixon Presidential Library and Museum, Yorba Linda, California (hereafter RNPL); Memo, George T. Bell to Richard M. Nixon, "Meeting with Executives of the Baptist World Alliance," November 23, 1970, Box 22, White House Special Files: Staff Member and Office Files: Meeting Files: Charles W. Colson, RNPL; Darrell M. Trent to Tom Melady, August 12, 1970, folder [EX] FO 8/1/70–8/31/70, Box 2, White House Central Files: Subject Files: FO Foreign Affairs, RNPL; Richard Nixon to Tom Melady, August 17, 1970, folder EX FO 5 7/1/70—[12/31/70], White House Central Files: Subject Files: FO Foreign Affairs, RNPL. See also Preston, *Sword*, 565.

38. Williams, *God's Own Party*, 3.

39. Preston, *Sword*, 565.

40. Conference on Security and Cooperation in Europe, *Final Act* (Helsinki, 1975), http://www.osce.org/mc/39501

41. Ibid.

42. Memorandum of Conversation, president's meeting with Henry A. Kissinger and Lt. General Brent Scowcroft, August 15 1974, Collection GRF-0314: Memoranda of Conversations (Nixon and Ford Administrations), 1973–1977, Gerald R. Ford Presidential Library, Ann Arbor, MI (hereafter GRFL), http://www.fordlibrarymuseum.gov/library/document/memcons/1552750.pdf; Gubin, "Between Regimes and Realism—Transnational Agenda Setting," 280; Snyder, "The Rise of the Helsinki Network: 'A Sort of Lifeline' for Eastern Europe," in *Perforating the Iron Curtain*, ed. Villaume and Westad, 179–80.

43. Morgan, "The United States and the Making of the Helsinki Final Act," in *Nixon in the World*, ed. Logevall and Preston, 165–66.

44. Newspapers and Christian periodicals reported on persecution in the Soviet bloc with increasing frequency beginning around 1973. See, for example, "Soviet Persecution of Christians Continues," *Applied Christianity* (March 1973): 35–37; "Repression in the U.S.S.R.," *Christianity Today* 18, no. 16 (May 10, 1974): 54–55; "Czech Crackdown," *Christianity Today* 18,

no. 15 (May 10, 1974): 51; Janice A. Broun, "Evangelism in the U.S.S.R.," *Christianity Today* 18, no. 19 (June 21, 1974): 11–16; James Robison, "Soviets still Persecute Us: Baptist Pastor," *Chicago Tribune* (February 15, 1975): B13; Russell Chandler, "Soviet Persecution of Christians Told," *Los Angeles Times* (February 22, 1975): A18.

45. "The Damper on Détente," *Christianity Today* 19, no. 11 (February 28, 1975): 33.

46. David H. Adeney, "Church in China: Praise amid Persecution," *Christianity Today* 22, no. 4 (November 18, 1977): 10–13; "Nixon, China, and Religious Freedom," *Christianity Today* 16, no. 9 (February 4, 1972): 20–21; James C. Hefley, "Beyond Martyrdom," *Christianity Today* 18, no. 12 (March 15, 1974): 52.

47. "Repression in the U.S.S.R.," 54–55; Carl F. H. Henry, "Human Rights and Wrongs," *Christianity Today* 21, no. 19 (July 8, 1977): 25. In addition, in 1975 the Baptist World Alliance formed a Study Commission on Religious Liberty and Human Rights, which presented its findings at the 13th Baptist World Congress. "Russian Baptists Disagree on Religious Freedom," *(BP)—Features: News of the Southern Baptist Convention* (July 18, 1975): 1.

48. See for example "Light on Rights," *Christianity Today* 22, no. 12 (March 24, 1978): 55–56; "Women Released, Appeal for Georgi Vins' Freedom," *Baptist Press* 75–132 (August 27, 1975): 1; "Soviets Still Repress Believers, Report Says," *Washington Post* (August 13, 1976): C6; Office of Senior Specialists (Congressional Research Service) and William Cooper, *Soviet-American Relations in 1977: A Chronological Summary and Brief Analysis*, Report No. 79-60 S, March 1, 1979, 45, 48.

49. See, for example, House Committee on International Relations, Subcommittees on International Political and Military Affairs and on International Organizations, *Religious Persecution in the Soviet Union*, 94th Cong., 2nd sess., June 24 and 30, 1976, 42, 130.

50. Broun, "Evangelism," 11; C. E. Bryant, "Nixon Visit Spotlights Baptists in Eastern Europe," *(BP)—Features: News of the Southern Baptist Convention* (May 30, 1972): 1; Fred Smolchuck, "Observations of Russia and the Ukraine During a Twenty—One Day Trip," October 9, 1974, Folder: Russia (1970–1979), Assemblies of God World Missions Archives, FPHC.

51. According to reports, Pentecostals suffered additional constraints. The AUCEB forbade them from speaking in tongues at church services and, worse yet, the state often committed those Pentecostals it caught engaging in glossolalia in underground churches to insane asylums. Broun, "Evangelism," 14; Smolchuck, "Observations."

52. "Russian Christians Don't Want to Leave." *Evangel* 65, no. 12 (August 25, 1975): 30; "Russian Christians Don't Want To Leave; They Want Freedom," *Baptist Press* 75–66 (April 25, 1975): 3–4.

53. "Russian Christians," 4.

54. "Revival and Risks in Romania," *Christianity Today* (October 22, 1976): 60.

55. Assemblyman Robert H. Burke to President Gerald Ford, September 11, 1974, Folder: CO 125 Romania 8/9/74–12/31/74 Executive, Box 43, WHCF Subject File, GRFL; Letter, Rev. Michael Bourdeaux to President Gerald Ford, September 4, 1975, Folder: CO 158 USSR 10/24/75–10/31/75, Box 52, WHCF Subject File, GRFL. The State Department also noted an uptick in attention from evangelical groups on Soviet persecution in 1975–76. See American Embassy Bucharest, Romania to United States Department of State, Washington, "Increased Interest in Situation of Baptists—Vladimir Hailo," October 6, 1976, Confidential Cable, State 248903, https://www.wikileaks.org/plusd/cables/1976STATE248903_b.html.

56. Philip M. Crane, Henry Helstoski, Alphonzo Bell, et al. to President Gerald Ford, July 22, 1975, Folder: TR 34–4 Bucharest, Romania, Box 58, WHCF Subject File, GRFL.

57. James H. Falk to The Honorable Robert H. Burke, October 18, 1974, Folder: CO 125 Romania 8/9/74–12/31/74 Executive, Box 43, WHCF Subject File, GRFL.

58. Charges, essentially, for administering to his church. "Soviet Court Convicts Dissident Baptist Leader," *Baptist Press* 75–19 (February 4, 1975): 1; "A Prophet in Peril," *Time* 105, no. 4 (January 27, 1975): 90. The Soviet government had also arrested, tortured, and imprisoned Vins from 1966 to 1969.

59. "World Baptist Leaders Ask Clemency for Prisoners," *(BP)—Features* 74–101 (December 19, 1974): 3

60. "Committee Urges Support for Persecuted Christians," *Baptist Press* 76–19 (January 29, 1976): 1.

61. W. Barry Garrett, "Congress Gets Resolution on Release of Georgi Vins," *Baptist Press* 76–63 (April 8, 1976): 2; "Christian Prisoners Inside Russia Walls: Free World Christians are taking a lesson from Free World Jews," *Playground Daily News* (Fort Walton Beach, FL), (May 12, 1976), 4.

62. W. Barry Garrett, "Baptists Urge Religious Liberty in Russia, India," *Baptist Press* 75–36 (March 6, 1975): 1–2; American Embassy Bucharest to United States Department of State, "Increased Interest," 1–2.

63. John Ashbrook, "Soviet Christians Persecuted Too," 93rd Cong., 2nd sess., *Congressional Record* 120 (July 29, 1974): 25632–25634; House, *Religious Persecution in the Soviet Union*; House Committee on International Relations, *Religious Repression in the Soviet Union: Dissident Baptist Pastor Georgi Vins*, 94th Cong., 2nd sess., 1976, Report No. 94-1464; Senate Committee on Foreign Relations, *Religious Freedom in the Soviet Union: The Case of Pastor Georgi Vins*, 94th Cong., 2nd sess., 1976, Report No. 94-1306. See also Preston, *Sword*, 573.

64. House Committee on International Relations, *Religious Persecution*, 29–33; W. Barry Garrett, "Congress Hears Report of Reform Russian Baptists," *Baptist Press* 76–105 (June 25, 1976): 2–4.

65. House Committee on International Relations, *Religious Persecution*, 48–50. Prior to his stint in Congress, Buchanan had served as a Baptist pastor. In his congressional testimony, Buchanan referenced information from evangelical organizations such as Religion in Communist Dominated Areas, the Baptist World Alliance, and Christian Prisoners' Release International. See also "Georgi Vins Resolution Moves Ahead in Congress," *Baptist Press* 76–148 (September 8, 1976): 3.

66. House Committee on International Relations, *Religious Persecution*, 51–52; Janis Johnson, "Movement Grows in Congress for Soviet Christian Support," *Washington Post* (July 31, 1976): A3.

67. H. Con. Res. 726, 94th Cong., 2nd sess.; S. Con. Res. 118, 94th Cong., 2nd sess. Buchanan introduced H. Con. Res 726 on August 31, 1976, with 140 sponsors (this resolution came after an original resolution, H. Con. Res. 606, which Buchanan had introduced with twenty-four sponsors). The House passed the measure with overwhelming support on September 20, 1976 (381–2) and the Senate passed it on October 1, 1976. See also W. Barry Garrett, "Congress Pressures USSR to Release Georgi Vins," *Baptist Press* 76–169 (October 8, 1976): 1–2; Janis Johnson, "Congress Decries Soviet Christian Persecution," *Washington Post* (October 8, 1976): B18.

68. The State Department acknowledged the expanding number of NGOs and interest groups expressing concern about religious dissidence in the USSR and noted that "there was a constant drumbeat of individual cases of persecution that came our way from Congressmen, NGO's and interested citizens" between 1975 and 1977. But State Department officials, especially Henry Kissinger, remained skeptical of the efficacy of international censure, and the newly created Office of Human Rights and Humanitarian affairs lacked adequate staff to address individual cases of persecution according to Wilson, who served as the first assistant secretary of state for that office from 1975 to 1977. James Wilson, "Diplomatic Theology—An Early Chronicle

of Human Rights at State," [August 1977], 11–12, 16, James Wilson Papers, Folder: Human Rights and Humanitarian Affairs—Wilson Memoir, Box 1, GRFL.

69. Wilson, "Diplomatic Theology," 16.

70. Ibid., 18, 41; Keys, "Congress," 839–40.

71. As Barbara Keys has argued, "by failing to develop a positive, proactive approach to human rights, Kissinger left it to Congress to implement a reactive, punitive, and unilateral approach that would set the human rights agenda long after the Ford administration. The end result of the conflict between Congress and Kissinger was that congressional leaders felt they had no choice but to enact increasingly restrictive legislation, producing precisely the outcome State Department officials wanted to avoid." Keys, "Congress," 825. See also Sikkink, *Mixed Signals*, 71, 106–7.

72. Bill Bright, "Your Five Duties as a Christian Citizen" (American Christian Voice Foundation, 1976). See also "Evangelicals in Washington: A Call to Action," *Christianity Today* 20, no. 13 (March 26, 1976): 36–37. Campus Crusade for Christ was a parachurch evangelistic organization and ministry for college students that Bill Bright founded in 1951 at UCLA.

73. Russell Chandler, "'Vote Christian' Impact on Elections Weighed: There Was a Wave of Religious Political Activity but Only a Few 'Born-Again' Challengers Won," *Los Angeles Times* (November 8, 1976): 3.

74. Ibid.; "Religious Leaders Score Group's Reported Effort to Elect Only Christians," *New York Times* (October 21, 1976): 44.

75. Diamond, *Spiritual Warfare*, 62; Joel Kotkin, "Ready on the Right," *Washington Post* (August 25, 1979): A10.

76. Harold O. J. Brown, "The Church of the 1970s: A Decade of Flux?," *Christianity Today* 23, no. 28 (December 21, 1979): 20–22.

77. Memorandum for Jessica Tuchman from Cord Meyer, Jr., "Subject: CIA Reports on Human Rights," May 25, 1977, JCPL, RAC Project Number NLC-28-10-3-1-6.

78. Jimmy Carter to Leonid Brezhnev, February 14, 1977, Folder: "U.S.S.R.—Carter/Brezhnev Correspondence [1/77–5/77]," Box 18, Zbigniew Brzezinski Collection, JCPL. Raymond Garthoff notes that even from the earliest days, the Carter administration demonstrated its interest in and commitment to human rights in its dealings with Soviet Union, including its willingness to publicly praise dissidents. Still, he notes that Vance and other members of the administration preferred quiet diplomacy. For this reason, many evangelicals found the administration wanting. See Garthoff, *Détente*, 569–71, 805.

79. Memorandum of Conversation between Jimmy Carter and Leonid Brezhnev, "Carter-Brezhnev Private Meeting," June 18, 1979, JCPL, RAC Project Number NLC-128-5-5-9-0.

80. Memorandum for Zbigniew Brzezinski from Global Issues, "Evening Report (U)," March 26, 1980, JCPL, RAC Project Number NLC-10-28-1-26-1.

81. Sikkink, *Mixed Signals*, 125–37.

82. Marjorie Hyer, "Soviets Spy on Churchgoers: Freed Dissident Tells Congressmen of Persecution," *Washington Post* (June 15, 1979): C20. Vins was the only religious dissident of the group.

83. "Georgi Vins Freed!" *Underground Evangelism* 20, no. 6 (June 1979): 4, folder "20-0 Underground Evangelism 1979 63/5/1," ID: 30515, FPHC.

84. "Carter-Brezhnev Private Meeting," 13.

85. Ibid.

86. "Marches, Rallies around World Turn Spotlight on Imprisoned Christians," *Underground Evangelism* (July 1976): 2, folder "20-0 Underground Evangelism 1976–1977 63/5/1," ID: 30515, FPHC; "Soviet Crackdown on Baptists—A Special Meaning for Carter," *U.S. News and World*

Report (April 18, 1977): 26–27; "After Long Vigil, Vins Is Free," *Underground Evangelism* (September 1979): 7, folder "20-0 Underground Evangelism 1979 63/5/1," ID: 30515, FPHC.

87. "Georgi Vins Special," *Underground Evangelism* (September 1979): 5.

88. Jim Newton, "Georgi Vins: Free to Tell of Russian Baptist Plight," *BP—Features* 79–92 (June 5, 1979): 1.

89. "Georgi Vins Special," 5.

90. Ibid.

91. Newton, "Georgi Vins," 1.

92. Robert Torth and John Goldman, "5 Freed Soviet Dissidents Vow to Continue Struggle: They Promise to Go on Seeking Political, Religious Freedoms, Express Amazement at Being in the U.S.," *Los Angeles Times* (April 29, 1979): SD1.

93. Robert Kaiser and Marjorie Hyer, "Brzezinski and Soviet Dissident Meet in White House Session," *Washington Post* (June 8, 1979): A7; Marjorie Hyer, "Soviets Spy on Churchgoers: Freed Dissident Tells Congressmen of Persecution," *Washington Post* (June 15, 1979): C20; Carol Franklin and Stan Hastey, "Vins: Pressure from West Resulted in His Release," *Baptist Press* 79–94 (June 7, 1979): 1.

94. Commission on Security and Cooperation in Europe, *Basket Three: Implementation of the Helsinki Accords, Hearing before the Commission on Security and Cooperation in Europe on Implementation of the Helsinki Accords: Pastor Georgi Vins on the Persecution of Reformed Baptists in the U.S.S.R.*, 96th Cong., 1st sess., June 7, 1979.

95. Georgi P. Vins to Bob Maddox, October 1, 1980, Folder: "Correspondence File 10/1/ 1980–10/5/1980 (Folder 5)," Box 101, Office of Anne Wexler, Special Assistant to the President— Bob Maddox Religious Liaison, JCPL.

96. The IRCEBCSU testified before Congress on numerous occasions, supported persecuted Soviet religious leaders, and published accounts of persecution in the USSR to keep U.S. evangelicals informed. After the collapse of the Soviet Union, Vins renamed the organization Russian Gospel Ministries, International, Inc., and focused more explicitly on evangelism in Russia. Daniel E. Gelatt, "Persecuted but Not Forsaken: An Interview with Georgi Vins," *Baptist Bulletin* (March 1981): 12–13; Georgi Vins, "Obey God, Don't Count the Cost," *Christianity Today* 26, no. 16 (October 8, 1982): 42–43; "Soviets Arrest Handicapped Woman for Letting Church Meet in Home," *Contact: Official Publication of the National Association of Free Will Baptists* (December 1986): 28; *Expressing Sense of Congress That the Soviet Union Should Proclaim a General Amnesty for Imprisoned Christians*, 100th Cong., 2nd sess., *Congressional Record* 134 (May 17, 1988): H 11320–321.

97. Commission on Security and Cooperation in Europe, *On the Right to Emigrate for Religious Reasons: The Case of 10,000 Soviet Evangelical Christians*, May 1, 1979, iv, 2–12, 29.

98. Central Intelligence Agency National Foreign Assessment Center, "Significant Developments Related to the U.S. Stand on Human Rights," April 21–27, 1978, JCPL, RAC Project Number NLC-31-39-1-17-6; Central Intelligence Agency Foreign Assessment Center, "Human Rights Performance: January 1977–July 1978," September 1978, JCPL, RAC Project Number NLC-28-17-15-9-8; Memorandum, [Redacted] to William Odom, "Human Rights Developments in the USSR, January—May 1978," May 25, 1978, JCPL, RAC Project Number NLC-6-79-6-15-7.

99. American Embassy Bucharest to United States Department of State, "Increased Interest," 1–2.

100. H. J. Res. 454, 96th Cong., 1st sess. (December 4, 1979), 2.

101. Carl Levin, "S. 2890 A bill for the relief of Maria and Timofei Chmykhalov, and for Lilia, Peter, Liubov, Lidia, and Augustina Vashchenko to the Committee on the Judiciary," 96th Cong., 2nd sess., *Congressional Record* (June 27, 1980): S 8678.

102. Ibid., S 8679.

103. Memorandum from Michael Hornblow to C. Arthur Borg, "Appeal to President Carter from Protestant Pentecostals in the Soviet Union," March 23, 1977, CO165 Executive 3/16/77–3/31/77 Folder 7, Box 57, WHCF—Subject File, JCPL.

104. Memorandum from Frank V. Ortiz and C. Arthur Borg to Zbigniew Brzezinski, "Appeal to President Carter from Protestant Pentecostals in the Soviet Union," March 21, 1977, CO165 Executive 3/16/77–3/31/77 Folder 7, Box 57, WHCF—Subject File, JCPL.

105. Zbigniew Brzezinski to B.S. Hrubý, January 19, 1979, CO 165 General 1/1/79–3/31/79 Folder 3, Box 63, WHCF—Subject File, JCPL; Douglas J. Bennet, Jr. to Representative Jim Weaver, April 20, 1979, CO 165 General 1/1/79–3/31/79 Folder 3, Box 63, WHCF—Subject File, JCPL.

106. As Sikkink has argued, human rights policy during the Carter administration shifted from an "active phase" in 1977 and 1978 to a "disenchantment phase" in 1979 and 1980 as a variety of foreign and domestic issues—including ongoing economic malaise, the Sandinista victory in Nicaragua, and Iran hostage crisis—rose to a higher priority than human rights compliance. Sikkink, *Mixed Signals*, 123–24.

107. Billy A. Melvin, "A Report from the National Association of Evangelicals," *Evangel* 71, no. 11 (August 10, 1981): 6–7; Robert Dugan to Anne Wexler, July 31, 1979, Folder 5: Correspondence File 8/1/79–8/14/79, Box 98, Office of Anne Wexler, Special Assistant to the President, Bob Maddox Religious Liaison, JCPL.

108. Not to mention the connections built with evangelical senators and representatives, more of whom had entered Congress with the rise of the religious right as a voting bloc.

109. Roger Jepsen to Richard Allen, February 23, 1981, Folder 6: Congressional Legislative File, Subject File, Foreign Relations, Christian Rescue Effort for the Emancipation of Dissidents (CREED) Briefing books, 1978–1981 (2 of 2), Box 127, JKP.

110. Roger Jepsen to Bob Maddox, October 14, 1980, Folder 6: Correspondence File 10/6/1980–10/15/1980, Box 101, Office of Anne Wexler, Special Assistant to the President, Bob Maddox Religious Liaison, JCPL.

111. CREED, Meeting Minutes, October 24, 1980, Fellowship House, Washington, D.C., Folder 5, Congressional Legislative File, Subject File, Foreign Relations, CREED Briefing books, 1978–1981 (1 of 2), Box 127, JKP.

112. Ibid., 5.

113. Ibid., 8.

114. Ibid., 8, 20–21.

115. Gen. 1:26–27 (New Revised Standard Version); Southern Baptist Convention, "Declaration of Human Rights," 1978, Folder 3.5 Human Rights, Box 3, Christian Life Commission Publication and Promotional Material Collection AR 140, SBHLA, Nashville, TN.

116. Jn. 3:16 (NRSV); Carl F. H. Henry, "Human Rights and Wrongs," *Christianity Today* 21, no. 19 (July 8, 1977): 25.

117. 2 Cor. 3:17 (NRSV); Henry, "Human Rights," 25.

118. Southern Baptist Convention, *Baptist Faith & Message* (1963), http://www.sbc.net/bfm2000/bfmcomparison.asp; Ronald D. Sisk, "The Atlanta Declaration: Articulating a Southern Baptist Commitment to Human Rights," unpublished manuscript (February 6, 1979), 13, Folder 51.9 Human rights, 1964–1980, Box 51, Christian Life Commission Resource Files AR 138–2, SBHLA.

119. Baptist World Alliance, "Declaration on Human Rights," 1980, http://baptiststudiesonline.com/wp-content/uploads/2007/02/bwa-declaration-on-human-rights.pdf

120. CREED, Meeting Minutes, 10; John Warwick Montgomery, "Should We Export the American Way?," *Christianity Today* 20, no. 15 (April 23, 1976): 58.

121. CREED, "Christian Solidarity International" and "Keston College," Briefing Book, folder 5, Congressional Legislative File, Subject File, Foreign Relations, CREED Briefing books, 1978–1981 (1 of 2), Box 127, JKP.

122. S. Con. Res. 60, 96th Cong., 2nd sess., November 24, 1980; S. Con. Res. 61, 96th Cong., 2nd sess., *Congressional Record* 125 (December 10, 1979), 35278.

123. Senate Committee on Foreign Relations, *Expressing the Sense of the Congress with Respect to the Treatment of Christians by the Union of Soviet Socialist Republics*, 96th Cong., 2nd sess., October 16, 1980, 6.

124. Ibid.

125. Ibid., 26.

126. Ibid., 38.

127. Bentley T. Elliot, "Campaign Builds to Aid Russian Christians," *Human Events* 41, no. 1 (January 3, 1981): 1.

128. Senate Committee on Foreign Relations, *Expressing*, 6.

129. Elliot, "Campaign," 1.

130. Ibid., 2.

4. Fighting Religious Persecution behind the Iron Curtain

1. William Hopkins and Eugenia Arensburger, Department of State, "Reagan-Gorbachev Meetings in Geneva November 1985," Memorandum of Conversation (November 20, 1985): 2, reproduced in Declassified Documents Reference System (hereafter DDRS) (Farmington Hills, MI: Gale, 2013), Document Number: CK2349539126.

2. Ibid.

3. Ibid.

4. Ibid.

5. "Dissent in the USSR," Briefing Paper, folder "Briefing Material for President Reagan— Gorbachev Meeting 11/27/85 (sic) (2/3)," Jack F. Matlock, Jr.: Files, Series III: US-USSR Summits, Box 47, Ronald Reagan Library.

6. Ibid.

7. Slavic Gospel Association, *Radio to Russia* newsletter (ca. 1985), SC-53 ISEES Collection, Box 38, Folder 14, WCSC.

8. "Dissent in the USSR," 6–7. See also Anderson, *Religion, State and Politics in the Soviet Union and Successor States*, 106, 128–30, 134; Sawatsky, "Protestantism in the USSR," in *Religious Policy in the Soviet Union*, ed. Ramet, 328–29.

9. See, for example, Bentley T. Elliot, "Campaign Builds to Aid Russian Christians," *Human Events* (January 3, 1981), 2; Robert Mackish, "God Is Working Mightily in Russia," *Pentecostal Evangel* (May 30, 1982): 16–17; Harry Genet, "The Soviet Union Has Failed to Stamp Out Christianity," *Christianity Today* (May 7, 1982), 38–39; Christian Solidarity International, "Revival Continues in Romania," *Intercession* (November-December 1982) 3–4.

10. The Siberian Seven case received extensive media coverage and congressional attention. For a small sampling of the newspaper coverage, popular books, and legislative hearings, see Craig R. Whitney, "U.S. still Giving Pentecostalists Soviet Asylum," *New York Times* (November 9, 1978): A13; Serge Schmemann, "Pentecostals Leave U.S. Embassy in Moscow after 4 Years' Asylum," *New York Times* (April 13, 1983): A1; Pollock, *The Siberian Seven*; Senate Committee on the Judiciary, Subcommittee on Immigration, Refugees, and International Law, *Relief of*

Seven Soviet Pentecostals Residing in the U.S. Embassy in Moscow Hearing Before the Subcommittee on Immigration and Refugee Policy and the Committee on the Judiciary, United States Senate on S. 312, 97th Congress, 1st sess., November 19, 1981.

11. Jeffrey Collins, EWNS Press material for 1982 Church and Media Exposition, February 8, 1982, Collection 309 Records of the National Religious Broadcasters, Box 98, Folder 41, BGCA, Wheaton, IL; Eric Malnic and Russell Chandler, "International Christian Aid Founder: L. Joe Bass—A Man on a Mission or a Power Trip?," *Los Angeles Times* (April 8, 1985): A2–3, 18.

12. East/West News Service, pamphlet included in *East/West News Service Packet* (February 1982), Collection 309 Records of the National Religious Broadcasters, Box 98, Folder 41, BGCA. Many other evangelical activist groups, including Religion in Communist Dominated Lands and Underground Evangelism, published similar accounts.

13. "Religious Freedom Russian Style! Profile of a Raid on a Church," *Underground Evangelism* (May 1978): 7.

14. Roger Arnold, "From Romania," *CSI Reports* 1, no. 2 (Summer 1980): 1; "Russian Pastor Rumachik Arrested," "Fourth Conviction for Brother Khorev—Five Years in Prison," "Twenty Russian Christians Imprisoned Since Last November," "Calciu Sentenced to 10 Years in Rumanian Prison," *EWNS News* (September 1980): 1–2, 4–5, Collection 309 Records of the National Religious Broadcasters, Box 98, Folder 41, BGCA; "Christian Prisoners in the USSR 1979–1982," *Religion in Communist Dominated Lands* 10, no. 1 (February 1982): 81–83; Ron Branson, "Soviet Authorities Confiscate Believer's Property," excerpt from *EWNS News* reprinted in *The Alert Sheet* (August 1981), folder 4, Alert Sheet Ministries, HH2314, Box 15–1, MS76.15 CRR, Gordon Hall and Grace Hoag Collection of Dissenting and Extremist Printed Propaganda, John Hay Library, Special Collections, Brown University, Providence, RI; "Printing Press Seized," *Religion in Communist Lands* 9, 1–2 (February 1981): 72.

15. By reporting on Soviet abuses, the EWNS affirmed "the Biblical command to 'Remember them that are in bonds as bound with them, and them which suffer adversity as being yourselves also in the body,'" a reference to Hebrews 13:3 (King James Version). East/West News Service, pamphlet (February 1982).

16. Roger Jepsen to Rev. Jerry Falwell, January 27, 1982 and Jack Kemp and Roger Jepsen to Phillip Spiess, September 16, 1983, FAL 5–2 Series 1 Folder 6, Correspondence with Senators: 1982, Liberty University Archive, Lynchburg, VA.

17. "Focus on Soviet Union at Madrid Review," *EWNS* (November 1980): 3, Collection 309 Records of the National Religious Broadcasters, Box 98, Folder 41, BGCA.

18. Ronald Reagan, "Republican National Convention Acceptance Speech," July 17, 1980, Ronald Reagan Library, https://www.reaganlibrary.gov/7-17-80; Brands, *Reagan*, chap. 31.

19. Dochuk, *From Bible Belt to Sunbelt*, 392–96; Allison O'Neill, "At Calvary Road, Reagan: Majority," *Washington Post* (November 3, 1980): D1, D3.

20. Kengor, *God and Ronald Reagan*, 58–59, 141–42; Freiling, *Reagan's God and Country*, 24–25, 48–51; Diggins, *Ronald Reagan*, 28. Reagan's mother, Nelle, raised him in the evangelical Disciples of Christ church. During his years as a Hollywood actor, he drifted somewhat from the devout evangelical faith of his upbringing, but returned to the church in the late 1950s when he launched his political career. He joined a Presbyterian church in the mid-1960s and, in the late 1970s, began identifying himself as a born-again Christian. That said, in addition to his core Christian beliefs, he also "harbored a rather more unorthodox spiritualism, such as a belief in ghosts." Preston, *Sword of the Spirit, Shield of Faith*, 579.

21. Ronald Reagan, "Labor Day Speech at Liberty State Park, Jersey City, New Jersey," September 1, 1980, Ronald Reagan Library, https://www.reaganlibrary.gov/9-1-80; Ronald Reagan, "Ronald Reagan/John Anderson Presidential Debate," September 21, 1981, Ronald

Reagan Library, https://www.reaganlibrary.gov/sspeeches/9-21-80. See also Freiling, *Reagan's God*, 24–25; Preston, *Sword*, 584. Reagan made this link explicit in a letter he wrote in the late 1960s to the president of the Freedom Foundation at Valley Forge, stating: "God meant America to be free because God intended each man to have the dignity of freedom." Ronald Reagan to Kenneth Wells, ca. 1967–68, reprinted in *Reagan: A Life in Letters*, ed. Reagan, Skinner, Graebner Anderson, and Anderson, 257.

22. Kengor, *God*, 90–92. The phrase "a city upon a hill" derives from Matthew 5:14, in the parable of Salt and Light. In 1630, John Winthrop incorporated this phrase into his sermon, "A Model of Christian Charity," asserting that the Massachusetts Bay colony "shall be as a city upon a hill. The eyes of all people are upon us." Scholars have explored how this idea influenced later U.S. leaders and the notion of exceptionalism. See, for example, Tuveson, *Redeemer Nation*; Cherry, *God's New Israel*; Walker, *National Security and Core Values*.

23. Kengor, *God*, 94, 201–6; Leffler, *For the Soul of Mankind*, 339–42.

24. Ronald W. Reagan, "A Strategy for Peace in the '80s," televised address, October 19, 1980, Ronald Reagan Library, https://www.reaganlibrary.gov/10-19-80; Reagan, "Election Eve Address, 'A Vision for America,'" November 3, 1980, Ronald Reagan Library, https://www.reaganlibrary.gov/11-3-80; "1980 Ronald Reagan/Jimmy Carter Presidential Debate," October 28, 1980, Ronald Reagan Library, https://www.reaganlibrary.gov/10-28-80debate. See also Sikkink, *Mixed Signals*, 19, 148; Caleb Rossiter and Anne-Marie Smith, "Human Rights: The Carter Record, the Reagan Reaction," *International Policy Report* (September 1984); Aryeh Neier, "Human Rights in the Reagan Era: Acceptance in Principle," *Annals of the American Academy of Political and Social Science* 506 (November 1989): 30–31.

25. This foreign policy orientation derived in part from the ideas that Jeane Kirkpatrick, whom Reagan appointed as the U.S. ambassador to the United Nations in 1981, set forth in her well-known 1979 *Commentary* article "Dictatorships and Double Standards." Her essay condemned the Carter administration for its "lack of realism about the nature of traditional versus revolutionary autocracies and the relation of each to the American national interest," which is to say, for its assumption that supporting left-leaning leaders rather than authoritarian regimes would encourage democratization, modernization, and observance of human rights. Kirkpatrick asserted that, repugnant though they might be, autocratic regimes had a better chance of evolving into democracies than did totalitarian ones. She also claimed that Marxist regimes perpetrated more systemic, totalizing forms of human rights abuses. The Kirkpatrick Doctrine found a number of adherents in the Reagan administration; in the Senate hearings regarding his nomination as secretary of state, Haig similarly criticized the Carter administration for targeting human rights abuses in authoritarian regimes while failing to condemn those totalitarian regimes "who were the greatest violators of human rights." See Jeane Kirkpatrick, "Dictatorships and Double Standards," *Commentary* (November 1979): 34–45; Jeane Kirkpatrick, "Human Rights and the Foundations of Democracy," *World Affairs* 144, no. 3, A U.S. Offensive at the U.N. (Statements by the U.S. Delegation before the General Assembly) (Winter 1981/82): 196–203; Senate Committee on Foreign Relations, *Nomination of Alexander M. Haig, Jr.: Hearings before the Committee on Foreign Relations, United States Senate*, 97th Congress, 1st sess., January 9, 10, 12, 13, 14, 15, 1981, Part 2 (Washington, DC: U.S. Government Printing Office, 1981), 44.

26. Ronald Reagan, interview by Walter Cronkite, *CBS News* (March 3, 1981), https://www.reaganlibrary.gov/research/speeches/30381c.

27. Elliot, "Campaign Builds," 1.

28. Ethics & Policy Center, "About," accessed September 25, 2014, http://eppc.org/about/.

29. In his testimony, he called into question the efficacy of laws that imposed human rights compliance as a condition for normalized trade relations. Ernest Lefever, "Statement of

Ernest W. Lefever, Director of the Ethics and Public Policy Center, Georgetown University: The Trivialization of Human Rights," in House Committee on Foreign Affairs, *Human Rights And U.S. Foreign Policy: Hearings before the Subcommittee on International Organizations of the Committee on Foreign Affairs, House of Representatives*, 96th Cong., 1st sess., May 2, June 21, July 12, and August 2, 1979 (Washington, DC: U.S. Government Printing Office, 1979): 239.

30. Ernest Lefever, "The Trivialization of Human Rights," *Policy Review* no. 3 (Winter 1978): 15; Senate Committee on Foreign Relations, *Nomination of Ernest W. Lefever: Hearings before the Committee on Foreign Relations*, 97th Cong., 1st sess., May 18, 19, June 4, and 5, 1981 (Washington, DC: U.S. Government Printing Office, 1981), 3–5, 83–84, 199; Leon Howell, "Ernest Lefever at the Edge of Power: A Profile in Consistency," *Christianity and Crisis* (March 2, 1981), 36–37.

31. Ibid., 25–30. A selection of letters from supportive evangelical leaders were inserted into the hearing record.

32. Carl F. H. Henry to the Senate Committee on Foreign Relations, March 10, 1981, reprinted in Senate Committee on Foreign Relations, *Nomination of Ernest W. Lefever*, 30; Arthur L. Beals to the Senate Committee on Foreign Relations, March 17, 1981, reprinted in Senate Committee on Foreign Relations, *Nomination of Ernest W. Lefever*, 25; Robert Lincoln Hancock to the Senate Committee on Foreign Relations, April 12, 1981, reprinted in Senate Committee on Foreign Relations, *Nomination of Ernest W. Lefever*, 29–30.

33. Robert P. Dugan, Jr. to the Senate Committee on Foreign Relations, April 16, 1981, reprinted in Senate Committee on Foreign Relations, *Nomination of Ernest W. Lefever*, 27.

34. Robert P. Dugan, Jr., "Prepared Statement of Robert P. Dugan, Jr.," Senate Committee on Foreign Relations, *Nomination of Ernest W. Lefever*, 307.

35. Ibid., 307–8.

36. Ibid., 307.

37. Ibid., 308.

38. Dugan, "Prepared Statement," 308; Carl F. H. Henry to the Senate Committee on Foreign Relations, March 10, 1981; Robert Lincoln Hancock to the Senate Committee on Foreign Relations, April 12, 1981; Letter, Dr. Franklin H. Littell to the Senate Committee on Foreign Relations, March 11, 1981, reprinted in Senate Committee on Foreign Relations, *Nomination of Ernest W. Lefever*, 31.

39. Dugan, "Prepared Statement," 309.

40. Paul Wolfowitz and Lawrence Eagleburger to Alexander Haig, "Human Rights Policy," Action Memorandum, October 2, 1981, released by the Freedom of Information Act (FOIA), http://foia.state.gov/searchapp/DOCUMENTS/StateChile3/00005F2D.pdf.

41. Ibid.

42. Richard Kennedy to Alexander Haig, "Reinvigoration of Human Rights Policy," Memorandum, October 26, 1981, released by FOIA.

43. Barbara Crossette, "Strong U.S. Human Rights Policy Urged in Memo Approved by Haig," *New York Times* (November 5, 1981): A10; Snyder, *Human Rights Activism and the End of the Cold War*, 140–41.

44. Sarah Snyder has argued that the Senate Foreign Relations Committee's rejection of the Lefever nomination "should be seen as a significant victory for those determined to maintain a commitment to human rights as an element of U.S. foreign policy." Even though Reagan administration *rhetoric* about human rights shifted after Elliot Abrams became the assistant secretary of state for Human Rights and Humanitarian Affairs and George Shultz replaced Alexander Haig as secretary of state, Reagan still focused most of his attention regarding human rights issues on the Soviet Union and other totalitarian states, as he had asserted he would during his campaign. He also tended to ignore abuses that occurred in authoritarian regimes friendly

to the United States. Snyder, "The Defeat of Ernest Lefever's Nomination," in *Challenging U.S. Foreign Policy*, 136, 153.

45. Snyder, "The Defeat," 150–51; Senate Committee on Foreign Relations, *Nomination of Elliot Abrams: Hearing before the Committee on Foreign Relations, United States Senate*, 97th Cong., 1st sess., November 17, 1981 (Washington, DC: U.S. Government Printing Office, 1981), 1–3.

46. Whereas Lefever seemed flummoxed by policy-specific questions in his hearings (often stating he had not yet reviewed the issues fully enough to take a position), Abrams offered specific, feasible policy recommendations. Senate Committee on Foreign Relations, *Nomination of Ernest W. Lefever*, 85, 131, 155; Senate Committee on Foreign Relations, *Nomination of Elliot Abrams*, 4–5, 7–11.

47. Senate Committee on Foreign Relations, *Nomination of Elliot Abrams*, 9.

48. Ibid., 13–14, 19. For example, he acknowledged the abysmal human rights conditions in El Salvador, but argued that public condemnation from the United States only worsened the situation there, whereas private diplomacy offered the State Department more leverage to encourage change. Yet he called for continued public attention to Soviet abuses because he did not believe that the United States had as much power to influence the Soviet leadership to change their internal policies through private negotiations.

49. William Safire, "Human Rights Victory," *New York Times* (November 5, 1981), A27; Jack Kemp, "Human Rights Victory," *Congressional Record* 127:21 (November 13, 1981), E27470–71.

50. The case of the Siberian Seven has received relatively sparse historical analysis, but see Preston, *Sword of the Spirit*, 594–98; Snyder, *Human Rights Activism*, 141–46. Those who have covered the case well have focused on top-level overviews of Reagan's concern for and quiet diplomacy on behalf of the two families. Preston has focused on the role of the Siberian Seven case in the larger narrative of the end of the Cold War, whereas Snyder has emphasized the case as part of a shift in U.S. expectations for Soviet human rights compliance. Adding in an analysis of the role that evangelical NGOs played in spurring grassroots and legislative activism helps to explain the sustained attention the case received. It also highlights the tensions this focus on the Siberian Seven sparked between advocates for religious freedom (congressional as well as NGO) and the State Department, which did not approve of activist tactics.

51. Two U.S. evangelical leaders had invited the Vashchenkos and Chmykhalovs to emigrate to the United States in the 1970s after hearing about the persecution they faced in the Soviet Union for their Pentecostal faith. The families applied for emigration based in part on these invitations and took refuge in the embassy only after Soviet officials denied their applications. Ernest Gordon, "Prepared Statement of Dr. Ernest Gordon, President, CREED," in United States Senate, *Relief of Seven Soviet Pentecostals Residing in the U.S. Embassy in Moscow Hearing before the Subcommittee on Immigration and Refugee Policy of the Committee on the Judiciary, United States Senate*, 97th Cong., 1st sess., November 19, 1981 (Washington, DC: U.S. Government Printing Office, 1982), 157.

52. Anthony Austin, "Pentecostals Hold Fast in Moscow Embassy," *New York Times* (June 24, 1979): 3.

53. Timofei Chmykhalov to supporters, February 27, 1981, SC-52 Siberian 7 Collection, Box IB2, Folder: Correspondence I.B., WCSC.

54. Austin, "Pentecostals," 3.

55. "Message from the Vashchenkos through Christian Solidarity International to Dr. Billy Graham and Dr. Walter Smith, Zurich, Switzerland," Telex (April 22, 1982), Collection 17 Records of the BGEA: Crusade Activities, Box 157, Folder: USSR 1982, BGCA; "Hunger Strike Overshadows Long-Awaited Grant for Additional Room for Siberian Seven," *EWNS* (January 15, 1982), 2–3, Collection 309 Records of the National Religious Broadcasters, Box 98, Folder 41, BGCA.

56. In 1979, Reagan discussed their plight on his syndicated radio program. In November 1981, when he first met with Jack Matlock, his adviser on Soviet affairs, he emphasized the importance of their case and his desire to see them leave the Soviet Union. Ronald Reagan, "Vlasenko, October 2, 1979," in *Reagan, In His Own Hand*, ed. Reagan et al., 177–78; Matlock, *Reagan and Gorbachev*, 54–59.

57. Some, such as executive director of Christian Solidarity International Rev. Roger Arnold, described the Siberian Seven situation explicitly as a "test case" for bringing religious persecution cases to public and congressional attention. U.S. Congress, House, *Religious Persecution as a Violation of Human Rights: Hearings and Markup Before the Committee on Foreign Affairs and Its Subcommittee on Human Rights and International Organizations, House of Representatives*, 97th Cong., 2nd sess., On H. Con. Res. 100, 378, 428, 433, and 434, H. Res. 269, S. Con. Res. 18, February 10, March 23, May 25, July 27 and 29, August 5 and 10, September 23, December 1 and 14, 1982 (Washington, DC: U.S. Government Printing Office, 1983), 353.

58. Kent Hill, "Statement of Kent Hill, Professor of Russian History, Seattle-Pacific University," in House, *Religious Persecution*, 301. Hill was a leading evangelical intellectual and an expert on religion and religious freedom in Russia.

59. Roger Jepsen, "Statement of Hon. Roger W. Jepsen, a U.S. Senator from the State of Iowa," in Senate, *Relief of Seven Soviet Pentecostals*, 28.

60. The Senate sent the bill to the House of Representatives, which referred it to the House Judiciary committee. Barney Frank (D-MA) then introduced HR 1588, *A bill for the relief of Maria and Timofei Chmykhalov, and Lilia, Peter, Liubov, and Augustina Vashchenko* in February 1983. Ultimately, the Soviet Union allowed the Siberian Seven to emigrate before the House took further action. Larry M. Eig, "Analysis under Domestic and International Law of Proposed Legislation (S.312) to Grant Certain Pentacostalists Residing in the United States Embassy in Moscow Permanent Resident Immigration Status and Other Relief" (December 6, 1982), in *Siberian Seven: Hearing before the Subcommittee on Immigration, Refugees, and International Law of the Committee on the Judiciary House of Representatives*, 97th Cong., 2nd sess., on HR 2873 and S. 312, December 16, 1982 (Washington, DC: U.S. Government Printing Office, 1983), 73; for related bills see, for example, U.S. Congress, House, *A concurrent resolution expressing the sense of the Congress with respect to the situation of two Soviet families, known as the Siberian Seven, who have sought refuge in the United States Embassy in Moscow because of the discrimination of their Pentecostal faith by the Union of Soviet Socialist Republics*, H.CON.RES.251, 97th Cong., 2nd sess. (1982).

61. Olga Hruby, "Statement of Olga S. Hruby," House Committee on Foreign Affairs, *Religious Persecution*, 329–30.

62. Roger Arnold, "Statement of Rev. Roger Arnold, Executive Director, Christian Solidarity International," House Committee on Foreign Affairs, *Religious Persecution*, 327.

63. Carl Levin, "Statement of Hon. Carl Levin, A U.S. Senator from the State of Michigan," *Religious Persecution*, 257–58.

64. Bonker, House Committee on Foreign Affairs, *Religious Persecution*, 322.

65. National Religious Broadcasters, "Resolution" and "Petition to Save the Siberian Seven," (February 1982), folder "National Religious Broadcasters (2 of 4)," Morton C. Blackwell Files, Series III: Religion Liaison Box 38, Ronald Reagan Library.

66. Ben Armstrong to Dr. L. P. Dorenbos, December 30, 1982, Collection 309 Records of the National Religious Broadcasters, Box 31, Folder 5, BGCA.

67. Alexander S. Haraszti, interview by Dr. Lois Ferm, June 16, 1982, Transcript of tape 1, Collection 141 BGEA: Oral History Project, Box 45, Folder: O.H.I.—Final Copy: Haraszti, Alexander S. (Dr.) (#357-3); 1982 (45-3), 4–7, BGCA.

68. American Embassy in Moscow to Secretary of State in Washington, D.C., February 9, 1982, Cable regarding Soviet preparations for Moscow's 1/26–28/82 World Peace Conference,

reproduced in DDRS, Document: CK2349469887. See also Walter J. Stoessell, Jr. to Ronald Reagan, "Presidential Intervention to Prevent Dr. Billy Graham from Attending Moscow 'Peace Conference,'" Memorandum, February 11, 1982, Jack F. Matlock, Jr.: Files, Series II: USSR Subject File, Box 40, Folder: US/USSR Rel [Jan–April 1982], Ronald Reagan Library; William L. Stearman to William P. Clark, "Billy Graham and the Moscow 'World Peace Conference,'" Memorandum, February 10, 1982, White House Office of Records Management (hereafter WHORM): Subject File, FO008, Case File #048718SS, Ronald Reagan Library; Archbishop Arnolds Lusis, The Evangelical Lutheran Church of Latvia in Exile to Dr. Billy Graham, April 16, 1982, Collection 16 BGEA: Crusade Activities, Box 157, Folder: USSR—Visit May 1982 (General), BGCA.

69. Alexander S. Haraszti, interview by Dr. Lois Ferm, March 15, 1984, Transcript of tape 1, Collection 141 BGEA: Oral History Project, Box 45, Folder: O.H.I.—Final Copy: Haraszti, Alexander S. (Dr.) (#357-6); 1984 (45-6), BGCA, 11–13; James W. Nance to Ronald Reagan, "Visit by Dr. John Akers and Dr. Walter Smith, Assistants to Dr. Billy Graham," Memorandum, February 4, 1982, WHORM Subject File FO008, Folder 048718, Ronald Reagan Library.

70. Harry Genet, "Graham Will Preach in Moscow: An Agonizing Decision After Weighing the Pros and Cons," *Christianity Today* (April 9, 1982): 44. Graham received many supportive letters from individual evangelicals, agencies involved in activism for the Siberian Seven, and international religious leaders. See Collection 17 BGEA: Crusade Activities, Box 157, Folder: USSR—Visit May 1982 (General), BGCA.

71. Horace Russell to John Poindexter, "Talking Paper for Visit with Billy Graham," Memorandum, March 26, 1982, WHORM Subject File, ND018, Box 3, Case File #071087, Ronald Reagan Library.

72. George H. W. Bush to Ambassador Hartman, "Billy Graham's Visit," Memorandum (ca. March 1982), reproduced in DDRS, Document: CK2349707679.

73. Billy Graham, "The Christian Faith and Peace in a Nuclear Age," address prepared for delivery at the World Conference: Religious Workers for Saving the Sacred Gift of Life from Nuclear Catastrophe, Moscow, USSR, May 11, 1982, Collection 17 BGEA: Crusade Activities, Box 157, Folder: USSR 1982, BGCA.

74. "Graham in the Soviet Union," *Christianity Today* (June 18, 1982): 42–43.

75. Ibid., 42.

76. Ibid.

77. Billy Graham Team Office, "Graham Exhausted but Exhilarated," Press Release, Collection 345 BGEA: Records of the Media Office, Box 76, Folder: News Release—Moscow, Russia May 13, 1982, BGCA, 1.

78. Haraszti, interview by Ferm, March 15, 1984, 11.

79. Alexander S. Haraszti, interview by Dr. Lois Ferm, June 3, 1983, Transcript of tape 2, Collection 141 BGEA: Oral History Project, Box 45, Folder: O.H.I.—Final Copy: Haraszti, Alexander S. (Dr.) (#357-5); 1983 (45-5), 3, BGCA.

80. Jim Gallagher, "Graham in Moscow, preaches obedience," *Chicago Tribune* (May 10, 1982): A1; Robert Gillette, "Saw No Soviet Repression of Religion, Graham Says," *Los Angeles Times* (May 13, 1982): B1. Graham's defenders rebuked these reporters for taking the preacher's statements out of context and misrepresenting the circumstances under which he preached. "Graham Cites Trip 'Misquotes,'" *Washington Post* (May 18, 1982): A19; Edward Plowman, "Correcting the Record on Billy Graham," *Congressional Record* 128:10 (June 16, 1982), H13920–21.

81. Plowman, "Correcting," H13921.

82. "Communists Reject 100,000 Bibles." *Underground Evangelism* 19, no. 2 (February 1978): 2–3; "Second Romanian Bible Freighter Found," *EWNS* (February 1, 1982): 16. These activities contributed to what the State Department referred to as "friction between the government and

religious groups" in the Soviet bloc. See Gary Matthews, "Prepared Statement of Gary Matthews, Deputy Assistant Secretary of State for Human Rights and Humanitarian Affairs," *Human Rights in Romania: Hearing before the Subcommittees on Europe and the Middle East and on Human Rights and International Organizations of the Committee on Foreign Affairs, House of Representatives*, 99th Cong., 1st sess., May 14, 1985 (Washington, DC: U.S. Government Printing Office, 1985), 109.

83. Denton Lotz, "Religion in the USSR: How Much Freedom Is Enough? Don't Suffer, Settle for Some," *Christianity Today* (October 8, 1982).

84. Council for Religious Affairs Attached to the USSR Council of Ministers, Moscow to the Central Committee of the Communist Party of the Soviet Union, "On the Publication of the Bible," December 1, 1982, in *Religion in the Soviet Union: An Archival Reader* (New York: New York University Press, 1996), 285–86.

85. Memorandum of Conversation between U.S. Secretary of State Alexander M. Haig and U.S.S.R. Foreign Minister Andrei A. Gromyko, September 28, 1981, William P. Clark Files, Box 3, Ronald Reagan Library, 24.

86. Ronald Reagan, George Shultz, and Anatoly Dobrynin, Memorandum of Conversation, February 15, 1983, William P. Clark Files, Box 8, Folder: US-Soviet Relations Papers Working File, Ronald Reagan Library, 2.

87. George Shultz to Ronald Reagan, "USG-Soviet Relations—Where Do We Want to Be and How Do We Get There?," Memorandum, March 3, 1983, William P. Clark Files, Box 8, Folder: US-Soviet Relations Working File: Contains Originals (3), Ronald Reagan Library, 1, 5.

88. Reagan, Shultz, and Dobrynin, Memorandum, February 15, 1983, 2–3.

89. Ronald Reagan, "Message to Lidiya and Augustina Vashchenko, Hunger Strikers in the United States Embassy in Moscow," January 29, 1982, Reagan Presidential Library, https://www.reaganlibrary.gov/research/speeches/12982d.

90. In his account of the negotiations, Jack Matlock reported that after Reagan and Dobrynin met to discuss the case, Max Kampelman, the U.S. ambassador to the CSCE coordinated with Soviet diplomat Sergei Kondrashev. Kondrashev provided secret assurances to the Vashchenko and Chmykhalov families that if they consented to emigrate to Israel first before going on to the United States, Soviet officials would grant them permission to leave the Soviet Union. Matlock, *Reagan and Gorbachev*, 57–59.

91. "Update on the State-of-Play of Lidia Vashchenko's Emigration," April 7, 1983, Jack F. Matlock, Jr.: Files, Series II: USSR Subject File, Box 30, Folder: USSR-Pentecostals (3/4), Ronald Reagan Library; Paula Dobriansky to William P. Clark, "USG Posture on Pentecostals," Memorandum, July 21, 1983, Jack F. Matlock, Jr.: Files, Series II: USSR Subject File, Box 30, Folder: USSR-Pentecostals (4/4), Ronald Reagan Library.

92. Ronald Reagan, *The Reagan Diaries*, ed. Brinkley, 215.

93. Draft letter to Senator Dan Quayle, ca. 1983, Jack F. Matlock, Jr.: Files, Series II: USSR Subject File, Box 30, Folder: USSR-Pentecostals (4/4), Ronald Reagan Library.

94. Ibid.; Charles Hill to William P. Clark, "Recommended USG Posture on the Emigration of the Embassy Pentecostals," July 20, 1983, Jack F. Matlock, Jr.: Files, Series II: USSR Subject File, Box 30, Folder: USSR-Pentecostals (4/4), Ronald Reagan Library.

95. Nicholas Platt to Robert McFarlane, "Secretary's Talking Points for Shevardnadze Meeting," Memorandum, September 23, 1985, Jack F. Matlock, Jr.: Files, Series III: US-USSR Summits, Box 45, Folder: Shultz-Shevardnadze Mtg. in New York, September 23, 1985 (1 of 3), Ronald Reagan Library.

96. Ronald Reagan, "Remarks at the Annual Convention of the National Association of Evangelicals," March 8, 1983, Ronald Reagan Library, https://www.reaganlibrary.gov/research/speeches/30883b.

97. Georgi Vins to Ronald Reagan, October 7, 1985, U.S. Department of State FOIA, http://foia.state.gov/searchapp/DOCUMENTS/foiadocs/5075.PDF; Alexa Popovici to Ronald Reagan, June 30, 1985, WHORM: Subject File, CO130 Romania, Case File #292913, Ronald Reagan Library.

98. Jerry K. Rose, "Statement of Jerry K. Rose, President, Christian Communications of Chicagoland, Inc.," Senate Committee on Foreign Relations, *Human Rights: Hearing before the Committee on Foreign Relations, United States Senate*, 98th Cong., 1st sess., November 9, 1983 (Washington, DC: U.S. Government Printing Office, 1983), 130.

99. Ibid., 132.

100. Senate Committee on Foreign Relations, *Human Rights*, 2.

101. "Report from the Advisory Council on Religious Rights in Eastern Europe and the Soviet Union," *Congressional Record* 98th Cong., 2nd sess. 130:2 (February 21, 1984): S2689; "Two Former Presidents and Four Former Secretaries of State Join Solon in Urging USSR to End Bias," *Jewish Telegraphic Agency* (October 25, 1984), http://bit.ly/1sCxTRX.

102. Jack Kemp to George Shultz, September 7, 1983, Box 119, Folder 8, Subject File, Foreign Relations, Soviet Union, 1983–1988, Jack Kemp Papers.

103. Ibid.

104. Ibid.

105. See, for example, Jack Kemp to George Shultz, January 4, 1984 Box 127, Folder 9, Jack Kemp Papers; Jack Kemp to Ambassador Micea Malitza, July 29, 1983, Box 127, Folder 9, Jack Kemp Papers.

106. Shultz to Reagan, "USG-Soviet Relations," 5; Jack Kemp, "Dear Colleague Letter," August 2, 1982, Box 127, Folder 8, Jack Kemp Papers.

107. Helsinki Watch, "Human Rights in Romania: A Report Prepared for the Most Favored Nation Hearings in the U.S. Congress," *A Helsinki Watch Report*, August 1984, 17; Wayne Van Gelderen, "Statement of Wayne Van Gelderen, Past President and Member, Executive Committee, Christian Legal Defense and Education; also, Pastor, Marquette Manor Baptist Church, Downers Grove, Ill.," *Extension of MFN Status to Romania, Hungary, and the People's Republic of China: Hearings before the Subcommittee on Trade of the Committee on Ways and Means, House of Representatives*, 97th Cong., 2nd sess., July 12 and 13, 1982, Serial 97–78 (Washington, DC: U.S. Government Printing Office, 1982): 203, 208–9. See also Ramet, *Social Currents in Eastern Europe*, 165–66.

108. "Revival and Repression in Romania," *Christianity Today* 19, no. 4 (November 22, 1974): 52–55; Alan Scarfe and Robert D. Linder, "Revival and Risks in Romania," *Christianity Today* (October 22, 1976), 57.

109. Ibid.; Alan Scarfe, "Romanian Baptists and the State," *Religion in Communist Lands* 4, no. 2 (1976): 15–16, 17–18. See also R. E. Davies, "Persecution and Growth: A Hundred Years of Baptist Life in Romania," *Baptist Quarterly* 33, no. 6 (April 1990): 269–70.

110. Embassy Bucharest to Secretary of State in Washington, D.C., "Human Rights 1976 Reporting," Cable, March 10, 1976, WikiLeaks, https://www.wikileaks.org/plusd/cables/1976BUCHAR01217_b.html; Frank Church to Department of State, "Concern for Josef Ton, A Baptist Pastor in Romania," February 25, 1975, P 740014–2117_b, Central Foreign Policy Files, 1973–79/P-Reel Printouts, RG 59: General Records of the Department of State, National Archives.

111. Jeffrey Collins, "Statement of Jeffrey A. Collins, Director, East/West News Service, accompanied by Radu Capusan, Former Spokesman, Romanian Christian Committee, Bucharest, Romania," *Extension of MFN Status to Romania*, 181. See also *Human Rights in Romania*, 6, 118.

112. Senate Committee on Finance Subcommittee on International Trade, *MFN Status for Hungary, Romania, China, and Afghanistan*, 99th Cong., 1st sess., July 23, 1985, 97–102.

113. Ibid., 71–72, 84, 96, 428–33; Senate Committee on Finance Subcommittee on International Trade, *Continuing Presidential Authority to Waive Freedom of Emigration Provisions*, 98th Cong., 2nd sess., August 8, 1984, 242.

114. Don Kyer, "Testimony of Rev. Don Kyer, Founder/Director, Frontline Fellowship, Fredericksburg, Virginia," *MFN Status for Hungary, Romania, China, and Afghanistan*, 75.

115. Senate, *Continuing Presidential Authority*, 308–9.

116. Ibid., 241.

117. Congressman Matthew Rinaldo to Ronald Reagan, May 28, 1982, WHORM: Subject File, CO130 Romania, Case File #082053, Ronald Reagan Library; William Armstrong et al. to Ronald Reagan, June 4, 1982, Case File #082573, Ronald Reagan Library.

118. Mark Siljander to Ronald Reagan, April 29, 1985, WHORM: Subject File, CO130 Romania, Case File #314073, Ronald Reagan Library. Sundseth later joined CRI as a board member. "Senator Nickles, Sundseth Join CRI Board," *CRI Response* (May–June 1985): 3, Case File #314073, Ronald Reagan Library.

119. Siljander to Reagan, April 29, 1985.

120. "C.R.I. Romanian Intervention," *CRI Response* (May–June 1985): 1, Case File #314073, Ronald Reagan Library.

121. Siljander to Reagan, April 29, 1985.

122. Ibid. He also assured his readers that by pledging their support for CRI, "You'll be blessed as much as those whom you are helping!"

123. "C.R.I. Romanian Intervention," 4.

124. House Committee on Ways and Means, *Extension of MFN Status to Romania, Hungary, and the People's Republic of China*, 97th Cong., 2nd sess., July 12, 1982, 5; Tom Lantos and John Porter, Letter from U.S. Congress Congressional Human Rights Congress to President Ronald Reagan, May 14, 1984, in Senate, *Continuing Congressional Authority*, 473.

125. Frank Carlucci, "Talking Points for Rep. Wolf," Memorandum, WHORM: Subject File, CO130 Romania, Case File #514906, Ronald Reagan Library.

126. Robert Dugan to George Shultz, May 19, 1986 and Robert Dugan to Richard Schifter, May 19, 1986, Carolyn Sundseth Files, Series II: Subject File, Box 2, Folder: National Association of Evangelicals, Ronald Reagan Library.

127. National Security Decision Directive 75, "U.S. Relations with the U.S.S.R.," January 17, 1983, William P. Clark Files, Box 8, Folder: US-Soviet Relations Papers Working File, Ronald Reagan Library.

128. William P. Clark to Ronald Reagan, "Draft of NSDD on 'United States Policy Toward Eastern Europe,' NSC Meeting 11:15 A.M. July 21, 1982," memorandum, July 20, 1982, Executive Secretariat: Meeting Files, NSC 56-70, Box 7, Folder NSC 00056, July 21, 1982, Ronald Reagan Library; Senate, *MFN Status*, 51.

129. Ibid.

130. Ronald Reagan, "Message to the Congress on Trade with Romania, Hungary, and China," June 3, 1986, Ronald Reagan Library, https://www.reaganlibrary.gov/research/speeches/60386f.

131. Ibid. See also: Ronald Reagan, "Message to the Congress on Trade with Romania, Hungary, and China," June 2, 1987, Ronald Reagan Library, https://www.reaganlibrary.gov/research/speeches/060287g.

132. Senate, *MFN Status*, 45.

133. Ibid., 44, 46; Senate, *Congressional Record*, 100th cong., 1st sess. (June 26 1987): 17742.

134. Reprinted in Senate, *MFN Status*: Letter from Congressmen Tony Hall, Christopher Smith, and Frank Wolf to Stefan Andrei, Minister of Foreign Affairs of the Socialist Republic of Romania, July 16, 1985, 278–80; Letter from Don Nickles, Christopher Dodd, and 17 other

US Senators to His Excellency Nicolae Ceauşescu, July, 24 1985, 165–66, and Letter from 46 US Congressmen to His Excellency Nicolae Ceauşescu, August 8, 1985, 168–71.

135. The House voted 232 to 183. "Trade and International Economic Policy Reform Act of 1987, Roll no. 76," *Congressional Record* 100th cong., 1st sess. (April 30, 1987): 10694–95. The Senate voted 57 to 23: "Omnibus Trade and Competitiveness Act of 1987, Roll call Vote no. 16," *Congressional Record* 100th cong., 1st sess. (June 26, 1987): 17761.

136. Commission on Security and Cooperation in Europe, *State of Human Rights in Romania (An Update)*, CSCE Serial No. CSCE 100-2-38: 2.

137. Ronald Reagan, "Letter to the Speaker of the House of Representatives and the President of the Senate on Trade with Hungary and China," June 3, 1988, Ronald Reagan Library, https://www.reaganlibrary.gov/research/speeches/060388d.

138. Edward Greenspon, "PIONEER FAITH Growth of Dissident Baptist Church Signals Romanian Spiritual Revival," *Globe and Mail* (March 28, 1988).

139. Robert White, "The Church Is Alive and Well in Romania," *Save Our World* 28, no. 4 (Winter 1989): 1, 16.

140. Christopher Moree, "Christian Literature in the Eastern Bloc," *Save Our World* 29, no. 4 (Winter 1990): 2; "A Record Year for Missions," *Pentecostal Evangel* (October 7, 1990): 10–11.

141. On Soviet stagnation and political transition during the 1980s, see Brown, *The Rise and Fall of Communism*, 587–602; Brown, *Seven Years That Changed the World*; Brown, *The Gorbachev Factor*; Kotkin, *Armageddon Averted*; Wilson, *The Triumph of Improvisation*, 202–4; Leffler, *For the Soul of Mankind*; Westad, *The Global Cold War*; Zubok, *A Failed Empire*.

142. On the emergence of civil society in the USSR, see Hosking, "The Beginnings of Independent Political Activity," in *The Road to Post Communism*, ed. Hosking, Aves, and Duncan; Hosking, *The Awakening of the Soviet Union*; Sawatsky, "Protestantism in the U.S.S.R.," 335–45. On the relationship between the Helsinki network and the end of the Cold War, see Snyder, *Human Rights Activism*.

143. "Dissent in the USSR," Briefing Paper, 4–7. Evangelicals in the United States supported Soviet religious dissidents through a variety of means, including radio broadcasts. See "Medium with a Message: UE Radio Mission Reaches Millions Daily," *Underground Evangelism* 25, no. 5 (September/October 1984): 3–5; "Around the World with the Church of God," *Save Our World* 25, no. 2 (Summer 1986): 14–15.

144. Wilson, *The Triumph*, 42–59, 82, 87–88; Zubok, *A Failed Empire*, 265–79.

145. Ibid.

146. Foglesong, *The American Mission*, 194; Bourdeaux, "Introduction," in *The Politics of Religion in Russia and the New States of Eurasia*, ed. Bourdeaux, 7–9.

147. Still, as late as 1987 many believers in Russia, especially Pentecostals and unregistered Baptists, indicated that the changes Gorbachev had promised had not much altered their day-to-day experiences of religious persecution (though, as Bourdeaux notes in *The Politics of Religion*, the reforms had at least included the release of many religious prisoners). See Bourdeaux, "Introduction," 7–9; U.S. Senate Committee on Banking, Housing, and Urban Affairs, "Report on the visit to the Soviet Union of the senate delegation led by Senator John Heinz: exploration of the condition of human rights and 'democratization' and economic reform initiatives undertaken by the Soviet Union," 100th Cong., 1st sess., October 1987 (Report No. 100-52): 4–8.

148. Steve Goldstein, "A Millennium for Christianity: Russian Church Defies Years of Communism, Gains Acknowledgment under Gorbachev," *Washington Post* (May 28, 1988): C16.

149. Ibid; Dev Murarka, "Religion in Russia Today: Renewal and Conflict," *Economic and Political Weekly* 28, no. 51 (December 18, 1983): 2846.

150. Goldstein, "A Millennium," C16; Plowman, *The Changing State of the Church*, 3, SC-53, ISEES Collection, Box 36, Folder 5, WCSC.

151. Senate, "Report on the visit to the Soviet Union," 6; Nina Shea, "State-Stamped Religion Isn't Free: Overtures to Russian Orthodox Church Hide Repression," *Los Angeles Times* (June 8, 1988): D7; "Religious Persecution in the Soviet Union," *State Department Bulletin* (November 1986): 77–83.

152. Jack Kemp, "Draft Speech on Foreign Policy and Defense," November 28, 1987, Box 130, Folder 11, Jack Kemp Papers; U.S. Senate Committee on Banking, Housing, and Urban Affairs, "Report," 4–8.

153. As one memorandum notes, "the question of religious freedom was foremost on our agenda" in meetings with Gorbachev and Soviet Minister of Foreign Affairs Eduard Shevardnadze at the 1988 Moscow Summit. Juanita Dugga to Katherine Chumachenko, "Human Rights at Moscow Summit," Memorandum, July 26, 1988, Katherine Chumachenko Files, Box 7, USSR: Religion/HR, Ronald Reagan Library. See also "Dissent in the USSR," Briefing Paper, 7; George Shultz to Ronald Reagan, "Progress in the US-Soviet Bilateral Relationship," Memorandum, November 5, 1986, European and Soviet Affairs Directorate, US-USSR Bilateral RAC Box 14, Ronald Reagan Library; "1986 Reagan-Gorbachev Summit: Public Diplomacy Strategy," Jack F. Matlock, Jr.: Files, Series II: USSR Subject Files, Box 44, USIA Conference on Public Diplomacy, London, March 3–4, 1986, Ronald Reagan Library; Memorandum of Conversation, "The President's First One-on-One Meeting with General Secretary Gorbachev," May 29, 1988, DDRS, Document CK2349550863.

154. *Operation Friendship: A Training Manual for Evangelism in the Soviet Union*, ca. 1986, 2, Collection 459 Records of the Fellowship Foundation, Box 264, Folder 29, BGCA. See also The All Union Council of Evangelical Christians U.S.S.R., *Information Bulletin*, no. 7 (August 1986), and The All Union Council of Evangelical Christians U.S.S.R., *Information Bulletin*, no. 11 (October 1986), Collection 459 Records of the Fellowship Foundation, Box 264, Folder 29, BGCA; Nesdoly, *Among the Soviet Evangelicals*, 201–7.

155. Pam Parry, "Soviet Union Commended for 'religious freedoms,'" *Baptist Press* 88, no. 160 (October 6, 1988): 3.

156. Ibid. Schifter presented this information to the Baptist Joint Committee on Public Affairs during their annual meeting. In his panel discussion, he reviewed Soviet reforms and commented on the "significant movement" that the USSR had made toward granting religious freedom.

157. Ibid., 3–4.

158. Art Toalston, "Christians in Soviet Union still praying for Gorbachev," *Baptist Press* 91, no. 71 (May 9, 1991): 2.

159. Gloria Robinett, "Soviet Pentecostals Need Your Help," Foreign Missions Mail-o-gram (ca. 1988–89), Folder: Russia (1986–1991), Assemblies of God World Missions Archives, FPHC.

160. Jim Burton, "Soviet Union grants permit for more Bibles," *Baptist Press* 88, no. 193 (December 6, 1988): 5.

161. Robert Mackish, "The Emerging Church," *Mountain Movers* (September 1988): 5–6; Joyce Wells Booze, "A New Day in the U.S.S.R." *Pentecostal Evangel* (January 21, 1990): 8–9; "A Record Year for Missions," 10–11.

162. Ibid.; Warren Flattery to Ed Nelson, January 10, 1988, Folder: Russia (1986–1991), Assemblies of God World Missions Archives, FPHC; Fred Smolchuck to Dr. Joseph R. Flower, February 9, 1990; and Fred Smolchuck to Dr. Joseph R. Flower, Robert Mackish, Loren Triplett, et al., July 13, 1990, Folder: Russia (1992–1999) Independent Country, Assemblies of God Missions Archives, FPHC.

163. Mk. 13:10.

164. "A/G teenager's Letter to Gorbachev One of 27 Published in *Pravda*," *Pentecostal Evangel* (February 21, 1988): 13.

165. Anderson, *Religion*, 97–98, 140; Snyder, *Human Rights*, 53–78.

166. Hosking, "The Beginnings of Independent Political Activity," in *The Road to Post Communism*, ed. Hosking, Aves, and Duncan. On the emergence of civil society in the USSR, see Hosking, *The Awakening of the Soviet Union*; Sawatsky, "Protestantism in the U.S.S.R.," 335–45. On the relationship between the Helsinki network and the end of the Cold War, see Snyder, *Human Rights Activism*.

167. Gorbachev, *Memoirs*, 349. He noted, "they left their mark—if not on our political structures, then on our minds."

168. Michael Parks, "Stick to Reform Path, Gorbachev Urges Party," *Los Angeles Times* (July 3, 1990): A11. See also Brown, *The Gorbachev Factor*, 206.

169. Brown, *Communism*, 523–24.

170. For works that examine the dynamics of Western NGO involvement in the Soviet Union and interaction with local organizations and leaders before, during, and after the collapse, see Foglesong, *The American Mission*, 196–218; Sundstrom, *Funding Civil Society*; Wedel, *Collision and Collusion*; Mendelson, "Democracy Assistance and Political Transition in Russia," 68–106; Mendelson and Gerber, "Activist Culture and Transnational Diffusion," 50–75; Roberts, "Doing the Democracy Dance in Kazakhstan," 308–30.

171. P. Davis Szymczak, "Ukrainian Tries To Build A Bridge To His Homeland," *Chicago Tribune* (May 1, 1992). The invitation bears the signatures of four members of the Supreme Soviet. Project Christian Bridge, "U.S. Evangelical Protestant Leaders Meet with President Mikhail Gorbachev and Other Leaders of the U.S.S.R.," press release (November 7, 1991), SC-53 ISEES Collection, Box 38, Folder 7, WCSC.

172. Konstantin Lubenchenko, Georgii Shahnazarov, Tamara Tiurina, Sergei Belozertsev, and Igor Sorokin, "Appeal to the leaders of the Christian movement in the USA," September 19, 1991, reprinted in Yancey, *Praying*, 10–11.

173. Morgulis had ties to Lubenchenko through his former university professor Vladimir Zotz, who served as assistant for religious affairs to the deputy for education, youth, and religion during Gorbachev's tenure as general secretary. Morgulis met Lubenchenko in August 1989 in Washington, D.C., while Lubenchenko was in town to observe the workings of the U.S. Congress. Margulis was there attending the NRB convention with Slavic Missionary Service executive director Alex Leonovich. By chance, Morgulis, Leonovich, and Lubenchenko were staying at the same hotel; they met serendipitously, and Leonovich invited Lubenchenko to attend the National Prayer Breakfast with President George Bush. Lubenchenko apparently remembered the visit (and Morgulis) fondly. See Christian Reformed Church in North America, "Russian Language Ministries," *Agenda for Synod* (June 9 to 19, 1992), 24, http://www.calvin.edu/library/database/crcnasynod/1992agendaacts.pdf; Felicity Barringer, "Soviet Visitors Learn from Congress," *New York Times* (August 25, 1989); Yancey, *Praying with the KGB*, 24; Souder and Bright, *Alex Leonovich*, 199–200.

174. Szymczak, "Ukrainian Tries to Build a Bridge to His Homeland." Peter Deyneka Sr., a Russian émigré and evangelical activist who studied at the Moody Bible Institute in Chicago, founded the Slavic Gospel Association (originally the Russian Gospel Association) in 1934. See "SGA History," http://www.sga.org/about/history/; Billy Graham Center Archives, "Records of the Slavic Gospel Association—Collection 237—Historical Background," http://www2.wheaton.edu/bgc/archives/GUIDES/237.htm.

175. Szymczak, "Ukrainian"; Christian Reformed Church in North America, "Russian," 24.

176. Project Christian Bridge to Supreme Soviet in Yancey, *Praying*, 93–95.

177. Yancey, *Praying*, 13.

178. Project Christian Bridge, "U.S. Evangelical," 2.

179. Yancey, *Praying*, 11, 21–26; Carey Kinsolving, "Soviets Seen Welcoming Evangelical Christians," *Washington Post* (November 30, 1991): C7; "Evangelical Delegation from U.S. Meets with Soviet Leaders," *Pentecostal Evangel* (January 12, 1992): 24; Project Christian Bridge, "U.S. Evangelical."

180. Yancey, *Praying*, 26.

181. Ibid., 25–26.

182. Ibid., 32–33; "Evangelical Delegation," 24.

183. Yancey, *Praying*, 66; "Evangelical Delegation," 24.

184. Project Christian Bridge, "U.S. Evangelical," 1. See also fn. 187.

185. Yancey, *Praying*, 68.

186. Project Christian Bridge to the Supreme Soviet, September 1991, reprinted in Yancey, *Praying*, 91–95.

187. Foglesong, *The American Mission*, 211–13; Shelley, *Church History in Plain Language*, 485–87.

188. Philip Yancey, "Praying with the KGB," *Christianity Today* (January 13, 1992): 19. Gorbachev also echoed this call for morality in meetings with other religious leaders. In his memoirs, he recounts discussing the relationship between morality and democracy with Pope John Paul II during their meeting at the Vatican in December 1989, during which he stated, "I have been thinking about the developments of the past years and have come to the conclusion that democracy alone is not enough. We also need morality. Democracy can bring both good and evil—there is no denying it. . . . For us, it is essential that morality should become firmly established in society—such universal, eternal values as goodness, mercy, mutual aid. We start from the principle that the faith of believers must be respected. This applies both to Orthodox believers and to representatives of other religions, including Catholics." Gorbachev, *Memoirs*, 509.

189. Kent Hill, president of the Institute on Religion and Democracy, accepted an invitation to spend a semester teaching about Christianity and democratic governance at the Moscow State University and Academy of Social Sciences. Kinsolving, "Soviets," 7; "Bloc Breakup Forces Ministries to Change Course," *Christianity Today* (November 25, 1991): 54. Peter and Anita Deyneka, who had previously led the Slavic Gospel Association, launched USSR ministries in Moscow (they changed the name of their organization to Peter Deyneka Russian Ministries after the collapse of the USSR). The Deynekas planned for their ministry "to serve as a liaison and expeditor between Western evangelistic organizations interested in working in Russia and churches and parachurch organizations in the former Soviet Union." Billy Graham Center Archives, "Interview with Peter Simon Deyneka, Jr.—Collection 381," http://www2.wheaton.edu/bgc/archives/GUIDES/381.htm. See also "Deynekas Leave Slavic Gospel, Form New Ministry," *Christianity Today* (October 7, 1991): 45; Hill, *The Soviet Union on the Brink*, 313–14.

190. Participants included representatives from some of the most prominent evangelical NGOs and denominations in the United States: World Vision, Campus Crusade for Christ, InterVarsity, the Christian Broadcast Network, the National Religious Broadcasters, World Evangelical Fellowship, the American Bible Society, the International Bible Society, Prison Fellowship, Slavic Gospel Association, the Southern Baptist Convention, the Assemblies of God, and others. Brian F. O'Connell, Meeting Minutes, "Evangelical Fellowship of Missions Agencies and the National Association of Evangelicals. Consultation on the Commonwealth of Independent States (CIS)," January 6, 1992, folder: Russia (1992–1999) Independent Country, Assemblies of God World Missions Archives, FPHC.

191. O'Connell, Meeting Minutes, 6.

192. Ibid., 1, 6–7.

193. Ibid., 4–6.

194. Ibid., 2.

195. O'Connell, Meeting Minutes, 2.

196. Ibid., 3.

197. Ibid., 6.

198. Gary Speer, "NAE's Melvin Challenges Christians to Fill 'Spiritual Vacuum,'" *Pentecostal Evangel* (January 12, 1992): 25; Brian O'Connell, "Strategic Response Needed by Mission Agencies in the Former USSR," *News Network International* (January 17, 1992): 21–22.

199. "Church of God Seeing Open Door of Ministry in Russia," *Cleveland Daily Banner* (November 6, 1992): 4; "Church of God Signs Agreement in Russia," *Chattanooga News-Free Press* (November 7, 1992): B5.

200. "New Church Planted in Minsk, Belarus," *Cleveland Daily Banner* (April 2, 1993): 3.

201. Christine Lehmann, "Russian Army Needs God, General Says," *Washington Post* (November 14, 1992): G12.

202. Carla Gwaltney, "High-Ranking Russian Officials in Meeting Here," *Cleveland Daily Banner* (January 20, 1993): 9.

203. Anita Deyneka, "Rethinking Our Russian Mission," *Christianity Today* (April 4, 1994): 21.

204. Ibid. Deyneka stressed, in particular, the fact that many Russians associated Western intervention with "rising crime, pornography, and drug use," in the CIS, and also criticized some sects for the "cultural insensitivity" of their evangelization strategies.

205. Serge Schmemann, "Russia May Curb Foreign Religions," *New York Times* (July 16, 1993): A9; "Russia Weights Restrictions on Missionaries," *Washington Post* (July 31, 1993): C6; Patricia Lefevere, "Theologian Decries Russia's Move on Evangelists," *Washington Post* (August 14, 1993): C6; Gerald Seig, "Religious Revival in Russia Riles Some Nationalists," *Wall Street Journal* (August 25, 1993): A10. On the Russian Orthodox Church's efforts to apply the language of democratization and antitotalitarianism to its fight against religious "cults," see Emily B. Baran, "Negotiating the Limits of Religious Pluralism in Post-Soviet Russia: The Anticult Movement in the Russian Orthodox Church, 1990–2004," *Russian Review* 65, no. 4 (October 2006): 637–56.

206. Anita Deyneka, "Stepping Back from Freedom: The New Law Restricting Religion Is Part of Russia's Struggle to Redefine Itself," *Christianity Today* (November 17, 1997): 10–11.

207. Christopher Moree, "Setting the Record Straight on Eastern Europe," *Save Our World* 29, no. 2 (Summer 1990): 2.

208. Jerry Parsley to Jimmy Turner, December 28, 1991, Assemblies of God World Missions Archives, Russia (1992–1999) Independent Country, FPHC.

5. Supporting a "Brother in Christ" in Guatemala

1. Frederic Chapin, United States Embassy, Guatemala to United States Department of State, Washington, "Coup Sitrep No. 5," March 23, 1982, Confidential Cable 002106, Digital National Security Archive (hereafter DNSA); Frederic Chapin, United States Embassy, Guatemala to United States Department of State, Washington, "Coup Sitrep No. 13," March 24, 1982, Confidential Cable 002115, DNSA, 2.

2. Chapin, "Coup Sitrep No. 13," 2.

3. Anfuso and Sczepanski, *He Gives—He Takes Away*, 111. Global Outreach church, which established el Verbo in Guatemala in 1976, published this account shortly after a coup removed Ríos Montt from power in August 1983. Curriculum Vitae del Gral. Ríos Montt (March 25,

1982), in Whitehead, ed., *Latin American History and Culture. Series 5, Civil War, Society and Political Transition in Guatemala: The Guatemala News and Information Bureau Archive, 1963–2000,* Roll 13.

4. Carlos Ramirez, interview by Bonnie Anderson and John Hart, "Headline: Guatemala / Rios Montt," *NBC Evening News,* March 27, 1982, http://tvnews.vanderbilt.edu/program.pl?ID=522679.

5. Bonnie Anderson and John Hart, "Headline: Guatemala / Rios Montt," *NBC Evening News,* March 27, 1982; Anfuso and Sczepanski, *He Gives,* 114–15, 117; Frederic Chapin, United States Embassy, Guatemala to United States Department of State, Washington, "Piedra / Carbaugh Visit: Impressions of President Rios Montt," May 19, 1982, Confidential Cable 003591, DNSA.

6. Paul Taylor, United States Embassy, Guatemala to United States Department of State, Washington, "The Rios Montt Presidency: A First Assessment," June 16, 1982, Confidential Cable 004301, DNSA.

7. Adolfo Aguilar Zinser, "De La Tierra Arrasada a La Aldea Estratégica," Crie Documentos Guatemala 4 (September 1982), Archivo de la Coordinadora Alemana de Solidaridad con Guatemala, Cartapacio No. 156 Coleccion Infostelle Del 13.01.06 Al 13.01.07, Centro de Investigaciones Regionales de Mesoamérica (hereafter CIRMA), Antigua, Guatemala.

8. "Así lo dijo anoche en su mensaje por televisión el general Ríos Montt," *Prensa Libre* (December 27, 1982), Publicación Diario El Imparcial, Serie: La Morgue (recortes de periódicos), Presidente: Gral. Ríos Montt (1982–1983), Ramo: Gob, CIRMA.

9. Broder and Lambek, "Military Aid to Guatemala," 111; "$6.7 Billion Foreign Aid Bill Signed by President," *Los Angeles Times* (November 2, 1977): B4; Pub. L. No. 95-148, § 503B. Broder and Lambek cite the 1975 Harkin Amendment to the Foreign Assistance Act of 1961 and the International Financial Institutions Act of 1977. In addition, the International Security Assistance and Arms Export Control Act of 1976 included an amendment to section 502B of the Foreign Assistance Act of 1961 mandating that the State Department prepare a human rights report for each country seeking security assistance. This requirement led to immediate and lasting tensions in U.S.-Guatemala relations. According to the NSC, the Guatemalan government "rejected future U.S. military assistance in 1976 in sharp reaction to the U.S. required human rights report." Although Guatemala remained eligible to receive USAID support for economic development projects, ongoing military efforts to quash the insurgency contributed to a dire need for materiel, training, and funding. In 1979, the Guatemalan government began requesting military aid from the United States again; Congress blocked these requests on human rights grounds. See Memorandum from the National Security Council to the Vice President, et al., "SCC Meeting on Central America," July 19, 1979, Jimmy Carter Presidential Library, RAC Project Number NLC-20-25-1-1-0.

10. Frank V. Ortiz, Jr., United States Embassy Guatemala to United States Department of State, "A Human Rights Strategy for Guatemala," March 10, 1980, Confidential Cable 001620, DNSA, 5.

11. Ronald Reagan, "A Strategy for Peace in the '80s," televised address, October 19, 1980, Ronald Reagan Presidential Library, https://www.reaganlibrary.gov/10-19-80; "1980 Ronald Reagan / Jimmy Carter Presidential Debate," October 28, 1980, Ronald Reagan Presidential Library, https://www.reaganlibrary.gov/10-28-80debate; Reagan, "Election Eve Address, 'A Vision for America,'" November 3, 1980, Ronald Reagan Presidential Library, https://www.reaganlibrary.gov/11-3-80.

12. Scholars of religion, sociology, political science, and history have examined this period in Guatemalan history from various perspectives. Those that explore evangelicalism and the Ríos Montt regime focus on how this dynamic played out in Guatemala exclusively, though some discuss the role of U.S. evangelicals within Guatemala and their ties with the Reagan administration. This chapter builds on works that expose the involvement of U.S. evangelicals in supporting the

Ríos Montt regime, but shifts the focus to examine this phenomenon from the perspective of U.S. international relations and foreign policymaking. In viewing these events through the lens of recent scholarship on NGOs and internationalist Christian outreach, it links the evangelistic aims of U.S. Christians with geopolitical developments abroad, offering new insight into how evangelicals affected U.S.-Central American relations. For the definitive book on Ríos Montt's presidency, counterinsurgency campaigns, and genocide against the Maya, see Garrard-Burnett, *Terror in the Land of the Holy Spirit*. On the role of evangelicalism in the Guatemalan Civil War and Ríos Montt's counterinsurgency strategy, see Melander, *The Hour of God*; Stoll, "Evangelicals, Guerrillas, and the Army," in *Harvest of Violence*. For recent work on evangelical internationalism, see Preston, "Evangelical Internationalism," in *The Right Side of the Sixties*: 221–42.

13. National Oceanic and Atmospheric Administration, National Geophysical Data Center, "February 4, 1976 Los Amateos Guatemala Earthquake," https://www.ngdc.noaa.gov/hazard images/#/all/9.

14. Orlando Olcese, "The Guatemala Earthquake Disaster of 1976: A Review of its Effects and of the Contribution of the United Nations Family" (Guatemala: United Nations Development Programme, 1977): 1.

15. Russell Chandler, "Church Relief Agencies Move Quickly to Aid Guatemala Earthquake Victims," *Los Angeles Times* (February 21, 1976): A26.

16. Ibid. U.S. religious organizations have long seen the provision of humanitarian aid as a core aspect of their mission, especially in cases of natural disasters and other crises. For background on this history, see Curtis, *Holy Humanitarians*; Stamatov, *The Origins of Global Humanitarianism*; Irwin, *Making the World Safe*; Tyrrell, *Reforming the World*.

17. Pew Research Center: Religion & Public Life, "Religion in Latin America: Widespread Change in a Historically Catholic Region," (November 13, 2014), https://www.pewforum.org/2014/11/13/religion-in-latin-america/.

18. "Declaró Billy Graham Tras su Recorrido," *Diario El Imparcial* (February 14, 1976), Publicación Diario El Imparcial, Serie: La Morgue (recortes de periódicos), GRAHAM, Billy, Ficha: S/7158 (2) 1–9, Ramo: Biográficos, CIRMA.

19. Ibid.

20. Ibid.

21. Mt. 28:16–20 (NRSV), "the great commission." See also Mt. 24:14; Mk. 13:10, 16:15.

22. "The Lausanne Covenant," in *Let the Earth Hear His Voice*, 8.

23. Wilmore, *Last Things First*, 47–48.

24. Mt. 24:14 (NRSV); Mk. 13:10 (NRSV), referenced in "The Lausanne Covenant," 9.

25. Tizon, *Transformation after Lausanne*, 54–58; Robert, "The Great Commission in an Age of Globalization," in *The Antioch Agenda*, 6–7; Jenkins, *The Next Christendom*.

26. Harold Lindsell, "Lausanne 74: An Appraisal," *Christianity Today* (September 13, 1974), 21–25.

27. Donald McGavran, "The Dimensions of World Evangelization," in *Let the Earth Hear His Voice*, 95.

28. Ibid., 96.

29. Ibid.

30. The ICOWE inspired increased outreach from Western evangelicals and also encouraged indigenous evangelism within Guatemala from Guatemalan religious leaders seeking to evangelize Ladinos and rural Mayans. See The Lausanne Committee for World Evangelization, "Evangelization in Central America Today," *World Evangelization Information Bulletin* 17 (February 1980), Collection 309 Records of National Religious Broadcasters, Box 101, Folder 13 LCWE Bulletins 1978–1983, BGCA, Wheaton, IL.

31. Cox, *Fire from Heaven*, 171. Cox notes that conversion to the Pentecostal faith requires an often radical change in lifestyle, as believers must conform to its moral precepts. He argues that their "reputation for sobriety, punctuality, and honesty" makes Pentecostals sought after employees. In this manner, the cultivation of the so-called Protestant work ethic has prepared such workers to participate in modern industrial capitalism. See also Berger, "Introduction: The Cultural Dynamics of Globalization," in *Many Globalizations*, 8. For the data Berger draws on linking Pentecostalism with social mobility, see Talavera, "Trends toward Globalization in Chile," in *Many Globalizations*, 271–74.

32. Samandú, Fuentes, and Salazar, *El protestantismo en Guatemala*, 61. Most other Guatemalans belonged to the Catholic Church and/or followed traditional Mayan spiritual practices.

33. Samandú, Fuentes, and Salazar, *El protestantismo*, 61. The authors noted that this percentage represented over 1.65 million people. Protestant sects continued to grow through the 1980s, comprising nearly 2.7 million, or 31.5 percent of the population, by 1988. Current estimates of the Protestant population in Guatemala range from 25 to 40 percent.

34. Melander, *The Hour of God?*, 74.

35. Loren Triplett, "Guatemala—Earthquake," and "Mrs. Haydus Shares Some Letters," (February 4, 1976), Guatemala: Guatemala earthquake, 1976 5/5/4 ID: 50135, FPHC.

36. "Pray for Guatemala Crusades," *Pentecostal Evangel* (November 13, 1977): 17.

37. On the ways in which competition in the "religious economy" leads to higher levels of religious observance, see Finke and Stark, *The Churching of America*, 9–11.

38. Medina, "The New Jerusalem versus Social Responsibility: The Challenges of Pentecostalism in Guatemala," in *Perspectives in Pentecostal Eschatologies*, 326.

39. Ibid., 327.

40. Garrard-Burnett, *Protestantism*, 121–23.

41. Ibid., 123.

42. Garrard-Burnett, *Protestantism*, 122; Cox, *Fire*, 15; O'Neill, *City of God*, 23. These authors note that due to its size and organizational structure, the Catholic church could not offer the small-scale, responsive outreach and individualized attention that evangelical groups did. These services proved enormously appealing to newly arrived migrants, many of whom were nominally Catholic. That Pentecostal worship helped migrants cope with city life was not a new observation; it has been well documented in the sociological literature. Rather it is this phenomenon coupled with the scale of migration that followed the earthquake that made this situation in Guatemala so transformative. For earlier accounts of this phenomenon, see Roberts, "Protestant Groups and Coping with Urban Life in Guatemala City," 761.

43. O'Neill, *City*, 24; Cox, *Fire*, 101.

44. Cox, *Fire*, 101–2.

45. Smith, "Pentecostal Presence, Power and Politics in Latin America," 224–25.

46. Guatemala Task Force, "Biography of Carlos Ramirez, Pastor of Verbo Christian Church in Guatemala Fact Sheet," Press Release, n.d. [ca. 1982–1983], *Guatemala* in *The North American Congress on Latin America (NACLA) Archive on Latin Americana* (Wilmington, DE: Scholarly Resources, 1998): Roll 19, File 90, Frames 907–8; Anfuso and Sczepanski, *Efrain Rios Montt, Servant or Dictator?*, 77. Ramirez, a U.S. citizen of Colombian origin, had joined the Gospel Outreach Church in 1971 and became an ordained minister in the church in 1975.

47. Cristobal Vargas, "Guatemala: A New Jerusalem?," *Latinamerican Press* 3 (February 1983): 3–4, in Whitehead, *Latin American History and Culture*, Roll 13.

48. Anfuso and Sczepanski, *Efrain Rios Montt*, 81, 83.

49. Ibid., 87. Ríos Montt's wife and children converted as well. Prior to conversion, the family had been Catholic.

50. In 1954, the CIA and right-wing military leader Carlos Castillo Armas overthrew the democratically elected Jacobo Arbenz, reversing ten years of popular reforms and unleashing a wave of repression and political instability. The resultant civil war lasted from 1960 to 1996, during which a succession of right-wing presidents, nearly all hailing from the military, waged a protracted battle against left-leaning insurgents over issues related to land tenure and economic justice. Through a combination of brutal state violence and incremental reform, the military had temporarily succeeded in subduing the insurgency by the early 1970s.

51. Garrard-Burnett, *Terror*, 42–43; Stoll, "Guatemala," 28.

52. United States Defense Intelligence Agency, "Biographic Information on Leader of March 1982 Coup in Guatemala," March 28, 1982, Confidential Cable, DNSA; Anfuso and Sczepanski, *He Gives*, 64–81.

53. Garrard-Burnett, *Terror*, 34–35, 42.

54. Ibid., 45, 48–49.

55. Ibid., 27–30. As Garrard-Burnett notes, many of the leftist guerrilla groups did have links to Cuba.

56. Damage from the earthquake had forced the closure of the original school buildings. Escuela Politécnica, "Historia," http://www.politecnica.edu.gt/history and "Directores," http://www.politecnica.edu.gt (accessed September 7, 2019); Anfuso and Sczepanski, *He Gives*, 78–79.

57. Anfuso and Sczepanski, *He Gives*, 79–80.

58. Ibid., 86–87. In interviews, Ríos Montt stated that his conversion to evangelicalism allowed him to shed his bitterness because he came to "see God's hand" in the events of 1974. Harry Genet and Stephen Sywulka, "You Heard It Right: The Dictator Is an Evangelical Christian," *Christianity Today* 26, no. 8 (April 23, 1982): 33.

59. The Jesus Movement blended Charismatic and evangelical forms of Christianity with the hippie counterculture of the 1960s. Allitt, *Religion in America Since 1945*: 133–37; Eskridge, *God's Forever Family*.

60. Gospel Outreach, "Gospel Outreach Fact Sheet," Press Release, n.d. [ca. 1982–1983], *Guatemala* in *The NACLA Archive*, Roll 19, File 90, Frame 892.

61. Ibid., Frames 892–93; Paul Goepfert, "The Lord and Jim Durkin: How Eureka became the religious capital of Guatemala," *Data Center Files* (February 1983), in Whitehead, *Latin American History and Culture*, Roll 13.

62. "Gospel Outreach Fact Sheet," Frame 893. During the mid-1970s, Gospel Outreach evolved into a nondenominational neo-Pentecostal church.

63. Ibid., Frames 893–95.

64. Ibid., Frame 895; Goepfert, "The Lord," 1.

65. Guatemala Task Force, "Biography of Carlos Ramirez," Frame 908.

66. Anfuso and Sczepanski, *Efraín Rios Montt*, xiii.

67. Most, though certainly not all. Progressive and leftist evangelicals did have a voice in Guatemala, and some worked with leftist evangelical groups in the United States, such as the Association for Public Justice. For recent work on the evolution of a radical evangelical left in Central America in this period, see Coeller, "Beyond the Borders: Radicalized Evangelical Missionaries in Central America from the 1950s through the 1980s." 2012); Kirkpatrick, *A Gospel for the Poor*.

68. Influential Catholic theologian Gustavo Gutiérrez advocated a theology of liberation at the Latin American Episcopal Council meetings held in 1968 in Medellín, Colombia and in 1979 in Puebla, Mexico, where he coined the phrase "a preferential option for the poor." See Eagleson and Scharper, *Puebla and Beyond*, 264; Smith, *The Emergence of Liberation Theology*, 25–50.

69. Public Relations Secretariat of the Presidency, "The Right to Clarification: The Political Jesuits Lie in order to Contribute to Subversion. They Put Aside the Cassock to Engage in Politics," *El Grafico* (January 17, 1980), in Whitehead, *Latin American History and Culture*, Roll 62.

70. These tensions stemmed, in part, from the success of Protestant missionary efforts in the predominantly Catholic country. Garrard-Burnett, *Protestantism*, 88.

71. Cor Bronson, "Guatemala's Coup: A Protestant's Perspective," (1982), 3, in Whitehead, *Latin American History and Culture*, Roll 12.

72. Ibid.

73. Washington Office on Latin America, "The Military Coup in Guatemala of the 23 March 1982," Press Release (March 30, 1982): 1, in Whitehead, *Latin American History and Culture*, Roll 13.

74. Chapin, "Coup Sitrep No. 5," 2.

75. Anderson and Hart, "Headline," *NBC Evening News*.

76. Bonnie Anderson and John Chancellor, "Headline: Guatemala," *NBC Evening News* (March 24, 1982); Frederic Chapin, United States Embassy, Guatemala to United States Department of State, "Piedra/Carbaugh Visit: Impressions of President Rios Montt," May 19, 1982, Confidential Cable 003591, DNSA.

77. Efraín Ríos Montt, quoted in Genet and Sywulka, "You Heard It Right," 34.

78. "Ríos Montt se dirige a los guatemaltecos sobre el tema de las presentes navidades," *Prensa Libre* (December 20, 1982), Publicación Diario El Imparcial, Serie: La Morgue (recortes de periódicos), Presidente: Gral. Ríos Montt (1982–1983), Ramo: Gob, CIRMA.

79. Washington Office on Latin America, "The Military Coup," 2; Iglesia Guatemalteca en el Exilio, "El Golpe de Estado, Otra Fraude Contra el Pueblo de Guatemala," *Boletin*, no. 11 (February–March 1982): 9–11, in Whitehead, *Latin American History and Culture*, Roll 62.

80. Washington Office on Latin America, "The Military Coup," 2.

81. "Así lo dijo," *Prensa Libre* (December 27, 1982).

82. Frente Popular 31 de Enero, "Hablan los Cristianos" and Comite Pro-Justicia y Paz de Guatemala, "Ríos Montt, Falso Profeta" (Guatemala: Enero 1983), Archivo del Comite Holandés de Solidaridad con Guatemala, Cartapacio No. 33 Justicia y Paz II, CIRMA; "Ríos Montt: Falso Profeta; Coordinadora Cristiana de Solidaridad con la Lucha del Pueblo de Guatemala," Crie Documentos Guatemala 4 (September 1982): 10–11, Archivo de la Coordinadora Alemana de Solidaridad con Guatemala, Cartapacio No. 156 Coleccion Infostelle Del 13.01.06 Al 13.01.07, CIRMA.

83. Peter Browning, "Scorched Earth in Guatemala," *Sojourners* 11 (October 1982): 10–12.

84. El Verbo elder Henry Gómez framed these struggles using the language of spiritual warfare, noting in an interview, " [we] aren't fighting a battle of flesh, blood and bone. We're combating the hordes that invade the spirit." This notion resonated deeply with evangelicals in the United States. Henry Gómez, interview with Julia Preston, in Julia Preston, "God and War in Guatemala," *Rolling Stone* (May 13, 1982): 24.

85. Jim and Jean Woolsey, newsletter, May 1982, Assemblies of God World Missions Archives, Guatemala (1980–1989), FPHC.

86. Jim Durkin, "A Letter From . . ." *Radiance Monthly* (April 1982): 1, in Whitehead, *Latin American History and Culture*, Roll 13.

87. *CBS Reports: Guatemala*, CBS, September 9, 1982. This news report includes a clip from the *700 Club* that aired one week after the coup, from which this quote was drawn.

88. Chapin, "Piedra/Carbaugh Visit" 2; Frederic Chapin, United States Embassy, Guatemala to United States Department of State, "Congressional Staff Del Ofnwoodward [sic], Ross and Cameron Have Dinner Meeting with Junta President Rios Montt and Aides Bianchi and Contreras," May 20, 1982, Confidential Cable 003640, DNSA.

89. Chapin, "Piedra/Carbaugh Visit," 5.

90. Chapin, "Congressional Staff."

91. Raymond Bonner, "Guatemala Junta's Chief Says God Guides Him," *New York Times* (June 10, 1982): A9.

92. Ibid.; Jim DeGolyer, interview by Ed Rabel, *CBS Reports: Guatemala*, CBS, September 9, 1982.

93. Anfuso and Sczepanski, Efrain Rios Montt, 151; Jim DeGolyer, interview by Jim Lehrer and Charlene Hunter Gault, PBS, *MacNeil/Lehrer Report*, October 25, 1982.

94. Ibid.

95. Council on Hemispheric Affairs, "COHA's Interim Human Rights Report on Guatemala: March 1982—September 1982" (September 28, 1982), Colección de Robert Trudeau sobre Política de Guatemala, Serie: Documents, Document RHT 829, CIRMA.

96. The delegation included Jim Durkin and Jim DeGolyer. Frederic Chapin, United States Embassy, Guatemala to United States Department of State, "Gospel Outreach Ministers Close to Rios Montt Visit," April 6, 1982, Confidential Cable 02517, released by the Freedom of Information Act (FOIA), document C05468282.

97. Patricia Hollis, "Save Guatemala, Save America!," *Mission to America* (November 1982): 3, ID #119015 WHORM: Subject File CO 060, Ronald Reagan Library; Sandra Rowland, "Guatemala: A First-Hand View of Government Fighting to Restore the Confidence of People," *Save Our World* 22, no. 2 (Spring 1983): 3; "Clevelander Visits Guatemala with Evangelical Team," *Cleveland Daily Banner* (January 2, 1983): 17.

98. Garrard-Burnett, *Terror*, 19.

99. Ibid.; U.S. Director of Intelligence, *President Jose Efrain Rios Montt and the Spiritual Rebirth of Guatemala: An Intelligence Assessment* (December 1982): 5, Folder "Guatemala—Oliver L. North, NSC Staff (1 of 3)," Box 12, Oliver L. North Files, Ronald Reagan Library.

100. Missionary News Service, "Guatemala Junta Leader a Christian," *Missionary News Service* 29, no. 9 (May 1, 1982), Collection 309 Records of National Religious Broadcasters, Box 103, Folder 1, Missionary News Service 1980–1982, BGCA; National Security Council, "Issues and Objectives for President's Latin America Trip," Meeting Minutes (November 23, 1982), Folder "NSC 00067 23 November 1982 [President's Trip], Box 91284," Executive Secretariat: Meeting Files NSC 56–70, Box 7, Ronald Reagan Library; Paul Taylor, United States Embassy, Guatemala to United States Department of State, Washington, "Congressional Hearing on Guatemala," August 22, 1982, Cable 05655, released by FOIA, document C18632632.

101. Jim Lehrer and Charlene Hunter Gault, PBS, *MacNeil/Lehrer Report*, October 25, 1982.

102. Ed Rabel, *CBS Reports: Guatemala*, CBS, September 9, 1982; Frederic Chapin, United States Embassy, Guatemala to United States Department of State, "Violence and Human Rights Report: April 1982," June 3, 1982, Confidential Cable 003956, DNSA.

103. Bureau of Intelligence and Research, "Guatemala's Guerrillas Retreating in the Face of Government Pressure," Secret Report (March 3, 1983): 7, reproduced in DDRS, Document CK2349695455.

104. Ibid., 1, 7.

105. Ibid., 7; Garrard-Burnett, *Terror*, 19.

106. Bureau of Intelligence and Research, "Guatemala's Guerrillas," 7; Garrard-Burnett, *Terror*, 20.

107. Chapin, "Piedra/Carbaugh Visit," 3. Ríos Montt also told Ambassador Chapin that Pat Robertson intended to produce a film about developments in Guatemala for broadcast on his television network "for the purpose of raising funds and recruiting volunteers." See United States

Embassy, Guatemala to United States Department of State, "Plans of President Rios Montt to Enlist US Christians in Guatemalan Development," May 20, 1982, Confidential Cable, released by FOIA, document C05468284, 2.

108. George Shultz to Ronald Reagan, "Your Meeting with Guatemalan President Rios Montt on December 4 [Includes Talking Points]," Secret Memorandum, November 20, 1982, DNSA; Fred Ikle to Caspar Weinberger, "Resumption of Commercial Sales to Guatemala" (December 20, 1982), DDRS, Document CK2349664307; Bureau of Intelligence and Research, "Guatemala's Guerrillas"; Frederic Chapin, United States Embassy, Guatemala to United States Department of State, "Analysis of Rios Montt Government after Eleven Months," February 18, 1983, Confidential Cable 001353, DNSA.

109. Frederic Chapin, United States Embassy, Guatemala to United States Department of State, "Meeting between President Reagan and President Rios Montt," November 18, 1982, Top Secret Cable 008703, DNSA.

110. Donna Eberwine, "To Ríos Montt, with Love Lift," *The Nation* 236, no. 8 (February 26, 1983): 238; Rabel, *Guatemala*, CBS, September 9, 1982; Goepfert, "The Lord"; Jack Anderson, "Latin Strongman May Embarrass Reagan, Falwell," *Washington Post* (September 29, 1982): PMd. 17.

111. Ibid.

112. Robert M. Pittenger to Edwin Meese, August 18, 1982, ID #094920 CO060, WHORM: Subject File, Ronald Reagan Library. Pittenger, a member of Campus Crusade for Christ, attended the meeting.

113. Ibid. Those involved included Billy Graham, Bill Bright of Campus Crusade for Christ, Senator Roger Jepsen, Congressman Jack Kemp, and Senator Bill Armstrong.

114. José Efraín Ríos Montt to Dr. Jerry Falwell, July 2, 1982, FAL 5–7 Series 1 Folder 1, Correspondence with Foreign Political Leaders: 1980–1984, Liberty University Archive, Lynchburg, VA; Ben Armstrong to José Efraín Ríos Montt, December 7, 1982, Collection 309 Records of National Religious Broadcasters, Box 63, Folder 3, International Banquet/Guests '83 Convention, BGCA.

115. Eberwine, "To Ríos Montt," 238.

116. Guatemala Task Force, "Biography of Carlos Ramirez," Frames 907–08. The Guatemala Task Force was an arm of the Gospel Outreach Church.

117. Carlos Ramirez, "God's miracle in Guatemala has opened a door . . ." International Love Lift fundraising letter (September 1, 1982), reprinted in *El Parcial* "Las sectas protestantes en Centroamérica," una documentacion de prensa 29 (Octubre de 1991): 105–6, Coleccion Infostelle, Del 23.02.07 al 23.03.01, Signatura 240, CIRMA.

118. Guatemala Task Force, "Guatemala Task Force Fact Sheet," n.d. [ca. 1982], *Guatemala in The NACLA Archive*, Roll 19, File 90, Frame 909. This group included pastors from Gospel Outreach, Gospel Relief Missions, and Calvary Church.

119. Ibid., Frame 910.

120. Ibid.

121. Pat Robertson, *700 Club*, CBN, January 31, 1983. The Ríos Montt regime routinely claimed that the guerrillas bore the responsibility for the mass killings and displacement of rural Guatemalans from their villages; outside of supporters for the regime, the bulk of the extent evidence exposes the speciousness of these allegations.

122. Jack Kemp, letter, July 30, 1982, reprinted in *CounterSpy* (March–May 1983): 49, Archivo de la Coordinadora Alemana de Solidaridad con Guatemala, Cartapacio No. 156, Coleccion Infostelle Del 13.01.06 Al 13.01.07, CIRMA.

123. See, for example, Central Intelligence Agency, "Central American Overview," January 31, 1983, Secret Report, DDRS, Document CK2349663734; George P. Shultz to United States Embassy, Guatemala, "FMS Cash Sales to Guat[e]mala," January 6, 1983, Confidential Cable 003022, DNSA; William P. Clark to Ronald Reagan, "Support for Guatemala," Top Secret Memorandum for the President, n.d. [ca. 1983], DDRS, Document CK2349611860; Paul Taylor, United States Embassy, Guatemala to United States Department of State, Washington, "An Evangelical Missionary's View of Current Guatemalan Situation," December 21, 1982, Confidential Cable 09543, released by FOIA, document C18632611.

124. "Summary Schedule of the President's Trip to South and Central America November 30—December 4, 1982," folder "Trip of President Reagan to Brazil, Colombia, Costa Rica and Honduras, 1982," Box 5, William Sittmann Files, Ronald Reagan Library.

125. National Security Council, "Issues and Objectives," 5.

126. National Security Council, "Supplementary Issues and Objectives for the President's Visit to Central America," Folder "NSC 00067, November 23, 1982 [President's Trip] Box 91284," Executive Secretariat: Meeting Files NSC 56–70, Box 7, Ronald Reagan Library.

127. For the longer history of congressional human rights advocacy in the 1960s and 1970s, see Snyder, *From Selma to Moscow*; Keys, *Reclaiming American Virtue*.

128. McCormick, "Freedom Tide?," 61–63.

129. Frederic Chapin, U.S. Embassy Guatemala to U.S. State Department, Draft Memorandum of Conversation: Bilateral Between President Reagan and the President of Guatemala, Rios Montt (December 6, 1982), folder "Guatemala, Vol. I, 1/20/81–7/31/84 [2 of 5]," Executive Secretariat, NSC: Country File, Latin America, Box 52, Ronald Reagan Library.

130. General José Efraín Ríos Montt, "Mensaje del presidente Ríos Montt, durante su primer ano del gobierno" (December 1982): 1, Archivo de Inforpress Centroamerica, Serie: Documentos, Documento 1512, CIRMA. This document was included in the "Este Gobierno Tiene el Compromiso de Cambiar" folder.

131. Ibid., 2–3.

132. Fred Francis and Chris Wallace, "Headline: Reagan/Guatemala Aid," *NBC Evening News*, December 5, 1982. For an earlier interview wherein Ríos Montt attributes massacres and displacement to the guerrillas rather than to his army, see Efraín Ríos Montt, interview with Ed Rabel, *CBS Reports: Guatemala*, CBS, September 9, 1982.

133. Francis and Wallace, "Headline." The extant evidence on the Guatemalan army's responsibility for the killings, kidnappings, and displacement is staggering. See Rothenberg, *Memory of Silence*; Recovery of Historical Memory Project, *Guatemala: Never Again! The Official Report of the Human Rights Office, Archdiocese of Guatemala*; Tribunal Permanente de Los Pueblos, Sesion Sobre Guatemala (Madrid, 27 al 31 de Enero de 1983), Archivo del Comité Holandés de Solidaridad con Guatemala, Caja No. 86, Tribunal Permanente de los Pueblos, 1979–1990, CIRMA; House Committee on Foreign Affairs and its Subcommittee on Human Rights and International Organizations, *Religious Persecution as a Violation of Human Rights: Hearings and Markup*, 97th Cong., 2nd sess. (Washington, DC: U.S. Government Printing Office, 1982): 698–784.

134. Garrard-Burnett, *Terror*, 6–7. Garrard-Burnett notes that this figure is an estimate based on two truth commission reports.

135. Ibid., 6.

136. Francis and Wallace, "Headline."

137. Ibid.

138. United States, Department of State, "President's Statement Following Meeting with Guatemalan President Rios Montt," November 22, 1982, DNSA; Ikle to Weinberger, "Resumption of Commercial Sales."

139. William P. Clark, "Memorandum of Conversation: U.S. Relations with Guatemala," Confidential Memorandum (May 3, 1983), DDRS, Document CK2349561878, 3.

140. Loren Triplett to Ronald Reagan, December 15, 1982, Triplett, Loren (Mildred) (–1989), Assemblies of God World Missions Archives, FPHC; W. S. McBirnie to Ronald Reagan, December 17, 1982, ID #115961, Senator Roger Jepsen to William P. Clark, September 17, 1982, ID #129022, and Daniel Crane to Ronald Reagan, September 24, 1982, ID #100944, CO060, WHORM: Subject File, Ronald Reagan Library. (In this latter piece of correspondence, Representative Crane forwarded a letter from an evangelical constituent to the White House; the Reagan Library contains a number of similar forwarded letters from constituents of other congressmen, including Roger Jepsen.)

141. McBirnie to Reagan, December 17, 1982.

142. Patricia Hollis to James Baker, November 29, 1982, ID #119015, CO060, WHORM: Subject File, Ronald Reagan Library.

143. Hollis, "Save Guatemala," 3.

144. Ronald Reagan to Patricia Hollis, January 10, 1983, ID #119015, CO060, WHORM: Subject File, Ronald Reagan Library.

145. J. Philip Hogan to John Bueno and Loren Triplett, Memorandum, January 7, 1983, "Guatemala (1980–1989)," Assemblies of God World Missions Archives, FPHC.

146. Ibid.

147. Ibid.

148. Christopher Moree, "Missions Editor Visits Guatemala.," *Evangel* 73, no. 3 (April 11, 1983): 18.

149. Hogan, Memorandum, 2.

150. Ibid.

151. Ibid.

152. Washington Office on Latin America, "Guatemala: State Department Policy after the March 23 Coup," Archivo de Inforpress Centroamericana, Documento ICA 1167, CIRMA; Council on Hemispheric Affairs, "COHA Report Marks Shameful Reagan-Rios Montt Meeting," Press Release (December 4, 1982), Colección de Robert Trudeau sobre Política de Guatemala, Serie: Documentos, Documento RHT 833, CIRMA; Vargas, "Guatemala," 3–4; Francis and Wallace, "Headline"; Juan Martin La Rotta, "Tierra Arrasada, Plan Del Regimen Guatemalteco," *Juventud Rebelde* (May 13, 1982), in Whitehead, *Latin American History and Culture*, Roll 13; United States Department of State, "Guatemala: Reports of Atrocities Mark Army Gains," August 1982, Secret Report, DNSA; Mark Whitaker and Beth Nissen, "Guatemala: Beans-and-Bullets Politics," *Newsweek* (December 13, 1982): 56.

153. Hogan, Memorandum, 2; Moree, "Missions," 18.

154. Hogan, Memorandum, 3.

155. Moree, "Missions," 18.

156. Ibid., 26.

157. J. Philip Hogan, "A Visit to 'The New Guatemala,'" *Pentecostal Evangel* (February 27, 1983): 8.

158. Rowland, "Guatemala," 2–4; "Clevelander Visits Guatemala with Evangelical Team."

159. J. Philip Hogan to Gene Taylor, January 11, 1983, "Hogan, J. Philip (Virginia)," Assemblies of God World Missions Archives, FPHC.

160. Gene Taylor to William Clark, January 25, 1983, "Hogan, J. Philip (Virginia)," Assemblies of God World Missions Archives, FPHC.

161. William P. Clark to Congressman Gene Taylor, February 7, 1983, Folder "[Guatemala] (3)," Box 2, Alfonso Sapia-Bosch Files, Ronald Reagan Library.

162. Guatemalan troops killed four people, including Abel Ortiz Jacinto, Obispo Santos, Patricio Ortiz Maldonado (who worked for USAID), and Catarina Ortiz. "Employee of U.S. Dies in Guatemala," *New York Times* (March 11, 1983): A7; Frederic Chapin, United States Embassy, Guatemala to United States Department of State, Washington, "Ambassador's Comments on the Information concerning the Deaths of the Three AID Project Related Persons," November 15, 1983, Confidential Cable 009871, DNSA; William Chislett, "Peace Prospects poor in Guatemala," *ISLA* (March 23, 1983): 30, in Whitehead, *Latin American History and Culture*, Roll 13.

163. American el Verbo pastor Jim DeGolyer insisted that U.S. lawmakers misinterpreted the situation in Guatemala, as he claimed that the extrajudicial killings actually "were part of the government's program to apply the law with vigor and justice and not, as previous regimes had done, with 'savagery' and illegality." Frederic Chapin, United States Embassy, Guatemala to United States Department of State, Washington, "Verbo Pastor on Executions and Catholic Church," March 10, 1983, Cable 01865, released by FOIA, document C18632601. Congress viewed such assertions as extremely unconvincing.

164. Reagan's allies in Congress included Robert Lagomarsino (R-CA), Henry Hyde (R-IL), and Douglas Bereuter (R-NE), all of whom visited Guatemala in February 1983, to meet with Ríos Montt and his evangelical advisers. House Committee on Foreign Affairs, *United States Policy toward Guatemala and El Salvador*, 98th Cong., 1st sess., February 20–26 1983, 2–25; House Committee on Foreign Affairs, *U.S. Policy toward Guatemala: Hearing Before the Subcommittee on Western Hemisphere Affairs*, 98th Cong., 1st sess., March 9, 1983, 1–6, 66–78.

165. Shultz, "FMS Cash Sales," 2. Interestingly, the Guatemalan government declined this offer; according to Serrano, "a Christian friend in Canada had obtained the parts for [them] at 1/10 the cost" of obtaining them from the United States, using money that International Love Lift donated to them. Clark, "Memorandum of Conversation" (May 3, 1983), 2. See also Ronald Reagan to Brigadier General José Efraín Ríos Montt, June 17, 1983, DDRS, Document CK2349620588; John Goshko and Lewis Diuguid, "U.S. to Sell Guatemala Copter Gear, White House Sees Criticism Softening on Rights Record," *Washington Post* (January 2, 1983): A1, A18.

166. James W. Connally to Alfonso Sapia-Bosch, "Helo Spare Parts for Guatemala," memorandum, Folder "Guatemala [2]," Box 2, Alfonso Sapia-Bosch Files, Ronald Reagan Library.

167. Clark, "Memorandum of Conversation" (May 3, 1983), 2; William Clark to Alfonso Sapia-Bosch, Memorandum (May 31, 1983), DDRS, Document CK2349561309; "Mercy Helicopters for Rios Montt," *CounterSpy* (March–May 1983): 47–49, Archivo de la Coordinadora Alemana de Solidaridad con Guatemala, Cartapacio No. 156 Coleccion Infostelle Del 13.01.06 Al 13.01.07, CIRMA; Alfonso Sapia-Bosch and Oliver North to William P. Clark, "Guatemala," Memorandum, August 1, 1983, Folder "Guatemala—Jul—Dece 83," "[Guatemala] (3)," Box 2, Alfonso Sapia-Bosch Files, Ronald Reagan Library; Al Sapia-Bosch to Bud McFarlane, cable, August 5, 1983, Folder "Guatemala—Jul—Dece 83," "[Guatemala] (3)," Box 2, Alfonso Sapia-Bosch Files, Ronald Reagan Library; Mark Thompson, "Lawmaker questions Bell sales," *Fort Worth Star-Telegram* (December 3, 1982), 1–2.

168. Clark, "Memorandum of Conversation" (May 3, 1983), 2.

169. Infoprensa, "Guatemala: La Contrainsurgencia de Rios Montt," *Informe* (June 1983), manuscript, Archivo del Comité Holandés de Solidaridad con Guatemala, Revistas/Investigaciones Documentos no seleccionados etc. 1983–1988, Caja No. 85, CIRMA; Iglesia Guatemalteca en el Exilio, "Reconstruir con permiso del rey," *Informe Especial: FUNDAPI* (June 1983), Archivo del Comité Holandés de Solidaridad con Guatemala, I.G.E. Signatura 31, Document 55, CIRMA; John Ross, "Despite Ríos Montt's Overthrow Eureka Church to Continue Guatemalan Strategic Hamlet Aid," *San Francisco Bay Guardian* (August 17, 1983): 17, 22–23; Stoll, "Evangelicals, Guerrillas, and the Army," 109; Melander, *Hour of God*, 225.

170. Ibid.

171. United States Embassy, Guatemala to United States Department of State, Washington, "Plans of President Rios Montt to Enlist US Christians in Guatemalan Development," May 20, 1982, Cable 03637, released by FOIA, document C05468284.

172. Richard Stone to Thomas Enders, "Repatriation of Guatemalan Refugees," memorandum, March 10, 1983, Folder "[Guatemala] (3)," Box 2, Alfonso Sapia-Bosch Files, Ronald Reagan Library.

173. William Conard, "An Interview with Guatemala's President," *Moody Monthly* (April 1983): 117; Raymond Bonner, "Guatemala Leader Reports Aid Plan," *New York Times* (May 20, 1982): A6.

174. Ross, "Despite Rios Montt's Overthrow," 17.

175. Guatemala Task Force, "Guatemala Situation Fact Sheet," *Guatemala* in *The NACLA Archive*, Roll 19, File 90, Frame 899.

176. Ibid.; "Disputed Guatemala Villages Get U.S. Funds," *San Francisco Examiner* (December 13, 1984): A22.

177. Frederic Chapin, United States Embassy, Guatemala to United States Department of State, Washington, "More Rumors of an MLN Coup" (July 26, 1982), Folder "Guatemala, Vol. I, 1/20/81–7/31/84 [2 of 5]," Box 52, NSC Executive Secretariat: Country File, Latin America, Ronald Reagan Library; Frederic Chapin, United States Embassy, Guatemala to United States Department of State, Washington, "Coup Rumors," March 24, 1983, Folder "Guatemala, Vol. I, 1/20/81–7/31/84 [2 of 5]," Box 52, NSC Executive Secretariat: Country File, Latin America, Ronald Reagan Library; Memorandum, Alfonso Sapia-Bosch to William P. Clark, "Guatemala," July 14, 1983, Folder "Guatemala, Vol. I, 1/20/81–7/31/84 [5 of 5]," Box 52, NSC Executive Secretariat: Country File, Latin America, Ronald Reagan Library.

178. Paul Taylor, United States Embassy, Guatemala to United States Department of State, Washington, "Disturbances of June 29: Sitrep 4," June 29, 1983, Secret Cable 005231, DNSA; Defense Intelligence Agency, "BG Rios Montt, Vulnerable and under Attack," June 14, 1983, Confidential Cable, DNSA.

179. Defense Intelligence Agency, "BG Rios Montt" 1.

180. Paul Taylor, U.S. Embassy, Guatemala to U.S. Department of State, Washington, "Disturbances of June 29: Sitrep 5," June 29, 1983, Secret Cable 005231, DNSA.

181. Paul Taylor, United States Embassy, Guatemala to United States Department of State, Washington, "The State of Government—A Week and a Half after the Crisis Broke into the Open," July 8, 1983, Confidential Cable 005514, DNSA.

182. Director of Intelligence, "Guatemala: Prospects for Political Moderation: An Intelligence Assessment" (August 1983): v, Folder "Guatemala—Oliver L. North, NSC Staff (3 of 3)," Box 12, Oliver North Files, Ronald Reagan Library.

183. Ibid.

184. Director of Intelligence, *President*, 5.

185. Memorandum, Charles Hill to William P. Clark, "Working Visits for Foreign Leaders: July–December 1983," April 11, 1983, Folder "[Guatemala]: Rios Montt Working Visit (Guatemala)," Alfonso Sapia-Bosch files, Ronald Reagan Library.

186. Hugh Montgomery to George P. Shultz, "Coup in Guatemala Deposes Rios Montt," August 8, 1983, Secret Information Memorandum, DNSA, 1.

187. Robert McFarlane to Ronald Reagan, "Memorandum from Secretary of State Shultz Concerning our Relations with Guatemala" (December 8, 1983), DDRS, document CK2349554630; Department of State Bureau of Intelligence and Research, "Guatemala: Death Squads Resume Activity," November 21, 1983, Confidential Analysis, DNSA.

188. Douglas Coe to General Ríos Montt, May 16, 1985, Collection 459 Records of the Fellowship Foundation, Box 223, Folder 43 "Guatemala 1985," BGCA; Ríos Montt to Douglas Coe, December 5, 1986, and Douglas Coe to Ríos Montt, December 23, 1986, Collection 459 Records of the Fellowship Foundation, Box 223, Folder 44, "Guatemala 1986–1987," BGCA.

189. Dean G. Peerman, "What Ever Happened to Ríos Montt?," *Christian Century* 102, no. 28 (September 25, 1985): 819–20.

190. Although the Guatemalan court convicted Ríos Montt of genocide and crimes against humanity on May 10, 2013, the Constitutional Court of Guatemala vacated the conviction on technical grounds. The trial was set to resume, but Ríos Montt died in 2018. For excellent coverage of the trial and the tremendous amount of evidence that the prosecutors presented to support the allegations of genocide and crimes against humanity, see The Open Society Justice Initiative, "The Trial of Efrain Rios Montt & Mauricio Rodriguez Sanchez," accessed September 22, 2013, http://www.riosmontt-trial.org.

191. Moree, "Missions," 17–18.

6. The Challenge of South African Apartheid

1. South African Mission to the United States, Chicago, to the director-general of the Department of Foreign Affairs and Information of South Africa, Pretoria, "Situation Report: Activities of USA Churches Regarding South Africa," Confidential letter, September 22, 1981, Folder: Chicago SA Kommul-General—Chicago, Box 4, Collection K382 E5/53-54, National Archives of South Africa, Pretoria, South Africa (hereafter SA KAB), 1–9.

2. Ibid., 1, 9–10.

3. Ibid., 10.

4. Stewart, "Amandla! The Sullivan Principles," 62–64; Schmidt, *Decoding Corporate Camouflage*; Nesbitt, *Race for Sanctions*.

5. Jerry Falwell, "Why Did We Go to South Africa?," *Fundamentalist Journal* "Special Report: The Untold Story: South Africa," (1985): 1, 6–10, Falwell Family Papers, Jerry Falwell Initiatives Collection, FAL 3-1 Series 1 Folder 2A, South Africa Trip 1985: Folder 1, Liberty University Archive, Lynchburg, VA; Christian Life Commission, "A Call to Concern About Apartheid" (1985), Folder: 164.18 Race—Apartheid Conference, 1985, Box 164, Christian Life Commission Resource Files AR 138-2, SBHLA; David Wilkinson, "CLC Meeting on Apartheid Issues 'Call to Concern,'" *Baptist Press* 85–159 (December 18, 1985): 1–2.

6. "South Africa: What Is Really Happening?," *Evangel* 77, no. 6 (May 1987): 18–19; Falwell, "South Africa," 1, 5, 12, 16; Texas Baptist Christian Life Commission, "The South African Crisis," CLC Briefing Paper (November 1985), Folder: 55.15 Race—Apartheid, 1981–1984, Box 55, Christian Life Commission Resource Files AR 138-2, SBHLA.

7. Or, at the very least, claimed to understand this in their public statements. National Association of Evangelicals, "Apartheid," Policy Resolution (1986); Falwell, "South Africa," 1; Christian Life Commission, "A Call to Concern About Apartheid"; Michael Cassidy, "A South African Christian Confronts Apartheid," *Christianity Today* (November 19, 1971): 3–6.

8. Ed Louton, "The Crisis of Christian Credibility in South Africa" (August 1983): 1–6, Folder: South Africa (1980–1989), Assemblies of God World Missions Archives, FPHC; Mangosuthu Buthelezi, "Remarks at the KwaZulu Legislative Assembly 12th Prayer Breakfast," March 22, 1985, http://archive.ifp.org.za/MGButhelezi/DOC0053.pdf; Robert O'Brien, "MasterLife Turns

Despair into Hope in South Africa," *Baptist Press* 85–140 (November 7, 1985): 3. As a note, under apartheid, the RSA classified mixed-race individuals as "colored."

9. A view so widespread that even *Penthouse* published an article censuring evangelical leaders for their stance on South Africa. Larry Kickham, "How U.S. Evangelicals Bless Apartheid," *Penthouse* (March 1988): 43, 118, 120.

10. The religious right was (and is) predominantly white. Despite similarly conservative theological perspectives, black and white evangelicals tend not to align politically. Since the 1960s, African Americans have voted more consistently for Democratic candidates, while white evangelicals have become a reliable voting bloc for Republican candidates. For work that explores the range of political and theological reasons for this divide, as well as for explanations of why scholars differentiate between black and white evangelicalism, see Lockerbie, "Race and Religion," 1146; Noll, *God and Race in American Politics*; Lincoln and Mamiya, *The Black Church in the African-American Experience*; McDaniel and Ellison, "God's Party? Race, Religion, and Partisanship Over Time," 180–91; Turner Jr., "Black Evangelicalism," 40–53.

11. Kenneth Bredemeier and Michel Marriott, "Fauntroy Arrested in Embassy," *Washington Post* (November 22, 1984): A1, A24; Karlyn Barker and Michel Marriott, "Protest Spreads to Other U.S. Cities: Anti-Apartheid Protest Widens," *Washington Post* (December 4, 1984): A1, A8. A small sampling of the voluminous reports on the violence in South Africa in 1984–85 includes "10 South Africans Killed in Protests: Police Open Fire to Disperse Crowds in Black Townships," *New York Times* (November 6, 1984): A1, A13; Alan Cowell, "Boy, 4, Killed in Continued South Africa Violence," *New York Times* (March 31, 1985): A8; Peter Honey, "A Year of Violence Brings Little Change in South Africa," *Los Angeles Times* (September 10, 1985): B5; "South Africa Police Tear-Gas Parishioners," *Chicago Tribune* (December 6, 1985): 6. There is a growing literature on anti-apartheid activism in the United States as well as abroad. Some recent works include Skinner, *The Foundations of Anti-Apartheid*; Hostetter, *Movement Matters*; Nesbitt, *Race for Sanctions*; Johnson, "Rethinking the Emergency of the Struggle for South African Liberation in the United States," 171–92; Culverson, *Contesting Apartheid*; Bratyanski, "Mainstreaming Movements: The U.S. Anti-Apartheid Movement and Civil Rights Memory."

12. Hostetter, *Movement Matters*; Robinson, "Doing Good and Doing Well," in *The Quiet Hand of God*, ed. Wuthnow and Evans, 346–51.

13. Falwell, "South Africa," 1; Jack Kemp to Libba Barnes, October 1, 1985, Folder 7, Congressional Legislative File, Leg. Assist., Brunette, Subject File, Foreign Relations, South Africa, 1985–1987, Box 119, Jack Kemp Papers.

14. For literature on evangelicals in South Africa, and the tremendous variation in opinion about apartheid that existed among South African Pentecostals, Baptists, and other evangelicals, see McAlister, *The Kingdom of God Has No Borders*; Balcomb, "Apartheid to the New Dispensation," 5–38; Anderson, "Pentecostals and Apartheid in South African during Ninety Years 1908–1998." Sociologist Stephen Offut has placed the expansion of evangelicalism in contemporary South Africa and the emergence of evangelical anti-apartheid activists in the late 1980s within the context of evangelical growth in the Global South. See Offutt, *New Centers of Global Evangelicalism*. R. Drew Smith has argued that U.S. evangelicals, particularly Jerry Falwell and Pat Robertson, lent support to the South African government and to Reagan's policies because of the RSA's anticommunism and as part of an effort to expand their own ministries in the United States. See Smith, "American Evangelists and Church-State Dilemmas in Multiple African Contexts," in *Freedom's Distant Shores*, ed. Smith and Lutiniko, 143–54; Smith, "U.S. Evangelicals, Racial Politics, and Social Transition in Contemporary South Africa," in *Freedom's Distant Shores*, 169–88. This chapter moves beyond Smith's conclusions by exploring evangelical

rhetoric, activism, and collaboration with policymakers from a transnational perspective, emphasizing the relationship between evangelical support for Reagan administration policies and their international missionary aims. It also examines a far larger and more diverse group of evangelical leaders than Smith covers, demonstrating that evangelical engagement extended well beyond Falwell and Robertson.

15. Cassidy, "Apartheid," 4–5.

16. Ibid., 6. That said, he also strongly advocated political involvement.

17. Ibid. In the article, Cassidy cited the "Ministry of Reconciliation" section of 2 Corinthians 5, "in Christ God was reconciling the world to himself." 2 Cor. 5:19 (NRSV). By referencing Sten-guns and Molotov cocktails, he rebuked the RSA police and military forces, which carried the submachine guns and used them to suppress dissent (most notoriously in the 1960 Sharpeville massacre) as well as the ANC.

18. By the late 1980s, even those evangelical denominations that had espoused apolitical views in the 1970s had come around to openly opposing apartheid and supporting efforts for peaceful reconciliation. Balcomb, "Apartheid," 8, 17.

19. Ibid., 11–15; Rom. 13 (NRSV). These groups represented a small percentage of the overall evangelical population.

20. Balcomb, "Apartheid," 27–32.

21. Though certainly many rank-and-file evangelicals took up the apolitical stance of their Charismatic and Pentecostal brethren. See fn. 5 for examples of U.S. evangelicals whose views aligned with the South African conservative and progressive perspectives.

22. The AFM established itself in South Africa in 1908, the Church of God in 1910, and the Assemblies of God in 1917. See Anderson, "New African Initiated Pentecostalism and Charismatics in South Africa," 67–68; Alex Thompson, "Sixty Years of Spiritual Conquest," *Evangel* 60, no. 3 (April 13, 1970): 20; Hilda Olsen, "History of the Assemblies of God USA in South Africa: Beginnings to 1985," manuscript, Folder 10–61–16 South Africa History of the Assemblies of God USA in South Africa Beginnings to 1985/Hilda Olsen 5/8/1, FPHC, 4, 14.

23. Anderson, "New African," 70. The Lausanne Movement grew out of Billy Graham's 1974 International Congress on World Evangelization. See Chapter 1 for the tremendous revival of evangelical missionary work that this event inspired.

24. "South African Baptists Announce 1966 Crusade," *Baptist Press* (October 1, 1965): 4; Baptist Mission in South Africa, "Significant Events in 1978," Annual Report, Folder 5: South Africa, Administration: Reports: Annual, 1978–1987, Box 138, AR. 551–1 Southern Baptist Convention, International Mission Board Mission minutes and reports, 1849–2005, SBHLA.

25. Jones, "Divided Evangelicals in South Africa," in *Religious Resurgence*, ed. Sahliyeh, 108. Jones notes that "from 1970 to 1980, the number of South Africans involved in Pentecostal churches tripled." Allan Anderson estimates that by 1991, approximately thirty percent of the South African populace belonged to a Pentecostal church. Anderson, "Dangerous Memories for South African Pentecostals," in Anderson and Hollenweger, *Pentecostals after a Century*, 89.

26. Anderson, "Dangerous Memories," 90–104. Under apartheid, the South African government delineated four racial classifications: white, black, Indian (citizens of Indian descent), and colored (citizens of mixed-raced heritage).

27. Michael Cassidy, "South African Group Report," in *Let the Earth Hear His Voice*, 1438.

28. Ibid., 1437.

29. Ibid.

30. The scholarship on evangelicalism in South Africa during the 1970s and 1980s paints a complex picture of race relations and religious life. For the most part, white South Africans held the leadership positions in the various evangelical denominations. At the same time, Zionist and

Apostolic independent African churches with Black leadership flourished as well. The internal mission histories of the Assemblies of God and the Church of God detail the decisions that the South African denominations made, first to segregate then, in the 1990s, to integrate. R. Drew Smith states that the U.S. denominations exerted some "light" pressure on their South African counterparts to integrate, noting, "significantly, a number of U.S.-related Evangelical churches and parachurch ministries, many of which arrived or were organized in South Africa during the 1970s and 1980s, also operated on a largely nonsegregated basis within their ministries. . . . Nevertheless, with respect to racial policies at the broader societal level, these newer Evangelical ministries and older ones such as the Assemblies of God were characterized by an overall acquiescence to the racially oppressive status quo—despite whatever racial integration may have existed within their church ministry structures and practices." Smith, "U.S. Evangelicals," 175. See also Anderson, "New African," 70–71; Thompson, "Sixty Years," 20; Watt, *From Africa's Soil*, 72–79.

31. Cassidy, *Bursting the Wineskins*, 32–41; Livingston, *A Missiology of the Road*, 316n97.

32. Cassidy, "Limitations of Mass Evangelism and Its Potentialities," *International Review of Mission* 65, no. 258 (April 1, 1976): 202; Ranger, *Evangelical Christianity and Democracy in Africa*, 204.

33. Steele, *Destined to Win: A Biography of Ray McCauley*, 55.

34. Ibid., 55–79, 97, 149–54.

35. Francis Grim, "Mobilize to Evangelize," *Encounter* 2, no. 10 (May 1977): 3, Q.734, Cape Town Serials, National Library of South Africa (hereafter NLSA); "South Africa: Nation on Trial," *Family Protection Scorecard* (BNS Publications, ca. 1986), Folder: [Foreign Affairs]: South Africa (3), Box 5, Series II: Subject File, Carl Anderson Files, Ronald Reagan Library; Smith, "U.S. Evangelicals," 175.

36. See Chapter 1 for background on Coe and the Fellowship Foundation, an organization that worked to spread the gospel and build a worldwide evangelical fellowship of political, business, and religious leaders through legislative and national prayer breakfasts as well as the establishment of "core" groups abroad. See also Sharlet, *The Family*.

37. Doug Coe to Michael Cassidy, February 23, 1965, Collection 459 Records of the Fellowship Foundation, Box 254, Folder 26: South Africa 1965–1973, BGCA.

38. Michael Cassidy to Doug Coe, August 20, 1971, Collection 459 Records of the Fellowship Foundation, Box 254, Folder 26: South Africa 1965–1973, BGCA.

39. Ibid.

40. Michael Cassidy, "South African Congress on Mission & Evangelism," planning memorandum (March 6, 1972), Collection 459 Records of the Fellowship Foundation, Box 254, Folder 26: South Africa 1965–1973, BGCA.

41. Members of these core groups met regularly, coordinated local legislative and national prayer breakfasts, and reported back to foundation leaders in Washington. Doug Coe to Chief Leabua Jonathan, April 19, 1972; Doug Coe to Chief Buthelezi, April 25, 1972; Rev. I. Ross M. Main to John Dellenback and Doug Coe, October 5, 1973, Collection 459 Records of the Fellowship Foundation, Box 254, Folder 26: South Africa 1965–1973, BGCA.

42. Main to Dellenback and Coe, October 5, 1973, 2–3. The National Party was the conservative, white minority ruling party that implemented and enforced apartheid. It governed South Africa from 1948 to 1994.

43. I.R.M. Main to Louis Kramp, "Visit of John Dellenback and Dick Hightower to South Africa and Botswana, November 20–24, 1973," December 5, 1973, Collection 459 Records of the Fellowship Foundation, Box 254, Folder 26: South Africa 1965–1973, BGCA.

44. Ibid.

45. In one letter, Washington Core member James Bell reminded Main that "There is no such thing as a 'confidential' memorandum, and leakage always seems to occur," and "further,

when the Movement has moved into delicate areas involving reconciliations (*e.g.*, political, racial or people) such events have always been misunderstood by 'outsiders.' As a result of very bitter experiences, therefore, we have learned *never* to commit to paper any discussions or negotiations that are taking place." James F. Bell to Ross I. Main, May 19, 1975, Collection 459 Records of the Fellowship Foundation, Box 254, Folder 27: South Africa 1974, BGCA.

46. Ross Main to Doug Coe, June 19, 1975, Collection 459 Records of the Fellowship Foundation, Box 254, Folder 27: South Africa 1974, BGCA.

47. Ross Main to Doug Coe, February 24, 1975, Collection 459 Records of the Fellowship Foundation, Box 254, Folder 27: South Africa 1974, BGCA.

48. Graham McIntosh to Doug Coe, May 21, 1976, Collection 459 Records of the Fellowship Foundation, Box 254, Folder 28: South Africa 1976, BGCA; Jim Bell to Doug Coe, Richard Halverson, Ross Main, John Dellenback, Howard Hughes, et al., Memorandum, April 14, 1976, Collection 459 Records of the Fellowship Foundation, Box 254, Folder 29: South Africa 1976–1979, BGCA.

49. Fellowship Foundation, Statement of Expenditure of Fellowship Foundation Cheque Received, March 1 to December 31, 1974, Collection 459 Records of the Fellowship Foundation, Box 254, Folder 27: South Africa 1974, BGCA.

50. Bell to Coe, et al., April 14, 1976, 5.

51. Ibid.

52. Rev. I.R.M. Main, "Finding God's Will for South Africa," essay for *Natal Mercury* (July 23, 1977), Collection 459 Records of the Fellowship Foundation, Box 254, Folder 29: South Africa 1976–1979, BGCA.

53. Thomson, *U.S. Foreign Policy towards Apartheid South Africa*, 90. The exact numbers of dead and wounded remain in dispute.

54. United Nations Security Council Resolution 392 (1976), June 19, 1976.

55. Ibid.; United Nations Security Council Resolution 181 (1963), August 7, 1963.

56. Thomson, *U.S. Foreign Policy*, 79.

57. Borstelmann, *The Cold War and the Color Line*, 234–35; Minter, *King Solomon's Mines Revisited*, 222; Westad, *The Global Cold War*, 208–13. White House memoranda between Kissinger and Nixon reveal that, while the administration did seek to convey to Prime Minister Vorster the need for a peaceful resolution to South Africa's racial problems, their core focus remained on encouraging desirable RSA engagement with its neighboring countries. Henry Kissinger to Richard Nixon, "Reply to the Prime Minister of South Africa," Memorandum, June 30, 1972, Folder [EX] CO 135 South Africa, Republic of 1/1/71–, Box 66, White House Central Files: Subject Files: CO (Countries), Richard Nixon Presidential Library and Museum, Yorba Linda, California.

58. Thomson, *U.S. Foreign Policy*, 66, 90. Thomson notes the importance of early (1969–71) anti-apartheid actions in Congress for the development of the broader anti-apartheid movement, but states that "it would still be more than a decade before South Africa would generate significant and sustained debate in the federal legislature. Indeed, it could be argued that, at this time, conservative views on southern Africa held greater sway amongst members of Congress" (66). Thomson attributes congressional sympathy toward South Africa in the early 1970s to corporate and South African lobbying as well as to anticommunist impulses. For examples of early anti-apartheid action in Congress, see House Committee on Foreign Affairs, Subcommittee on Africa, *Policy toward Africa for the Seventies: Hearings*, 91st Cong., 2nd sess., March, May, June, September–December 1970 (Washington, DC: U.S. Government Printing Office, 1970); House Committee on Foreign Affairs, Subcommittee on Africa, *U.S. Business Involvement in Southern Africa*, 92nd Cong., 1st sess., May–July 1971 and September–December 1971 (Washington, DC: U.S. Government Printing Office, 1972 and 1973). See also Borstelmann, *The Cold War*, 234.

59. See, for example, Senate Committee on Foreign Relations, Subcommittee on African Affairs, *South Africa, Hearings on South Africa-U.S. Policy and the Role of U.S. Corporations*, 94th Cong., 2nd sess., September 1976 (Washington, DC: U.S. Government Printing Office, 1977); House Committee on International Relations, *United States-South African Relations: Internal Change in South Africa*, 95th Cong., 1st sess., June 3, 1977 (Washington, DC: U.S. Government Printing Office, 1978).

60. House Committee on International Relations, *Report of Secretary of State Kissinger on His Visits to Latin America, Western Europe, and Africa, Hearing*, 94th Cong., 2nd sess., June 17, 1976 (Washington, DC: U.S. Government Printing Office, 1976), 18; Senator John Tunney, "South Africa and Secretary Kissinger's Meeting with Prime Minister Vorster," *Congressional Record*, 94th Cong., 2nd sess., June 23, 1976, 19971-2; House Committee on International Relations, *Urging the President Not to Extend Diplomatic or Other Recognition to the Transkei Territory*, House Report no. 94-1463, 94th cong., 2nd sess., September 2, 1976.

61. Representative Solarz, speaking on H. Res. 1509, on September 21, 1976, 94th Cong., 2nd sess., *Congressional Record* 122, pt. 24: 31586.

62. Representative Collins, speaking on H. Res. 1509, on September 21, 1976, 94th Cong., 2nd sess., *Congressional Record* 122, pt. 24: 31591.

63. Thomson, *U.S. Foreign Policy*, 89–90, 99.

64. Stevens, "'From the Viewpoint of a Southern Governor': The Carter Administration and Apartheid, 1977–81": 845, 874–76; Thomson, "The Diplomacy of Impasse," 107.

65. Stevens, "Viewpoint," 846; Thomson, "Diplomacy," 107–8.

66. "Billy Graham against Apartheid in Africa," *Baptist Press* 77-15 (January 27, 1977): 5.

67. Ibid.

68. "Church Officials Visit Areas in Southern Africa," *Cleveland Daily Banner* (May 1, 1978): 10, Subject Files: Church of God (Cleveland, TN)—South Africa, Dixon Pentecostal Research Center, Cleveland, TN.

69. Ibid.

70. Don Bonker to Mangosuthu Buthelezi, September 21, 1978, Collection 459 Records of the Fellowship Foundation, Box 255, Folder 1: South Africa 1978, BGCA.

71. The term "petty apartheid" referred to the various pieces of legislation that imposed racial segregation, instituted the odious pass system that prevented black South Africans from traveling into white areas, outlawed interracial marriage and schooling, and the like. "Grand apartheid," meanwhile, institutionalized racial categorizations and included legislation such as the Group Areas Act of 1950, the Bantu Authorities Act of 1951, and the Bantu Homelands Citizenship Act of 1970, which forcibly resettled nonwhite citizens in segregated neighborhoods and separate homelands (Bantustans) and, with the latter act, revoked the citizenship of blacks in the Bantustans. Botha's reforms included the legalization of trade unions and the desegregation of some public accommodations and sports. Thomson, *U.S. Foreign Policy*, 90; Central Intelligence Agency, "South Africa: The Politics of Racial Reform," January 4, 1981, Document 0000568199, CIA FOIA Reading Room, http://www.foia.cia.gov/document/0000568199.

72. Carey Winfrey, "Premier's New Ideas Surprise South Africa," *New York Times* (October 28, 1979): 14. See also Thomson, *U.S. Foreign Policy*, 90.

73. CIA, "South Africa," 1.

74. Thomson, *U.S. Foreign Policy*, 90.

75. Rev. Ross Main to James F. Bell, March 29, 1978 and Rev. Ross Main to Doug Coe, March 29, 1978, Collection 459 Records of the Fellowship Foundation, Box 255, Folder 1: South Africa 1978, BGCA.

76. James F. Bell to Messrs. Dellenback, Hardman, Holladay, Bonker, Van Egmond, and Coe, April 6, 1978, Collection 459 Records of the Fellowship Foundation, Box 255, Folder 1: South

Africa 1978, BGCA. Holladay worked as the Fellowship Foundation's European Director and southeastern U.S. coordinator until 1980; he later served in the Reagan White House as associate director of Public Liaison and director of the South African Working Group for Public Diplomacy. Biographical details on Holladay from United States and Ronald Reagan, *Public Papers of the Presidents of the United States, Ronald Reagan, 1986*, 927–28.

77. Baptist Mission in South Africa, "Significant Events in 1978."

78. "1976 Charismatic Leadership Conferences," *New Vision* 1, no. 6 (Nov./Dec. 1976): 11, Folder: 20-00 New Vision (Christian Interdenominational Fellowship of South Africa), 60/8/2 ID: 54879, FPHC. Bhengu, a black Pentecostal preacher who launched the massive "Back to God" evangelistic movement in the 1950s, grew disenchanted with anti-apartheid political activism; he believed that the power of the gospel and black self-sufficiency would alleviate the suffering of black South Africans. Anthony Balcomb notes that this made Bhengu unpopular with "many educated blacks as well as politically active clergymen," though his crusade, one of the largest evangelical movements in the country, had nearly a million adherents. Balcomb, "Apartheid," 23–27.

79. "1976 Charismatic Leadership Conferences," 11.

80. Ken Crider to Davis L. Saunders, April 12, 1979 (with enclosed SACLA, "South African Christian Leadership Assembly" information packet, ca. 1979), Folder 7: South Africa, Associations: African Enterprise, 1978, 1979, Box 138, AR. 551-1, SBHLA; "SACLA-An Idea Whose Time Has Come," *AE News* (June 1979): 1, Collection 459 Records of the Fellowship Foundation, Box 255, Folder 2: South Africa 1979, BGCA. Cassidy raised a substantial amount of money for SACLA from U.S. evangelical donors. Board members of AE included the leaders of U.S. evangelical organizations World Vision, the Fellowship Foundation, and the Billy Graham Evangelistic Association. SACLA's executive members included the leadership of the Full Gospel Church of South Africa, the Apostolic Faith Mission, the Assemblies of God, the SACC and Youth for Christ, as well as Nicolas Bhengu and Ross Main, among other influential evangelicals.

81. SACLA "South African Christian Leadership Assembly" information packet, 1.

82. Ramsey Collins to Jim F. Bell, November 19, 1979, Collection 459 Records of the Fellowship Foundation, Box 255, Folder 2: South Africa 1979, BGCA.

83. Christian League of Southern Africa, *SACLA: The Wrong Road*, pamphlet (1979), AP 1980–679, NLSA.

84. Offut, *New Centers*, 78.

85. CIA, "South Africa" 17.

86. Ibid., 2–3.

87. Ibid., 3.

88. Ibid., 5.

89. Joseph B. Treaster, "Reagan Is Critical of Carter on Rights," *New York Times* (June 10, 1977): 5; Robert Shogan, "Reagan Warns of Soviet Domination in Africa," *Los Angeles Times* (March 18, 1978): A17; Richard Burt, "Presidential Candidates Stake out Divergent Ground on Foreign Policy," *New York Times* (October 19, 1980): 1.

90. Culverson, *Contesting Apartheid*, 87–88.

91. Crocker, "South Africa: Strategy for Change," 325.

92. Ibid., 345. See also Davies, *Constructive Engagement?*

93. Ibid., 333–37.

94. Ibid., 346.

95. Gleijeses, *Visions of Freedom*, 178–79; Borstelmann, *The Cold War*, 261; Thomson, *U.S. Policy*, 114–15; Culverson, *Contesting Apartheid*, 88–89; Minter, *King Solomon's Mines*, 306, 312.

96. "Tutu Says US Attitude to SA Is Worrying SACC," *Citizen* (March 28, 1981): 12, LÊER KK6/1 Kommissie van ondersoek na die Suid-Afrikaanse Raad van Kerke, Inligtings Versameling,

Publisiteit: Koerantknipsels INEG—1981, Box 22, Collection K382 E5/53–54, SA KAB. [This folder title translates to "Commission of Inquiry into the South African Council of Churches, Information Collection, Advertising, Newspaper Clippings." The RSA Justice Department gathered these materials as evidence in an investigation of the SACC Botha ordered that November.]

97. Ibid. The NCC invited Bishop Tutu and coordinated the trip. "Courtesy Visit," *Citizen* (March 27, 1981): 9, LÊER KK6/1 Kommissie, van ondersoek na die Suid-Afrikaanse Raad van Kerke, Inligtings Versameling, Publisiteit: Koerantknipsels INEG—1981, Box 22, Collection K382 E5/53-54, SA KAB.

98. "Tutu stands firm on sanctions for change," *Post* (October 26, 1979): 12, LÊER KK6/1 Kommissie van ondersoek na die Suid-Afrikaanse Raad van Kerke, Inligtings Versameling, Publisiteit: Koerantknipsels INEG—1979, Box 18, Collection K382 E5/53-54, SA KAB.

99. "Bishop Leaves Politics to the Politicians," *Sowetan* (April 21, 1981): 6, LÊER KK6/1 Kommissie van ondersoek na die Suid-Afrikaanse Raad van Kerke, Inligtings Versameling, Publisiteit: Koerantknipsels INEG—1981, Box 122, Collection K382 E5/53-54, SA KAB.

100. "Church and State," *Cape Times* (June 4, 1980): 8, LÊER KK6/1 Kommissie van ondersoek na die Suid-Afrikaanse Raad van Kerke, Inligtings Versameling, Publisiteit: Koerantknipsels INEG—1980, Box 123, Collection K382 E5/53-54, SA KAB.

101. Hostetter, *Movement Matters*, 58–63.

102. Transcript of meeting between Prime Minister Botha, Desmond Tutu, and others, August 7, 1980, Binder: PM, Box 45, Collection K382 E5/53-54, SA KAB.

103. Ibid.

104. P. W. Botha to Bishop Desmond Tutu, March 3, 1981, Binder: PM, Box 45, Collection K382 E5/53-54, SA KAB.

105. P. W. Botha to Reverend Peter Storey/SACC, June 24, 1981, Binder: PM, Box 45, Collection K382 E5/53-54, SA KAB. See also Smith, *Disruptive Religion*, 128–29. The RSA restored Tutu's passport after an outpouring of international criticism.

106. Mungazi, *In the Footsteps of the Masters*, 93–94; "Government Judicial Commission on SACC Represents Phase in Church-State Conflict," *Ecunews* 3/1982 (February 19, 1982): 21, Binder: Attitudes, Box 37, Collection K382 E5/53-54, SA KAB. The *Ecunews* article noted that the SACC received 90 percent of its funding from foreign sources. See also Smith, *Disruptive*, 128–29; Allen, *Desmond Tutu*, 197–99.

107. De Gruchy, *The Church Struggle in South Africa*, 107.

108. Folder: Kommissie van ondersoek na die sa raad van kerke, inligtingsversameling: Skriftelike getuienis File: KK 6/3/1 parts 1 and 2, Box 129 and Folder: Kommissie van ondersoek na die sa raad van kerke, inligtingsversameling: instansies genader om inligting, File: KK 6/6 part 1, Box 131, SA KAB.

109. Dorothea Scarborough to Eloff Commission, January 26, 1981, Folder: Kommissie van ondersoek na die sa raad van kerke, inligtingsversameling: Skriftelike getuienis File: KK 6/3/1 part 1, Box 129, Collection K382 E5/53-54, SA KAB. The Gospel Defence League was a right-wing South African evangelical organization that communicated with evangelical and fundamentalist leaders in the United States such as Jerry Falwell and Jimmy Swaggart.

110. J. H. Martin to Eloff Commission, March 26, 1982 and Isaac Mokoena to Eloff Commission, August 16, 1982, Folder: Kommissie van ondersoek na die sa raad van kerke, inligtingsversameling: Skriftelike getuienis File: KK 6/3/1 part 2, Box 129, Collection K382 E5/53-54, SA KAB.

111. "The Truth about Rev Shaw: Info gave him R10 000 'licence to libel,'" *Sunday Express* (September 9, 1979): 1, LÊER KK6/1 Kommissie van ondersoek na die Suid-Afrikaanse Raad van

Kerke, Inligtings Versameling, Publisiteit: Koerantknipsels INEG—1979, Box 18, Collection K382 E5/53-54, SA KAB.

112. Congress of the United States Committee on Foreign Affairs to Honorable H. J. Coetsee, September 22, 1982, Kommissie van ondersoek na die sa raad van kerke, inligtingsversameling: instansies genader om inligting, File: KK 6/6 part 2, Box 132, Collection K382 E5/53-54, SA KAB.

113. Ibid.

114. The Institute on Religion and Democracy, "IRD Executive Committee Statement on South Africa," February 22, 1982 and "A Statement by the Institute on Religion and Democracy to the Eloff Commission of Inquiry into the South African Council of Churches," August 20, 1982, Box 5, Collection K382 E5/53-54, SA KAB.

115. Mungazi, *In the Footsteps*, 94; Commission of South Africa, *Report of the Commission of Inquiry into South African Council of Churches* (Pretoria: Govt. Printer, 1983).

116. *Republic of South Africa Constitution Act 110 of 1983*, September 22, 1983, http://www.gov. za/documents/constitution/republic-south-africa-constitution-act-110-1983.

117. "South Africa Debates New Constitution," *Baltimore Afro-American* (May 14, 1983): 8. As a note, in 1983 South Africa's population included 4.5 million whites, 2.5 million colored people, 900,000 Indians, and some 25 million blacks.

118. Peter Wilhelm, "South Africa Plan to Let Nonwhites Vote Opposed by Liberals and Right Wingers," *Wall Street Journal* (October 24, 1983): 34.

119. Ibid.; Jack Fosie, "South Africa to Put New Constitution Before Its Voters," *Los Angeles Times* (October 29, 1983): B8.

120. Seventy-six percent of eligible voters voted in the referendum. Jack Fosie, "S. African Vote Backs Voice for Asians, Colored," *Los Angeles Times* (November 4, 1983): B1.

121. Ibid.

122. Unrest bubbled up throughout the year, with spikes during important anniversaries (such as Soweto), around the time that voting for representatives in the new parliament commenced, and in response to increasing police violence against peaceful demonstrators. For a brief selection of news headlines see Allen Cowell, "Tear Gas and Subdued Crowd as Soweto Remembers," *New York Times* (June 17, 1984): A10; "South African Police Use Tear Gas in Melee," *New York Times* (July 17, 1984): A7; "Violence Mars Voting in S. Africa," *Chicago Tribune* (August 29, 1984): 3; "S. Africa Simmering with Unrest," *Chicago Tribune* (September 6, 1984): 11; Lawrence Schlemmer, "South Africa: A Time of Violence," *Washington Post* (September 18, 1984): A19; "Riots Resume in South Africa," *New York Times* (September 28, 1984): A14.

123. Thomson, *U.S. Policy*, 123–24; Sanford Unger, "A Hollow 'Success' in Africa," *Chicago Tribune* (April 15, 1984): D3.

124. Ibid.; Senate Committee on Foreign Relations, *U.S. Policy on South Africa: Hearing before the Subcommittee on African Affairs*, 98th Cong., 2nd sess., September 26, 1984 (Washington, DC: U.S. Government Printing Office, 1985), 2–4, 15–19

125. Culverson, *Contesting Apartheid*, 127.

126. Most evangelicals opposed the sanctions movement but not all. The predominately African American Pentecostal denomination Church of God in Christ and the Progressive National Baptist Convention began pushing hard for sanctions and disinvestment in the 1970s. See Linda A. Wyche, "Andrew Young: Now Ambassador for Christ," *Norfolk Journal and Guide* (November 23, 1979): 1.

127. Letter quoted in House Committee on Foreign Affairs, *Economic Sanctions and Their Potential Impact on U.S. Corporate Involvement in South Africa, Hearing before the Subcommittee on Africa*, 99th Cong., 1st sess., January 31, 1985 (Washington, DC: U.S. Government Printing Office, 1985), 1.

128. *Anti-Apartheid Act of 1985*, HR 1460, 99th Cong., 1st sess., March 7, 1985. This bill was followed by the *Comprehensive Anti-Apartheid Act of 1986*, HR 4868, 99th Cong., 2nd sess., October 2, 1986. See also House Committee on Foreign Affairs, *The Current Crisis in South Africa: Hearing Before the Subcommittee on Africa*, 98th Cong., 2nd sess., December 4, 1984 (Washington, DC: U.S. Government Printing Office, 1985); House Committee on the District of Columbia, *South Africa Divestment: Hearing and Markups before the Subcommittee on Fiscal Affairs and Health*, 98th Cong., 2nd sess., January 31 and February 7, 1984 (Washington, DC: U.S. Government Printing Office, 1984).

129. "Southern Africa Status Report," 1–4, Folder: NSDD 187—South Africa (1 of 4), Box 6, RAC Box 15, African Affairs Directorate, NSC: Records, Ronald Reagan Library.

130. National Security Decision Directive Number 187, "United States Policy toward South Africa," September 7, 1985, 1, Folder: NSDD 187—South Africa (2 of 4), Box 6, RAC Box 15, African Affairs Directorate, NSC: Records, Ronald Reagan Library.

131. Ibid.

132. Ibid., 3.

133. Mona Charen to Pat Buchanan, "Framing the Argument on S. Africa," memorandum, July 29, 1985, Folder: CO141 (South Africa) (275000–275949), Box 165, WHORM Subject Files, Ronald Reagan Library. See also Chester Crocker and Robert Smalley to Michael Armacost, "Special South and Southern Africa Public Diplomacy Working Group," memorandum, August 21, 1985, Folder: South Africa: Public Diplomacy (8/09/1985–9/05/1985), Box 9, African Affairs Directorate, NSC: Records, Ronald Reagan Library.

134. J. Douglas Holladay to Doug Coe, John R. Dellenback, Leighton Ford, Ronald J. Sider, et al., November 26, 1985, Folder: CO141 (South Africa) (437500–438349), Box 171, WHORM Subject Files, Ronald Reagan Library; United States Department of State, "Sustaining a Public Diplomacy Program on South Africa," secret memorandum, November 15, 1985, Item Number: SA01966, DNSA; George Shultz, "Statement of/Briefing by The Honorable George P. Shultz Secretary of State on the Appointment of Advisory Committee on South Africa," December 19, 1985, Folder: South Africa Advisory Committee: [09/09/1985–01/02/1986], Box 6, African Affairs Directorate, NSC: Records, Ronald Reagan Library. Former senator, Fellowship Foundation member, and director of the Christian College Coalition John Dellenback was one of the members of the Advisory Committee.

135. J. Douglas Holladay to Chester Crocker, April 11, 1985, Folder: FG006-01 (426057–426096), Box 130, WHORM Subject Files, Ronald Reagan Library.

136. J. Douglas Holladay to Linas Kojelis, "List for Vice Presidential Briefing on U.S. Policy toward South Africa," memorandum, January 24, 1985, Folder: South Africa Briefing Box 11521, Box 5, Series I: Subject File, Linas Kojelis Files, Ronald Reagan Library. Including Pentecostal Rev. Sam Hines and black prison minister Rev. John Staggers, Executive Director of World Vision Thomas Getman, Doug Coe, and John Dellenback, among others.

137. J. Douglas Holladay to Albert Quie, "Strategy Paper for the Office of Public Diplomacy for South Africa," Memorandum, January 3, 1986, Folder: CO141 (South Africa) (440313–440873), Box 171, WHORM Subject Files, Ronald Reagan Library.

138. Ibid., 2.

139. Ibid., 3.

140. Ibid., 11.

141. Mangosuthu Buthelezi, "Some Thoughts Expressed to President Ronald Reagan, President of the United States of America, on the Emerging American Policy of Constructive Engagement in South Africa," February 4, 1985, Folder: CO141 (South Africa) (270000–274999), Box 165, WHORM Subject Files, Ronald Reagan Library.

142. Chief Buthelezi to Ronald Reagan, July 11, 1986, Folder: CO141 (South Africa) (405690–406296), Box 169, WHORM Subject Files, Ronald Reagan Library.

143. Bishop B. E. Lekganyane to Ronald Reagan, October 22, 1985, Folder: CO141 (South Africa) (343237–344299), Box 167, WHORM Subject Files, Ronald Reagan Library; Pat Buchanan to Ronald Reagan, "Press and South Africa," memorandum, August 6, 1986, Folder: CO141 (South Africa) (405690–406296), Box 169, WHORM Subject Files, Ronald Reagan Library.

144. Department of State Bureau of African Affairs, chronological outline of Public Affairs initiatives, ca. October 1985, Folder: CO141 (South Africa) (339352) (1), Box 167, WHORM Subject Files, Ronald Reagan Library.

145. J. Douglas Holladay to Chester Crocker, "Briefing on South Africa, September 13 for religious leaders," memorandum, September 4, 1985, Folder: Briefing for Religious Leaders on South Africa, 09/13/1985, Box 13, Series V: Events OA 12267, J. Douglas Holladay Files, Ronald Reagan Library.

146. *Comprehensive Anti-Apartheid Act of 1986*, HR 4868, 99th Cong., 2nd sess., May 21, 1986.

147. George Shultz, "The Church as a Force for Peaceful Change in South Africa," address before the Conference on South Africa for American Religious Leaders, Department of State, Washington, D.C., June 2, 1986, *Current Policy* no. 841 (Washington, DC: Bureau of Public Affairs, Office of Public Communication, Editorial Division, 1986).

148. J. Philip Hogan, "Speech at School of Missions," 1986, 2, Folder: Hogan, J. Philip (Virginia) (–2001), Assemblies of God World Missions Archives, FPHC.

149. Ibid.

150. Ibid.

151. O. W. Polen, "U.S. State Department's Conference on South Africa," *Evangel* 76, no. 11 (August 11, 1986): 2.

152. In 1985, the Christian Life Commission of the SBC held a Consultation on Racial Reconciliation, Human Rights, and Justice, and issued a "Call to Concern about Apartheid," which recommended divestment. Many SBC members disagreed with the CLC's recommendations. See Christian Life Commission, "A Call to Concern About Apartheid"; Marv Knox, "Racial Statements distort SBC Stand, Ethicist Says," *Baptist Press* 88-156 (September 29, 1988): 2–3.

153. "Falwell and Jackson Debate South Africa," in *Fundamentalist Journal* "Special Report: The Untold Story: South Africa" (1985): 16. See also "Falwell, Jackson Accuse Each Other of Racism on S. Africa," *Los Angeles Times* (August 21, 1985): 2. During the debate with Jackson, Falwell referred to Bishop Tutu as a "phony," setting off a torrent of angry media responses and letters to Falwell as well as to the Reagan administration (though Falwell had no official relationship with the president, the U.S. public associated them, and the constructive engagement policy, closely enough that Reagan was included in the firestorm). Falwell estimated donations to his ministry dropped by nearly $1 million after the remarks, suggesting that not all evangelicals and fundamentalists shared his views. "Falwell Gifts Slip After Tutu Remark," *Washington Post* (September 26, 1985): A33.

154. "Falwell and Jackson," 16.

155. "Foreign Minister Botha Seeks Reason and Reform," in *Fundamentalist Journal* "Special Report: The Untold Story: South Africa" (1985): 10; Jack Kemp to Libba Barnes, October 1, 1985, Folder 7, Congressional Legislative File, Leg. Assist., Brunette, Subject File, Foreign Relations, South Africa, 1985–1987, Box 119, Jack Kemp Papers.

156. Charen to Buchanan, "Framing the Argument on S. Africa."

157. Christopher Moree, "The Church in South Africa: Conversation between Christopher Moree & Dr. Alex Thompson, President of the Full Gospel Church of God in South Africa," *Save Our World* 24, no. 4 (Winter 1985–86): 1–2, 15; Ben Armstrong to Ronald Reagan, May 28,

1986, Folder: CO141 (South Africa) (403000–405689), Box 168, WHORM Subject Files, Ronald Reagan Library.

158. "Comments from the Fact-Finding Team," in *Fundamentalist Journal* "Special Report: The Untold Story: South Africa," (1985): 5.

159. Ronald Reagan, "Message to the House of Representatives Returning without Approval a Bill Concerning Apartheid in South Africa," September 26, 1986, https://www.reaganlibrary.gov/research/speeches/092686h.

160. Carol Hornby to Mari Maseng, "Religious Group Activities on South Africa," September 24, 1986, Folder: [Foreign Affairs]: South Africa Working File October 1986 (2), Box 5, Series II: Subject File, Carl Anderson Files, Ronald Reagan Library.

161. Ibid.

162. Carl Anderson to Mari Maseng, "South Africa Update (12:00 pm)," memorandum, September 29, 1986, Folder: [Foreign Affairs]: South Africa Working File October 1986 (2), Box 5, Series II: Subject File, Carl Anderson Files, Ronald Reagan Library.

163. Carl Anderson to Mari Maseng, "South Africa Update (5:00 pm)," memorandum, September 29, 1986, Folder: Foreign Affairs]: South Africa Working File October 1986 (2), Box 5, Series II: Subject File, Carl Anderson Files, Ronald Reagan Library.

164. Public Law No. 99-440.

165. Ronald Reagan, "Statement on the Comprehensive Anti-Apartheid Act of 1986," October 2, 1986, https://www.reaganlibrary.gov/research/speeches/100286d.

166. Davies, *Constructive Engagement?* 62.

167. Kickham, "How U.S. Evangelicals," 43; Anthony Lewis, "Marching for Pretoria: Kemp's Bill Would Back South Africa," *New York Times* (October 31, 1985): A27.

168. Alex Thomson argues that policymaker opinion about apartheid grew less heated after the CAAA passed, in part because P. W. Botha cracked down on unrest in the townships, drastically reducing the number of graphic newscasts about South African violence that Americans saw. Although some legislators wanted to impose additional sanctions on South Africa in 1988, Congress ultimately voted against a bill "that would have imposed a total economic embargo against the Republic." See Thomson, *U.S. Foreign Policy*, 150.

169. Frank C. Carlucci to Ronald Reagan, "South African Sanctions: First Annual Report to the Congress on the Impact of Sanctions," memorandum, October 1, 1987, Folder: CO141 (South Africa) (506970) (1), Box 173, WHORM Subject Files, Ronald Reagan Library; Thomson, *U.S. Foreign Policy*, 152–54.

170. Thomson, *U.S. Foreign Policy*, 150–53.

171. Ibid., 158.

172. Baptist Mission in South Africa, "Annual Narrative Report to the Foreign Mission Board, SBC—1985," 1986, Folder 5: South Africa, Administration: Reports: Annual, 1978–1987, Box 138, AR. 551-1, SBHLA.

173. Baptist Mission in South Africa, "Annual Narrative Report to the Foreign Mission Board, SBC—1986," 1987, Folder 5: South Africa, Administration: Reports: Annual, 1978–1987, Box 138, AR. 551-1, SBHLA.

174. Fellowship Foundation, "South African Trip—March 12–21," ca. 1987, Collection 459 Records of the Fellowship Foundation, Box 255, Folder 9, South Africa 1986–1987, BGCA.

175. Michael Cassidy to Doug Coe, June 25, 1987, Collection 459 Records of the Fellowship Foundation, Box 255, Folder 10, South Africa 1987, BGCA.

176. Dudley and Elizabeth Foord, "Reflections from South Africa," April 1987, Collection 459 Records of the Fellowship Foundation, Box 255, Folder 10, South Africa 1987, BGCA.

177. Concerned Evangelicals, *Evangelical Witness in South Africa*, 17–18.

178. Ibid., 25–26.

179. Ibid., 26–28.

180. Relevant Pentecostal Witness, "Questions People Frequently Ask," pamphlet, 1988, and Joanne Shephard Smith, "Pentecostals Take the Plunge and Form Group to Fight Apartheid," *Sunday Tribune* (November 27, 1988), Folder: Records of the Relevant Pentecostal Witness, 1988–1989, HR028, Yale University Divinity Library Special Collections, New Haven, CT.

181. Steele, *Destined*, 178.

182. Becky Wells to Linas Kojelis, September 12, 1986 and Mike Evans to Carolyn Sundseth, August 8, 1986, Folder: CO141 (South Africa) (448400–449499), Box 172, WHORM Subject Files, Ronald Reagan Library; Nina May, et al. "Renaissance Women 'Fact-Finding' Trip to South Africa," in Senate Committee on Foreign Relations, *United States Policy toward South Africa: Hearings before the Subcommittee on African Affairs*, 100th Cong., 1st sess., October 22, 1987 and June 22, 23, and 24, 1988 (Washington, DC: U.S. Government Printing Office, 1989), 688–89.

183. Bruce Barron, "The Charismatic Path to South African Brotherhood," *Wall Street Journal* (July 5, 1990): A10; Doug Bandow, "Public Politics and Religious Values," *Chicago Tribune* (August 2, 1990): N23.

184. Barron, "The Charismatic," A10.

185. Ibid.; Bandow, "Public," N23.

186. Concerned Evangelicals, *Evangelical Witness*, 38–39, 42–45.

187. Bill Bangham, "Baptists Seek Redemptive Acts in South Africa Today," *Baptist Press* 89–36 (March 3, 1989): 1–2.

188. Pat Cole, "South African Baptist Cites Church Influence," *Baptist Press* 90–37 (March 14, 1990): 16.

189. "Young Evangelicals Prepare to Lead," *Washington Post* (July 2, 1988): E7.

190. Molebatsi, "Social Concern and Evangelism III," in *Proclaim Christ until He Comes*, ed. International Congress on World Evangelization and Douglas, 294.

191. Donald D. Martin, "Missionaries Freed to Cross Racial Barrier in South Africa," *Baptist Press* 92-20 (February 4, 1992): 5; Craig Bird, "South African Churches Reflect Society's Moods," *Baptist Press* 90-51 (April 9, 1990): 2–6.

192. Knox, "Racial Statements," 2; Lynda Richardson, "Southern Baptists Seek Recruits among Blacks," *Washington Post* (July 15, 1990): A3. Despite this, the CLC reelected the trustee to the board.

193. Knox, "Racial statements," 3.

194. Martin, "Missionaries," 5–6.

195. Central Intelligence Agency, "South Africa's Brokers of Ballots and Bullets, Andries Treurnicht, Conservative," March 1, 1990, Document 0000417148, CIA FOIA Reading Room, https://www.cia.gov/library/readingroom/document/0000417148.

196. L. L. Rowlands, "Church in South Africa Moves toward Full Integration," *Save Our World* 32, no. 2 (Summer 1993): 19.

197. *Rustenburg Declaration: National Conference of Churches in South Africa* (Pretoria, South Africa: National Initiative for Reconciliation, 1990); David B. Ottawny, "South African Churches Seeking Reconciliation," *Washington Post* (November 6, 1990): A15.

198. Ibid.; Cassidy, *A Witness For Ever*, 98–99; "Church Leaders Condemn Apartheid," *Christianity Today* 4, no. 18 (December 17, 1990): 54; Balcomb, "Apartheid," 15–19.

199. Cassidy, *A Witness*, 100–105; Balcomb, "Apartheid," 19–22; Anderson, "Pentecostals and Apartheid," 29.

200. Cassidy, *A Witness*, 102–3.

201. Baptist Mission in South Africa, "Annual Narrative Report to the Foreign Mission Board, SBC—1994," Folder 30: South Africa, Administration: Reports: Annual, 1992–1995, Box 306 South Africa, AR. 551–1, SBHLA.

202. Ibid.

Conclusion

1. See, for example, House Committee on Foreign Affairs, Subcommittee on International Security, International Organizations, and Human Rights, *Religious Persecution*, 103rd Cong., 2nd sess., October 28, 1993 and March 9, 1994 (Washington, DC: U.S. Government Printing Office, 1994); House Committee on International Relations, *Persecution of Christians Worldwide: Hearing before the Subcommittee on International Operations and Human Rights*, 104th Cong., 2nd sess., February 15, 1996 (Washington, DC: U.S. Government Printing Office, 1996).

2. Commission on Security and Cooperation in Europe, *CSCE to Examine Repression against Evangelicals in Former Soviet Union*, February 16, 1994 (Washington, DC: CSCE, 1994); David Neff, "Our Extended, Persecuted Family," *Christianity Today* 40, no. 5 (April 29, 1996): 14; Kim A. Lawton, "The Suffering Church," *Christianity Today* 40, no. 8 (July 15, 1996): 54–64; Peter Steinfels, "Evangelicals Lobby for Oppressed Christians," *New York Times* (September 15, 1996): 26; Laurie Goodstein, "Evangelical Christians Seek Action: Administration, Congress react to call to fight persecution," *Washington Post* (September 22, 1996): A3.

3. Hertzke, *Freeing God's Children*, 29. See also Iverson, *Foreign Policy in God's Name*, 27; den Dulk, "Evangelical 'Internationalists' and U.S. Foreign Policy during the Bush Administration," in *Religion and the Bush Presidency*, ed. Rozell and Whitney, 215–18.

4. Mt. 28:19 (NRSV).

5. Evangelicals rooted such beliefs in their reading of scripture, including Romans 8:18 (NRSV)—"I consider that the sufferings of this present time are not worth comparing with the glory about to be revealed to us"—and the Beatitudes from the Sermon on the Mount in Mt. 5:3–12 and the Sermon on the Plain in Lk. 6:20–22.

6. Collection 459 Records of the Fellowship Foundation, Billy Graham Center Archives, Wheaton, IL.

7. See The Southern Baptist Convention Christian Life Commission, "Declaration of Human Rights" (Atlanta, GA: 1978), http://www.sbc.net/resolutions/623/declaration-of-human-rights; "The Lausanne Covenant," in *Let the Earth Hear His Voice*, 8; "Treatment of Christians by the Soviet Union," *Congressional Record* 126 pt. 23: S15041–46.

8. Robert P. Dugan, Jr., "Prepared Statement of Robert P. Dugan, Jr.," Senate Committee on Foreign Relations, *Nomination of Ernest W. Lefever: Hearings before the Committee on Foreign Relations, United States Senate*, 97th Cong., 1st sess., May 18, 19, June 4, and 5, 1981 (Washington, DC: U.S. Government Printing Office, 1981), 305.

9. "The Lausanne Covenant," 4–6, 8.

10. Jn. 3:16 (NRSV); 2 Cor. 3:17 (NRSV); Rom. 8:18 (NRSV); Mt. 5:3–12 (NRSV); Carl F. H. Henry, "Human Rights and Wrongs," *Christianity Today* 21, no. 19 (July 8, 1977): 25.

11. See Amstutz, *Evangelicals and American Foreign Policy*.

12. Preston, *Sword of the Spirit; Shield of Faith*; Inboden, *Religion and American Foreign Policy*; Herzog, *The Spiritual-Industrial Complex*.

Bibliography

Archival Collections

United States

Billy Graham Center Archives, Wheaton, IL (BGCA)

Billy Graham Evangelistic Association: Crusade Activities, Collection 17
Billy Graham Evangelistic Association: International Conference for
Itinerant Evangelists, Collection 253
Billy Graham Evangelistic Association: Media Office Records, Collection
345
Billy Graham Evangelistic Association: Oral History Project, Collection
141
Evangelical Foreign Missions Association (EFMA), Collection 165
International Congress on World Evangelization, Collection 53
Interviews with Carlos René Padilla, Collection 361
Interview with Peter Simon Deyneka, Jr., Collection 381
Mission Aviation Fellowship. Collection 136
Records of the Fellowship Foundation, Collection 459

Records of the National Religious Broadcasters, Collection 309
Records of the Slavic Gospel Association, Collection 237
Records of the World Evangelical Fellowship, Collection 338

Brown University, John Hay Library Special Collections, Providence, RI

Gordon Hall and Grace Hoag Collection of Dissenting and Extremist
Printed Propaganda

Dixon Pentecostal Research Center, Cleveland, TN

Church of God Subject Files
J. H. Walker Jr. Papers

Flower Pentecostal Heritage Center, Springfield, MO (FPHC)

Assemblies of God World Missions Archives
Flower Pentecostal Heritage Center Archives

Gerald R. Ford Presidential Library, Ann Arbor, MI (GRFL)

Collection GRF-0314: Memoranda of Conversations (Nixon and Ford
Administrations), 1973–1977
James Wilson Papers
White House Central Files

Jimmy Carter Presidential Library, Atlanta, GA (JCPL)

Office of Anne Wexler, Bob Maddox Religious Liaison Files
Office of Public Liaison, Jane Wales Subject Files
RAC Project Files
White House Central Files
Zbigniew Brzezinski Collection

Liberty University Archive, Lynchburg, VA

Falwell Family Papers

The Library of Congress, Washington, DC

Jack Kemp Papers (JKP)

Richard Nixon Presidential Library and Museum, Yorba Linda, CA (RNPL)

Charles W. Colson Files
White House Central Files
White House Special Files

Ronald Reagan Presidential Library, Simi Valley, CA

African Affairs Directorate, NSC: Records
Alfonso Sapia-Bosch Files
Carl Anderson Files
Carolyn Sundseth Files
European and Soviet Affairs Directorate Files
Executive Secretariat: Meeting Files
Executive Secretariat, NSC: Country Files
J. Douglas Holladay Files
Jack F. Matlock, Jr. Files
Linas Kojelis Files
Katherine Chumachenko Files
Morton C. Blackwell Files
Oliver North Files
White House Office of Records Management (WHORM): Subject Files
William P. Clark Files
William Sittmann Files

Southern Baptist Historical Library and Archives, Nashville, TN (SBHLA)

AR 138–2: Christian Life Commission Resource Files
AR 140: Christian Life Commission Publication and Promotional Material Collection
AR. 551–1 Southern Baptist Convention International Mission Board Mission minutes and reports, 1849–2005
AR 551–8: Southern Baptist Convention Foreign Mission Board Historical Files
AR 711: John David Hughey Papers

United States National Archives, College Park, MD

RG 59: General Records of the Department of State

Wheaton College Special Collections, Buswell Library, Wheaton, IL (WCSC)

Institute of Soviet and East European Studies (ISEES) Collection
Intercessors for the Suffering Church Collection
National Association of Evangelicals (NAE) Records
Siberian 7 Collection

Yale University Divinity Library Special Collections, New Haven, CT

Records of the Relevant Pentecostal Witness, 1988–1989

Guatemala

Centro de Investigaciones Regionales de Mesoamérica, Antigua, Guatemala

Archivo de Inforpress Centroamericana
Colección de donantes anónimos sobre la historia política, económica y social de Guatemala
Archivo del Comité Holandés de Solidaridad con Guatemala
Archivo de la Coordinadora Alemana de Solidaridad con Guatemala
Colección CIRMA
Colección de Robert Trudeau sobre Política de Guatemala
Publicación Diario El Imparcial

South Africa

National Library of South Africa, Cape Town, South Africa (NLSA)

Cape Town Serials

National Archives of South Africa, Pretoria, South Africa (SA KAB

Collection K382, E5/53-54, Eloff Commission

Government Publications, Public Laws, and Legislation

Commission on Security and Cooperation in Europe. *Basket Three: Implementation of the Helsinki Accords. Hearing before the Commission on Security and Cooperation in Europe. Pastor Georgi Vins on the Persecution of Reformed Baptists in the U.S.S.R.*, 96th Cong., 1st sess., June 7, 1979.

Commission on Security and Cooperation in Europe. *On the Right To Emigrate for Religious Reasons: The Case of 10,000 Soviet Evangelical Christians.* Washington, DC: The Commission, 1979.

Commission on Security and Cooperation in Europe. *State of Human Rights in Romania (An Update).* CSCE Serial No. CSCE 100-2-38. Washington, DC: U.S. Government Printing Office, 1989.

Commission on Security and Cooperation in Europe. *The Status of Religious Liberty In Russia Today: Hearing Before the Commission On Security and Cooperation In Europe.* 106th Cong., 2nd sess., February 17, 2000.

Congressional Record. Washington, DC: U.S. Government Printing Office.

Office of Senior Specialists (Congressional Research Service) and William Cooper. *Soviet-American Relations in 1977: A Chronological Summary and Brief Analysis.* Report No. 79–60 S. March 1, 1979.

Olcese, Orlando. *The Guatemala Earthquake Disaster of 1976: A Review of Its Effects and of the Contribution of the United Nations Family.* Guatemala: United Nations Development Programme, 1977.

Public Law No: 990-440, October 2, 1986

Public Law No: 105-292, October 27, 1998

Republic of South Africa. *Commission of South Africa, Report of the Commission of Inquiry into South African Council of Churches.* Pretoria: Govt. Printer, 1983.

Republic of South Africa. *Republic of South Africa Constitution Act, No. 110, 1983.* Pretoria: Govt. Printer, 1983.

Shultz, George P. "The Church as a Force for Peaceful Change in South Africa." Address before the Conference on South Africa for American Religious Leaders, Department of State, Washington, D.C., June 2, 1986. *Current Policy* no. 841. Washington, DC: Bureau of Public Affairs, Office of Public Communication, Editorial Division, 1986.

United Nations. Security Council Resolution 181 (1963), August 7, 1963.

United Nations. Security Council Resolution 392 (1976), June 19, 1976.

United States and Ronald Reagan. *Public Papers of the Presidents of the United States, Ronald Reagan, 1986.* Washington, DC: U.S. Government Printing Office, 1989.

U.S. Commission on International Religious Freedom. "Russia: Unruly State of Law: Findings from a Visit of the U.S. Commission on International Religious Freedom." *Policy Brief.* Washington, DC: USCIRF, 2013.

U.S. Congress. House. *Anti-Apartheid Act of 1985.* HR 1460, 99th Cong., 1st sess. March 7, 1985.

U.S. Congress. House. *Comprehensive Anti-Apartheid Act of 1986.* HR 4868, 99th Cong., 2nd sess. May 21, 1986.

U.S. Congress. House. Committee on Foreign Affairs. Subcommittee on Human Rights and International Organizations. *Religious Persecution as a Violation of Human Rights: Hearings and Markup before the Committee on Foreign Affairs and Its Subcommittee on Human Rights and International Organizations.* 97th Cong., 2nd sess., February 10, March 23, May 25, July 27 and 29, August 5 and 10, September 23, December 1 and 14, 1982.

U.S. Congress. House. Committee on Foreign Affairs. Subcommittee on International Security, International Organizations, and Human Rights. *Religious Persecution.* 103rd Cong., 2nd sess., October 28, 1993 and March 9, 1994.

U.S. Congress. House. Committee on Foreign Affairs. Subcommittee on International Organizations. *Human Rights and U.S. Foreign Policy: Hearings before the Subcommittee on International Organizations of the Committee on Foreign Affairs.* 96th Cong., 1st sess., May 2, June 21, July 12, and August 2, 1979.

U.S. Congress. House. Committee on Foreign Affairs. *Economic Sanctions and Their Potential Impact on U.S. Corporate Involvement in South Africa, Hearing before the Subcommittee on Africa.* 99th Cong., 1st sess., January 31, 1985.

U.S. Congress. House. Committee on Foreign Affairs. *United States Policy toward Guatemala: Hearing before the Subcommittee on Western Hemisphere Affairs of the Committee on Foreign Affairs.* 98th Cong., 1st sess., March 9, 1983.

U.S. Congress. House. Committee on Foreign Affairs. *United States Policy toward Guatemala and El Salvador.* 98th Cong., 1st sess., February 20–26, 1983.

U.S. Congress. House. Committee on Foreign Affairs, Subcommittee on Africa. *Policy Toward Africa for the Seventies: Hearings.* 91st Cong., 2nd sess., March 17–19, 23–24, May 19–21, June 4, September 30, October 1, November 18, and December 3, 1970.

U.S. Congress. House. Committee on Foreign Affairs, Subcommittee on Africa. *U.S. Business Involvement in Southern Africa: Hearings.* 92nd Cong., 1st sess., May 5, June 2–3, 15–16, 30, July 15, September 27, November 12, December 6–7, 1971.

U.S. Congress. House. Committee on Foreign Affairs. Subcommittee on Africa. *The Current Crisis in South Africa: Hearing Before the Subcommittee on Africa.* 98th Cong., 2nd sess., December 4, 1984.

U.S. Congress. House. Committee on Foreign Affairs. Subcommittees on Europe and the Middle East and on Human Rights and International Organizations. *Human Rights in Romania: Hearing.* 99th Cong., 1st sess., May 14, 1985.

U.S. Congress. House. Committee on International Relations. *Religious Repression in the Soviet Union: Dissident Baptist Pastor Georgi Vins.* 94th Cong., 2nd sess., September 2, 1976. H. Report No. 94-1464.

U.S. Congress. House. Committee on International Relations. *Report of Secretary of State Kissinger on His Visits to Latin America, Western Europe, and Africa*: Hearing. 94th Cong., 2nd sess., June 17, 1976.

U.S. Congress. House. Committee on International Relations. *United States-South African Relations: Internal Change in South Africa.* 95th Cong., 1st sess., June 3, 1977.

U.S. Congress. House. Committee on International Relations. *Urging the President Not to Extend Diplomatic or Other Recognition to the Transkei Territory.* 94th cong., 2nd sess., September 2, 1976; House Report no. 94-1463.

U.S. Congress. House. Committee on International Relations. Subcommittee on International Operations and Human Rights. *Persecution of Christians Worldwide: Hearing.* 104th Cong., 2nd sess., February 15, 1996.

U.S. Congress. House. Committee on International Relations. Subcommittees on International Political and Military Affairs and on International Organizations. *Religious Persecution in the Soviet Union.* 94th Cong., 2nd sess., June 24 and 30, 1976.

U.S. Congress. House. Committee on the District of Columbia. Subcommittee on Fiscal Affairs and Health. *South Africa Divestment: Hearing and Markups before the Subcommittee on Fiscal Affairs and Health.* 98th Cong., 2nd sess., January 31 and February 7, 1984.

U.S. Congress. House. Committee on the Judiciary. Subcommittee on Immigration, Refugees, and International Law. *Siberian Seven: Hearing.* 97th Cong., 2nd sess., December 16, 1982.

U.S. Congress. House. Committee on Ways and Means. *Extension of MFN Status to Romania, Hungary, and the People's Republic of China.* 97th Cong., 2nd sess., July 12, 1982.

U.S. Congress. House. Committee on Ways and Means. Subcommittee on Trade. *Extension of MFN Status to Romania, Hungary, and the People's Republic of China: Hearings.* 97th Cong., 2nd sess., July 12 and 13, 1982. Serial 97-78.

U.S. Congress. House. *Comprehensive Anti-Apartheid Act of 1986.* HR 4868, 99th Cong., 2nd sess., October 2, 1986.

U.S. Congress. House. *A concurrent resolution expressing the sense of the Congress with respect to the situation of two Soviet families, known as the Siberian Seven, who have sought refuge in the United States Embassy in Moscow because of the discrimination of their Pentecostal faith by the Union of Soviet Socialist Republics.* H.CON.RES.251. 97th Cong., 2nd sess. Washington, DC: U.S. Government Printing Office, 1982.

U.S. Congress. Senate. Committee on Banking, Housing, and Urban Affairs. *Report on the visit to the Soviet Union of the senate delegation led by Senator John Heinz: Exploration of the condition of human rights and "democratization" and economic reform initiatives undertaken by the Soviet Union.* 100th Cong., 1st sess., October 1, 1987. Report No. 100-52.

U.S. Congress. Senate. Committee on Finance. Subcommittee on International Trade. *Continuing Presidential Authority To Waive Freedom of Emigration Provisions.* 98th Cong., 2nd sess., August 8, 1984.

U.S. Congress. Senate. Committee on Finance. Subcommittee on International Trade. *MFN Status for Hungary, Romania, China, and Afghanistan.* 99th Cong., 1st sess., July 23, 1985

U.S. Congress. Senate. Committee on Foreign Relations. *Expressing the Sense of the Congress with Respect to the Treatment of Christians by the Union of Soviet Socialist Republics.* 96th Cong., 2nd sess., October 16, 1980.

U.S. Congress. Senate. Committee on Foreign Relations. *Human Rights: Hearing before the Committee on Foreign Relations, United States Senate, Ninety-Eighth Congress, First Session, on the Promotion and Protection of Human Rights in Eastern Europe and the Soviet Union.* Chicago, IL. 98th Cong., 1st sess., November 9, 1983.

U.S. Congress. Senate. Committee on Foreign Relations. *Nomination of Alexander M. Haig, Jr.: Hearings before the Committee on Foreign Relations, United States Senate, Ninety-Seventh Congress, First Session, on the Nomination of Alexander M. Haig, Jr., to Be Secretary of State, Part 2.* 97th Cong., 1st sess., January 9–10, 12–15, 1981.

U.S. Congress. Senate. Committee on Foreign Relations. *Nomination of Elliot Abrams: Hearing before the Committee on Foreign Relations, United States Senate, Ninety-Seventh Congress, First Session, on the Nomination of Elliot Abrams, of the District of Columbia, to*

Be Assistant Secretary of State for Human Rights and Humanitarian Affairs. 97th Cong., 1st sess., November 17, 1981.

U.S. Congress. Senate. Committee on Foreign Relations. *Nomination of Ernest W. Lefever: Hearings before the Committee on Foreign Relations, United States Senate, Ninety-Seventh Congress, First Session, on the Nomination of Ernest W. Lefever to Be Assistant Secretary of State for Human Rights and Humanitarian Affairs.* 97th Cong., 1st sess., May 18–19, June 4–5, 1981.

U.S. Congress. Senate. Committee on Foreign Relations. *Religious Freedom in the Soviet Union: The Case of Pastor Georgi Vins.* 94th Cong., 2nd sess., September 24, 1976. S. Report No. 94-1306.

U.S. Congress. Senate. Committee on Foreign Relations. *S. 1868: The International Religious Freedom Act of 1998: Hearings Before the Committee on Foreign Relations of the United States Senate.* 105th Cong., 2nd sess., May 12 and June 17, 1998.

U.S. Congress. Senate. Committee on Foreign Relations. *U.S. Commission on International Religious Freedom: Findings on Russia, China, and Sudan; and Religious Persecutions in the World.* 106th Cong., 2nd sess., May 16 and September 7, 2000.

U.S. Congress. Senate. Committee on Foreign Relations. Subcommittee on African Affairs. *South Africa: Hearings on South Africa-U.S. Policy and the Role of U.S. Corporations.* 94th Cong., 2nd sess., September 8–9, 16–17, 22–23, 29–30, 1976.

U.S. Congress. Senate. Committee on Foreign Relations. Subcommittee on African Affairs. *U.S. Policy on South Africa: Hearing.* 98th Cong., 2nd sess., September 26, 1984.

U.S. Congress. Senate. Committee on Foreign Relations. Subcommittee on African Affairs. *United States Policy toward South Africa: Hearings.* 100th Cong., 1st sess., October 22, 1987 and June 22, 23, and 24, 1988.

U.S. Congress. Senate. Committee on the Judiciary. Subcommittee on Immigration, Refugees, and International Law. *Relief of Seven Soviet Pentecostals Residing in the U.S. Embassy in Moscow Hearing before the Subcommittee on Immigration and Refugee Policy and the Committee on the Judiciary, United States Senate on S. 312.* 97th Cong., 1st sess., November 19, 1981.

U.S. Department of State. *Bulletin.*

USSR Council for Religious Affairs Attached to the USSR Council of Ministers. Moscow to the Central Committee of the Communist Party of the Soviet Union. "On the Publication of the Bible." December 1, 1982. Reprinted in *Religion in the Soviet Union: An Archival Reader,* edited by Felix Corley, 285–86. New York: New York University Press, 1996.

Wurmbrand, Richard. *Communist Exploitation of Religion: Hearing.* 89th Cong., 2nd sess. May 6, 1966. Washington, DC: U.S. Government Printing Office, 1966.

Memoirs, Diaries, and Contemporaneous Publications

American Jewish Congress. "Executive Director's Report." *Congress bi-Weekly: A Journal of Opinion and Jewish Affairs* 40, no. 8 (May 18, 1973): 15

Anfuso, Joseph and David Sczepanski. *Efrain Rios Montt, Servant or Dictator?: The Real Story of Guatemala's Controversial Born-Again President.* Ventura, CA: Vision House, 1984.

———. *He Gives—He Takes Away: The True Story of Guatemala's Controversial Former President Efrain Rios Montt.* Eureka, CA: Radiance Publications, 1983.

Armstrong, Ben. *The Electric Church.* Nashville: T. Nelson, 1979.

Bourdeaux, Michael. *Faith on Trial in Russia.* New York: Harper & Row, 1971.

Bright, Bill. "Your Five Duties as a Christian Citizen." American Christian Voice Foundation, 1976.

Brumback, Carl. *Suddenly . . . from Heaven: A History of the Assemblies of God.* Springfield, MO: Gospel Publishing House, 1961.

Bühlmann, Walbert. *The Coming of the Third Church: An Analysis of the Present and Future of the Church.* Maryknoll, NY: Orbis Books, 1977.

Cassidy, Michael. *Bursting the Wineskins.* London: Hodder and Stoughton, 1983.

———. *A Witness For Ever: The Dawning of Democracy in South Africa—The Stories behind the Story.* London: Hodder & Stoughton, 1995.

Cerillo, Augustus and Murray W. Dempster. *Salt and Light: Evangelical Political Thought in Modern America.* Grand Rapids, MI: Baker Book House, 1989.

Cho, David J. "My Pilgrimage in Mission." Last modified September 10, 2010. Accessed December 18, 2013. http://davidcho.org/archives/282.

Christian Reformed Church in North America. "Russian Language Ministries." Agenda for Synod (June 9 to 19, 1992). http://www.calvin.edu/library/database/crcnasynod/1992agendaacts.pdf.

Concerned Evangelicals. *Evangelical Witness in South Africa: A Critique of Evangelical Theology and Practice by South African Evangelicals.* Grand Rapids, MI: William B. Eerdmans Publishing Company, 1986.

Crocker, Chester A. "South Africa: Strategy for Change." *Foreign Affairs* 59, no. 2 (Winter 1980): 323–51.

Douglas, J. D., ed. *Let the Earth Hear His Voice: International Congress on World Evangelization, Lausanne, Switzerland Official Reference Volume.* Minneapolis, MN: World Wide Publications, 1975.

———. *Proclaim Christ until He Comes: Calling the Whole Church to Take the Whole Gospel to the Whole World.* Minneapolis, MN: World Wide Publications, 1990.

Eagleson, John, and Philip J. Scharper. *Puebla and Beyond: Documentation and Commentary.* Maryknoll, NY: Orbis Books, 1979.

Engel, James F. *Contemporary Christian Communications: Its Theory and Practice.* Nashville, TN: Thomas Nelson Publishers, 1979.

Engstrom, Ted W. *What in the World Is God Doing? The New Face of Missions.* Waco, TX: World Books Publisher, 1978.

Falwell, Jerry, Ed Dobson, and Ed Hinson. *The Fundamentalist Phenomenon: The Resurgence of Conservative Christianity.* Garden City, NY: Doubleday, 1981.

Friedman, Murray. "Intergroup Relations and Tensions in the United States." In *American Jewish Yearbook*, 73 (1972), the American Jewish Committee, edited by Morris Fine and Milton Himmelfarb, 97–153. Philadelphia: Jewish Publication Society of America, 1973.

Graham, Billy. *Just as I Am: The Autobiography of Billy Graham*. New York: HarperCollins, 1997.

Gorbachev, Mikhail Sergeevich. *Memoirs*. New York: Doubleday, 1996.

Harris, Rosemary. *Christian Prisoners in Russia*. Wheaton, IL: Tyndale House Publishers, 1972.

Helsinki Watch. "Human Rights in Romania: A Report Prepared for the Most Favored Nation Hearings in the U.S. Congress." A Helsinki Watch Report, August 1984.

Hill, Kent R. *The Soviet Union on the Brink: An Inside Look at Christianity & Glasnost*. Portland, OR: Multnomah, 1991.

International Congress on World Evangelization Research Committee. *World Congress Country Profiles*. Monrovia, CA: Missions Advanced Research & Communication Center, 1974.

Jesus to the Communist World. *Baptists! Thousands of Your Brethren Are in Red Prisons!* Glendale, CA: Jesus to the Communist World, 1969.

Jones, C. W. "As It Was Then—Christmas Day 1931." *Andex International* 1, no. 12 (December 1974): 1, 4. http://www.ontheshortwaves.com/HCJB/ANDEX/1974/Dec_1974.pdf.

Kirkpatrick, Jeane. "Dictatorships and Double Standards." *Commentary* (November 1979): 34–45.

——. "Human Rights and the Foundations of Democracy." *World Affairs* 144, no. 3, A U.S. Offensive at the U.N. (Statements by the U.S. Delegation before the General Assembly) (Winter 1981/82): 196–203.

Lefever, Ernest. "The Trivialization of Human Rights." *Policy Review*, no. 3 (Winter 1978): 11–26.

Matlock, Jack. *Reagan and Gorbachev: How the Cold War Ended*. New York: Random House Trade Paperbacks, 2005.

McGavran, Donald, ed. *Eye of the Storm: The Great Debate in Mission*. Waco, TX: Word Books, 1972.

Missions Advanced Research and Communications Center. *Unreached Peoples: A Preliminary Compilation*. Monrovia, CA: MARC, 1973.

Molebatsi, Caesar. "Social Concern and Evangelism III: Reaching the Oppressed." In *Proclaim Christ until He Comes: Calling the Whole Church to Take the Whole Gospel to the Whole World*, edited by International Congress on World Evangelization and J. D. Douglas, 294–97. Minneapolis, MN: World Wide Publications, 1990.

National Conference of Churches in South Africa. *Rustenburg Declaration*. Pretoria, South Africa: National Initiative for Reconciliation, 1990.

Neely, Lois. *Come up to This Mountain: The Miracle of Clarence W. Jones & HCJB*. Wheaton, IL: Tyndale House Publishers, 1980.

Nesdoly, Samuel J. *Among the Soviet Evangelicals: A Goodly Heritage*. Carlisle, PA: The Banner of Truth Trust, 1986.

Plowman, Edward E. *The Changing State of the Church amid Communism's Collapse*. Roanoke, VA: National & International Religion Report, 1991.

Pollock, John. *The Siberian Seven*. Waco, TX: World Books, 1980.

Reagan, Ronald. *In His Own Hand: The Writings of Ronald Reagan That Reveal His Revolutionary Vision for America.* Edited by Kiron K. Skinner, Annelise Graebner Anderson, and Martin Anderson. New York: Free Press, 2001.

——. *Reagan: A Life in Letters.* Edited by Kiron K. Skinner, Annelise Graebner Anderson, and Martin Anderson. New York: Free Press, 2003.

——. *The Reagan Diaries: Volume I January 1981–October 1985.* Edited by Douglas Brinkley. New York: HarperCollins, 2009.

Recovery of Historical Memory Project. *Guatemala: Never Again! The Official Report of the Human Rights Office, Archdiocese of Guatemala.* Maryknoll, NY: Orbis Books, 1999.

Rohrer, Norman B., and Peter Deyneka, Jr. *Peter Dynamite "Twice Born Russian": The Story of Peter Deyneka—Missionary to the Russian World.* Grand Rapids, MI: Baker Book House, 1977.

Samandú, Luis, Claudia Dary Fuentes, and Vitalino Similox Salazar. *El Protestantismo en Guatemala.* Guatemala: Universidad de San Carlos de Guatemala, Dirección General de Investigación, 1989.

Sawatsky, Walter. *Soviet Evangelicals since World War II.* Kitchener, Ontario: Herald Press, 1981.

Schmidt, Elizabeth. *Decoding Corporate Camouflage: U.S. Business Support for Apartheid.* Washington, DC: Institute for Policy Studies, 1980.

Souder, Patricia, and Bill Bright. *Alex Leonovich: A Heart for the Soul of Russia.* Camp Hill, PA: Horizon Books, 1999.

Steele, Ron. *Destined to Win: A Biography of Ray McCauley.* Tulsa, OK: Praise Books, 1987.

Stoll, David. "Guatemala: The New Jerusalem of the Americas?" *Cultural Survival Quarterly* 7, no. 1 (March 31, 1983): 28–31.

Stott, John. *Making Christ Known: Historic Mission Documents from the Lausanne Movement 1974–1989.* Carlisle, Cumbria: Paternoster Publishing, 1996.

Voronaeff, Paul. *Pastor Paul Voronaeff's "Firsthand Report of Communist Persecution of Christians behind the Iron Curtain."* Tulsa, OK: Christian Crusade, 1969.

Wurmbrand, Richard. *Tortured for Christ.* Glendale, CA: Diane Books, 1969.

Yancey, Philip. *Praying with the KGB: A Startling Report from a Shattered Empire.* Portland, OR: Multnomah, 1992.

Zotz, Vladimir. "Personal Spiritual Orientations: Atheism and Religiousness in the Soviet Union." *Occasional Papers on Religion in Eastern Europe* 12, no. 3 (June 1992): 11–22.

Microfilm Collections

North American Congress on Latin America, et al. *Guatemala North American Congress on Latin America (NACLA) Archive of Latin Americana.* Wilmington, DE: Scholarly Resources, 1997.

Whitehead, Amanda, ed. *Latin American History and Culture. Series 5, Civil War, Society and Political Transition in Guatemala: The Guatemala News and Information Bureau Archive, 1963–2000*. Woodbridge, CT: Primary Source Microfilm, 2004.

Newspapers, Periodicals, and Newsletters

Action: World Association for Christian Communication Newsletter
AE News (African Enterprise)
Applied Christianity
The Baltimore Afro-American
Baptist Bulletin
Baptist Press
Baptist Standard
Baptist Quarterly
(BP)—Features: News of the Southern Baptist Convention
The Bulletin (Bend, OR)
Call of the Andes
Calvin Theological Journal
The Cape Times (South Africa)
Chattanooga News-Free Press
Chicago Daily Defender
Chicago Defender
Chicago Tribune
Church Growth Bulletin
Christian Century
Christian Messenger: Ghana's Oldest Christian Paper
Christian Solidarity International Reports
Christianity and Crisis
Christianity Today
The Citizen (South Africa)
Cleveland Daily Banner (Cleveland, TN)
Concordia Theological Monthly
Contact: Official Publication of the National Association of Free Will Baptists
CounterSpy
The Daily Telegraph (London)
East/West News
Economic and Political Weekly

Ecunews
El Grafico (Guatemala)
Encounter (South Africa)
Evangel
Fundamentalist Journal
Gallup News
The Globe and Mail (Canada)
Gospel Call
Human Events
Intercession
International Review of Mission
Jewish Telegraphic Agency
Komsomolskaya Pravda
Los Angeles Times
Missionary News Service
Moody Monthly
Mountain Movers
The Nation
New York Times
New Vision (Christian Interdenominational Fellowship of South Africa)
News Network International
Newsweek
Norfolk Journal and Guide
Pentecostal Evangel
Penthouse
Playground Daily News (Fort Walton Beach, FL)
Post (South Africa)
Prensa Libre (Guatemala)
Radiance Monthly
Religion in Communist Dominated Lands
Religion in Communist Lands
Rolling Stone
The San Francisco Bay Guardian
San Francisco Examiner
Save Our World
St. Petersburg Times (St. Petersburg, FL)
Sunday Express (South Africa)
The Sowetan (South Africa)

Time
Underground Evangelism
U.S. News and World Report
The Washington Post
The Wall Street Journal
WEF Communications Report
World Vision Magazine

Online Sources

Baptist Studies Online: http://baptiststudiesonline.com
Billy Graham Center Archives, Documents of the First Lausanne Congress (1974): http://www2.wheaton.edu/bgc/archives/docs/Lausanne/704/704.htm
Central Intelligence Agency Freedom of Information Act Electronic Reading Room: http://www.foia.cia.gov
Conference on Security and Cooperation in Europe, Text of Final Act (Helsinki, 1975): http://www.osce.org/mc/39501
Declassified Documents Reference System: https://www.gale.com/c/us-declassified-documents-online (DDRS)
Digital National Security Archive: http://nsarchive.chadwyck.com (DNSA)
Escuela Politécnica (Guatemala): http://www.politecnica.edu.gt
Global Recordings Network: http://globalrecordings.net
Inkatha Freedom Party Archives: http://www.ifp.org.za/documents/archives/
Institute for the Study of American Evangelicals: http://www.wheaton.edu/ISAE
Lausanne Movement Content Library: http://www.lausanne.org/category/content
National Association of Evangelicals Policy Resolutions: http://www.nae.net/fullre solutionlist
National Oceanic and Atmospheric Administration, National Geophysical Data Center: http://www.ngdc.noaa.gov/
The National Security Archive: http://nsarchive.gwu.edu/index.html
Open Society Justice Initiative: http://www.riosmontt-trial.org
Pat Robertson: http://www.patrobertson.com
Public Papers of the President: Ronald Reagan, 1981–1989: https://www.reaganlibrary.gov/sspeeches
Russian Radio Bible Institute Christian Ministries: http://rrbiworld.com/
Southern Baptist Convention Resolutions: http://www.sbc.net/resolutions/search/
Southern Baptist Historical Library and Archives, Baptist Press Archives from 1948 to 1996: http://www.sbhla.org/bp_archive/index.asp
United Nations Documents: http://www.un.org/en/documents
U.S. Department of State Freedom of Information Act (FOIA) Virtual Reading Room: http://foia.state.gov/

Vanderbilt Television News Archive: http://dev-tvnews.library.vanderbilt.edu/
WikiLeaks Public Library of U.S. Diplomacy: https://www.wikileaks.org/plusd/

Secondary Sources

Abzug, Robert H. *Cosmos Crumbling: American Reform and the Religious Imagination.* Oxford: Oxford University Press, 1994.

Allen, John. *Desmond Tutu: Rabble-Rouser for Peace.* Chicago: Free Press, 2006.

Allitt, Patrick. *Religion in America Since 1945: A History.* New York: Columbia University Press, 2003.

Amstutz, Mark R. *Evangelicals and American Foreign Policy.* New York: Oxford University Press, 2013.

Anderson, Allan. "Dangerous Memories for South African Pentecostals." In *Pentecostals after a Century: Global Perspectives on a Movement in Transition,* edited by Allan H. Anderson and Walter J. Hollenweger, 89–107. Sheffield, England: Sheffield Academic Press, 1999.

——. "New African Initiated Pentecostalism and Charismatics in South Africa." *Journal of Religion in Africa* 35, no. 1 (February 2005): 66–92.

——. "Pentecostals and Apartheid in South African during Ninety Years 1908–1998." *Cyberjournal for Pentecostal-Charismatic Research* (September 2000). http://www.pctii.org/cyberj/cyberj9/anderson.html.

Anderson, John. *Religion, State and Politics in the Soviet Union and Successor States.* Cambridge: Cambridge University Press, 1994.

——. *Conservative Christian Politics in Russia and the United States.* New York: Routledge, 2015.

Balcomb, Anthony. "Apartheid to the New Dispensation: Evangelicals and the Democratization of South Africa." *Journal of Religion in Africa* 34, no. 1/2 (February–May, 2004): 5–38.

Balmer, Randall H. *Blessed Assurance: A History of Evangelicalism in America.* Boston: Beacon Press, 1999.

——. *Thy Kingdom Come: How the Religious Right Distorts the Faith and Threatens America, an Evangelical's Lament.* New York: Basic Books, 2006.

Baran, Emily B. "Negotiating the Limits of Religious Pluralism in Post-Soviet Russia: The Anticult Movement in the Russian Orthodox Church, 1990–2004." *Russian Review* 65, no. 4 (October 2006): 637–56.

Barfoot, Chas H. *Aimee Semple McPherson and the Making of Modern Pentecostalism, 1890–1926.* London: Equinox, 2011.

Bays, Daniel H., and Grant Wacker. *The Foreign Missionary Enterprise at Home: Explorations in North American Cultural History.* Tuscaloosa: University of Alabama Press, 2003.

Bebbington, David W. *Evangelicalism in Modern Britain: A History from the 1730s to the 1930s.* London: Unwin Hyman, 1989.

Berger, Peter L. "Four Faces of Global Culture." *National Interest* 49 (Fall 1997): 23–30.

——. "Introduction: The Cultural Dynamics of Globalization." In *Many Globalizations: Cultural Diversity in the Contemporary World*, edited by Peter L. Berger and Samuel P. Huntington, 1–16. Oxford: Oxford University Press, 2002.

Berggren, J., and N. C. Rae. "Jimmy Carter and George W. Bush: Faith, Foreign Policy, and an Evangelical Presidential Style." *Presidential Studies Quarterly* 36, no. 4 (December 2006): 606–32.

Beuttler, Fred W. "Evangelical Missions in Modern America." In *The Great Commission: Evangelicals and the History of World Missions*, edited by Martin Klauber and Scott Manetsch, 108–32. Nashville, TN: B & H Publishing Group, 2008.

Borgwardt, Elizabeth. *A New Deal for the World: America's Vision for Human Rights*. Cambridge, MA: Belknap Press of Harvard University Press, 2005.

Borstelmann, Thomas. *The Cold War and the Color Line: American Race Relations in the Global Arena*. Cambridge, MA: Harvard University Press, 2001.

Bourdeaux, Michael, ed. *The Politics of Religion in Russia and the New States of Eurasia*. Armonk, NY: M.E. Sharpe, 1995.

Bon Tempo, Carl. "From the Center-Right: Freedom House and Human Rights in the 1970s and 1980s." In *The Human Rights Revolution: An International History*, edited by Akira Iriye, Petra Goedde, and William I. Hitchcock, 223–44. New York: Oxford University Press, 2012.

——. "Human Rights and the U.S. Republican Party in the Late 1970s." In *The Breakthrough: Human Rights in the 1970s*, edited by Jan Eckel and Samuel Moyn, 146–65. Philadelphia: University of Pennsylvania Press, 2014.

Boyer, Paul S. *When Time Shall Be No More: Prophecy Belief in Modern American Culture*. Cambridge, MA: Belknap Press of Harvard University Press, 1992.

Brands, H. W. *Reagan: The Life*. New York: Doubleday, 2015.

Broder, Tanya, and Bernard Lambek. "Military Aid to Guatemala: The Failure of U.S. Human Rights Legislation." *Yale Journal of International Law* 13, no. 1 (Winter 1988): 111–45.

Brown, Archie. *The Gorbachev Factor*. Oxford: Oxford University Press, 1996.

——. *Seven Years That Changed the World: Perestroika in Perspective*. Oxford: Oxford University Press, 2007.

——. *The Rise and Fall of Communism*. New York: HarperCollins, 2009.

Bratyanski, Jennifer. "Mainstreaming Movements: The U.S. Anti-Apartheid Movement and Civil Rights Memory." PhD diss., University of North Carolina at Greensboro, 2012.

Carpenter, Joel A. *Revive Us Again: The Reawakening of American Fundamentalism*. New York: Oxford University Press, 1997.

Castelli, Elizabeth. "Praying for the Persecuted Church: US Christian Activism in the Global Arena." *Journal of Human Rights* 4, no. 3 (2005): 321–51.

Chapman, Alister. "Evangelical International Relations in the Post—Colonial World: The Lausanne Movement and the Challenge of Diversity, 1974–89," *Missiology: An International Review* 37, no. 3 (July 2009): 355–68.

Cherry, Conrad. *God's New Israel: Religious Interpretations of American Destiny*. Chapel Hill: University of North Carolina Press, 1998.

Cmiel, Kenneth. "The Emergence of Human Rights Politics in the United States." *Journal of American History* 86, no. 3 (December 1999):1231–50.

——. "The Recent History of Human Rights." *American Historical Review* 109, no. 1 (February 2004): 117–35.

Coeller, Rodney A. "Beyond the Borders: Radicalized Evangelical Missionaries in Central America from the 1950s through the 1980s." PhD diss., American University, 2012.

Coleman, Simon. *The Globalisation of Charismatic Christianity: Spreading the Gospel of Prosperity*. Cambridge: Cambridge University Press, 2000.

Comaroff, Jean, and John L. *Of Revelation and Revolution*, Volume 1: *Christianity, Colonialism, and Consciousness in South Africa*. Chicago, IL: University of Chicago Press, 2008.

Cox, Harvey. *Fire from Heaven: The Rise of Pentecostal Spirituality and the Reshaping of Religion in the Twenty-First Century*. Cambridge, MA: Da Capo Press, 1995.

Critchlow, Donald T. *Phyllis Schlafly and Grassroots Conservatism: A Woman's Crusade*. Princeton, NJ: Princeton University Press, 2005.

Culverson, Donald R. *Contesting Apartheid: U.S. Activism, 1960–1987*. Boulder, CO: Westview Press, 1999.

Curtis, Heather. *Holy Humanitarians: American Evangelicals and Global Aid*. Cambridge, MA: Harvard University Press, 2018.

Dallek, Robert. *Nixon and Kissinger: Partners in Power*. New York: HarperCollins, 2007.

Davies, J. E. *Constructive Engagement? Chester Crocker & American Policy in South Africa, Namibia & Angola, 1981–8*. Oxford: Oxford University Press, 2007.

De Gruchy, John W. *The Church Struggle in South Africa*. Minneapolis: Fortress Press, 2005.

Den Dulk, Kevin R. "Evangelical 'Internationalists' and U.S. Foreign Policy during the Bush Administration." In *Religion and the Bush Presidency*, edited by Mark J. Rozell and Gleaves Whitney, 213–34. New York: Palgrave Macmillan, 2007.

Deweese, Charles W. "International Baptist Perspectives on Human Rights." *Baptist History and Heritage* 43 no. 2 (Spring 2008): 60–69.

Diamond, Sara. *Not by Politics Alone: The Enduring Influence of the Christian Right*. New York: Guilford Press, 1998.

——. *Spiritual Warfare: The Politics of the Christian Right*. London: Pluto, 1989.

Diggins, John P. *Ronald Reagan: Fate, Freedom, and the Making of History*. New York: W.W. Norton, 2007.

Dochuk, Darren. *From Bible Belt to Sunbelt: Plain-folk Religion, Grassroots Politics, and the Rise of Evangelical Conservatism*. New York: W.W. Norton, 2011.

Dow, Philip E. "Romance in a Marriage of Convenience: The Missionary Factor in Early Cold War U.S.-Ethiopian Relations, 1941–1960." *Diplomatic History* 35, no. 5 (November 2011): 859–95.

Dunch, Ryan. "Beyond Cultural Imperialism: Cultural Theory, Christian Missions, and Global Modernity." *History and Theory* 41, no. 3 (October 2002): 301–25.

Duranti, Marco. *The Conservative Human Rights Revolution: European Identity, Transnational Politics, and the Origins of the European Convention*. New York: Oxford University Press, 2017.

Eckel, Jan, and Samuel Moyn. *The Breakthrough: Human Rights in the 1970s*. Philadelphia: University of Pennsylvania Press, 2014.

Edwards, Mark. "Rethinking the Failure of Fundamentalist Political Antievolutionism after 1925." *Fides et Historia* 32, no. 2 (Summer/Fall 2000): 89–106.

Erickson, Hal. *Religious Radio and Television in the United States: 1921–1991*. Jefferson, NC: McFarland, 1992.

Eskridge, Larry. *God's Forever Family: The Jesus People Movement in America*. Oxford: Oxford University Press, 2013.

Fairbank, John King. *The Missionary Enterprise In China and America*. Cambridge, MA: Harvard University Press, 1974.

Farr, Thomas F. "America's International Religious Freedom Policy." In *Rethinking Religion and World Affairs*, edited by Timothy Samuel Shah, Alfred C. Stepan, and Monica Duffy Toft, 262–78. Oxford: Oxford University Press, 2012.

Feingold, Henry L. *"Silent No More": Saving the Jews of Russia, The American Jewish Effort, 1967–1989*. Syracuse: Syracuse University Press, 2007.

Ferrari, Silvio. "Proselytism and Human Rights." In *Christianity and Human Rights: An Introduction*, edited by John Witte, Jr. and Frank S. Alexander, 253–66. Cambridge: Cambridge University Press, 2010.

Finke, Roger and Rodney Stark. *The Churching of America, 1776–2005: Winners and Losers in Our Religious Economy*. New Brunswick, NJ: Rutgers University Press, 2005.

Foglesong, David S. *The American Mission and the "Evil Empire": The Crusade for a "Free Russia" since 1881*. New York: Cambridge University Press, 2007.

Fox, Richard Wightman. "Experience and Explanation in Twentieth-Century American Religious History." In *New Directions in American Religious History*, edited by Harry S. Stout and D. G. Hart, 394–413. New York: Oxford University Press, 1997.

Freiling, Tom. *Reagan's God and Country: A President's Moral Compass: His Beliefs on God, Religious Freedom, the Sanctity of Life, and More*. Ann Arbor, MI: Vine Books, 2000.

Garrard-Burnett, Virginia. *Terror in the Land of the Holy Spirit: Guatemala under General Efraín Ríos Montt, 1982–1983*. Oxford: Oxford University Press, 2010.

——. *Protestantism in Guatemala: Living in the New Jerusalem*. Austin: University of Texas Press, 1998.

Gayraud S. Wilmore. *Last Things First*. Philadelphia: Westminster Press, 1992.

Gleijeses, Piero. *Visions of Freedom: Havana, Washington, Pretoria and the Struggle for Southern Africa, 1976–1991*. Chapel Hill: University of North Carolina Press, 2013.

Gordon Conwell Theological Seminary Center for the Study of Global Christianity. "Christianity in its Global Context, 1970–2020: Society, Religion, and Mission." June 2013. http://www.gordonconwell.edu/resources/Global-Context-of-Christianity.cfm.

Grabill, Joseph. *Protestant Diplomacy and the Near East: Missionary Influence on American Policy, 1810–1927*. Minneapolis: University of Minnesota Press, 1971.

Grenz, Stanley J. *Renewing the Center: Evangelical Theology in a Post-Theological Era*. Grand Rapids, MI: Baker Academic, 2006.

Gubin, Sandra L. "Between Regimes and Realism—Transnational Agenda Setting: Soviet Compliance With CSCE Human Rights Norms." *Human Rights Quarterly* 17, no. 2 (1995): 278–302.

Gunn, T. Jeremy. *Spiritual Weapons: The Cold War and the Forging of an American National Religion.* Westport, CT: Praeger, 2009.

Hanhimäki, Jussi. *The Flawed Architect: Henry Kissinger and American Foreign Policy.* Oxford: Oxford University Press, 2004.

Harris, Paul W. "Cultural Imperialism and American Protestant Missionaries: Collaboration and Dependency in Mid—Nineteenth—Century China." *Pacific Historical Review* 60, no. 3 (August 1991): 309–38.

Hart, D. G. "Mainstream Protestantism, 'Conservative' Religion, and Civil Society." In *Religion Returns to the Public Square: Faith and Policy In America*, edited by Hugh Heclo and Wilfred M McClay, 195–225. Washington, DC: Woodrow Wilson Center Press, 2003.

Hatch, Nathan. *The Democratization of American Christianity.* New Haven: Yale University Press, 1989.

Hertzke, Allen D. "Evangelicals and International Engagement." In *Public Faith: Evangelicals and Civic Engagement*, edited by Michael Cromartie, 215–35. Oxford: Rowman & Littlefield, 2003.

——. *Freeing God's Children: The Unlikely Alliance for Global Human Rights.* Lanham, MD: Rowman & Littlefield, 2004.

——. *Representing God In Washington: The Role of Religious Lobbies In the American Polity.* Knoxville: University of Tennessee Press, 1988.

Herzog, Jonathan P. *The Spiritual-Industrial Complex: America's Religious Battle against Communism in the Early Cold War.* New York: Oxford University Press, 2011.

Heyrman, Christine Leigh. *Southern Cross: The Beginnings of the Bible Belt.* New York: Knopf, 1997.

Hill, Patricia R. "Religion as a Category of Diplomatic Analysis." *Diplomatic History* 24, no. 4 (Fall 2000): 633–40.

Hofrenning, Daniel J. B. *In Washington but Not of It: The Prophetic Politics of Religious Lobbyists.* Philadelphia: Temple University Press, 1995.

Hollinger, David A. *Protestants Abroad: How Missionaries Tried to Change the World but Changed America.* Princeton, NJ: Princeton University Press, 2017.

——. *After Cloven Tongues of Fire: Protestant Liberalism In Modern American History.* Princeton: Princeton University Press, 2013.

Horne, Adele. *The Tailenders.* Bucksport, ME: Northeast Historic Film, 2013.

Hosking, Geoffrey A. "The Beginnings of Independent Political Activity." In *The Road to Post Communism: Independent Political Movements in the Soviet Union 1985–1991*, edited by Geoffrey A. Hosking, Jonathan Aves, and Peter J. S. Duncan, 1–28. London: Pinter Publishers, 1992.

——. *The Awakening of the Soviet Union.* Cambridge, MA: Harvard University Press, 1990.

Hostetter, David L. *Movement Matters: American Antiapartheid Activism and the Rise of Multicultural Politics.* New York: Routledge, 2006.

Hunt, Michael H. *Ideology and U.S. Foreign Policy.* New Haven: Yale University Press, 1987.

Hunter, James Davison. *Culture Wars: The Struggle to Define America.* New York: Basic Books, 1991.

Hunter, James Davison, and Joshua Yates. "In the Vanguard of Globalization: The World of American Globalizers." In *Many Globalizations: Cultural Diversity in the Contemporary World*, edited by Peter L. Berger and Samuel P. Huntington, 323–58. Oxford: Oxford University Press, 2002.

Hutchinson, Mark, and John Wolffe. *A Short History of Global Evangelicalism*. Cambridge: Cambridge University Press, 2012.

Hutchison, William R. *Errand to the World: American Protestant Thought and Foreign Missions*. Chicago: University of Chicago Press, 1987.

Inboden, William. *Religion and American Foreign Policy, 1945–1960: The Soul of Containment*. Cambridge: Cambridge University Press, 2008.

Iriye, Akira, Petra Goedde, and William I. Hitchcock. *The Human Rights Revolution: An International History*. New York: Oxford University Press, 2012.

Irwin, Julia. *Making the World Safe: The American Red Cross and a Nation's Humanitarian Awakening*. New York: Oxford University Press, 2013.

Iverson, Ivar A. *Foreign Policy in God's Name: Evangelical Influence on U.S. Policy towards Sudan*. Oslo: Norwegian Institute for Defence Studies, 2007.

Jenkins, Philip. *The Next Christendom: The Coming of Global Christianity*. New York: Oxford University Press, 2007.

Johnson, Charles Denton. "Rethinking the Emergency of the Struggle for South African Liberation in the United States: Max Yergan and the Council on African Affairs, 1922–1946." *Journal of Southern African Studies* 39, no. 1 (March 2013): 171–92.

Jones, Lawrence. "Divided Evangelicals in South Africa." In *Religious Resurgence and Politics in the Contemporary World*, edited by Emile Sahliyeh, 107–19. Albany: State University of New York Press, 1990.

Katzenstein, Peter J., ed. *The Culture of National Security: Norms and Identity in World Politics*. New York: Columbia University Press, 1996.

Kaufman, Robert G. *Henry M. Jackson: A Life in Politics*. Seattle: University of Washington Press, 2000.

Kengor, Paul. *God and Ronald Reagan: A Spiritual Life*. New York: Regan Books, 2004.

Keys, Barbara. "Congress, Kissinger, and the Origins of Human Rights Diplomacy." *Diplomatic History* 34, no. 5 (November 2010): 823–52.

——. *Reclaiming American Virtue: The Human Rights Revolution of the 1970s*. Cambridge, MA: Harvard University Press, 2014.

Kidd, Thomas S. *The Great Awakening The Roots of Evangelical Christianity in Colonial America*. New Haven, CT: Yale University Press, 2007.

King, David. "The New Internationalists: World Vision and the Revival of American Evangelical Humanitarianism, 1950–2010." *Religions* 3, no. 4 (September 2012): 922–49.

Kirkpatrick, David C. *A Gospel for the Poor: Global Social Christianity and the Latin American Evangelical Left*. Philadelphia: University of Pennsylvania Press, 2019.

Kochavi, Noam. "Insights Abandoned, Flexibility Lost: Kissinger, Soviet Jewish Emigration, and the Demise of Détente." *Diplomatic History* 29, no. 3 (2005): 550–72.

Kotkin, Stephen. *Armageddon Averted: The Soviet Collapse, 1970–2000*. Oxford: Oxford University Press, 2001.

Lahr, Angela M. *Millennial Dreams and Apocalyptic Nightmares: The Cold War Origins of Political Evangelicalism.* New York: Oxford University Press, 2007.

Lazarowitz, Arlene. "Senator Jacob K. Javits and Soviet Jewish Emigration." *Shofar: An Interdisciplinary Journal of Jewish Studies* 21, no. 4 (2003): 19–31.

Leffler, Melvyn P. "National Security." In *Explaining the History of American Foreign Relations,* edited by Michael J. Hogan and Thomas G. Paterson, 123–36. Cambridge: Cambridge University Press, 2004.

——. *For the Soul of Mankind: The United States, the Soviet Union, and the Cold War.* New York: Hill and Wang, 2007.

Lincoln, C. Eric, and Lawrence H. Mamiya. *The Black Church in the African American Experience.* Durham, NC: Duke University Press, 1990.

Lindsay, D. Michael. "Is the National Prayer Breakfast Surrounded by a 'Christian Mafia'? Religious Publicity and Secrecy Within the Corridors of Power." *Journal of the American Academy of Religion* 74, no. 2 (June 2006): 390–419.

——. "Organizational Liminality and Interstitial Creativity: The Fellowship of Power." *Social Forces* 89, no. 1 (September 2010): 163–84.

Litwak, Robert S. *Détente and the Nixon Doctrine: American Foreign Policy and the Pursuit of Stability, 1969–1976.* Cambridge: Cambridge University Press, 1984.

Livingston, J. Kevin. *A Missiology of the Road: Early Perspectives in David Bosch's Theology of Mission and Evangelism.* Eugene, OR: Pickwick Publications, 2013.

Lochte, Robert H. *Christian Radio: The Growth of a Mainstream Broadcasting Force.* Jefferson, NC: McFarland, 2006.

Lockerbie, Brad. "Race and Religion: Voting Behavior and Political Attitudes." *Social Science Quarterly* 94, no. 4 (December 2013): 1145–58.

Lynerd, Benjamin T. *Republican Theology: The Civil Religion of American Evangelicals.* Oxford: Oxford University Press, 2014.

Marsden, George M. "The Evangelical Denomination." In *Piety and Politics: Evangelicals and Fundamentalists Confront the World,* edited by Richard John Neuhaus and Michael Cromartie, 55–68. Washington, DC: Ethics and Public Policy Center, 1987.

——. *Understanding Fundamentalism and Evangelicalism.* Grand Rapids, MI: W.B. Eerdmans, 1991.

——. *The Twilight of the American Enlightenment: the 1950s and the Crisis of Liberal Belief.* New York: Basic Books, 2014.

Martin, William C. *With God on Our Side: The Rise of the Religious Right in America.* New York: Broadway Books, 1996.

——. "The Christian Right and American Foreign Policy." *Foreign Policy,* no. 114 (1999): 66–80.

Marty, Martin E. *Protestantism in the United States: Righteous Empire.* New York: Scribner's, 1986.

Mazower, Mark. "The Strange Triumph of Human Rights, 1933–1950." *Historical Journal* 47, no. 2 (June 2004): 379–98.

McAlister, Melani. *The Kingdom of God Has No Borders: A Global History of American Evangelicals.* New York: Oxford University Press, 2018.

——. "The Persecuted Body: Evangelical Internationalism, Islam, and the Politics of Fear." In *Facing Fear: The History of an Emotion in Global Perspective*, edited by Michael Francis Laffan and Max Weiss, 133–61. Princeton: Princeton University Press, 2012.

——. "What Is Your Heart For? Affect and Internationalism in the Evangelical Public Sphere." *American Literary History* 20, no. 4 (September 2008): 870–95.

——. *Epic Encounters: Culture, Media, and U.S. Interests in the Middle East, 1945–2000*. Berkeley: University of California Press, 2001.

McDaniel, E. L., and C. G. Ellison. "God's Party? Race, Religion, and Partisanship Over Time." *Political Research Quarterly* 61, no. 2 (June 2008): 180–91.

McGirr, Lisa. *Suburban Warriors: The Origins of the New American Right*. Princeton, NJ: Princeton University Press, 2001.

Mead, Walter Russell. "God's Country?" *Foreign Affairs* 85, no. 5 (September/October 2006): 24–43.

——. *Special Providence: American Foreign Policy and How It Changed the World*. New York: Routledge, 2002.

Medina, Néstor. "The New Jerusalem versus Social Responsibility: The Challenges of Pentecostalism in Guatemala." In *Perspectives in Pentecostal Eschatologies: World Without End*, edited by Peter Althouse and Robby Waddell, 315–39. Eugene, OR: Wipf & Stock Publishers, 2010.

Melander, Veronica. *The Hour of God?: People in Guatemala Confronting Political Evangelicalism and Counterinsurgency (1976–1990)*. Uppsala: Swedish Institute of Missionary Research, 1999.

Mendelson, Sarah Elizabeth. "Democracy Assistance and Political Transition in Russia: Between Success and Failure." *International Security* 25, no. 4 (Spring 2001): 68–106.

Mendelson, Sarah Elizabeth, and Theodore P. Gerber. "Activist Culture and Transnational Diffusion: Social Marketing and Human Rights Groups in Russia." *Post-Soviet Affairs* 23, no. 1 (January–March 2007): 50–75.

Miller, Steven P. *The Age of Evangelicalism: America's Born-Again Years*. Oxford: Oxford University Press, 2014.

Minter, William. *King Solomon's Mines Revisited: Western Interests and the Burdened History of Southern Africa*. New York: Basic Books, 1986.

Morgan, Michael Coty. "The Seventies and the Rebirth of Human Rights." In *The Shock of the Global: The 1970s in Perspective*, edited by Niall Ferguson, Charles Maier, Erez Manela, and Daniel Sargent, 237–50. Cambridge, MA: Belknap Press of Harvard University Press, 2010.

——. "The United States and the Making of the Helsinki Final Act." In *Nixon in the World: American Foreign Relations, 1969–1977*, edited by Fredrik Logevall and Andrew Preston, 164–83. New York: Oxford University Press, 2008.

Moyn, Samuel. *Christian Human Rights*. Philadelphia: University of Pennsylvania Press, 2015.

——. "Imperialism, Self-Determination, and the Rise of Human Rights." In *The Human Rights Revolution: An International History*, edited by Akira Iriye, Petra Goedde, and William I Hitchcock, 159–78. New York: Oxford University Press, 2012.

——. *The Last Utopia: Human Rights in History*. Cambridge, MA: Harvard University Press, 2010.

Muldoon, James. *The Americas in the Spanish World Order: The Justification for Conquest in the Seventeenth Century*. Philadelphia: University of Pennsylvania Press, 1994.

Mungazi, Dickson. *In the Footsteps of the Masters: Desmond M. Tutu and Abel T. Muzorewa*. Westport, CT: Greenwood Publishing Group, 2000.

Nelson, Keith L. *The Making of Détente: Soviet-American Relations in the Shadow of Vietnam*, Baltimore, MD: Johns Hopkins University Press, 1995.

Nesbitt, Francis Njubi. *Race for Sanctions: African Americans Against Apartheid, 1946–1994*. Bloomington: Indiana University Press, 2004.

Nichols, Joel A. "Evangelicals and Human Rights: The Continuing Ambivalence of Evangelical Christians' Support for Human Rights." *Journal of Law & Religion* 24, no. 2 (2009): 629–62.

Noll, Mark A. *America's God: From Jonathan Edwards to Abraham Lincoln*. Oxford: Oxford University Press, 2002.

——. *American Evangelical Christianity: An Introduction*. Oxford: Blackwell, 2000.

——. *Protestants in America*. Oxford: Oxford University Press, 2000.

——. *The Rise of Evangelicalism: The Age of Edwards, Whitefield, and the Wesleys*. Downers Grove, IL: Intervarsity Press, 2003.

Offutt, Stephen. *New Centers of Global Evangelicalism in Latin America and Africa*. New York: Cambridge University Press, 2015.

O'Neill, Kevin Lewis. *City of God: Christian Citizenship In Postwar Guatemala*. Berkeley: University of California Press, 2010.

Peck, James. *Ideal Illusions: How the U.S. Government Co-Opted Human Rights*. New York: Henry Holt, 2010.

Pew Research Center: Religion & Public Life. "Global Christianity: A Report on the Size and Distribution of the World's Christian Population." http://www. pewforum.org/files/2011/12/Christianity-fullreport-web.pdf.

—— "Religion in Latin America: Widespread Change in a Historically Catholic Region." https://www.pewforum.org/2014/11/13/religion-in-latin-america/.

Pierson, Paul E. "The Rise of Christian Mission and Relief Agencies." In *The Influence of Faith: Religious Groups and U.S. Foreign Policy*, edited by Elliot Abrams, 151–70. Lanham, MD: Rowman & Littlefield, 2001.

Poewe, Karla. *Charismatic Christianity as a Global Culture*. Columbia: University of South Carolina Press, 1994.

Porter, Andrew. *Religion versus Empire?: British Protestant Missionaries and Overseas Expansion, 1700–1914*. Manchester: Manchester University Press, 2004.

Preston, Andrew. "Bridging the Gap between the Sacred and the Secular in the History of American Foreign Relations." *Diplomatic History* 30, no. 5 (November 2006): 783–812.

——. "Evangelical Internationalism: A Conservative Worldview for the Age of Globalization." In *The Right Side of the Sixties: Reexamining Conservatism's Decade of Transformation*, edited by Laura Jane Gifford and Daniel K. Williams, 221–40. New York: Palgrave Macmillan, 2012.

———. *Sword of the Spirit. Shield of Faith: Religion in American War and Diplomacy.* New York: Alfred A. Knopf, 2012.

Rabe, Valentin H. *The Home Base of American China Missions, 1880–1920.* Cambridge, MA: Council on East Asian Studies, Harvard University Press, 1978.

Ramet, Sabrina P. *Social Currents in Eastern Europe: the Sources and Consequences of the Great Transformation.* Durham, NC: Duke University Press, 1995.

Ranger, Terence O. *Evangelical Christianity and Democracy in Africa.* Oxford: Oxford University Press, 2008.

Reed, James. *The Missionary Mind and American East Asia Policy, 1911–1915.* Cambridge, MA: Harvard University Press, 1983.

Ribuffo, Leo. "Religion and American Foreign Policy: The Story of a Complex Relationship." *National Interest* 52 (1998 Summer): 36–51.

Robeck, Cecil M., Jr. *The Azusa Street Mission & Revival: The Birth of the Global Pentecostal Movement.* Nashville, TN: Thomas Nelson Publishers, 2006.

Robert, Dana L. "Shifting Southward: Global Christianity Since 1945." *International Bulletin of Missionary Research* 24, no. 2 (April 2000): 50–58.

———. "The Great Commission in an Age of Globalization." In *The Antioch Agenda: The Restorative Church at the Margins. Celebrating the Life and Work of Orlando Costas,* edited by D. Jeyaraj, R Pazmino, and R Petersen, 5–22. New Delhi, India: Indian Society for the Promotion of Christian Knowledge, 2007.

———. *Christian Mission: How Christianity Became a World Religion.* Malden, MA: Wiley-Blackwell, 2009.

Roberts, Bryan R. "Protestant Groups and Coping with Urban Life in Guatemala City." *American Journal of Sociology* 73, no. 6 (May 1968): 753–67.

Roberts, Sean R. "Doing the Democracy Dance in Kazakhstan: Democracy Development as Cultural Encounter." *Slavic Review* 71, no. 2 (Summer 2012): 308–30.

Robinson, Lynn D. "Doing Good and Doing Well: Shareholder Activism, Responsible Investment, and Mainline Protestantism." In *The Quiet Hand of God: Faith-Based Activism and the Public Role of Mainline Protestantism,* edited by Robert Wuthnow and John H. Evans, 343–63. Berkeley: University of California Press, 2002.

Rothenberg, Daniel. *Memory of Silence: The Guatemalan Truth Commission Report.* New York: Palgrave Macmillan, 2012.

Rotter, Andrew J. "Christians, Muslims, and Hindus: Religion and U.S.-South Asian Relations, 1947–1954." *Diplomatic History* 24 (Fall 2000): 593–613.

Sawatsky, Walter. "Protestantism in the USSR." In *Religious Policy in the Soviet Union,* edited by Sabrina Petra Ramet, 233–75. Cambridge: Cambridge University Press, 1993.

Schäfer, Axel R. *Countercultural Conservatives: American Evangelism from the Postwar Revival to the New Christian Right.* Madison: University of Wisconsin Press, 2011.

Schlesinger, Arthur Jr. "The Missionary Enterprise and Theories of Imperialism." In *The Missionary Enterprise in China and America,* edited by John K. Fairbank, 336–73. Cambridge, MA: Harvard University Press, 1974.

Schlozman, Kay Lehman, and John T. Tierney. *Organized Interests and American Democracy.* New York: Harper & Row, 1986.

Schlozman, Kay Lehman, Sidney Verba, and Henry E. Brady. *The Unheavenly Chorus: Unequal Political Voice and the Broken Promise of American Democracy*. Princeton, NJ: Princeton University Press, 2012.

Settje, David E. *Lutherans and the Longest War: Adrift on a Sea of Doubt about the Cold and Vietnam Wars, 1964–1975*. Lanham, MD: Lexington Books, 2007.

Sharlet, Jeff. *The Family: The Secret Fundamentalism at the Heart of American Power*. New York: HarperCollins, 2008.

Shaw, Mark. *Global Awakening: How 20th Century Revivals Triggered a Christian Revolution*. Downers Grove, IL: InterVarsity Press, 2010.

Shelley, Bruce L. *Church History in Plain Language*. Dallas, TX: Word Pub, 1995.

Shibley, Mark A. "Contemporary Evangelicals: Born-Again and World Affirming." *Annals of the American Academy of Political and Social Science* 558, no. 1 (July 1998): 67–87.

Sikkink, Kathryn. *Mixed Signals: U.S. Human Rights Policy and Latin America*. Ithaca, NY: Cornell University Press, 2004.

Skinner, Rob. *The Foundations of Anti-Apartheid: Liberal Humanitarians and Transnational Activists in Britain and the United States, c. 1919–64*. Hampshire, England: Palgrave Macmillan, 2010.

Smith, Calvin L. "Pentecostal Presence, Power and Politics in Latin America." *Journal of Beliefs & Values: Studies in Religion & Education* 30, no. 3 (December 2009): 219–29.

Smith, Christian. *American Evangelicalism: Embattled and Thriving*. Chicago: University of Chicago Press, 1998.

——. *Disruptive Religion: The Force of Faith in Social Movement Activism*. New York: Routledge, 1996.

——. *The Emergence of Liberation Theology: Radical Religion and the Social Movement Theory*. Chicago: University of Chicago Press, 1991.

Smith, R. Drew, and Pedro Lutiniko. *Freedom's Distant Shores: American Protestants and Post-Colonial Alliances with Africa*. Waco, TX: Baylor University Press, 2006.

Smith, Timothy. "The Evangelical Kaleidoscope and the Call to Christian Unity." *Christian Scholars Review* 15, no. 2 (1986): 125–40.

Snyder, Sarah. "The Defeat of Ernest Lefever's Nomination: Keeping Human Rights on the United States Foreign Policy Agenda." In *Challenging U.S. Foreign Policy: America and the World in the Long Twentieth Century*, edited by Bevan Sewell and Scott Lucas, 136–61. New York: Palgrave Macmillan, 2011.

——. *From Selma to Moscow: How Human Rights Activists Transformed U.S. Foreign Policy*. New York: Columbia University Press, 2018.

——. *Human Rights Activism and the End of the Cold War: A Transnational History of the Helsinki Network*. New York: Cambridge University Press, 2011.

——. "The Rise of the Helsinki Network: 'A sort of lifeline' for Eastern Europe." In *Perforating the Iron Curtain: European Détente, Transatlantic Relations, and the Cold War, 1965–1985*, edited by Poul Villaume and Odd Arne Westad, 179–93. Copenhagen, Denmark: Museum Tusculanum Press, University of Copenhagen, 2010.

Stamatov, Peter. *The Origins of Global Humanitarianism: Religion, Empires, and Advocacy*. New York: Cambridge University Press, 2013.

Stern, Paula. *Water's Edge: Domestic Politics and the Making of an American Foreign Policy.* Westport, CT: Greenwood Press, 1979.

Stewart, James B. "Amandla! The Sullivan Principles and the Battle to End Apartheid in South Africa, 1975–1987." *Journal of African American History* 96, no. 1 (Winter 2011): 62–89.

Stevens, Simon. "'From the Viewpoint of a Southern Governor': The Carter Administration and Apartheid, 1977–81." *Diplomatic History* 36, no. 5 (November 2012): 843–80.

Stoll, David. "Evangelicals, Guerrillas, and the Army: The Ixil Triangle Under Rios Montt." In *Harvest of Violence: Maya Indians and the Guatemalan Crisis,* edited by Robert M. Carmack, 90–116. Norman: University of Oklahoma Press, 1988.

Stoneman, Timothy H. B. "Global Radio Broadcasting and the Dynamics of American Evangelicalism." *Journal of American Studies* 51, no. 4 (November 2017): 1139–70.

——. "Preparing the Soil for Global Revival: Station HCJB's Radio Circle, 1949–1959." *Church History* 76, no. 1 (March 2007): 114–55.

Sundstrom, Lisa McIntosh. *Funding Civil Society: Foreign Assistance and NGO Development in Russia.* Stanford, CA: Stanford University Press, 2006.

Suri, Jeremi. *Henry Kissinger and the American Century.* Cambridge, MA: Harvard University Press, 2007.

Sutton, Matthew Avery. *Aimee Semple McPherson and the Resurrection of Christian America.* Cambridge, MA: Harvard University Press, 2009.

——. *American Apocalypse: A History of Modern Evangelicalism.* Cambridge, MA: Harvard University press, 2014.

Swartz, David. "Embodying the Global Soul: Internationalism and the American Evangelical Left." *Religions* 3, No. 4 (September 2012): 887–901.

Talavera, Arturo Fontaine. "Trends toward Globalization in Chile." In *Many Globalizations: Cultural Diversity in the Contemporary World,* edited by Peter L. Berger and Samuel P. Huntington, 250–95. Oxford: Oxford University Press, 2002.

Thomas, Scott M. *The Global Resurgence of Religion and the Transformation of International Relations: The Struggle for the Soul of the Twenty-first Century.* New York: Palgrave Macmillan, 2005.

Thomson, Alex. "The Diplomacy of Impasse: The Carter Administration and Apartheid South Africa." *Diplomacy & Statecraft* 21, no. 1 (March 2010): 107–24.

——. *U.S. Foreign Policy towards Apartheid South Africa, 1948–1994.* New York: Palgrave Macmillan, 2008.

Tizon, Al. *Transformation after Lausanne: Radical Evangelical Mission in Global—Local Perspective.* Eugene, OR: Wipf & Stock, 2008.

Turner Jr., William C. "Black Evangelicalism: Theology, Politics, and Race." *Journal of Religious Thought* 45, no. 2 (Winter/Spring 1989): 40–53.

Tuveson, Ernest Lee. *Redeemer Nation: The Idea of America's Millennial Role.* Chicago: University of Chicago Press, 1968.

Tyrrell, Ian. *Reforming the World: The Creation of America's Moral Empire.* Princeton, NJ: Princeton University Press, 2010.

Varg, Paul A. *Missionaries, Chinese, and Diplomats: The American Protestant Missionary Movement In China, 1890–1952.* Princeton, NJ: Princeton University Press, 1958.

Wacker, Grant. *Heaven Below: Early Pentecostals and American Culture.* Cambridge: Harvard University Press, 2003.

Wagner, Benjamin A. "'Full Gospel' Radio: Revivaltime and the Pentecostal Uses of Mass Media, 1950–1979." *Fides et Historia* 35, no. 1 (Winter/Spring 2003): 107–22.

Walker, William O. *National Security and Core Values in American History.* Cambridge: Cambridge University Press, 2009.

Walls, Andrew F. *The Cross-Cultural Process in Christian History: Studies in the Transmission and Appropriation of Faith.* Maryknoll, NY: Orbis Books, 2002.

Watt, Peter. *From Africa's Soil: The Story of the Assemblies of God in Southern Africa.* Cape Town, South Africa: Struik Christian Books, 1992.

Weber, Paul J., and T. L. Stanley. "The Power and Performance of Religious Interest Groups." *Quarterly Review* 4 (1984): 28–43.

Wedel, Janine R. *Collision and Collusion: The Strange Case of Western Aid to Eastern Europe, 1989–1998.* New York: St. Martin's Press, 1998.

Westad, Odd Arne. *The Global Cold War: Third World Interventions and the Making of Our Times.* Cambridge: Cambridge University Press, 2005.

Wilcox, Clyde. "Laying up Treasures in Washington and in Heaven: The Christian Right and Evangelical Politics in the Twentieth Century and Beyond." *OAH Magazine of History* 17, no. 2 (January 2003): 23–29.

Williams, Appleman William. *The Tragedy of American Diplomacy.* New York: W.W. Norton, 1972.

Williams, Daniel K. *God's Own Party: The Making of the Christian Right.* Oxford: Oxford University Press, 2010.

Wilson, James Graham. *The Triumph of Improvisation: Gorbachev's Adaptability, Reagan's Engagement, and the End of the Cold War.* Ithaca, NY: Cornell University Press, 2014.

Woodberry, Robert D. "The Missionary Roots of Liberal Democracy." *American Political Science Review* 106, no. 2 (May 2012): 244–74.

Wuthnow, Robert. *Boundless Faith: The Global Outreach of American Churches.* Berkeley: University of California Press, 2009.

Zubok, Vladislav. *A Failed Empire: The Soviet Union in the Cold War from Stalin to Gorbachev.* Chapel Hill: University of North Carolina Press, 2007.

Index